THE CAT BIBLE

THE
CAT

BIBLE

Everything Your Cat Expects You to Know

TRACIE HOTCHNER

GOTHAM BOOKS

GOTHAM BOOKS
Published by Penguin Group (USA) Inc.
375 Hudson Street, New York, New York 10014, U.S.A.
Penguin Group (Canada), 90 Eglinton Avenue East, Suite 700, Toronto, Ontario M4P 2Y3, Canada (a division of Pearson Penguin Canada Inc.); Penguin Books Ltd, 80 Strand, London WC2R 0RL, England; Penguin Ireland, 25 St Stephen's Green, Dublin 2, Ireland (a division of Penguin Books Ltd); Penguin Group (Australia), 250 Camberwell Road, Camberwell, Victoria 3124, Australia (a division of Pearson Australia Group Pty Ltd); Penguin Books India Pvt Ltd, 11 Community Centre, Panchsheel Park, New Delhi–110 017, India; Penguin Group (NZ), 67 Apollo Drive, Rosedale, North Shore 0745, Auckland (a division of Pearson New Zealand Ltd.); Penguin Books (South Africa) (Pty) Ltd, 24 Sturdee Avenue, Rosebank, Johannesburg 2196, South Africa

Penguin Books Ltd, Registered Offices: 80 Strand, London WC2R 0RL England

Published by Gotham Books, a member of Penguin Group (USA) Inc.

First printing, October 2007

10 9 8 7

Gotham Books and the skyscraper logo are trademarks of Penguin Group (USA) Inc.

LIBRARY OF CONGRESS CATALOGING-IN-PUBLICATION DATA

Hotchner, Tracie.
   The cat bible : everything your cat expects you to know / Tracie Hotchner.
      p. cm.
   ISBN 978-1-592-40325-7 (pbk.)
   1. Cats. I. Title.
   SF447.H673   2007
   636.8–dc22   2007009791

Printed in the United States of America
Set in New Baskerville

Dedicated to Tim,

my completely

wonderful brother

CONTENTS

FOREWORD

By Dr. Dawn D. Stelling, D.V.M.

Cats are not small dogs. I realize this may sound like a foolish statement, but as a veterinarian, I'm surprised at the number of people who think getting a cat is like getting a dog, only less work. This couldn't be further from the truth. Although most cats are litter-trained and don't need to be taken for walks, many require more attention and care than dogs, only in different ways.

Providing care to cats in all walks of life is part of my daily routine as a vet. However, these cats do not come into my office by themselves. Each cat is attached to a person with his or her own individual set of concerns and questions. It is my job to provide people with all the information I have, discuss all of the options, and allow the owner to make the best decisions for their cat.

Tracie's book is designed in a similar manner. Tracie provides up-to-date, often thought-provoking ideas and information that will empower you to make educated choices for you and your cat. Some of the facts and theories she presents may shock you and even cause you to disagree. In fact, I reacted that way myself in several spots, but then I realized that controversy and disagreement can often be healthy. New ideas and information challenge us to evaluate how or why we do things, and may even result in change for the better.

Ultimately, what is important is what is best for *your* cat. Tracie's approach in this book is to give you information that you can use in your own cat's best interests. Each cat is a special, unique individual with her own set of needs. *The Cat Bible* provides you with the tools to make the best possible life for your kitty. Use this book to tailor your own personal approach to nurturing your bond with your cat. May you enjoy many happy, healthy years together.

Dawn D. Stelling, D.V.M.
Southampton, New York 2007

Dawn D. Stelling got her B.S. in Animal Science at Cornell and went on to get her degree as a Doctor of Veterinary Medicine at Cornell University. She practices at a small animal hospital in Southampton, New York, where she lives with her husband, Robert, their three small, darling children, Shawn, Ryan, and Summer, and two young dogs, Hobie and Hula—none of which interests her cats, Moet and Jazz, who are certain she cares more about them than anything else. But, being cats, of course they would think that.

FOREWORD

Stephanie Shain, Director of Companion Animal Outreach,
The Humane Society of the United States (HSUS), Washington, D.C.

Are you a cat person? After years spent living with and adoring dogs and cats (and a selection of rodents), the realization that I am primarily a cat person came as a total shock to me. I was having a conversation with my husband about the latest antics in our 4-dog, 6-cat household and which critters were responsible for what minor disasters of the day when he proclaimed my feline bias. I was stunned, since I had always thought of myself as an "everyone" person. But since that day I have come to see clearly that I lean toward cats, and what it is about cats that (in spite of my doggie affections) that makes me a "cat person." It's that my cats are more like my friends, while my dogs are more like my kids. I know my cats love me, but they don't hang on my every word and action. They are more my equals, not adoring fans. Although I know my cats love me and that their safe and happy life requires just as much from me as my dogs do, they just *seem* less needy.

The fact is that cats are seen as more independent—more "I can take care of myself," if you will—and their welfare may suffer because of that image. Cats are often thought of as low-maintenance pets, and perhaps, compared to a dog who has to be walked 3 times a day, that's true. But too many people mistake low maintenance for no maintenance—cats still need love, attention, and a healthy dose of protection to thrive and be happy. We tend to trust that cats will somehow be fine on their own. No responsible dog person would let their pooch out in the morning when they go to work and expect him to take care of himself all day, yet we treat our cats this way and consider it normal, if not vital, to their happiness. (It is neither!)

Think about it. If you see a dog wandering alone in your neighborhood, you most likely think the dog is lost and you try to intervene. Loose cats are seen as just out for the day, and the intervention that might save them often doesn't come. While dogs would surely be thrilled to have the day to themselves for checking out garbage cans and tussling with other neighborhood dogs, we don't allow them to roam alone because we know it's not safe. Lost dogs are searched for immediately, while lost cats are often given a couple of days to "go off hunting" before we start hunting for *them.* This is a catastrophic mistake in many cases. We should offer our pet cats that same level of protective care.

There are more pet cats in America than there are pet dogs, a shift that happened in the 1990s and continues today. But being popular hasn't necessarily equaled a happy ending for cats. While millions of cats are loved and adored, millions more are abandoned or neglected. Cats are adopted from shelters in fewer numbers than dogs. In most parts of the country, we still have a "kitten season," a time in the late spring/early summer when litters upon litters of unwanted kittens surge into shelters. Lost cats are reunited with their owners far less often than their canine counterparts because we don't routinely put collars and ID tags on cats, as we do with dogs. In a recent publicized case in which a large number of dogs and cats were taken away from people who had kept them in cruel conditions, of the more than 100 dogs and 26 cats who were rescued, only 1 cat was adopted, but there was a waiting list to adopt all the dogs. That is a sad reality to face. Saving cats from the myriad of cruelties and tough circumstances they face will take more than the efforts of a national group such as The Humane Society of the United States and all the animal shelters combined. The lasting solutions will come only when a groundswell of cat lovers joins with these types of groups to learn more and then take action to proactively help cats.

I trust that you, as a reader of *The Cat Bible,* either are a cat person or are on your way to being one. I know that as you read on, you'll learn many wonderful things to help you better understand and care for your cat. I hope that you'll also take particular note of the portions that talk about less fortunate cats, and that you'll decide to extend your concern to those felines as well. Whether by helping to spay and neuter feral cats in your neighborhood or volunteering to pet and groom cats at your local shelter, there are so many opportunities to help, but not nearly enough of us cat people are pitching in and doing it. And really, I think we're all cat people . . . some of us just don't know it yet.

Stephanie Shain is the Director of Companion Animal Outreach for The Humane Society of the United States. She oversees programs dedicated to keeping pets and their people together through challenges such as behavior problems, allergies, and rental housing issues. Stephanie also directs campaigns to stop puppy mills, promote adoption, and assist feral cats. She lives in Washington, D.C., with her husband, two daughters, dogs, guinea pigs, and of course some remarkable cats.

THE CAT BIBLE

INTRODUCTION

As a cat-lover, you'll find that there are so many reasons you need this book. It can help you to understand the creature who shares your home, it will enhance the quality of your cat's life and the quality of your relationship with her, and it can also help you to avoid and solve problems. Cats are majestic, ancient creatures who have managed to share their lives with humans without ever compromising or forsaking their essential catness—a fundamental quality that we can all admire about them.

One of the biggest challenges for people living side by side with cats is that there are so few guidelines and guideposts about what cats need to make them truly content. For example, nobody gives you good information about how to make a cat's life stimulating, or ensure that her litter box is the *only* place she'll do her business, or even what a cat should be eating for a long, healthy life. People try to guess or chat among themselves, swapping cat stories in hopes of shedding light on these often-baffling, always-fascinating creatures who can share their lives with us for decades, often without giving up any of their secrets. Sometimes you can't help wishing that your kitty came with an owner's manual!

Consider this book that long-awaited guide to all things feline. Think of me as your cat's best friend, someone who wanted to find answers to questions on everything from a cat's basic physical needs to her complex psychological ones, all with the goal of creating a satisfying environment for your cat and in the process making her an even more delightful companion for you. A selfish motivation for this book was to unlock those mysteries for myself, because I have to confess that I used to feel a bit like an outsider in the world of cats, as though I was on the outside looking in, wondering what makes them tick. I love to watch cats, stroke them, marvel at them, yet I didn't have a sense of understanding them from the inside out. Does that happen to all cat lovers? Do all of us wonder, "How does my kitty *really* feel? What makes her truly content? What is she thinking now?" Or does a top-flight cat person—the most true-blue kind of cat-lover—never have that sense of otherness with his cats? Maybe it's just my fantasy, but I've always imagined that other people felt more deeply connected and in tune with the feline part of their family. Either way, I wanted to get closer to that interspecies wavelength myself, and this book made that possible.

But I didn't write this just for me. The more altruistic reason I steeped myself in everything there was to know about cats is because of what would happen with cat-lovers at book signings with my previous book, *The Dog Bible: Everything Your Dog Wants You to Know.* People who love cats would lurk at the edges of these all-about-dogs gatherings, looking both forlorn and hopeful. "I was just wondering if you're doing a *Cat Bible,*" many of them asked. "Our cats really need a book like this!"

Before embarking on another such ambitious endeavor, I wanted to see what books already existed with practical, reliable advice along with insights into the mysteries of feline behavior. I could sure see why cat-lovers were so hungry for satisfying information—it's a desert out there. Many cat books seem focused on what cats are *not,* explaining cats as "not being like dogs" (as in "unlike a dog, a cat would never . . ."), which makes about as much sense to me as saying that cats aren't anything like dandelions or chipmunks, either. Tens of millions of people own both dogs and cats, but I don't think anyone wants to relate to his or her cat in terms of all the doggish things she does *not* do. Why would anyone want to disrespect the essence of a cat by looking at her through the lens of the dog, or measure her by some canine yardstick? I want this book to offer a proper perspective from which to learn everything possible about your cat.

I also found an awful lot of books that seemed to assume that cat people are all a little nutty, believing that their cat can understand human language or can read their thoughts through interspecies psychic communication. Instead, this book treats a cat-lover as an intelligent, realistic person who wants to get closer to his or her cat or offer her a better existence but does not believe that she can literally understand long conversations directed at her. If you are someone who is more comfortable reading about a cat's "personality" than having it referred to as her "catsonality," then this is the book for you—and your cat.

So we know what a cat is *not*: She is *not* subservient, *not* all over us (usually) with affection or demands for it from us, *not* dependent on our behavior for her emotional well-being and *not* eager to chow down on everything we put in her bowl (in fact, she may not even eat at all if she doesn't like the bowl itself). The deeper I got into the research—from veterinary medical publications, interviewing vets and owners and combing through stacks of books—the more pieces of the puzzle came together. As I continued the search for information and theories about cats and their behavior, the more I learned about their physical and emotional development, their health and illnesses, nutrition, exercise and most of all communication both between them and us, and among their own kind. The more facts I accumulated, the more fascinating cats became to me.

No matter how many cats you have had in your life and how close you have felt to them, there has to be a great deal that you never had the need or opportunity to learn. You've probably been quite happy in your blissful cohabitation with your cat(s), maybe curious to learn more but not feeling compelled to dig around for explanations, information and advice. But now I've done it for you: collected every last scrap of fact and speculation about those mesmerizing felines, information that I hope will amaze, delight, help and surprise you, while also reconfirming what you have always imagined and believed about those special felines who share your home.

One of the best reasons I heard for writing this book came from Celia Sack, co-owner of the Noe Valley Pet Company in San Francisco. When my previous book, *The Dog Bible,* was first published, the very first book signing I had was at this charming store. "Oh, great!" Celia exclaimed when I said I was already at work on *The Cat Bible.* "Cat people *really* need you." I was a little surprised by the ardor with which she said this. "There is just so little for them," she explained. "First of all, there isn't a comprehensive book that seriously covers all aspects of cohabiting with cats and sharing the planet with them. So *The Cat Bible* will go a long way toward solving that. But there is the problem of cats from the retail perspective: the challenge of figuring out what to buy to make your cat happier. It's a problem because I can't honestly recommend anything for them to buy. It's bad enough that cats are such finicky eaters that people can work their way straight across the food shelf without finding anything their cat will eat with enthusiasm. But on top of that frustration, they can't even buy a bed for their cats. Cats won't set foot on most beds, so how can I recommend some attractive, costly cat bed? What I *could* sell is a cardboard box full of old cashmere sweaters—now *that* would definitely be a successful item! Plus, people can't buy fun stuff for their cats because there aren't many toys that interest cats—how can I, in good conscience, sell a $14 cat toy to someone when I know that what their cats really want are bottle caps and rings from plastic water bottles and milk jugs? There isn't a cat around who wouldn't rather bat a plastic water bottle lid around on the floor than almost anything."

This book is here to give you practical folk wisdom like that, as well as the newest studies about cat behavior and the most up-to-date information about medical conditions, vaccinations and parasite products, along with controversial topics such as indoor versus outdoor living and what to feed for long-term health.

One of the great attractions about cats is that they are the proverbial conundrum: an "enigma wrapped in a mystery." This book does not intend to diminish the mystical effect that cats can have on us, but it will peel away some of the layers for a greater understanding. You owe it to your cat to get this book, if for no other reason than as a guide to demystifying cats in practical situations where—once you understand the natural forces at work—you can join forces with your cat to find solutions, rather than working against her inborn feline nature.

◆ How to Use This Book

Until *The Cat Bible,* there was no single resource guide that could explain all about your cat's mind and body while also steering you toward the best ways to feed and care for her—one volume to answer all your questions while also giving you reliable information about things you might not have even considered. Let's just say that this is the one book you'd need if you were stranded in a mountain cabin with your cats—which I hope never befalls you unless it's a lifestyle choice you want to make.

The book has a detailed table of contents at the front to steer you in the right direction, and

then a super-duper index in the back with every topic broken down into the smallest possible fragments so that you can find it in a flash.

So dip into this book for curiosity and pleasure, or grab it for quick feedback and explanations. You may never read all of it, or you may not be able to put it down until you have, but however you use *The Cat Bible*, your cat will be glad you did. She expects you to know what's in here for her own good. And what's more important than your cat's happiness, right?

Chapter 1

CHOOSING YOUR CAT

Some Questions to Ask Yourself Pre-Cat

Before we run through all the ways and places you can find a cat, the responsible thing to do is ask yourself some hard questions about whether you can give a cat a good home. I know, it may rub you the wrong way to be put on the spot. You may wonder why you should have to answer a bunch of questions when there are so many cats waiting for a home, so many who might even be euthanized if they aren't adopted. But that doesn't change the fact that not all people are in a position to offer a good home to a pet—even though they might think they are. Animal shelters can get very crowded, and the usual reason that animals get turned in is because people couldn't deal with them. Some of the questions that follow may be ones you wouldn't even think to ask yourself, but if you want to be part of the solution and not the problem, then ask yourself in all honesty whether *you* would want to be a cat in your home.

There are a number of practical considerations about your lifestyle that you need to review before you take on the responsibility of a feline family member. Some you may have already realized before deciding to get a cat or kitten, while others you may not have considered.

THE BASIC QUESTIONS

♦ Does Your Lease Allow Cats?

If you own your own home, then you need no permission to get a cat, but if you rent an apartment or own a condominium or co-op, you must make sure ahead of time that having a pet is allowed under your lease or the rules of your building or community. If your contract does not specifically forbid you from having a pet, then you should be all right—but most leases do specify something on this topic. Even with a no-pets clause in a contract, many people will say, "It's only a cat, the landlord will never know," but you are putting yourself and your cat-to-be at risk. Landlords *do* find out about pets—if they come to fix or check something in the house or apartment, it's too easy to get caught. The real question is this: If your landlord finds out and tells you to either leave or get rid of the cat, would you be willing to move to keep that cat? Because if you aren't sure, or if the answer is no, then don't be selfish and put that cat at risk of being homeless. If she came from a shelter, going back there is more than stressful for her. It is harder for an orphaned animal who finds a new home and then loses it than it is for a cat who never has that chance at being in a family. Unless you're willing to stick with her through thick and thin, don't introduce a cat into your life. If you get the okay to have a cat, get it in writing, as managers may come and go and you want to be protected.

✦ Any Allergies in the Family?

If you have a partner, children, or roommates, you need to ask if they have allergies and whether a cat will aggravate their allergic condition. If anyone isn't sure, then take the time to arrange a test: Put that person in a room with any cat to see if he or she gets itchy and watery eyes, sneezing, constriction of the throat and so on. This will tell you how the person responds to a cat right now, but in reality some allergies take months to develop and exhibit symptoms. Although there are remedies, from antihistamine tablets to allergy shots, you need to ask if that person is willing to accommodate the cat. There are numerous suggestions in Chapter 8, "Humans and Cats," about ways to lessen allergic reactions. No matter what, make sure that the allergic person is willing to make the personal sacrifice to live with a cat.

✦ Does 10 to 20-Plus Years Sound Good to You?

A young, healthy cat who lives indoors can live for that long—does that appeal to you, or does it feel like too big a commitment?

✦ Do You Have Preschool-Age Children?

Very young children may have a hard time understanding how to be gentle to and respectful of a cat. This can result in scratches to the child or emotional disturbance and even physical harm for the cat. If you have small children, do you feel you can teach them how and when to pick up a cat—or even not to lift a cat but only stroke her in certain ways and at certain times?

✦ Do You Have the Financial Means to Support a Cat for 20 Years?

Cats may not seem like a costly luxury to you, but they cost money in ways you may not immediately think of. Of course everyone knows cats have to eat, but you may not consider that they need to have a lot of protein in their diet—and that can be costly. The same with litter—seems cheap, but those bags add up over a year, too. And then there is the serious cost of veterinary care: If you are wise (and able), you should sign a new cat up for pet insurance the minute you bring her home. If you don't believe that veterinary insurance is a good financial move for you, it will seem like a bargain after you get your first vet bill and the insurance covers most of it. Advances in veterinary care and the cost of it all can be ruinously expensive, but once you're in love with a cat and that animal gets hurt or sick, emotionally you'll want to do anything you can to make that cat better. Some people just wing it, hoping nothing bad will happen. But it's probably wiser to think about whether you have the ability to pay for medical care—or how you would feel about not being able to afford it. I certainly hope nothing bad ever happens to your kitty, but this is a cost you need to consider when making your decision. Have a look at the pet insurance section below and make a decision that suits your situation.

THE CAT LEFT ALONE: LIFESTYLE ISSUES

◆ Do You Have Very Long Hours out of the House?

Whether for work, recreation, or travel, do you spend more time outside than you do in your house? Contrary to popular misconception, cats are *not* happy when left alone for long periods and can get as depressed and anxious as any other living being when they have no company or stimulation. If you want a cat, then you have to be willing to spend time with her—otherwise what's the point of having an animal share your life?

◆ Cats Do *Not* Like to Be Left Alone

If one of the reasons you're thinking of getting a cat is because you've heard that they are no trouble and can be left alone for days, *think again*. People have been terribly unkind to their cats—unknowingly—in accepting the idea that cats are happy being left alone for long hours or even days at a time. People hear that cats are so independent that they don't even care if people are around, and so they add a cat to their home as though it were an adornment they can interact with or not. I guess we've chosen to accept this clearly illogical misinformation as being the truth—in part because it makes cat ownership so much easier.

◆ Put Yourself in the Cat's Place

Shouldn't we stop to consider what kind of thinking, feeling creature on this earth would really *want* to be totally alone if it could choose? The only family pet that might be perfectly happy spending days at a time by itself is a python (but I don't even know that for sure, and probably never will since there is no *Python Bible* in the works). It may be that a cat won't visibly sulk or act depressed from being left alone for long chunks of time, but she's got to be feeling the boredom and loneliness. Whether a cat just keeps that unhappiness inside or exhibits her boredom or anxiety in other ways, such as overgrooming or litter box problems, the only really kind way to have a cat if you will be out of the house a great deal of the time is to have another cat as a companion for her. This is especially true for a cat who is going to be entirely indoors, which is now the recommended lifestyle for cats.

◆ Do You Already Have a Cat?

Before deciding that you want another cat, be sure that decision is fair to the cat or cats you already have. Take a good look at the section on multiple cats in Chapter 11 even if you are already a multi-cat household. It's important to keep in mind that cats are very territorial, so if you are going to bring more of them into your home, you need to introduce the cats properly (more on this later). You need to have enough room for multiple litter boxes and high and low places for cats to have "alone time" and get the solitude and quiet they crave. If you cannot provide that, then you aren't doing any of the cats a favor—not the one(s) already living with you, nor the one you are thinking of adding, whose life will be hellish if her reception is hostile. No matter how much you love the idea of having more than one cat, and even if you have one cat who might seem lonely to you, be sure you try to view the introduction of a new cat from your existing cat's perspective. Even though it may seem jolly to you, your cat(s) may feel quite the opposite—especially if you have an older cat and are thinking of making her life truly miserable by "giving" her a kitten to irritate her night and day.

◆ An Exception: Getting Two Kittens/Cats at Once
Two cats are company for each other, which makes for a much better life for them when you are out. It also relieves guilt you might feel, which makes the cat less of an emotional burden for you, especially if you're out of the house a lot. If you are getting a kitten, the best gift you can give her is to take home one of her siblings at the same time. The two already know each other and can settle into life at your house with confidence and companionship.

PET HEALTH INSURANCE
I recommend that all cat owners buy pet insurance before they do another thing for their pets. When you get a new cat, signing her up *immediately* for insurance is vitally important. I have had so many people tell me that they thought insurance was a good idea but had procrastinated about getting it—only to kick themselves later, because the day came when they needed serious medical care for their cat and did not have insurance coverage to help with the astronomical costs of veterinary care today. All it takes is one not particularly complicated episode of urinary blockage (to which cats are particularly prone) and you will be very grateful for the insurance safety net.

If you already have a cat and don't have her insured, consider it a lucky twist of fate that you are reading these words. Don't wait another minute. Accidents and illnesses happen when we least expect or are least prepared for them, so why tempt fate when having health insurance would make any problem more bearable?

◆ Are You a Person Who Generally Believes in Carrying Insurance?
You may have insurance for your car, home, belongings, death, disability and so on. Pet insurance may be another important investment you might want to make. Whatever it costs to insure a pet is much less than the amount you will get back if your pet has any kind of significant medical problems or procedures. As with any insurance, if you go through a year with no claims, then consider the premium a good investment in your peace of mind.

◆ Veterinary Care Is More Expensive than Ever
Big health decisions for your cat often ride on the cost of sophisticated medical diagnostic tools. Complicated surgeries that can be performed on cats have evolved to equal many of the procedures available for people. In fact, the first MRI and CAT scan machines that vets used were the

recently outdated models from human hospitals. Until vets had this technology, they could neither diagnose nor treat many animal infirmities without exploratory surgery, as was once true in human medicine.

Both of the tests mentioned above, as well as ultrasounds and X-rays, are often used to help veterinarians find answers to whatever is ailing your pet. But those are just the *tests*. After those diagnostic tests are done, an operation or medications might be recommended. So the big question is, would having pet insurance make a difference to you if the doctor were to tell you that she wanted to do an MRI on your sick cat—and the charge was going to be $1,000? If an MRI or CAT scan were suggested to diagnose your child, it's fair to say that your health insurance would cover it—or if you didn't have the coverage, you would find a way to pay for that test. But how would you feel if the patient was your kitty? Would you not do the testing because of the cost? Would you feel frustrated or guilty about not being able to do everything possible for her? Or would you pay the bill and kick yourself for not having gotten the insurance? Signing up *today* seems like it might be the best choice.

Because so many new insurance companies for pets are developing all the time, even though I have a list in Chapter 12, I will also maintain an up-to-date listing on the book's Web site, www.TheCatBible.com. This gives me the flexibility to add or remove companies as things evolve in the field.

◆ How Pet Insurance Generally Functions

Insurance Doesn't Cover Preexisting Conditions. If your cat has a complicated or expensive medical condition, the insurance company will request all of the cat's prior veterinary records when you make a claim, especially a large one. For example, when I adopted a cat in California and moved to New York soon after I had added her to my policy, the insurance company understandably wanted to see all of her prior veterinary records when a medical problem arose soon thereafter. They did pay the claim when it was clear that I had just adopted her and that her shelter medical records showed no sign of the problem.

There Is a 10-Day Waiting Period. After enrolling a pet you cannot make a claim during a waiting period, usually around 10 days. This is so people can't suddenly get coverage at the moment they need urgent medical care, which you wouldn't be able to do with health insurance for people, either. But once you sign, I wouldn't be surprised if you get a nervous sense of danger, of feeling you need to make sure your cat lives cautiously until those 10 days have passed.

There Is a Deductible and an Annual Limit on Claims. Insurance may not pay 100 percent of the bill, but it sure beats the alternative. When you are beside yourself with worry because your pet is ailing and you have a huge medical bill on top of it, you will be so grateful for any of the burden that the insurance relieves.

You Pay the Vet, Reimbursement Comes to You. One difference between pet and human insurance is that the vet does not have to participate in an insurance plan, and he does not do any billing on your behalf. The insurers ask you to get their form signed by the vet, with his diagnosis and treatment noted, and attach the doctor's bill (already paid by you). The insurance companies require that you return paperwork to them within a certain number of weeks or months for them to consider the claim, so if you're reasonably organized it shouldn't be a problem.

Insurance Companies Do Not Tell the Vet What to Do. Unlike in human medical coverage, a vet is not part of a health network overseen by the insurer. This is a beneficial difference between animal and human medical care because pet insurers have no impact on the vet's medical decision-making process. Each vet does what he believes is best for every animal without having to worry about an insurance company dictating his choices (as is now often the case in human medicine). There are already forward-thinking vets who are wondering what might happen when the pet insurers get more powerful.

There Is Often a Multiple-Pet Discount. If you have more than one dog and/or cat, you will probably pay a reduced fee for covering all of them. The fee per animal is based on age, with older animals costing substantially more to insure than younger ones. This is based on an actuarial table that shows more need for medical care as cats age. I would recommend that you not drop coverage on your older animals just because the premium goes up, even though you may figure that a senior citizen leads a safer, more sedentary life. All it takes is one bout of gastrointestinal upset with the lab tests, possible X-rays and medication to run up a serious bill.

When your cat has a problem beyond the capacity of your regular vet, he may refer you to a specialty veterinary hospital that is staffed entirely by subspecialists: vets who have been trained and received further degrees in ophthalmology (eyes), oncology (cancer) and so on. I have met pet owners in these waiting rooms who have spent $5,000 to $10,000 on their cat's care because they didn't have insurance. These are regular, working people who can ill afford such enormous bills, but they view their cats as family members and will pay anything to make them well or keep them alive.

There Is an Additional Premium for Cancer Care. It is understandable that an insurance company would charge an additional premium for a cancer endorsement or rider, given the high cost of treating the disease and the large numbers of cats and dogs who get some kind of cancer. You pay only a marginal additional premium, but if your pet does get cancer, you get more coverage for diagnosis and treatment. Given the current elaborate diagnostics and treatment for animal cancer and the sadly high statistics on pets getting cancer, it is a wise choice for most people.

Caveat Emptor: Beware a Few Loopholes. As grateful as I am for the existence of pet insurance companies, they are still insurance companies, and paying reimbursements is not the thing they like to do most. There are usually rules about how soon a claim must be submitted, payments may not be super-swift, they can be difficult to reach by phone, and when they refuse payment on a bill they require a written appeal from you and perhaps further documentation to reconsider reimbursement. It can be annoying, yes—but doesn't all of that sound just like the way insurance companies for people operate?

Choosing Your Cat

There's not much value to the idea of temperament testing for cats, since we all know they wouldn't submit to the test anyway unless they were in the mood. Dogs can be evaluated through a temperament test, but there is no such yardstick to evaluate cats, so you can't choose a cat or kitten based on a checklist of qualities. The truth is that there's really no way to pick the perfect cat for you, even if you knew what such a cat would be like. This is because one of the beautiful things about cats is that they do not reveal themselves all at once—getting to know them is a process, a gradual discovery of their enigmatic natures. Purebred cats are the only ones who tend to have somewhat predictable personalities and energy levels, but since only a small percentage of cat owners have purebreds, majority rules apply here.

WHAT CAN YOU TELL ABOUT A CAT AHEAD OF TIME?

Behaviorists who study cats have identified just two basic personality types for a cat, which you'll see below. But beyond that, there just aren't any clear guidelines that give you the ability to judge a cat's temperament ahead of time, other than sitting with a cat over one or more visits to discover how she interacts with you.

◆ Two Kinds of Cat Personality

Those who study cats generally agree that most cats' personalities can be divided into one of two groups, with subtle variations.

Type A cats are independent loners, aloof and maybe even reclusive. Type B cats are the kind of cats who will seek out people and other cats for companionship; they need affection and company.

◆ Don't Pick Extremes of Personality

When you go to the breeder—or, better yet, to a shelter—be wary of the cat cowering in the corner. If she's a kitten, that timidity may be her natural personality and nothing you can do will make much of a dent in it. If she is fearful and withdrawn, it may be that a trauma of some kind has driven her into a nervous state—in which case you're not going to have much effect there, either. When you're picking a cat, the best advice you can get is to avoid any extreme behavior—either very reticent or overly enthusiastic may spell trouble, so why ask for it?

WHAT KIND OF CAT PERSON ARE *YOU*?

When you try to imagine the perfect cat for you, what you also need to do is take a look at your side of the equation. In your imagination, what would your ideal cat look like? If you have a fantasy of the color and size of your dream cat, it's easy enough to accommodate the physical characteristics on your wish list—on any day of the week there are so many thousands of cats for adoption wherever you might turn (local shelters, breed rescues, Petfinder.com on the Internet, newspapers, etc.).

But what about personality and energy levels—do you have strong feelings about what those should be like in your cat? Kittens tend to zoom around and get into mischief, so they need to have their environment kitten-proofed while their personalities are developing and their energy mellows out. A grown cat will need less playtime and probably exhibit very little—if any—of the wild antics of a kitten.

When you meet an adult cat, you know in short order what her personality is. Does she like to sit on laps? Is she quiet and timid or bold and assertive? Shelters and rescue groups often know their cats very well and can help steer you to a compatible match if you have a sense of what qualities would be appealing to you in a cat.

But if you think about it, attraction often just happens. When you're dealing with another living, feeling being, there are two sides to the equation—and then the mysterious moment of being touched with that magical wand of mutual attraction: a glance, a stare in the eyes, something you can't even put your finger on. If you leave yourself open to that moment, you will know when it happens. For many people there is an "Aha!" moment—the "That's the one!" feeling—when they are attracted to a human partner. For some people this can happen with pets, too.

Call it animal magnetism, karma, fate or your "inner cat," and just go with it. What you'll be letting go of at that moment is the idea that you can mold a cat into what you want, or control her natural self.

AMOUNT OF GROOMING TIME REQUIRED

If you are attracted to cats with long hair, be prepared to brush your cat every single day. Purebred Persians or other long-coated breeds—or long-haired mixed-breed cats—often shed a lot, which can be helped by daily grooming. The other reason they need to be brushed for at least 5 to 10 minutes a day is that otherwise their coats will become matted. Mats can be painful for them, causing sores and infection or requiring a trip to the groomer or vet to have the mats shaved off.

So while you may love the look and feel of a long-haired cat, just make sure you have the necessary time, along with the desire, to devote to brushing that kitty every day.

DOES COLOR MATTER TO YOU?

There is a name for every one of the color variations that cats can be. If there is a particular coloration you like, now you'll know its name.

COLORS OF CATS

Classic tabby: broad stripes everywhere, including tail and legs
Ticked tabby: deerlike ticking everywhere, no stripes or spots (Abyssinian)
Spotted tabby: stripes on face, legs and tail with large spots on sides
Orange or marmalade: the typical all-over orange cat
Points: pale body, darker legs, tail and ears; always blue eyes (Siamese)
Tortoiseshell (tortie): black with patches of red (usually female)
Calico: white with patches of red and black (usually female)
Van: bicolor, with a white body and color on head and/or tail
Tuxedo: black with white on chest, stomach and feet

SHOULD YOU GET A MALE OR FEMALE?

People report very little difference in the relationship they have with one cat or another based on gender. Male cats who are neutered when they are young do not develop the kind of extremes of behavior that can happen with their unneutered counterparts. Unneutered males, or tomcats, are often off wandering, creating their own universe: fighting, spraying and looking for a receptive female. Females who aren't spayed have their personalities overridden by a biological drive to reproduce. However, once a kitten is spayed or neutered there is no way to distinguish between the sociability of either gender—and what you get is a cat who is much happier to hang out with you than go to the feline equivalent of a singles bar. If an owner decides to neuter later, the cat may retain some of the pre-neuter personality but nevertheless will settle down into a kinder, gentler cat.

If you do have a leaning toward one sex or the other, you should know that telling the difference between them when they are less than 7 weeks old may be difficult, even for professionals. Their genitals are located below where their tail joins their body. Below the anus there is another opening—just one for a female, but if the kitten is male it looks like two dots and there is more distance between them, a space into which the testicles will descend at about 7 weeks. Given how similar the two sexes look until that age, you're really best off to wait until then to figure it out. *Note:* To develop appropriate social skills, a kitten should remain in her litter with her mother until she is at least 8 weeks old. Breeders of pedigreed cats are encouraged by their breed organizations to keep kittens until they are 12 weeks old.

A YOUNG KITTEN, A MATURE KITTEN, OR A CAT?

Many people want a young kitten because they are so charming and entertaining, but folks often are not aware of the pros and cons of young kittens. An older kitten—9 or 10 months old—is more settled, may demonstrate more affection and will require less supervision, and if you have resident cats, the older kitten may make an easier transition. Before making your own decision about what age cat to consider, have a look at some of the issues to consider on the downside of little kittens.

A young kitten will be constantly on the go, darting around and under your feet. If you have any older folks in your home, this can be hazardous for them because they might trip and fall.

A little kitten can be destructive, because she is onto and into everything, causing breakables to break and materials to shred. She doesn't do it on purpose; it's just a factor of insatiable curiosity as she explores the world around her.

You have to watch a young kitten or keep her confined because she is going to be constantly getting into things that might harm her. Kittens need supervision so they don't do anything dangerous to themselves and also so they can learn what is expected of them, what is out of bounds, reminders about where the litter pans are and so on.

A young kitten may not be affectionate because she isn't that focused on you yet. After puberty and adolescence—around 9 to 10 months—she will settle down and become interested in her people. Until then, young kittens have too much energy to spend "quality time" with you.

A young kitten will require more vet visits for vaccinations, for sterilization and because kittens are frailer and more vulnerable to illness.

 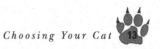

Kittens are more likely to nip and scratch when playing because they get more wound up and excited.

KITTEN TEMPERAMENT WARNING SIGNS

- ❏ A kitten who won't play with you may never play with you; she may not have been properly socialized.
- ❏ A kitten who cannot relax in your lap after you've had her there a few minutes may just be a tense individual who will always be uptight.
- ❏ A kitten who bites you may be destined to be a cat who bites or chews—there is no science to back this up, but why take the chance that a biting kitten may not outgrow it?

SIGNS OF PHYSICAL PROBLEMS IN KITTENS

- ❏ Very dry or oily coat (sickness or malnutrition)
- ❏ Bloated belly (intestinal worms)
- ❏ Signs of external parasites such as fleas or ticks
- ❏ Lameness or deformity of limbs or tail
- ❏ Discharge of any kind from any orifice
- ❏ Scratching ears—tarry substance in ears (mites)
- ❏ Oral problems such as odor, teeth missing, overbite or underbite
- ❏ Dirt or crust under the tail—signs of diarrhea

Ask your vet about a kitten with any of the above problems because many of these medical warning signs can be easily corrected.

WHERE TO FIND PUREBRED OR MIXED-BREED CATS

- ❏ Shelters, both private and public
- ❏ Strays
- ❏ Purebred breeders, "backyard experimenters" and private professionals
- ❏ Pet stores—from commercial "kitten mills"
- ❏ Purebred rescue groups
- ❏ Cat shows
- ❏ Classified ads in magazines or newspapers

Shelters: They Are Not All the Same

If you are like the vast majority of cat owners—who do not want purebreds—the best place to look for your special cat is from a local shelter or rescue group. You may also find a cat through ads on bulletin boards or in local papers, or just through word of mouth. But just as a famous bank robber explained that he robbed banks "because that's where the money is," your best bet to find cats in a wide selection of sizes, colors, and temperaments is where the cats are: shelters.

A shelter is a place where injured, lost, relinquished and abandoned animals are cared for and sometimes rehabilitated until some good soul comes along and gives them a second chance—a chance for a "forever home" where they can live out their lives with their new human family.

You want to visit as many rescue groups and shelters as you can because there can be a vast difference in the care they provide and in how the shelters are run. Some shelters are state-of-the-art in animal comfort and create a positive atmosphere for potential adopters, while others seem like draconian prisons where animals are cramped in depressing cages. But you cannot know where your cat could be waiting for you unless you visit as many as possible. Depending on how crowded a shelter is, there may be as little as a three-day waiting period before animals are humanely put to sleep because there just is not room enough to house them. If there are any purebred cats or kittens—which are in greater demand—they are usually not euthanized. So if you want to do the greatest good, adopt a mixed-breed cat and you'll know you have saved a life.

If you live in a fairly small community, you may only have one shelter near you—and with any luck it's a good one. You should patronize that shelter, even if after reading the checklist for shelters below you find that the facility is lacking in some respects. You should support your local shelter because it is part of your community and only with resident support will it be able to place animals in homes and make room for more. Even a somewhat deficient shelter is better than the alternative.

THE DIFFERENT KINDS OF SHELTERS

◆ Municipal Shelters

A shelter that receives money from a local municipality may also perform tasks such as picking up strays, going to the aid of trapped animals (domestic but sometimes wild, too) and investigating animal abuse. Municipal shelters are usually staffed by town or village employees; these people may have sought out the job of animal control officer (or whatever the local title is), or it may have simply been a job opening with decent benefits and job security. This means that the kind of staff you'll encounter in a publicly funded shelter can run the gamut from passionate animal advocates to civil servants punching a clock. While it would be great to encounter staff who fall into the first category, don't worry if you wind up with someone from the second category—you're not there to make human friends or get some hearty pat on the back for wanting to adopt a cat. At the end of the day what matters is how the animals are cared for and whether the shelter cares what kind of home you can offer.

◆ "Kill" or "No-Kill" Shelters

One distinction between shelters is whether a facility has a high volume of animals that come in and room enough to keep them until potential adopters can be found. Even though a no-kill shelter has a nicer ring to it (and you don't have to feel guilty that a cat will be put to sleep if you don't choose it), it would stand to reason that the kill shelters need your patronage even more because of their possible overcrowding. The staff and volunteers at the latter kind of shelter pay a steep emotional price for having to lose perfectly lovely animals due to lack of space, so when you adopt from such a shelter you are doing good for the humans in the equation, too.

Check the Humane Society of the United States Web site to learn more about how shelters are run: www.hsvs.org.

◆ A Private Rescue or Shelter

This kind of organization depends on private donations and fund-raising activities. This means that the facility and how it is run depend a great deal on how well the group is financed and who happens to be on the board of directors at any given time. As far as how you are treated when you go there to adopt, there can be as much variation here as in a public facility, from a chilly reception to a warm, welcoming one. Again, do not get caught up in the human end of the equation—you're here to give a cat a home and find a wonderful companion.

WHAT MATTERS IN A SHELTER

Cleanliness is probably the most important aspect because it indicates a level of respect and concern for the welfare of the animals and all the people working and volunteering there.

Cage conditions tell you everything about a shelter. Does each cat's cage have a litter box, a place for food and water, room to move around?

A *"living room"* is nice but not essential if cats are kept in small individual cages. Is there a time and place for the cats to get out of their small quarters? Is there a communal exercise area where cats can roam or play? Such living rooms usually have cat shelves, cubbies and/or perches to give cats a chance to be up high, which is important to them. Many rescue groups don't have the space for a living room but may take cats out of their cages into other spaces for playing and attention.

Compatibility of cats makes for harmony. Has the shelter figured out which cats can interact pleasantly with others and given them a place to do that? Dogs in a shelter can be walked by volunteers or let out in exercise pens, but it's not the same for cats. They deserve somewhere to stretch their legs and have a change of scenery, where they can also be comfortable amongst the other cats out with them.

Stimulation is really important for cats—they need activities to engage their minds. Some shelters have cat cages and/or communal spaces with bird feeders outside a window, which gives the cats a stimulating focus. Other shelters have well-protected fish in tanks or hamsters in inaccessible cages to keep the cats' minds occupied—the Humane Society of Knox County, Maine, has just such a setup and calls it "kitty TV." Volunteers have built screened patios for the cats where they can sit on shelves and watch "real-time kitty TV" in the world outside—making this innovative private shelter the very opposite of depressing.

A *sick room* is essential in a shelter because unless sick animals (coughing, sneezing, etc.) can be segregated until cured, all the animals are at risk for getting sick. It's really helpful if there is some kind of readily available veterinary care, such as regular visits from a vet or vet tech (veterinary technician).

YOUR EXPERIENCE AT THE SHELTER

It would be ideal to have a completely positive experience when deciding which cat to adopt. It would be nice to feel as though you and the staff are all on the same side, working to find a home for one of the unwanted cats. However, sometimes people coming to adopt feel they are being given the third degree, or the atmosphere is adversarial. If the shelter gives you a questionnaire or asks you a lot of personal questions, does it feel like they want you to adopt or that they're being too critical or judgmental? Does it feel like you're being interrogated harshly? Do staff or volunteers seem interested in helping you meet a cat, or do they make you feel like you're just interfering with their job?

You need to take a step back and realize this is not a personal attack. The reality of life for those on the other side of the desk is that many people like you want to adopt cats without understanding what they need to provide for them. Often the nicest shelters are the ones where they are most reluctant to just hand over cats for adoption—where they do put potential adopters through the wringer to make sure the cat they have been sheltering is never going to be in that position again. Please try to be patient and see it from the point of view of those temporary guardians: They want to do everything they can to prevent "bouncebacks," the return to the shelter of animals who were not placed carefully enough in new homes.

Think of it this way: You spend thirty or forty minutes in a shelter and see only the surface, but the volunteers and employees are there for months or years and see so much animal heartache. Please be patient with these devoted guardians and have some compassion for the tough emotional jobs they have: watching animals stuck for so long in their institution, only to finally find a home that may not appreciate their needs and may discard them all over again.

The easy way out is to get indignant at being questioned and declare that you're going to leave and look for your cat elsewhere. You could sound off and tell the people at the shelter that one of their cats has missed a chance at a loving home because they made you so uncomfortable. Maybe you think that will make them less intense with the next possible adopter—but maybe it will only justify their process. Half an hour of discomfort to you should be worth it for the sake of the deserving cat to whom you'll be giving a loving home for a lifetime.

Adopting a Stray Cat

Often a cat without an ID tag will hang around your house, hungry and bedraggled-looking. If you're in a position to adopt, that can be great, but you'll probably want a clear conscience about the cat's rightful owners. But even before you put up "Found Cat" signs, you will want to take that cat straight to the vet to be checked out. Cats can have diseases that are contagious to others or may have other underlying health problems. Your vet will want to scan the cat for a microchip ID; if that does not reveal the owner's name, then she will probably want to vaccinate the cat to protect against future illnesses and deworm the cat. You certainly need to test the cat for FeLV/FIV (which are explained in Chapter 13), especially if you already have cats.

Purebred Cats

There are several organizations that deal with purebred, or pedigreed, cats—the largest is the Cat Fanciers' Association (CFA), and smaller ones are the International Cat Association, the American Cat Association, the Cat Fanciers Federation, and the American Cat Fanciers Association. These groups are involved in regulating the showing of cats, describing what characteristics make a purebred and writing the rules governing these issues.

Only a small percentage of the cats in America are purebred—as few as 5 percent are registered as a breed, of which there are about 36 recognized by one of the cat registries, while another currently recognizes 39. If you are one of the few who is considering spending the time and money to find a specific breed of cat, there are some basics you should know about how cats get to the "marketplace." After you know the ins and outs of the purebred cat world, it really comes down to whether a physical type of cat attracts you.

BREED PERSONALITY

You may have been told by a breeder or breed enthusiast that there are personality traits associated with their breed, which may be part of what interests you. However, research has shown that the most significant influence on a cat's character—at least vis-à-vis people—springs from frequent handling during a kitten's early development. Almost all purebred cats have enthusiasts who make claims for their cats' excellent inborn temperaments, although there really aren't any scientific studies showing that the components of a cat's disposition (which she develops during her lifetime) can actually be passed on to her progeny (although there are studies showing that the disposition of the tomcat can affect the kittens). So if a breed of cat appears to be loving and playful, it may be a function of excellent kitten-rearing practices by the breeders—which might just as easily have a positive affect on any sort of kitten they might raise. And if the mother cat is relaxed rather than being tense and defensive, the kittens will follow in her footsteps.

On a genetic level, there are some definite differences in behavior and personality between one kind of cat and another, along with distinct colors and types of coat. From a strictly scientific perspective, there are no discernible anatomical differences between cats of most breeds—the exceptions being the Persian, with her flat face, or breeds with physical anomalies, such as the ears on the Scottish Fold.

HOW BREEDS HAVE EVOLVED

The way that breeds of cats (or any other domesticated animal) have developed is that people decided on certain physical and personality characteristics they wanted to emphasize, and then permitted only cats with those qualities to breed. Whatever specific variations were wanted in a breed would then be introduced in a carefully decided way.

Some of the oddest breeds have developed from accidental genetic mutations, which someone then meticulously bred to other cats with that same oddity (hairless, short-legged, odd-eared, flat-faced, etc.). Other breeds occurred naturally, such as the Maine Coon (see below), which some people have mistakenly imagined as a cross between a cat and raccoon—a misconception by people who didn't know that nature does not actually allow interspecies breeding!

INBREEDING

One of the concerns about any purebred animal is that if the gene pool is too small, people wind up breeding closely related cats, with negative consequences. For example, if two closely related cats are bred—such as a brother and sister—the kittens resulting from such a pairing are likely to die from birth defects or be sterile and unable to reproduce. This means that there cannot be much inbreeding in the cat world because any lines that are too closely bred will basically self-destruct before they can pass on any deleterious genes. However, there are still some hidden defects (known as recessive genetic traits) from inbreeding that slip through—and the eventual price to pay can be fertility problems, kittens that don't survive and inherited problems such as proneness to hip dysplasia and cancer.

One way that cat organizations have found to avoid these inbreeding problems is to broaden the gene pool of their breed by allowing what is called "outcrossing," or breeding to specified other purebred cats. This is particularly helpful in a breed that has few registrations and therefore a small gene pool to draw from. The Cat Fanciers' Association has allowances for certain breeds to be outcrossed with others—for example, the Devon Rex can be bred to British Shorthairs, Somalis can be crossed with Abyssinians, and domestic longhairs and shorthairs can be bred to American Curls.

DIFFERENCES IN PERSONALITIES AND PHYSICAL TRAITS

What follows are some of the personality types that some breeds—or groups of breeds—are believed to have by those who are devoted to them. It is not a complete listing of every recognized breed, since some are much less well known. When reading this list it helps to keep a healthy skepticism about whether there are true personality differences between breeds and/or dependable character traits. Please be aware that the description of personalities and other generalizations about each breed *are not proven.* Cats are first and foremost individuals, with their personalities shaped in great part by their early experiences, not their genes. Nonetheless, for the sake of thoroughness, I include these descriptions with the warning that the reader (or cat buyer) should beware.

◆ Abyssinian/Somali

This muscular, athletic cat has a close-lying coat that needs almost no grooming. Somalis are a medium-length-haired version of the Abyssinian with a coat that needs brushing about once a month. The cats are very energetic and enjoy interactive play. Some enthusiasts say they are really affectionate, although usually too active and on the go to be considered a lap cat. Others say that this Oriental breed is quite different from others because they are shy, do not trust strangers, and can be aloof and independent of people.

◆ American Shorthair

This is a muscular, stocky cat that can get quite big and comes in a vast array of coat colors. A laid-back breed, they are affectionate and want to be close to you. The short coat needs weekly brushing.

 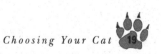

✦ Bald Cats

There are completely hairless cats such as the Sphynx, a naked-looking cat whose bald skin feels like suede and who is active and talkative and loves your lap, and the nearly bald Devon Rex and Cornish Rex, busy cats who like to play fetch and are very talkative. The totally bald ones have such greasy skin that you need to wash them every few days. The oil from their skin can stain the fabric of furniture and beds. The bathing doesn't have to be an elaborate process—a quick wash and dry is enough—but since these cats are easily chilled, they have to be kept warm until they are completely dry. They are also obviously sensitive to cold weather, and since they can also get sunburned, there is no doubt they should be kept strictly indoors.

✦ Birman

This is a long-bodied, large cat with white feet and dark blue eyes. They are an active, inquisitive breed and love to be with people, but they're not generally lap-sitters. Their silky longish hair does not mat and needs weekly brushing.

✦ Burmese

This Oriental breed tends to be outgoing and affectionate—even to the point of demanding their owner's time and affection. This is not a cat you leave alone at home all day. They crave a lot of attention because it is part of their genetic makeup—they like being the center of attention, and some will even react poorly if they are around people but are left out of the proceedings. To this end they are talkative, with a soft voice, and do not hesitate to initiate interactions with their humans. This is a muscular, elegant cat that is playful enough to want to play fetch but also happy to be a lap cat. Although devoted to people, they are not great with other cats and are often the aggressors in a fight.

✦ California Spangled

This cat has beautiful spotted markings and no wild blood—but the breed had a controversial beginning because the breeder who developed the cats marketed them through the Neiman Marcus Christmas catalogue for nearly $1,500 apiece. Cat-lovers thought it was disrespectful to any cat to sell them through a store catalogue as if they were a luxury accessory.

✦ Egyptian Mau

This spotted cat was bred to resemble the cats one sees in ancient Egyptian depictions of cats in art (*mau* means "cat" in Egyptian). It is a very active and chatty cat that likes to lap-sit. The short close-lying coat needs only a monthly hand combing.

✦ Maine Coon

These big, broad-chested cats are often enormous—the female averages 9 to 12 pounds and the male can go up to 20 pounds. They have a long shaggy coat that should be groomed a few times a week. An affectionate breed, they like not only children but dogs, too, and they love the *water*! They are considered doglike in that they will come when called, follow their people around and happily walk with harness and leash. Their voices are soft, their activity level is moderate and their fans are devoted.

+ **Manx**

This is the tailless cat with a compact, muscular body that can get quite large. They have either short or long hair but both require daily brushing. They are quiet, affectionate cats.

+ **Norwegian Forest Cat**

A large, muscular cat that has many different coat patterns in a long double coat with a dense undercoat that requires a commitment to extensive grooming. This cat talks quite a bit and is active and affectionate but is not a lap-sitter.

+ **Ocicat**

This breed resembles the Ocelot and was developed in the 1960s by breeding Siamese to Abyssinians and American Shorthairs. They are known for being outgoing, liking dogs and other cats and being amenable to leash walking. The Ocicat is a moderately large cat (females are around 10 pounds, males can get up to 14) with a powerful, muscular body. Some of them are chatty, others are not, but all enjoy being with their people.

+ **Persian, Himalayan**

Gentle, warm, calm and sweet-natured, the Persian's known problems with using the litter box and keeping clean are well tolerated by people who prize them for their other characteristics. They are prone to eye and sinus problems. They need to be brushed several times *a day*.

+ **Ragdoll**

This large-boned cat doesn't talk much, does not need much exercise and will look for a lap to sit in. They have a long coat with a wiry undercoat and so need a daily brushing.

+ **Russian Blue**

Long, fine-boned cats with a blue coat and silver tips, Russian Blues need grooming a few times a week. They don't need much exercise and, while affectionate, don't want to sit on your lap.

+ **Scottish Fold**

The ears on these cats are folded over, and they have a short, rounded body. They are affectionate and love children and dogs. They need to be with their people, mostly on a lap!

+ **Selkirk Rex**

This is a heavyset, large, muscular cat that likes people but doesn't want to lap-sit. They are modestly active and do not talk.

+ **Siamese**

This is a self-confident, highly active and playful breed that needs human interaction and mental stimulation or they can run a bit wild. They have a distinctive shorthaired beige coat with black points on the face, ears, legs and tail and need very little grooming. They are a very talkative breed—in fact, they talk more than any other type of cat—and can meow in dozens of different

 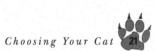

tones and timbres in what appears to be a genuine desire to connect, communicate and bond with people.

◆ Tonkinese
These are medium-sized, muscular cats that are active and can carry on a "conversation" with people. Their fine, short coat needs combing seasonally.

◆ Turkish Van
A long-bodied, active cat that talks quite a bit and is very affectionate.

◆ Turkish Angora
An imposing large breed that is very active and likes to retrieve objects like a dog. They chat a bit and are affectionate without liking to lap-sit.

WILD CAT CROSSES

There is a trend—frowned upon by some—to get wild-cat coloring in a domestic cat by cross-breeding with actual wild cats. The controlling registration organizations in the cat world have forbidden crossing any wild cat type with a domestic cat; they refuse to recognize any breed that has been created in this way. The object is to prevent breeders and amateurs from playing around with wild animals without understanding the potentially unpredictable consequences.

However, many of the cats with a spotted, leopard-like wild appearance do not have any wild blood. The California Spangled (see p. 20) is an example of a cat that resembles the wild cousins of cats but actually has no wild blood at all.

Generally speaking, the temperament of these wild-looking breeds is a middle-of-the-road energy level—they're neither couch potatoes nor hotwired dynamos.

◆ Bengal
This breed was created by crossing domestic cats with the wild Asian Leopard Cat. Some cat fanciers object to this breeding because a wild animal is unpredictable in so many ways, but those who have Bengals say that the cross has turned out to be both extremely attractive with leopard spots and really friendly. Breeders claim that generations of breeding only the most calm and sociable individuals has resulted in domesticated cats who have kept only the look of wildness without the problems of a wild nature.

PUREBRED PERSONALITY CHARTS

What follows is a chart identifying general personality traits of cats and the breeds known for possessing those qualities. There is no exact science to this chart, since every cat is an individual who is the product of her genetic background, her life in the litter and her earliest experiences. However, each of the breeds listed is definitely known for those qualities, so you can assume that a dedicated breeder will have influenced the selection of the breeding queen (which is what they call mama cats) and her spouse (tomcat) of the moment.

Active	Chatty	Affectionate/ Social	Lap-Sitting	Play Fetch and Other Doggish Things
Abyssinian/ Somali	Burmese	Abyssinian	Burmese	Cornish and Devon Rex
Birman	Cornish and Devon Rex	American Shorthair	Cornish and Devon Rex	Burmese (they act doglike and like dogs, too)
Cornish and Devon Rex	Egyptian Mau	Birman	Ocicat	Maine Coon (doglike)
Egyptian Mau	Norwegian Forest Cat	Maine Coon	Ragdoll	Scottish Fold (likes dogs)
Ocicat	Siamese	Manx	Siamese	Turkish Van
Siamese	Siberian	Norwegian Forest Cat	Sphynx	
Siberian	Sphynx	Persian	Tonkinese (prefer shoulder)	
Sphynx	Tonkinese	Himalayan		
Tonkinese	Turkish Angora	Russian Blue		
Turkish Angora	Turkish Van	Scottish Fold		
Turkish Van		Siberian		
		Tonkinese		
		Turkish Angora		
		Turkish Van		

Where to Find Purebred Kittens

PET STORES: THE TERRIBLE TRUTH

The best place to get a purebred cat is anywhere but a pet store. That's the long and the short of it. Pet stores that sell puppies and kittens are perpetuating the cruel, often barbaric warehousing of breeding dogs and cats that supply those stores. The purebred kittens in pet stores come from "kitten mills," which are mass breeding operations. We all hear a lot of bad press about "puppy mills," but the same kind of inhumane dollar-driven operations exist for cats, too.

The queens, or mother cats, are kept in dreadful confinement and forced to have litter after litter, without the benefit of human socialization, good nutrition or mental or physical stimulation for either mother or kittens. What you have are parent cats treated like breeding farm animals, and kittens born to malnourished mothers without the benefit of genetic screenings to avoid the problems of inbreeding.

But the good news is that there is a way to end the suffering of these poor cats. We are the ones who make selling pets a business: Vendors can charge whatever the marketplace will bear

 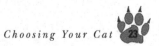

and, like any other business, it is based on supply and demand. The more requests there are for purebred cats from pet shops, the more kittens the commercial cat breeders will pump out into the pet stores. You may still be waiting to hear the positive side of this sorry story. It is that each one of us can have an impact on the animal-production business. If fewer people patronize pet stores, they will place fewer orders from the kitten mills—and with lower volume those "kitten factories" will have to reduce their prices and eventually stop production.

Do not even *think* that you can justify purchasing from a pet store by saying to yourself, "Oh, it's just one kitten, what difference can I really make? Besides, she is *so* adorable . . . blah blah." That is choosing the low road: justifying something that is going to perpetuate the cruel "animal factories" that kitten mills are. It's like buying clothes made in places where there is child labor and/or horrible work conditions: You can take a stand and not participate in that cycle by not purchasing, even going so far as to boycott the company or store that sells the stuff, or you can turn a blind eye and pretend you don't know, or buy the clothes on the twisted logic that they "are already in the store anyway" and "somebody else will buy them if I don't." But that doesn't make your participation any less immoral. Anyone who strives to live a conscious existence doesn't litter, doesn't shoplift, doesn't cheat or steal—all behaviors that any of us might consider for a moment before our moral compass sets us straight.

Do not even begin to think that you are being a hero and "saving the poor little kitten from the cage" in the pet store. If people stopped buying from pet stores, there would be no kittens and puppies in wire cages or hot window displays—and their poor mothers would not be hidden away in a much worse cage on some breeding farm somewhere. It is not just about you wanting this kitten right here and now—there is a bigger picture, and you can be an important piece in the mechanism to shut down the kitten production machinery. Your decision has a ripple effect that can be an example to others and inspire people to do the right thing. Every act of moral decency is felt in this world, and especially so in the world of animals who are completely our responsibility because they are brought into existence purely for our enjoyment. So if you want to be part of the solution rather than part of the problem, do not even walk inside a pet store that sells kittens. (Why tempt yourself? Would you go into a French bakery if you were on a diet?) And pass the word along—tell your friends to do the same.

Furthermore, illness is common in pet stores. Kittens are vulnerable to a number of illnesses when they are kept in close quarters with many others in a pet-store setting. Few pet stores have a good working knowledge of kitten health care, much less the skills or medication to promptly treat common but potentially fatal illnesses.

◆ Some of the Unreliable Claims Made by Pet Stores

"Our Kittens Come from Good, Reputable Breeders." It can't be true when a pet store assures you that its kittens are from "good" breeders, because responsible breeders belong to the nationally recognized organization of their breed. Good breeders would never subject their offspring to a pet-store setting and the unpredictability of where their kittens can wind up. But if you think they may be telling the truth, ask if you could have the name and phone number of this breeder to talk to them for yourself.

"Our Kittens Come from USDA-Licensed Brokers." This is a pointless claim since the USDA is the Department of Agriculture, a government agency that oversees livestock and doesn't even have enough inspectors to monitor the living conditions of animals that will go to our dinner tables. In any case, their criteria for evaluating a breeding facility are not applicable to pets. USDA rules and licenses have nothing to do with conscientious breeding practices for companion animals, nor with humane and beneficial kitten-rearing techniques.

"Health Guaranteed." You may feel reassured that a store would promise to pay for a kitten's care or replace it if anything should be physically wrong. However, many states have regulations for buyers of pets that were sick when purchased to be reimbursed for vet bills or receive a full refund—so this "guarantee" is pretty much required by law. If a pet store offers to replace a defective kitten as though it were a piece of equipment, doesn't that tell you everything you need to know?

"I'll Bring the Kitten to You." Avoid anyone offering to bring a kitten to your door "direct from the breeder." This is a middleman who has found a way to bypass the pet store to bring you a kitten of questionable origin, keeping the substantial profit for himself but denying you the recourse and backup of buying from an established retail outlet.

BACKYARD BREEDERS

Breeding cats is something best left to those who do it responsibly, as a vocation, not as a lark. "Backyard breeders" is the phrase commonly used to identify people who are breeding and selling cats with no plan in mind. Let's call them BYBs. They decide to mate their cat with another cat for fun—or profit. Some say it's to show their kids the "miracle of birth." But there are enough nature programs on television to satisfy any young person's curiosity. If BYBs want to teach their children something of value, it should be that it is not morally correct to bring 4 to 10 new kittens into a world where there are already thousands without homes. But I digress. The basic problem with BYBs is that they tend to be uninformed about the potential for genetic problems in all purebred cats. They breed without knowing how to make good decisions or find an appropriate mate for their cat.

BYBs generally aren't bad people—they can easily be people who love cats, enjoy kittens or want to make some extra money—but they are making a bad decision. They should not be trying to make a business of cat breeding when they are not educated about careful planning and attention to detail. Professional breeders often demand that their "pet-quality" offspring be neutered for this very reason: so owners don't suddenly decide they're going to breed on an impulse of "I'd love to make some dollars off my cat."

◆ Things to Know About Backyard Breeders

Participation in cat shows and/or competitions is a test of a breeder who takes what she is doing seriously. If a breeder is completely uninvolved in the cat show world—often true of BYBs—then she is not showing interest in top-quality breeding and the concerns of those who are doing it professionally.

No Knowledge of Genetic Defects. A sloppy breeder or a BYB may claim there are no defects in his breed, or that his cats are free of them. However, without testing and documentation this is an

empty claim (actually, more often a *lie*). Purebred animals are becoming increasingly at risk for horrible defects or life-threatening illnesses, many of which are not immediately discernible. You don't want to take on the heartbreak of painful medical problems if you can avoid it, nor do you want to encourage BYBs to breed their pets, which is exactly what you do by buying from them.

Handling the Kittens. The most important thing a breeder can do for kittens once they're born is to spend time every day handling and talking to them and later exposing them to as many different stimuli as possible. The important time for the kittens to learn from their littermates is in the sixth to eighth weeks. You want to avoid any breeder who does not know the importance of systematically socializing kittens from the earliest age or does not know how to stimulate them—all of which can be true of BYBs.

Selling the Kittens Too Young. Backyard breeders often give kittens away when they are only 5 or 6 weeks old, when they are too physically fragile to do well without their litter and have not gotten the full benefit of interacting with their mother and littermates. Although a kitten can leave her original family at 8 weeks, many professionals believe she should not leave her feline family before 12 weeks to get all the social benefits.

Failing to Register the Litter. Since there are three different cat registries, the failure of a breeder to document a litter anywhere is a sign something is not quite right. If a breeder tells you she hasn't had time, if nothing else it means that she does not take the business of breeding as seriously as she should.

PRIVATE (NONCOMMERCIAL) BREEDERS

Breeders who work on a small scale—as a hobby on the side or as their only business—are known as noncommercial breeders. I like to call them "private breeders" to contrast them with large-scale commercial cat farmers. These are the breeders you may hear about from word of mouth or through classified ads. They are people who have often devoted their lives to perpetuating the one breed (or maybe two) that they are passionate about. Obviously, just as in any small-scale business, some are much better at what they do, and take it more seriously than others. That's why I give you checklists and questions to ask: so that you can discover for yourself whether someone is bringing quality kittens into the breed you are interested in.

Keep in mind that cat breeding is a business—a business in which some breeders are more savvy salespeople than others. But once you are fortified with the information in this section, you should be able to pinpoint those private breeders whose devotion to their breed will give you the highest chance of getting a fantastic feline.

◆ Finding a Private Breeder

There are a number of ways, listed below, to find breeders of the kind of cat that interests you. Probably the most efficient and rewarding way is to go to a cat show, if there is one anywhere near where you live. But even if you do go to one, you can still explore some of the other options as well.

Cat Shows. Spectators get a chance to talk to breeders of cats that interest them, learning more in a short amount of time than they could any other way. If you have no idea what kind of cat appeals to you—or if you are certain of the one you want or curious about a few others—a cat show is a good way to see many of them.

Breed Clubs. There is a club somewhere in America for every breed. Contact the club and they should be able to tell you which breeders are closest to you. Buying from a breeder who belongs to a club gives you an extra perk: members have a code of ethics. It encourages honesty and adds incentive to do the best they can for their cats and potential customers. Cat clubs and some individual breeders are listed online. Just type in the breed of cat you're interested in and lots of choices appear. A word of warning: Don't be taken in by a slick Web site, because that tells you nothing about the actual kittens.

Breeders tend to belong to informal networks that provide them with information about what litters other breeders have or are expecting. If a breeder doesn't have a litter when you want a kitten, he will often be generous and send you to another breeder he knows who has a litter available. Because you are asking a favor of someone, be thoughtful about when you call. Figure out the time difference, if there is one, and avoid calling at dinnertime or too late or early. Do not leave your number on their answering machine unless you tell them to reverse the charges and return your call collect. You are asking for a recommendation of another breeder for which they will have no personal gain.

Veterinarians. Local vets can be a good source for cat breeders, and if there happens to be a vet in your area who specializes only in cats, she should be a good source to find breeders.

Cat Magazines. *Cat World* and *Cat Fancy* are the big commercial cat magazines that come out every month and seem awfully similar, which is no surprise since they are published by the same company. You can pick up copies at a newsstand and find a listing of virtually every cat show being held anywhere. There are also advertisements in the back of those magazines with classified and display ads for breeders.

Although the majority of breeders advertising in these magazines are reliable professionals, some breeders who advertise are *not* responsible and ethical. Have your antennae up when you speak to them on the phone, and use the list of questions for breeders to determine whether they are just trying to make a quick buck or are dedicated to turning out quality examples of their breed.

Newspaper Classified Ads. Many of the ads you'll see in the paper are not placed by high-quality, successful breeders, who often do not advertise in newspapers. Move cautiously. A lot of shady characters use ads to lure people into making deposits for cats that never even existed, so make sure you actually go visit any breeder who advertises and see what her cattery looks like. And ask for references from previous customers. This may seem paranoid, but unfortunately there are unsavory people who take advantage of others through pets.

There are phrases and buzzwords that are clues that an ad has been placed by an unknowledgeable or unreliable backyard breeder—or even someone posing as a cat breeder who is not.

If you see one or more of the following phrases in an ad (or the person says them to you), it is a tip-off that you are not dealing with a good, well-informed breeder.

"Shots and wormed." All kittens should have this done. Bragging about a basic health safeguard is unimpressive—and presumes the buyer doesn't know that.

"Registered," "purebred," or "pedigreed." All these words refer to the same thing—only a purebred cat with a pedigree can be registered.

"Championship lines." This can mean that the cat's grandfather or maybe only one or two other ancestors was a champion—meaning the breeder hasn't shown the kitten's parent(s). It must say "champion parents" or "champion sired" to show that the breeder has been taking her cats to shows and they have been judged as being of good quality.

"Rare color." This is a tip-off that the kittens may be from a careless breeding that resulted in colors that are unusual and not accepted in that breed's standards. Even if you don't intend to show your cat, the goal for any breeder is to conform to the breed standards.

Avoid anyone who pressures you to decide quickly. Cheap sales tactics such as insisting you make a decision about a kitten and buy it right away because "someone saw her earlier today and wants her" should be saved for used cars.

✦ Contact and Visit as Many Breeders as You Can

Try to visit as many breeders as you possibly can. Educate yourself. Comparison-shop, which is something you'd do with any important decision or purchase in your life—in this case, not for the price so much as for the right attitude. Visiting breeders lets you compare the physical qualities of the facilities for cleanliness, roominess, and whether the cats seem relaxed and happy in their environment. You need to visit a few breeders, if possible, because without a point of comparison it's hard to gauge what you are seeing and make an intelligent evaluation. You'll probably make a good decision if you trust your gut reaction, especially when something doesn't look or sound right to you.

E-mail is often the way contact is first established, but you can also make an old-fashioned phone call to get information about the cats a breeder has, using the recommendations in this section. Ask if you can meet the parents of the kittens. You should always be able to see the mother, although you may not be able to meet the father. But if the father is owned by another breeder and that cat lives elsewhere, that may be a good sign; it means time and money were spent to breed to that male. A good breeder makes informed choices about the best sire to enhance the qualities of his female and goes out of his way to breed to the right male—unlike a breeder who has males and females that he breeds because it's free and easy, even if that union might not result in optimal offspring.

Even the most successful breeders won't have what you might think of as a big, formal breeding facility; rather, the cats usually live right inside their house. Don't be alarmed if the house itself is untidy or a downright mess, because "animal people" often put their animals' well-being before their own. What matters is whether the cats' environment is clean, pleasant and equipped with toys, beds and clean water. There should be no bad odors, and especially not a smell of urine. The litter boxes should be clean or recently cleaned. Nothing should look dirty or broken or potentially hazardous.

Trust your intuition: If the place strikes you as not clean or safe, or if it's a place you'd never want to send a kitten back to, then walk away. No matter how far you might have come, you should turn around now and leave. It might seem rude not to be polite and at least go through the motions of looking, but it's only going to make you feel worse if you spend time with the kittens and then leave them in a place that seems awful to you.

◆ When the Kittens Can Go Home with You

Although many breeders of pedigreed cats let their kittens go by 8 weeks, their breed organizations encourage them to keep kittens until they are 12 weeks old. This is to ensure that the kitten does not come into contact with unvaccinated cats, although it's easy enough to keep a kitten indoors and away from other cats yourself. There is no absolute agreement on the best age for separating a kitten from her litter, since there are even some behaviorists who believe that 7 weeks of age—the age of natural weaning—is the perfect time for a kitten to bond with you during her greatest learning period.

The following qualities won't all apply to every breeder—but the breeder of your future cat should have a lot of these points.

WHAT A GOOD BREEDER DOES

- ❏ Is knowledgeable and enthusiastic about the breed
- ❏ Breeds only a few litters a year
- ❏ Breeds each female no more than once a year
- ❏ Breeds only one (maybe two) breeds
- ❏ Competes in cat shows
- ❏ Asks you questions about your lifestyle to be sure of a good home
- ❏ Wants to know if you have a dog or other cat
- ❏ Requires that you keep the cat indoors
- ❏ Answers your questions
- ❏ Doesn't pressure you to buy
- ❏ Has all the registration papers and records of the cat's health history and vaccinations
- ❏ Requires you to sign a spay/neuter contract if buying a "pet-quality" kitten
- ❏ Won't let any kitten leave before 12 weeks of age (or explains why)
- ❏ If you are not happy with the kitten, offers a refund, not just a replacement kitten
- ❏ Wants the kitten back if you can't keep her anymore for any reason at any time
- ❏ Tells you they'll take the kitten back if she develops any health issues (this is *not* a promise the breeder makes *instead of* genetic testing of the parents)
- ❏ Does not breed any nervous or aggressive cats, so as to get the best possible personality in any offspring

WHAT A BAD BREEDER DOES

- ❏ Doesn't show her cats or belong to a breed club
- ❏ Doesn't have registration papers for the litter from a cat association

❏ Doesn't show you the kitten's mother and littermates

❏ Doesn't have knowledge about the breed standards

❏ Doesn't know the problems or genetic defects in the breed (all breeds carry some risks)

◆ Questions to Ask a Breeder

The following is a list of questions to ask a breeder. Some breeders will be chatty and happy to answer questions; others will be annoyed if you bug them with too many. So start with the questions that interest you the most, see how the breeder responds, and go from there. How the breeder answers the questions tells you a lot about her as a person and as a businessperson. A breeder may not have thought about some of these questions before, but even the way she answers can reveal a great deal about how she views breeding and the kittens that result from it.

QUESTIONNAIRE FOR BREEDERS

❏ "How many cats do you have in your breeding program?"

❏ "How do you socialize the kittens?"

❏ "Do you breed more than one breed?"

❏ "How long have you been breeding?"

❏ "Do you participate in cat shows—and why or why not?"

❏ "Can I see where the cats live?"

❏ "What are the genetic problems in the breed and how do you avoid them?"

❏ "How do you guarantee the kitten's health?"

❏ "What do you do if she gets sick within the first week—or if genetic defects appear at any point?"

❏ "Can I get the kitten vet-checked before I make my final decision about buying?"

◆ A Few Other Safety Tips with Breeders

In addition, there are a few other safeguards that are helpful in determining whether your breeder is good one.

1. Ask for references from someone who bought one of the breeder's kittens recently—and also a buyer from a previous year. Take the time to call those people; it is worth it just to make sure they had no problems with their cat or that the breeder was responsive to any problems they did have. Also, if you have any doubt that the name the breeder gave you was really a prior kitten buyer and not just a friend or family member, ask the reference if he or she could send you a photo of their cat grown up. Almost everyone with cats has a photo of them. Even if the reference is reluctant to part with a photo, from the response you can tell right off the bat whether or not the person has a cat from this breeder—you don't really need the photo, just a sense that the cat exists and the owner is proud of her.

2. Some breeders give you a contract to sign that has restrictions on the buyer. Sometimes that contract gives the breeder/seller part ownership in the kitten, even after you have paid for her. In theory, that would have to do with breeding rights and future offspring. So find out whether you will actually own your kitten 100 percent—and don't sign a contract that you haven't read and understood.

3. Find out with which organization the breeder registers his litters. The big three organizations that register cats and hold shows are the Cat Fanciers' Association (CFA), the International Cat Association (TICA), and the American Cat Fanciers Association (ACFA). One of those groups is the standard for where a litter should be registered—if not, it is cause for suspicion. You would want to know why not.

◆ Questions the Breeder May Ask You

Below are some questions you might expect to hear from a breeder who takes seriously the kind of home his kitten is going to live in. Do not be offended by these questions, even if they make you feel defensive—they are the sign of a breeder who really cares. In fact, be wary of a breeder who does not ask you *some* questions about the life you have planned for his precious little kitty: Any caring breeder wants to have some sense that his youngster is going to have a good life. You can tell from these sample questions that the motivation behind them has to do with concern for the quality of life a cat that goes to live with you will have—since many people have misconceptions about the amount of companionship a cat optimally requires.

SAMPLE QUESTIONS FROM A BREEDER TO YOU

- ❐ "How many hours will the cat be left alone at home?"
- ❐ "Who is home during the day?"
- ❐ "Do you have young children?"
- ❐ "Can I visit your home?"
- ❐ "If you rent, could you get me a letter from your landlord okaying a cat?"
- ❐ "Have you had cats before—and what happened to them?"
- ❐ "Do you have any other animals at home?"

◆ The Cost of a Purebred Cat

Pedigreed cats who are "pet-quality"—meaning purebred but with even a slight imperfection compared to the written standards for the breed—can cost up to $1,000 and even beyond, depending on the rarity of the breed itself. A "show-quality" cat—meaning everything a judge should be looking for in that breed—can be $2,000 or more.

Even though this may sound like a ton of money (and compared to non-purebred kittens being given away free, it certainly is a pile of dough), don't think breeders are laughing all the way to the bank. If the owner of the queen doesn't own the male, he has to pay a stud fee—plus all the costs of pregnancy, birth and care of the kittens in the early weeks.

THE PUREBRED CAT REGISTRY ORGANIZATIONS

There are three different national organizations that hold cat shows, register litters of purebred kittens and recognize between 37 and 56 breeds of cats.

 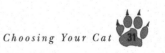

CFA (Cat Fanciers' Association) is the largest (sponsoring over 350 shows a year) and oldest (more than 100 years) of the registries. CFA recognizes 37 breeds of cats and can be accessed on the Web at www.cfainc.org or by calling 732-528-9797.

TICA (The International Cat Association) has been around only since 1979 but sponsors about as many shows as CFA and recognizes even more breeds (56). They can be reached at www.tica.org or 956-428-8046.

ACFA (American Cat Fanciers Association) is the smallest organization, around since 1955 but with only 50 shows a year and 49 breeds recognized. See www.acfacat.com or call 417-725-1530.

There is also the *Traditional Cat Association*, www.traditionalcats.com, and the Cat Fanciers Federation, www.cffinc.org, 937-787-9009.

PUREBRED RESCUE GROUPS

For every breed there is a network of rescue/foster groups that will take in unwanted cats of that breed and keep them until a suitable home can be found. Cats may find themselves without a home because of many human issues: People have to move, they may lose their jobs and have financial constraints or they may fall ill or develop allergies or share their life with someone who does.

Therefore, if you like a certain breed but can't afford the hefty price tag—or you prefer the idea of adopting and doing a good deed—you can contact one of the breed rescues and see whether they have any cats in your area.

The Purebred Cat Breed Rescue was formed as a nonprofit group in 2004 and coordinates efforts of cat fanciers in providing a safety net for purebred cats. They work to remove purebred cats from shelters and also assist animal control agencies who find situations with neglect, cruelty or large numbers of cats, helping to move the cats to foster homes.

You can try www.felinerescue.net; www.fanciers.com/rescue.html; www.purebredcatbreeds rescue.org. There may also be good kitties for adoption on www.petfinder.com. Try www .abyssinian-rescue.com for Abyssinians; www.geocities.com/bengalrescue for Bengals; www .burmesecat.org/rescue for Burmese; www.mainecoonrescue.net for Maine Coons; www.persian catrescue.org for Persians, www.scottishfoldrescue.net for Scottish Folds; www.siameserescue.org for Siamese.

Expect to pay between $100 and $200 for a rescued purebred, to cover costs incurred by these devoted foster families who have to do many things for these relinquished kitties.

Chapter 2

THE BASICS

 This chapter will fill you in on all the facts you'll need to better understand your cat, particularly because there are feline behaviors or activities that can be hard for us to decipher. After the first section, on how a kitten develops, the headings are alphabetical so that you can easily locate what interests you. Information about how a cat's body and senses function and what her body language may be communicating, should help you to more fully understand and appreciate your cat, bringing you closer to her.

Random Cat Facts

- A group of kittens is called a *kindle.*
- A group of adult cats is called a *clowder.*
- A mother cat is called a *queen* or a *dam.*
- A father cat is called a *tom* or a *sire.*
- A cat has 230 bones in her body, 10 percent of which are in her tail.
- The cat is the only species of animal that can walk while holding its tail vertical.

The Different Colors of Cats

The color of a cat is sometimes determined by the animal's sex.

Calico cats tend to be female, while **orange cats** are almost always males.

A **tortoiseshell** cat (also known as a "tortie") has a black coat with patches of yellow or orange.

A **calico** cat is a tortie with patches of white.

A **tricolored** cat is either a tortoiseshell with a diluted coat pattern where the black is replaced by gray, or a calico cat where the orange has been replaced by a cream color. Tricolored male cats are very rare—about 1 in 3,000. For a male to be tricolored there has to be a genetic flaw (having to do with chromosomes), and usually these males are sterile—but don't count on it, since some of these tricolored males have been known to become fathers. Apparently, there are people who believe that tricolored males have some special monetary value because they are unusual. This is just a myth, and unless you can find another person who is under the same delusion and wants to buy him, your cat has *not* just won the lottery for you. Simply enjoy your tricolored male for himself.

Kitten Development

THE FIRST TWO MONTHS

The initial 2 months of a kitten's life are referred to as "the sensitive period." During this period of development in a kitten's life, she learns to form social connections, whether with people or other animals—especially of her own species. If a kitten does not socialize during these 2 months she may never overcome a general reluctance or apprehension about interacting or socializing.

◆ Learning to Move

There's not much a kitten can do on her own in the first 2 weeks—she relies on her mother for absolutely everything. She can barely move for the first 2 weeks of life; after 2 or 3 weeks she begins a kind of preliminary walking movement. Because nature equips a kitten to be able to smell her mother's teats and feel her warmth, the kitten can maneuver over to her mom in a paddling fashion. By the time she reaches 3 to 4 weeks, the little one will have started to walk in a wobbly way to get to her mother and to move around a little.

When they reach 4 to 5 weeks of age, kittens start to run, but not until a kitten is 6 to 7 weeks old does she begin to use all the gaits of an adult cat. It is not until this stage of development that a kitten has the mobility to really start exploring her world.

◆ What They Eat

Kittens live solely on their mother's milk until they are a month old, after which time they begin to eat solid foods. However, there is no on-demand feeding in the cat world—the mother is the one who determines when the kittens will be allowed to feed.

◆ External Stimulation Is Necessary for Development

If a kitten is kept in a setting that does not challenge or stimulate her during the sensitive period, the result can be that the kitten never learns how to overcome a problem or even how to be interested in her environment.

◆ Early Handling by People

The amount of handling a kitten receives in her first 8 weeks will influence whether she becomes a friendly cat who seeks out the company and affection of humans. In order for a cat to become well socialized and feel at home with people, it is tremendously important that as a kitten she is handled gently and frequently by people (any person will do) between 2 and 7 weeks of age. Kittens handled frequently between 2 and 7 weeks of age are known to develop into people-oriented, outgoing, responsive cats. Studies show that kittens who are handled regularly and get used to people in the first 45 days of life seem to develop a willingness to be handled and a general inquisitiveness.

It is important to emphasize that it does not matter who does this handling—and it certainly does not have to be the people who will eventually give that kitten a home. All that matters is that humans have their hands on those little kitties.

Some people believe incorrectly that if you handle kittens at all in their early weeks, their mother will turn her back on them and refuse to nurse them. This is decidedly false. But it *is* true that if a mother cat perceives there is too much human intrusion into her litter, she may take her babies off and hide them. The best course of action, therefore, is to handle the kittens for only about a minute a few times a day.

◆ Too-Early Handling by People Is in Question

Some cat experts believe that handling kittens before they are 2 weeks old may make them less friendly. Other cat experts believe that picking up kittens from birth will make them more friendly to people—nothing more than taking a few minutes each day to lift each kitten, turn her around in their hands and stroke her. Those who subscribe to the theory that early handling impedes the cat-human relationship do not have any theories about why this is so, although they presume that the human contact interferes with the way that kittens learn.

Everyone seems to agree that litters of kittens born without human contact of any kind will hiss at people who try to handle them when they reach 2 or 3 months.

However, kittens do need to stay in their litters to develop properly. If kittens are bottle-fed, hand-reared (which can delay physical development while also causing a kitten to be frightened by and/or aggressive toward other cats) or taken from their mothers too early for any reason, it does not bode well for their personalities. They can develop into unpredictable cats who switch in a moment between friendliness and aggression toward people. So it is definitely

unwise to remove kittens from their mother and littermates before they reach 7 or 8 weeks; their physical, emotional and social development may be adversely affected by separating them before this age.

A MOTHER'S PART IN HER KITTENS' DEVELOPMENT

✦ An Ill Mother

If a kitten's mother is ailing or malnourished when she rears the litter, her illness leaves a lasting deficit, both physically and psychologically, on all of her kittens. A mother cat who is sick will probably be less attentive to her kittens and less able to do her maternal job of teaching social skills. The early skills that a mother teaches her kittens are essential to prepare them for later life. If that learning stage is compromised, those kittens will have personalities that reflect the deficit. This can lead to kittens becoming cats with behavior problems such as timidity, aggression and/or antisocial attitudes to other cats.

✦ Limited Milk Supply

If the mother has insufficient milk for her litter, the kittens will be smaller and weaker. This situation may also result in kittens who are lacking in social and physical skills. Kittens who have to spend extended amounts of time suckling, trying to get nourishment from their mother's limited milk supply, have less chance to learn how to interact with other cats or how to relax.

✦ Devotion in the Early Weeks

For the first 24 hours after birth, a mother cat stays right by her kittens. One reason for this devotion is that kittens cannot regulate their body temperature in the first 2 weeks, so their mother has to keep them warm with her body. She also has to stimulate all the kittens' elimination processes by licking their genitals and ingesting their waste. (And you thought *you* had a devoted mother!) By the time they are 3 weeks old, kittens can eliminate on their own and their mother will show them how to cover their waste.

✦ Sharing Prey She Catches

An important part of the feline maternal instinct is the strong drive to catch prey and bring it back to the kittens. When the kittens are only a few weeks old, a mother cat who has access to the outdoors (or who lives without human contact) will begin bringing live rodents to the kittens. She releases the animals in front of the kittens as a way to teach them to grab the prey themselves. If they do not succeed, she will often recapture the rodent and release it in front of them again. This maternal instinct to teach hunting skills is so powerful that a mother cat will do this no matter how hungry she may be herself. It also may explain why adult cats—even when all alone—will often play with a live animal they have caught, a habit that some people find cruel or disgusting but which clearly has its origins in their early development.

A KITTEN'S GROWTH

Weeks 1 and 2

- ❑ Birth weight 3 to 4 ounces; weight doubles in first week
- ❑ Umbilical cord drops off in 2 to 3 days
- ❑ Born deaf and with eyes shut
- ❑ Sense of smell highly developed

Weeks 2 to 4

- ❑ Eyes open between days 7 and 14
- ❑ Ears open between days 7 and 10
- ❑ Baby teeth start coming in between days 21 and 28
- ❑ At 14 days a kitten can crawl, stand, explore and play
- ❑ Play among kittens begins between the 3rd and 4th weeks
- ❑ At 21 days she can walk and swivel her ears

Weeks 4 to 8

- ❑ Weaning is complete by the 7th week
- ❑ Baby teeth have all appeared by the 8th week
- ❑ Can self-groom by 8 weeks
- ❑ Important socialization time—play gets rougher
- ❑ Begin to display adult responses—run, freeze and display aggression

Weeks 8 to 14

- ❑ Permanent eye color established around 12 weeks
- ❑ Adult teeth begin to come in at 14 weeks
- ❑ Socialization with littermates continues to be important until the 10th week

WHEN DO KITTENS BECOME CATS?

Kittens go through adolescence when they are between 4 and 8 months of age. Between 6 and 12 months they reach sexual maturity, and they reach social maturity between 18 months and 2 years of age, when they finally settle down into their personalities. From the ages of 9 to 12 months a kitten is in late adolescence and has finished growing. However, it still takes females 2 years and males 3 years to reach their full weight.

This chart has no useful application since our two species are completely different. But it makes up for all the time people only talked about "dog years" when discussing a canine's age relative to people. Now you can do the same for your cats: After two years, every cat year equals four human years.

Cat	Human
1 month	= 6 months
3 months	= 4 years
6 months	= 10 years
8 months	= 15 years
1 year	= 18 years
2 years	= 24 years
4 years	= 35 years
6 years	= 42 years
8 years	= 50 years
10 years	= 60 years
12 years	= 70 years
14 years	= 80 years
16 years	= 84 years

FERAL KITTENS

Feral colonies of cats spring up wherever cats have been abandoned—generally in fairly heavily populated areas—and the cats then live without human contact, breeding and surviving without the assistance of people. There is more on feral cats in the last chapter of the book, but their behavior has not been formally studied and it could be so illuminating. Much could be learned from feral cats about how cats live without human interference and how a cat's personality develops. So far there have been no scientific studies of feral kitten development, even though it might help us to understand the cats who share our lives.

However, we do know that our influence on growing kittens is powerful in molding them into the cats who live with us. A cat who grows up in a feral colony will probably share the uncivilized tendencies of her parents, even if adopted as a small kitten. I know this to be true from my own experience. When I was living in Rome with my family we took in a street kitten, Aurelia, but she couldn't make the transition to being a house cat. This sweet-looking little kitty took every opportunity she could to dash out the door (into Roman traffic, mind you), she climbed straight up the curtains, she relieved herself in any suitcase or container of any kind left uncovered and she

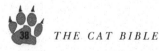

seemed to enjoy scaring the daylights out of our dog Pango, who would stand up to any other dog but tucked in his tail and hid when that cat gave him so much as a look.

Air-Righting: Landing on All Fours

The air-righting reflex in cats is an astonishingly complex reaction that occurs automatically when they are falling, allowing them to turn in midair so that they land on all fours. Air-righting is an entirely instinctive motor pattern that develops in kittens between 4 and 6 weeks of age. Researchers know the exact age at which this instinct develops because tests were done on 4-week-old kittens dropped upside down from 16 inches above a padded surface. At that age they were completely unable to turn themselves over before landing, but over the subsequent 2-week period they got consistently better at righting themselves, until by 6 weeks of age they hit the ground with all 4 feet every time they were dropped.

Cat Body Language

Each cat has her own set of actions and expressions that are a mirror of how she is feeling. The chart below matches the mood or state of mind with a standard list of body positions and physical signs that apply to all cats. However, each cat is an individual, so your own cat may have only some of these characteristics. How she expresses or exhibits them may also depend on the circumstances. So while this chart can help you to decipher what your cat may be thinking and feeling, you should make a point of watching your cat and learning her personal quirks so that you can better understand her.

You can use the following chart to identify your cat's frame of mind by looking at the groups of descriptive phrases and deciding which group she seems to fall into—or by observing some of your cat's behavioral characteristics and then trying to fit them into one of those categories. As you can see, there are a variety of possible attitudes that fit each frame-of-mind category, and that is because every cat is a unique individual and every situation varies. So your cat may have just one or even all of the behaviors listed. Even armed with this information, you will still have to do some observing and interpreting to get a clear picture of your own kitty.

Guide to Body Language

FRIENDLY/RELAXED

- Ears pricked slightly forward
- Whiskers stand straight out from the face
- Tail upright or relaxed
- Purring

- Hair smooth and flat
- Stalking
- Dilated pupils
- Chattering (if feeling playful)

FRIGHTENED

- Hair up on back and tail
- Tail lashing or held close to body
- Whiskers flattened against face
- Ears pulled flat against the head, pointed down
- Crouching sideways
- Hissing, growling or spitting

AGGRESSIVE

- Direct stare
- Constricted, narrow pupils
- Hair raised on shoulders and tail
- Facing front, butt in air (ready to pounce)
- Tail swishes or thumps the ground
- Lips curled in a snarl
- Hissing or screeching
- Ears flat and rotated backwards

ANNOYED

- Tip of tail twitches
- Whiskers pulled back tightly against face
- Ears flat against head

SICK

- Eyes half closed
- Tail between legs
- Whiskers and ears in abnormal positions for long periods
- Loud purring when stroked

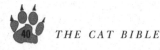

READING A CAT ONE PART AT A TIME

Learning to read your cat's body language is an important part of understanding her personality and reactions. But keep in mind that with cats there is rarely an absolutely clear answer; it is only by interpreting the sum of the parts that you can get the whole picture. It can be confusing or misleading to look at just one aspect of her demeanor and try to figure her out; only by taking into consideration her eyes, ears, tail, whiskers, body posture and voice can you get a complete understanding of what she's feeling.

The chart below gives you all the ingredients that make up a cat's full physical expression. It is a checklist to refer to when you can't quite figure out what's going on with your cat and you may not have considered all aspects of her body language. It can also help to factor in the circumstances in which your cat finds herself—the things in her environment to which she may be reacting.

BODY LANGUAGE CHECKLIST

- ❏ Whole-body position
- ❏ Tail position
- ❏ Ear position
- ❏ Eye shape
- ❏ Whiskers
- ❏ Hair
- ❏ Voice

⬧ Whole-Body Position or Posture

A cat's posture basically boils down to two possibilities: either she's indicating that it's fine to come on over or she's warning you (or another cat) to stay away. And that attitude can change very quickly, depending on how the other creature is conducting herself.

Tail Upright, Trotting Toward You. This is a confident, trusting cat who expects something positive from the encounter—it's the way that stray cats come running when a person who brings them food arrives. A cat will also give this greeting to another cat she knows and likes.

Arched Back with Hair Standing Up (Piloerection). This is the opposite of the posture above because it shows that the cat expects the worst, not the best. This classic "Halloween cat" posture can be either offensive or defensive, depending on what the other cat (or person) does. It gives this message to another cat: "Be forewarned, I'm not fooling around."

Stiff-Legged, Hind End Elevated. This is a purely offensive stance and challenges the other cat or person. Since a cat's hind legs are naturally longer than her front legs, it's a natural position for the cat to stand stiff-legged with her rump higher than her front end.

Crouching. This is a defensive position, with the tail often curled tightly around the body; it protects the tail and gives the impression that the cat is smaller and less threatening to an opponent.

If the crouching cat is frightened, she will flatten her ears back and down; a sign that she is really frightened would be if she is also drooling.

Belly Up. This is the ultimate passive position, indicating to an opponent that she is no threat at all. However, that is not entirely true, since a cat on her back can use her claws and teeth if the opposing cat does not respect her position of subordination and advances on her anyway. It all depends on the individual. A cat may also expose her belly to elicit play or stroking—it depends

Reading Cat Body Language

TAIL

- **Erect like a flagpole** = friendly, confident, content, ready to interact
- **Hairs on end (piloerection)** = heightened anxiety; passively aggressive
- **Wrapped around body** = wants to be left alone, possibly fearful
- **Inverted U** = defensive aggression (but in kittens can signal play)
- **Curled under body** = threatened
- **Arched over back with piloerection** = defensive aggression (may lower tail if other cat doesn't back off)
- **Arched over back *without* piloerection** = interested, aroused
- **Thumping** = conflicted, frustrated, irritated; may attack
- **Mild flicking** = ambivalence, changing her mind about what she is doing
- **Rapid flicking** = agitation, anxiety, growing arousal; for some, may be a stress reliever
- **Constant flicking** = reactive, a commentary on her surroundings
- **Lashing** = agitation in proportion to vigor of lashing: stay away!
- **Puffed up to twice its size** = unpredictable, can swing from retreat to attack
- **Between legs** = submissive
- **Lowered** = offensive (moving stiffly) or defensive aggression (moving loosely)
- **Half down, horizontal** = normal relaxed position of tail at rest

EARS

- **Pointed forward** = curious
- **Erect** = alert, even if dozing
- **Erect, forward-facing** = alert, interested
- **Forward facing and tilted slightly back** = friendly, relaxed
- **Turned sideways (like airplane wings)** = concern/fear over possible threat
- **Rotated sideways and downward** = defensive aggression, might attack
- **Rotated sideways and flattened against head** = extreme defensiveness, could attack
- **Rotated sideways, flattened and inner ear visible** = offensive aggression, will attack

EYE SHAPE

- **Round pupils** = excited, interested, fearful or defensive aggression
- **Slightly oval pupils** = relaxed
- **Droopy lids** = relaxed, trusting
- **Slowly closing eyes** = trust, affection
- **Constricted pupils** = offensive aggression
- **Unblinking stare** = challenging, defensive threat
- **Slow blinking** = opposite of stare: feels safe, comfortable and affectionate (some people "answer" by blinking back at their cats and call this interaction "cat kisses")

WHISKERS

- **Pointed forward** = interest or aggression (if ears are sideways or back this means aggression; if ears are erect this means interest in something she sees)
- **Relaxed, pointed to the side** = position at rest, relaxed
- **Flattened back against cheeks** = fear

HAIR

- **Hair erect (piloerection)** = defensive
- **Fluffed but not fully standing up** = uneasy, threatened or defensive

VOICE

- **Chattering** = excitement when seeing prey but unable to get to it
- **Chirp** = when expecting something desirable like a meal or treat; mother cat to kittens
- **Growl** = offensive or defensive low-pitched sound made with open mouth
- **Hiss** = openmouthed snakelike sound, usually defensive
- **Meow** = greeting just for people
- **Mew** = identify and locate another cat
- **Moan** = a long sad sound made before vomiting, when disoriented (senior cats), or when at door wanting to be let in or out
- **Murmur** = soft closed-mouth sound, accompanies purring or is a greeting
- **Purr** = contentment, anxiety (stress relief), or self-soothing when ill or injured
- **Shriek** = harsh high-pitched sound for pain or highly aggressive meetings
- **Snarl** = threatening expression with upper lip curled, showing teeth, may go with a growl
- **Spit** = sudden short popping sound, heard before or after a hiss
- **Squeal** = raspy high-pitched sound while expecting food; also occurs during play
- **Trill** = like a chirp but more musical, expressing happiness

on what the rest of her body signals are. If the cat adds a meow and stretches out with ears forward, those are signs of relaxation.

◆ The Environment Around the Cat

The circumstances surrounding a cat can influence her frame of mind, which can help you to understand her behavior and predict her reactions. There's obviously no way to list here what those environmental situations might be, since anything and everything can potentially affect a cat. A cat's behavior can be triggered by everything from another cat walking by outside the window to another cat in the house interacting with her, a move to a new house, new furniture or rearranged furniture, the addition or loss of a human or other animal in the household, human stress such as illness or divorce—you name it. You just need to be aware that each cat has issues in her environment that can affect her mood and behavior. The lists below can help you figure out just what that mood might be.

CAT BODY LANGUAGE YOU MIGHT MISUNDERSTAND

There are a few classic "cat moves" that people assume they understand—but which in some cases mean something quite different than we think. What follows are a few of these typical physical demonstrations and what the cat is *really* trying to communicate.

◆ Lying Down, Belly Exposed

Doesn't it look adorable and inviting when your kitty is on her back, feet in the air, waiting for her soft tummy to be rubbed? A cat who exposes her stomach is relaxed, but she is not necessarily "asking" for a belly rub—don't be fooled, even if she rolls over to expose more of her stomach. Showing her belly is a sign that a cat feels secure enough to put herself in the ultimate vulnerable position, but it is not always an invitation to touch. Sometimes, rubbing a cat's stomach can even trigger an automatic aggressive reflex, which can involve pushing you away with her feet and biting. This would explain all those times you may have thought a cat was "mean," "aggressive" or "tricky," when actually you didn't know cat etiquette or body signals.

◆ Sitting with a Closely Wrapped Tail

You know the classic cat pose—the elegant "statue" of the cat sitting close to the ground, her tail wrapped tightly around her feet so she's tucked into a neat package? The message there is "closed for business." This body posture is one that cats may use to keep other cats at a distance; it's not a hostile posture, just one that establishes she does not want any interaction. Although you may be tempted to go over and stroke a cat because she looks so serene and tranquil in this position, what you'll actually be doing is interrupting that tranquility by breaking through the invisible visual barrier she has put up by putting herself in this position.

Any resting position in which the cat has all her body parts tucked in sends the message "Give me my space." The cat would prefer not to be approached or disturbed—think of her as being in her own zone. And don't be fooled if the cat seems alert and her head is up; if her limbs and tail are all tucked in, her alertness does *not* mean she's inviting you over to her.

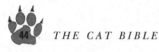

◆ **Tail Up**

When a cat's tail is straight up or even slightly curved over her back, this is a signal that she is ready for you to approach. In general, soft upright tail motions indicate a willingness to interact—in fact, if she raises her tail and waves it like a flag, this is an invitation to other cats (or to you) to come be with her.

◆ **Touching with Nose**

When cats are friendly to one another they greet by touching noses, a gesture that you can approximate with a cat by putting out one finger for her to touch and sniff. When two cats are doing the nose-to-nose greeting, they then share odors by depositing scent on each other. The cat will rub her cheek glands on you, rub against your leg with her whole body, raise her cheeks for you to scratch them and invite you to stroke her back by arching it. So when a cat comes up to you, extending your finger is the nicest, most catlike way of saying hello.

Ears and Hearing

Although their eyes open between the 7th and 10th days of life, kittens cannot hear until they are 2 weeks old, and a kitten's hearing does not become well developed until she is about a month old.

FREQUENCIES THEY CAN HEAR

Cats can hear sounds at a higher frequency than even dogs can. They can hear sounds up to 65,000 hertz (cycles per second). The absolute limit of human hearing is just 20,000 hertz. This allows cats to catch the high-pitched noises made by small rodents, which are their main prey. This keen hearing is yet another tool the cat has in addition to keen sight, which enables her to home in on prey and go right to it. The only animals with keener hearing than a cat are bats and certain insects such as moths, which can detect sounds up to 100,000 hertz.

THE DIRECTION OF SOUND

Dogs and cats can determine the direction a sound is coming from and pinpoint it more specifically than many other animals. The ability to locate the direction of a sound is partly determined by the distance between the ears. It is interesting to note that a great deal of a cat's brain must be devoted to hearing, since she can equal a dog's auditory performance but is much smaller (and therefore has less distance between her ears). A cat's hearing can outperform that of larger animals such as horses.

Your cat's hearing is so finely tuned that she can differentiate the sound of your car engine from others, or the way your footsteps sound coming toward the house. Some cats are responsive to music or to certain favorite types of music or instruments, so playing music for them can be soothing and relaxing.

THE PHYSICAL STRUCTURE OF THE EAR

The *pinna* is the external part of a cat's ear—the erect, triangular shape. There are 30 muscles controlling each of the ears, which funnel sound from the outside down into the inner ear. The pinnas on the two ears can rotate independently of each other, 180 degrees, which allows a cat to pick up sounds from every direction without even moving her head.

The ears are also essential to the cat's remarkable sense of balance. The semicircular canals inside the cat's ears are fluid-filled chambers that help her in precisely determining how she moves. The microscopic hairs that line the inside of the cat's ear chambers—called cilia—also assist the cat in determining her exact position in space.

DEAF CATS

Cats' other senses compensate for deafness: they can feel movement and vibration through the super-sensitive pads of their feet (see "Feet and Paws," below).

Some white cats are born deaf because of an inherited gene; apparently the deafness is a birth defect that goes along with the white pigmentation.

Eyes and Eyesight

DEVELOPMENT OF THE EYE AND VISION

♦ Eye Color

A kitten is born with closed eyes, which will first open when she is anywhere between 7 and 10 days old. All kittens have blue eyes when they are born. When a kitten reaches about a month in age, her eyes will begin to transform into their adult color, which can be in a kaleidoscopic variety of shades of blue with other colors mixed in, ranging from lavender to green, yellow and orange. Permanent eye color is usually set around 3 months of age. However, the color can continue to intensify until the cat reaches maturity.

♦ Eyesight Development

When a kitten first opens her eyes, some time after the first week of life, she still cannot really see things. In fact, it isn't for 3 weeks that her eyes can follow moving objects and she can orient herself using visual clues. Vision is still cloudy all the way until she reaches 5 weeks of age.

♦ Eye Size

A cat's eyes can often appear large in relation to the size of her head—which, interestingly, is also true of human babies. There is a theory that this ratio may play some part in people's attraction to cats. Cats actually have the largest eyes of any domestic animal in proportion to their size.

♦ Eyesight in Daylight

A cat cannot see particularly well, nor in great detail, in bright daylight. That is one of those times that she can rely on her whiskers to give her more information about what is in front of her or nearby.

✦ Twilight

Cats can see in light about 6 times dimmer than what we humans need, so when it is dusk for us it would seem like bright daylight to them. At that time the pupil is fully dilated to allow as much light into the eye as possible (which means the cat can focus less well on objects up close). Dusk is the time of day when cats traditionally hunt their rodent prey because this is the light in which they see best.

Cats and other mammals that are most active at night or at dawn and dusk have a visual system adapted to their hunting habits. Wondering how the cat's eye actually works? In low light the cat's pupil can open all the way up to 1/2 inch (1 cm) in diameter. This makes the whole eye look black. The muscles in the iris change the position of the pupil so that the right amount of light enters. In very bright light you might see only a very small dark strip of the pupil running vertically down the center of the cat's eye (remember those marbles called "cat's-eye"? That's the idea). This mechanism protects the delicate retina at the back of the eye from being overexposed to sunlight. Conversely, when there is very little light the iris changes position so that the pupil can dilate and let in more light.

✦ The Tapetum Lucidum

There is a layer of specialized, pigmented cells behind the retina that reflects back any light shined at it, like a mirror. This reflective quality essentially gives the cat's retina a "second chance" to see the image by bouncing it back through the retinal cells. When car headlights, a flashlight or the flash of a camera shines in a cat's eyes at night and you see that gold or greenish glow (called *eye shine*), that is the tapetum reflecting back at you.

STRENGTHS AND WEAKNESSES OF FELINE EYESIGHT

✦ Distance

Cats cannot focus very well on objects up close, nor can they focus on fine detail. Their best focal point is at a distance of anywhere from 2 yards to 6 or 7 yards (2 to 6 meters).

✦ Movement

Cats follow movement especially well—this is what their eyes are adapted to do for hunting. They have specialized nerve cells in their brains that respond to motion. Combined with a cat's super-fast reflexes, this gives the cat a great advantage over her prey. However, the prey has its own instincts that lead it to freeze when it senses it is being hunted—and once the movement ceases, a cat often loses sight of the prey. Fast reflexes and ability to judge distance accurately also contribute to cats' hunting skills.

DO CATS SEE COLOR?

Cats are usually thought to be color-blind, just like almost every other mammal except the primates. However, there has been disagreement in scientific studies, with some showing that cats have a full range of color vision similar to our own. According to prevailing scientific opinion, cats don't distinguish much in the way of color—apparently they are able to see mostly green

with some blue. Cones are the color-sensitive cells in the eye, and humans have 3 varieties of them along with the ability to distinguish over 100 different hues. However, cats have only 2 kinds of cones, and those are most sensitive to green and blue, respectively. That means that a cat sees red, orange, yellow and green as the same color, and all shades of blue and violet as a single other color. A yellow flower does not look white or gray to her, but she cannot distinguish between a red flower and a yellow one.

This inability to distinguish colors may have evolved because cats are night hunters and colors are not as discernible in reduced light. Cats don't really need to see color to hunt since a mouse or mole of any color is just fine by them.

EYES AS A "THERMOMETER" OF MOOD

A cat's eyes can give an indication of her emotional state. A cat's eyes are dilated (the pupils are open wide) when she is surprised, frightened or excited. If her pupils are constricted, it can be a sign of tension or potential aggressiveness. You can read more in this chapter about how a cat's eye and body posture reflect her emotional state.

SIAMESE EYES ARE DIFFERENT

Siamese cats have a different type of reflecting cell in their eyes. While other cats' eyes appear gold or green when a flashlight or car headlights are shined on them, a Siamese's blue eyes appear to have a red tinge to them when lit up.

Siamese cats do not have full binocular vision, which is the ability to form one image from information that comes into two eyes. This means that Siamese are not able to receive a complete visual picture and do not have vision that is as sharp as other cats, and it also means that they often have a cross-eyed appearance, which begins early in life as their brains try to correct for this deficit by moving the eye muscles. By the time Siamese are about 3 months old, their eye position has changed to compensate and their eye muscles get used to that position, creating a cross-eyed appearance.

BLINDNESS IN CATS

A visually impaired cat moves her head from side to side, sweeping her path with her whiskers. Blind cats can play and hunt by using their whiskers and by feeling the vibrations in their paw pads to determine where an object is without being able to see it. The toy or prey also makes some kind of noise, however faint, which the cat can pick up and use to orient herself.

Feet and Paws

THE PAW PADS

The paw pads are the pads at the bottom of a cat's foot that make up the actual surface she walks on. All cats have at least 4 toes (although a cat with extra toes—a *polydactyl*—has more; extra toes are passed on through the genes, so you can have a whole line of cats with additional toes), with a 5th toe called the dewclaw that is partway up the inside of each of the front feet and does not touch the ground. Underneath each of the toes that touch the ground is a small paw pad, with a larger central paw pad underneath each foot. There is also a small accessory pad behind the foot, up the back of the leg, although we don't really know what role that plays for the cat.

You can think of the paw pads as being roughly equivalent to the heels or balls of our feet, except that in the cat they are also much more than that since they are highly sensitive. A cat's pads are an important information-gathering system for her, serving as part of her exploratory equipment. You will often see a cat reach out to tap on an object or surface with the bottom of her foot, so that she can gauge its shape, texture and temperature with her paw pads.

◆ Sensitivities

The pads of a cat's feet are very sensitive to both touch and vibration. This sensitivity may explain why many cats do not like their pads being touched and will pull their foot away if you touch them. Even though the pads are touchy, they are not very sensitive to hot and cold.

The paw pads sense movement and vibration in the ground, making them an essential part of the cat's highly sensitive early-warning system to detect danger or prey. The pads also help a cat keep her balance and maintain her posture.

◆ Sweat Glands

The footpad is the only area of a cat's body that has sweat glands—nowhere else on her body is liquid sweat produced. But unlike the sweat glands in humans and other creatures that sweat all over, a cat's sweat glands are not intended to maintain body temperature (her respiration does that); however, they do serve as a sweating mechanism in severely hot conditions. A frightened or very hot cat may leave damp paw prints.

◆ Problems with the Paw Pads

Allergies. Footpad problems are fairly rare, but when they occur they are usually caused by an allergy to something a cat has touched, inhaled or eaten. An allergic reaction on the footpad will cause it to look red and swollen and be sensitive to the touch. If a bacterial infection has begun, a dark discharge and/or crustiness may occur, along with a nasty smell.

Calluses. Another problem that can arise is a callus that forms on the paw pad, which looks something like an extra nail. No one knows why these calluses form, and they usually don't cause problems. Your vet may want to cut the callus off, with the cat under a light anesthetic; stitches are usually not needed.

"MANUAL" DEXTERITY

Cats have a surprising variety of techniques for grasping and maneuvering objects. A cat can pierce an object with her claws, she can hold it between a paw and a claw and she can sometimes even hold something between two paw pads without even using her claws, all depending on the size and texture of the object.

Some cats are able to move the individual toes of their paws separately, an unusual fine-motor

control that you don't see in many other four-legged creatures. Although many of us have a mental image of raccoons as being exceptionally clever with their paws, don't underestimate your cat's dexterity at using her paws for many functions. When she reaches out to grip something, you may notice that she prepares her paw by curling it into the right shape to best be able to grip it, then closes her paw as she makes contact with the object, demonstrating a sophisticated fine motor control.

Hunting

PLAYING WITH THEIR FOOD

We don't know for sure why cats toss their prey around, but they aren't the only ones who do it—you'll see some dogs and other animals doing it, too. One possible answer is that something moving and squeaking is more interesting than a lifeless body. By throwing the prey around they amuse themselves and can generate possible signs of life in their victim, thereby keeping the game going a little longer. A dead victim loses all interest for a cat, who will just walk away and leave it.

✦ Their Mother Taught Them

You'd think a polite mother would teach a kitten *not* to play with her food, but just the opposite is true. If a cat was raised in an outdoor setting, then her mother would have followed her own strong instinct to bring back mice that are still moving so the youngsters could practice their hunting skills and learn how to execute a swift kill. However, if a kitten has *not* had this early training, then as an adult she may appear to be playing aimlessly with her prey—batting it around, throwing it with her mouth—when in fact she just never learned the proper fast-kill technique.

✦ Should You Rescue Prey Your Cat Catches?

Cats bring their hunting prizes to their people, and we don't fully understand why they do this. Do they have some primal instinct to bring the prey inside, so they can deal with it under our protection without threat from other animals? Or is the dead or half-dead rodent or bird an offering to us? In either case, these gutted or decapitated or still quivering little victims can leave you queasy, both physically and morally.

If the prey is still alive, do you get involved and try to take it away from the cat? Or do you let nature take its course? The answer depends on what shape the bird or mouse is in. Did the cat just snatch it and the prey is basically unharmed? If you think that is the case, don't try to chase the cat or force her to release the prey because you may just make her bite down or otherwise hurt the creature. Instead, try throwing some kind of cloth—a towel, dishcloth or piece of clothing—over the cat's head. In most cases this will cause her to let go. If this drama is taking place indoors, you will have to solve the problem of getting the prey out of the house once the cat has released it. I have chased field mice around my bedroom with a broom—behind bureaus, under the bed—trying to herd them out the door to freedom.

However, if the cat has had a chance to cause any bodily harm before presenting the prey to you, that probably means the little thing won't be able to survive back outside, even if you do manage to get the cat to release it. There are those of us who think we can nurse an injured bunny or bird, but I have tried to rescue both and failed miserably. You will only worry yourself and prolong the suffering because the animal inevitably dies anyway, either because it is too damaged, too stressed or too young.

Some people don't even have the stomach to try to make a close-up determination of the condition and possible fate of their cat's prisoners. If you fall into this group, you're better off not even attempting to get in the middle; just let the cat deal with it and hope she dispatches the prey quickly.

No matter how disgusted you are by the arrival of your cat's treasures, you should certainly not think ill of her for hunting and killing despite the fact that you feed her well. If you allow her to be an outdoor cat and you live in a place that gives her the opportunity to really hunt, you need to accept the fact that cats are hard-wired to be hunters.

The moral dilemma is really yours, not hers, and it relates to the question of whether domestic cats should be indoor or outdoor pet animals. You can read more about this later in the book, but suffice it to say there are numerous health and safety reasons for keeping a cat indoors. And there is also the highly debated public issue of whether house cats should be allowed outside. In many areas of the world where cats are free to hunt, there are virtually no small songbirds left alive.

HUNTING VERSUS HUNGER

It may bother you that your well-fed cat goes on search-and-destroy missions, but the two things have nothing to do with each other; the inborn desire to hunt has nothing to do with whether a cat's stomach is full. The two sensations—the drive to kill and the desire to eat—come from different parts of the brain of a cat. When a cat plays with toys or with us, the pouncing, leaping and biting she exhibits are all practice for the instinctive desire to hunt.

It is natural that at times cats will not eat what they capture. To our way of thinking, there is something morally askew about killing for the sake of killing, rather than to fill a physical need for food, but this behavior is quite natural for cats and other hunting animals. Cats will catch and kill moles and shrews but rarely eat them; mice or birds are more to their liking. What varies is that some cats will leave behind the small intestine and/or gallbladder of prey, while others will eat everything right down to the feathers. We don't know the reason for this stylistic difference in post-hunting appetites.

Mouth, Teeth and Gums

TONGUE

Besides using the papillae on her tongue to detect tastes (see the "Taste" section), a cat also uses her tongue as a spoon of sorts. Cats drink water by curling the outer edges of their tongue inward, to create a valley for the water.

DROOLING

Quite a few cats drool when they are having a pleasurable experience. Salivation (the production of saliva) is basically essential to eating because it lubricates the food and aids swallowing. But salivation has a special function for a nursing kitten because the saliva helps form an airtight seal between the mother's nipple and the kitten's mouth. Cats who drool when having a pleasurable sensation may also knead with their paws, which is another thing that small kittens do against their mother's belly when they nurse. This may be why drooling and kneading behavior will crop up in an adult cat who is being stroked or otherwise receiving pleasure—it triggers the memory of the pleasure of nursing.

There are also a number of mouth disorders and medical problems that can trigger drooling, but you have nothing to worry about if your cat does her drooling only when you are stroking or scratching her at a favorite spot.

TOOTH DEVELOPMENT IN KITTENS

When a kitten is born she has no visible teeth. When she is anywhere from 10 to 14 days old, her very tiny front teeth (the deciduous or baby incisors) begin to push through her gums. These 6 incisors in the front of her mouth, upper and lower, are designed for tearing small bits of meat off bones and extracting feathers from prey.

At 2 to 3 weeks of age, the 4 fangs at the corners of her jaws (the deciduous canine teeth) come in. The canines are the teeth a cat uses to sever the spinal cord of prey and to administer the killing bite.

A few days later, other teeth along the sides begin to push through. By the time a kitten is 2 months old, all 28 of her deciduous teeth will have arrived—which is 2 teeth fewer than what will be her final full count of permanent teeth. Just as with people, deciduous teeth are the temporary ones, the "baby teeth," and will fall out and be replaced with the permanent or adult teeth. In cats, this happens when the kitten reaches 3 to 4 months of age. The permanent teeth appear in the same sequence as the temporary ones came in, with the incisors first, the canine teeth next and lastly the teeth at her cheeks, the premolars and molars. Cats do not chew or grind the pieces of meat they cut off; they swallow them whole. These teeth are used to cut off larger pieces of meat from prey. All in all, a cat has 30 adult teeth, which should have erupted by the time the kitten is 5 or 6 months old.

ROUTINE DENTAL CHECKUPS

Cats are prone to certain gum and tooth problems that can cause serious difficulties—not the least of which is early tooth loss—unless found early and nipped in the bud. Since every cat's mouth and teeth have their own patterns and problems, when you have your first visit with the vet you should ask whether a once-yearly dental checkup is enough for your cat. For some cats, a yearly visit is plenty, while those with ongoing dental problems should be seen several times in a year.

TOOTH BRUSHING

Tooth brushing works for cats the way it does for us: it reduces the buildup of plaque and tartar, which can cause gum disease. Brushing also might prevent FORLs (see below)—one study showed that when cats had their teeth brushed twice weekly they did not develop these cavities. However, unless you start tooth brushing with a young, adaptable kitten, it's unlikely that an older cat is going to readily accept having her teeth brushed. Almost any adult cat will fight you tooth and nail when you try a toothbrush with even the most cat-friendly toothpaste on it.

FORL'S (FELINE ODONTOCLASTIC RESORPTIVE LESIONS)

A FORL is a pit that forms on a tooth near the gum line and erodes progressively—and is extremely painful. FORLs are so common that one-third of all cats will develop them during their lifetime, and while some cats show signs of discomfort, most of them grit their teeth and bear it (quite literally). This means that if your cat has a FORL, you'll have no idea how much she is suffering. These cavity-like craters in the tooth get worse over time; the tooth will often become so eroded that it breaks right off at the gum line. The cause of FORLs is not known, but there are a range of theories. Could they be triggered by the cat's body's response to a viral infection? Or an uncontrolled immune response? Too much vitamin D in cat food? A metabolic imbalance? None of these possibilities has been proven, and none of them has gotten doctors any closer to preventing or curing this chronic problem.

◆ Symptoms of FORLs

Some of the more common signs of a FORL to watch out for are tooth grinding, "chattering" of the teeth, and favoring one side when chewing.

◆ Treatment for FORLs

Sadly, the medical profession has not been able to come up with a solution to FORLs. They cannot even stop them from progressing. Finding the problem early is good, but the only treatment so far is to remove the tooth, which at least ends the pain for the cat. After the procedure, eating is reported to be no problem—even dry kibble and even for those cats who have undergone a full-mouth extraction. It sounds incredible that cats whose teeth have all been removed can still eat, but apparently they can and it's a whole lot more comfortable for them than the pain of FORLs.

THE GUMS

Some cats get dark spots on their gums but these are not a cause for concern. These spots are pigmentation, called *lentigines* (the singular is *lentigo*), and are usually found in orange cats. Lentigines are a sort of freckle—they are black and flat and the tissue is normal-looking. They have no relationship to melanomas, which are a cancerous kind of raised black growth with uneven edges. Fortunately, cats are not prone to melanoma.

Sleep

Cats sleep a whole lot—it's natural for them. If you've ever wondered if something is wrong with your cat because she is constantly snoozing, don't worry—it's just because she's a cat. In fact, all

felines, from the smallest domestic cat to the largest king of the jungle (and all the tigers and leopards in between), sleep away a good part of the day. The statistics for domestic cats range from 10 hours of daily sleep all the way to 18 hours a day in hot weather. The facts show that cats spend 85 percent of their time sleeping or resting, with 40 percent of that being regular sleep, 15 percent of it deep REM (rapid eye movement) sleep and 30 percent being resting or sitting. That leaves 10 percent of their day in which to be active, and 5 percent to perform vital functions such as eating, drinking, and eliminating.

SOME SLEEP FACTOIDS

- ❏ Fat cats sleep more than thin ones—and if they lose weight they will sleep less.
- ❏ Indoor cats sleep more than cats who go outside because there is less for an indoor cat to do. In particular, an indoor cat doesn't have to hunt since tasty (we hope) meals are served without her having to twitch a whisker.
- ❏ Newborn kittens sleep more than adult cats. In fact, it takes 3 months for a cat's sleeping pattern to establish itself, so a young kitten sleeps pretty much throughout the day and night. This pattern probably developed as a survival mechanism, since a kitten asleep in a den is not in the jeopardy she would be if she were out and about.

DIFFERENT KINDS OF CAT SLEEP

✦ Catnaps

Our use of the word *catnap* came about from the way that cats actually do sleep: indulging in brief, light snoozes that last about half an hour. A cat's body is not entirely peaceful when she sleeps, often giving the impression that she could be up and out in a shot if awakened.

✦ Night Sleep

Cats have two measurable sleep periods during the night. How soundly they sleep is affected by many things, including their diet, their age and their physical environment.

✦ Deep Sleep

Sometimes a cat will sleep deeply even during the day, and you can tell because typically she will be lying flat or curled up with her body completely relaxed. Her paws, legs and facial muscles may move and twitch, however, and people tend to think that the cat must be dreaming of chasing a mouse or running from a threat. But while experts do believe that domestic animals have a dream life, all we can do is guess at what they are dreaming about and whether it is pleasant or a nightmare.

Another sign of deep sleep, the same as in people, is rapid eye movement (also called REM), during which you can see the cat's eyeballs moving behind her closed lids.

CHANGE IN SLEEP HABITS IS A WARNING SIGN

Learn what is normal for your cat because any change in an established sleep pattern can be a sign that something is not quite right. Since cats establish a personal sleep pattern and pretty much stick to it throughout their lives, a sudden change in that rhythm can be a symptom of a serious health issue. Some sleep disturbances can be related to thyroid problems. A cat who suddenly starts sleeping less may have an infection, even something as serious as feline immunodeficiency virus (FIV). A cat who sleeps a lot more than usual could also have kidney disease or cancer; in an older cat, sleeping more can signal the onset of the feline equivalent of Alzheimer's disease.

Excessive sleeping—beyond what you know is normal for your cat—is a sign that you should make an appointment with the vet to see what might be going on.

If you notice your cat suddenly sleeping in a strange position that is unusual for her, this could be a sign that she has pain or discomfort somewhere in her body and is trying to compensate for it. Just remember that a cat does not show pain—masking pain is an inborn survival mechanism. So don't wait for your cat to come up to you whining and holding up her paw, asking for help—you may have to pick up on subtle clues. You should get her checked out if you have any doubts that she is completely herself.

Smell

Cats have a much keener sense of smell than we people do (14 times more sensitive, experts say), and many believe that a cat's sense of smell is comparable to a dog's in what it can accomplish. Researchers have many unanswered questions about how a cat's sense of smell really works since studies have left much unexplored.

Having a sharp sense of smell is valuable—even essential—to a cat because it allows her to identify her territory, alerts her to dangers such as another animal that may be an enemy, gives her information about the opposite sex and helps her locate prey.

FOOD AND THE SENSE OF SMELL

A well-developed sense of smell is important to a cat's health because it has a direct influence on her appetite: If she cannot smell, she will stop eating. Cats will often refuse to eat food that comes from the refrigerator since food gives off its aroma when it is at least at room temperature, which is why some people with a finicky cat will warm up their cat's food before they offer it.

KITTENS AND THE SENSE OF SMELL

A newborn kitten's sense of smell begins functioning very soon after birth, whereas her sight will not begin to develop until nearly a week after birth. A cat's nose has about 200 million odor-sensitive cells. When a kitten is born, those cells lining the nasal cavity can already collect and distinguish differences in molecules of air. In the early weeks, this allows her to seek out her mother's milk by its odor.

However, kittens are very impressionable where smell is concerned. If a kitten has a traumatic experience, she may associate an odor with the episode and react negatively to it throughout her

life. This can be the smell at the vet's office or at the groomer's, which is why positive early experiences are so important if a kitten is to become an adaptable, high-functioning cat. This is another reason why young cats need to be exposed to a variety of odors when they are small, along with frequent handling and early socialization.

JACOBSON'S ORGAN

Cats have a special part of their nose called the Jacobson's organ (or vomeronasal organ), two small sacs in the roof of their mouths, just above the hard palate. This organ has ducts that lead into both the nose and mouth, so its function is a cross between smelling and tasting: the cat inhales, opens her mouth and curls her upper lip, allowing her to pick up an odor. Then she moves her tongue to the roof of her mouth and sends the odor to the Jacobson's organ, where her brain analyzes the molecules that make up the scent.

FLEHMEN REACTION

The Flehmen reaction (also spelled Flehman) is the grimacing expression that a cat will make when sniffing certain scents. Your cat may curl her lips, squint her eyes, flatten her ears and even show her teeth. The official word for this action is *flehmening,* and it also involves rapid panting to move the scent molecules up into the Jacobson's organ to be identified.

The Flehmen reaction is most often seen when a male is smelling a female cat in heat—it is a reaction you'll also see in horses and other animals in the same circumstances—the male raises his head with his lips curled after smelling the female or her urine.

LEAVING A SCENT

The flip side of a cat's sense of smell is her ability to leave her own scent on surfaces and objects, either to mark them as her own or so that she can recognize them later herself.

There are scent glands on either side of a cat's forehead, on her chin and lips and beneath her front paws. So when a cat rubs against your legs, it may be a sign of affection, but it is also a gesture of marking you as her territory.

A cat will also sniff you when you return from elsewhere, picking up information from the odors clinging to your skin and garments.

Taste

The senses of smell and taste work so closely together that you could say a cat tastes what she smells. A cat's sense of taste is important to her health because it allows her to distinguish between food that is safe and healthy and food that might be rotten or poisonous. However, a cat's sense of taste is not highly developed: cats have fewer than 500 taste buds (470, to be exact), while dogs have 1,700 and people have a whopping 10,000. Kittens' taste receptors don't mature until a few weeks after birth.

The sense of taste lets cats decide how appetizing and safe a food is while also stimulating secretions of saliva, pancreatic fluids and gastric juices to aid digestion.

THE TONGUE

The tongue itself is covered with small, hook-shaped bumps called *papillae,* which is where the taste buds are located. The ability to taste is determined by these taste buds, which are also located in the mouth and pharynx. These raised projections help detect the texture of food as well. Furthermore, the papillae help a cat to groom herself by pulling the loose hairs from her coat. When your cat licks you, that rough, sandpapery feeling comes from the papillae on her tongue. In wild cats, whose papillae are even rougher, they are useful for licking and stripping the meat from the bones of prey.

NO TASTE FOR SWEETS

Cats can detect three different tastes—salty, bitter and sour (acidic)—but they have no receptors for sweetness. They are the only member of the animal kingdom without this receptor for sugary flavors. The reason for this is a bit of an evolutionary mystery to scientists, some of whom postulate that cats have no receptors for sweetness because they are fundamentally carnivores and so have no need to distinguish sweetness. But it isn't clear whether cats were meat-eaters first and lost the ability to distinguish sweetness from not using those receptors or there was something wrong with their receptors in the first place that caused them to become solely meat-eaters.

This may not make sense to people whose cats eagerly consume very sweet foods such as doughnuts and marshmallows. Scientists believe that the reason for this sweets consumption is not necessarily the taste. At least in the case of marshmallows, it may be the spongy texture. With doughnuts or rich desserts, it is thought that cats are attracted to the fat content and that is what they are enjoying. However, scientists do not pose the obvious question that comes to mind: Why would anyone give these foods to an animal in the first place? When humans choose to eat foods like this, they know they are unhealthy—but why inflict them on an unwitting cat?

A TASTE FOR EVERYTHING

Some cats are culinary adventurers: there doesn't seem to be any food they are not curious to try. Often these exotic ingredients have nothing to do with meat, which is the primary food that cats need and crave; this makes their culinary boldness even more surprising. Cats have been known to try anything—sips of drinks of any kind, and surprising foods such as melon, oatmeal, bread, vegetables, olives, pickles, yogurt, ice cream and spaghetti. (Some of them *love* spaghetti, like our Persian mix, Florence, who would park herself on the table right next to your pasta bowl and wait for you to fish her out one strand at a time.)

Touch

A cat has touch receptors all over her body, but especially sensitive ones on her tongue, her whiskers and the pads of her feet. You may have seen cats using their paws to explore or investigate something—cats rely heavily on the information they gather from their paws.

TOUCH SPOTS

A cat has areas all over her body that are covered in touch-sensitive nerves. You can see the touch spots reacting when a cat is sprayed with something and her skin seems to ripple with a physical reaction—those are the sensitive spots responding in sequence as the spray hits her body.

WHISKERS

A cat has whiskers on her face—12 on the upper lip, in 4 rows—and some on the sides of her face, above her eyes and on her chin. There are even some of these whiskers on a cat's elbows. Whiskers are actually a coarse type of hair that grows from a layer of skin that is deeper than where the ordinary hairs grow. Whiskers are highly sensitive and act like a finely tuned early warning system, picking up vibrations, breezes, and motion, magnifying even the smallest movement or disturbance of the air. When the hairs bend they can send messages about how fast the air is moving and from what direction. A cat depends on this sensory system to feel movement near her (mostly for hunting prey, which in theory is the most important skill for a cat's survival). Whiskers on the forelegs are used to sense the movement of prey she may have trapped under her front paws.

Whiskers also help a cat to navigate in the dark. People often say that cats have eyes that can see in the dark, which is not untrue since their eyes *are* designed for primarily low-light use. However, it is their upper whiskers, which extend beyond their head, as much as their night vision, that make it possible for a cat to get around so well in the dark. The whiskers feel and interpret the flow of air around objects, giving the cat information so that she will not bump into things; she can also use her whiskers to "feel" her prey's location just before she executes the final pounce with her teeth and claws.

PADS OF THE FEET

As mentioned earlier, the pads of a cat's feet are highly sensitive to both touch and vibration. This sensitivity may explain why many cats do not like their pads being touched and will pull their foot away if you touch it.

SPECIAL PHYSICAL SENSITIVITIES TO HOT AND COLD

Except for the nose and lips, a cat's body has little awareness of hot or cold extremes. This explains why a cat may not recognize that a stove or radiator is hot and jump right up onto it. To compare a cat's sensitivity to heat to our own, a person will move away from a source of heat once it reaches 110°F (44°C), which is when it can become uncomfortable and burn us. A cat can enjoy a heat source of up to 126°F (52°C) and will seek it out, curling up right next to a hot fire or even right on top of a hot radiator.

This sensitivity is already at work in a newborn kitten. The sensitivity of a tiny kitten's nose guides her to her mother's warmest place (the milk bar). Later on, this sensitivity permits the cat to figure out the temperature around her as well as her own body temperature.

Vocalizing: What the Sounds Mean

Cats make a wide variety of sounds, many of which are alien to us, but all of which help the cat to make the connections she needs to the humans and the other animals in her universe. The more you understand about the repertoire of sounds she is able to make, the more it will enhance and enrich your relationship with your cat. Here's a look at each of the sounds a cat is capable of making, along with their meanings.

PURRING

Purring is a natural form of expression for cats and a source of mystery for us.

◆ Where Does the Sound Come From?

There are several theories about how the phenomenon occurs, but no one really knows for sure. Here are some of the ideas on the subject of what makes the purr:

- ❏ It involves vibrations of the vocal cords.
- ❏ It emanates from the vibrations of the hypoid apparatus, a series of small bones connecting the skull and the larynx that offer support to the tongue.
- ❏ It may be the vibration of air in the larynx and diaphragm.
- ❏ It may be the movement of air in spasms through contractions of the diaphragm.
- ❏ It may be from rapid and regular nerve impulses sent directly from the central nervous system to the muscles of the diaphragm and to the vocal cords; the muscles are activated in bursts of 20 or 30 seconds, making them very well controlled tremors.
- ❏ It may be that air passes over and vibrates a pair of folds of skin called the false vocal cords, located at the back of the cat's throat.
- ❏ It may originate from the central nervous system.

◆ When Does a Cat Usually Purr?

We think of purring as a sound of contentment and pleasure for a cat, and it certainly does occur when a cat is being stroked or even when she hears the sound of your voice. But purring also occurs for many other reasons and at times you might not expect.

Mothers and Newborns. There is good evidence that the purr was initially a contact sound between a mother and her young. A newborn kitten purrs by the second day of life, well before she can even open her eyes. It is thought the kitten purrs to let her mother know she is getting enough milk, and the mother purrs back as a reassurance to the kitten. Some animal experts believe that communication between the mother and kitten was the original purpose of purring since kittens can feel their mother's purr, which helps them to locate her.

Communication with Other Cats. The purr can also be used to signal to other cats. A cat who is frightened and feels threatened by another cat may purr to appease the dominant cat, by indicating

that she is subordinate or submissive. Conversely, an aggressive cat may purr to let another cat know she is not going to attack.

Comfort and Self-Healing. Purring is a comfort behavior that cats use while recovering from illness; it may even be a self-healing mechanism. There is speculation that the vibration of purring may actually assist cats in healing themselves when they are sick or injured, in particular when there is a problem with bones. Studies have shown that all bones and muscles need stimulation for their health. However, cats are especially sedentary and spend a full two-thirds of their time sleeping and lying about. It is possible that the vibrations created by a cat's purring function like a low-energy mechanism to stimulate muscles and bones during the healing process. Cats also purr while in labor.

A Purr Before Dying. As strange as it may sound, veterinarians have witnessed cats who purr when they are close to dying. This may be a result of a euphoria that occurs when death is imminent—a euphoria we know about because terminally ill human patients have reported it.

OTHER CAT SOUNDS AND THEIR USES

Chirp: a soft, trill-like sound used as a greeting.

Chatter: a sound made by a cat who sees prey that she cannot get to, often on the other side of a window.

Growl: a low-pitched, continual warning sound.

Hiss: a defensive sound like that made by a snake, created with an open mouth and a burst of air forced out through an arched tongue. The cat uses the hiss as a warning to bluff the attacker into backing off and to prevent actual confrontation and violence.

Spitting: often accompanies hissing and is the result of being surprised or threatened.

Yowl: a loud cry of bewilderment, usually from older cats who are disoriented and anxious. It often happens at nighttime when everyone is asleep and the elderly cat is walking around the dark house, frightened and confused. A different kind of yowl is the one made by the female in heat, trying to attract a mate. It is a cry like fingernails on a blackboard—if you don't know all the other reasons to spay your cat, this sound may be enough!

Cats and Water

Although many cats do hate water, there are also cats who are fascinated by it. Tolerance for water varies enormously and is generally a personal like or dislike. Some cats will swirl a paw in a puddle or the edge of a pond, enjoying the sensation as well as the visual stimulation of the water in motion, while others will flee at the sound of water.

It's also a matter of habit, because show cats get frequent baths starting when they are kittens and most don't seem to mind it, accepting it as part of their normal routine.

PLAYING WITH A DRIPPING FAUCET

Some cats like to play in the sink or bathtub if there is water in the bottom or the faucet is dripping. They may be drawn to the sound or motion of the dripping water, and it can keep them amused for hours. Other cats enjoy drinking from a faucet and will come running when you turn it on.

TAKING A BATH WITH YOU

Some cats will sit on the edge of the bathtub while you are bathing, and they may actually enjoy it if you splash them with water. Other cats go right into the shower if someone is in there.

SOME BREEDS LIKE WATER MORE

Many purebred Manx cats (the breed that often has little or no tail) have a special affinity for water. This may be a reflection of their heritage, since the breed originated on the Isle of Man near Great Britain.

Turkish Vans are water lovers as well. This breed of domesticated cat originated near Lake Van in Turkey, and these cats often need no coaxing to go for a swim, whether in the bathtub, a swimming pool or a natural body of water.

CATS ARE NATURAL SWIMMERS

Whether a cat likes or detests water, she is born able to swim. It's not necessary to teach a cat anything—all cats can instinctively swim when placed in water.

WARNING: KEEP TOILET SEAT LIDS DOWN

Because some cats are so fascinated by water, you have to take care with an enticing but potentially deadly water source in your home. Some cats are fascinated by the water in the toilet and can reach in to play with the water—but they can also slip and fall in, and the slippery sides may make it impossible for them to get out. Make sure all toilet seat lids are down when not in use.

Chapter 3

A CAT-SAFE HOME

 This chapter will help you prepare your home ahead of time for the arrival of your cat. By making all the adjustments and arrangements beforehand, you make it easier for both of you; when your cat makes her entrance there will be all the comforts and conveniences to suit her needs and very few ways for her to get into trouble.

You may be surprised by all the myriad ways that a home can put a cat in jeopardy. While some of the warnings that follow might sound a bit paranoid and alarmist, there is some truth behind the old saying "curiosity killed the cat." There are so many places both high and low that cats can get to, and their fascination with small, shiny or moving objects compels them to put everything into their mouths. And cats have an added physiological problem: their rough, barbed tongues make it nearly impossible for them to spit something out. Once they start swallowing something such as thread or cord they cannot *stop* swallowing it—it just keeps going down. Cats and kittens also explore inside openings and can get trapped.

While I want you to pay attention to the warnings and suggestions that follow, I don't mean to make you crazy. You should take heart in that other well-worn saying about a cat having 9 lives. While you will do the best you can to protect her, remember that your cat will also undoubtedly have some of that inborn feline luck on her side.

This chapter is about how to eliminate the potential dangers to your cat in your home, including some suggestions about how to provide a safe and comfortable homecoming and a smooth and happy transition to living with you. The next chapter is about all of the products and equipment that exist to make life more entertaining and satisfying for your cat or kitten. Sometimes you can improvise rather than purchasing these products, but either way they will improve the quality of life you share with your cat.

General Household Dangers

Some of the items around your house can make a cat sick with a gastrointestinal disturbance, while others can actually kill her, depending on how much she ingests. The first chart here lists super-dangerous items, while the second chart lists items that can make a cat uncomfortable or ill, or—if not treated—can cause serious harm or even death. The third chart lists potentially deadly plants; this list is so long that you will probably conclude that the safest rule of thumb about cats and houseplants is not to have both in the same household! Having indoor greenery can either kill your cat or drive you nuts as your kitty digs up your houseplants, uses them as a toilet and so on. If you still want to keep your house plants despite these impediments, the best solution is to use Sticky Paws, which are plastic strips coated with adhesive. You can place them criss-cross across the top of a pot so that the cat can't get in there.

With household cleaning products, you will need to change your style of cleaning, making an effort to rinse any floor you have treated with a cleaning product because chemicals can be absorbed through a cat or kitten's paw pads. Make sure those floors or surfaces have dried completely before letting a kitten walk on them since youngsters are especially delicate and vulnerable. Also, cats will lick their paws and ingest the toxins.

Read the labels of anything you bring into the house, and be on alert with any product that says "Keep out of the reach of children" or "Wear rubber gloves or protective eye wear." Especially with a young kitten, you want to keep her far, far away from the harmful ingredients in products such as these. Consider using products that are less toxic or more environmentally friendly, for the sake of your family's health, too.

Potentially Fatal Household Items

Acetaminophen (Tylenol)

Alcohol

Antifreeze

Apricot, cherry and apple seeds, stems and leaves (in sufficient amounts can cause rapid death)

Automatic garage doors (can come down on cats, who are too small to trigger the safety sensors)

Bells from cat toys

Bones from cooked poultry

Car engines (cats may sleep under the hood, seeking warmth, so check before starting the car)

Cellophane cigarette wrappers (can cut the intestine)

 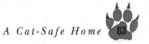

Gasoline, motor oil

Fishing hooks and lines

Household cleaners such as Lysol, Windex, Mr. Clean, and bleach (a cat may lick these off her paws, so use "green" products instead)

Liquid potpourri (deadly if any is on the cat and she licks it)

Medications prescribed for people

Paint, paint thinner

Poisons for rats and mice (or a dead rodent that ate poison)

Rose plant treatments with disulfoton

Slug baits (metaldehyde)

String (dental floss, balloon string, kitchen twine)

Dangerous Household Items

Aspirin, ibuprofen (Advil) (cause gut problems; high doses can cause kidney failure)

Cocoa mulch for gardening

Electrical cords (can cause shock and/or fires when chewed)

Fabric softener (remains on a towel and can coat a cat's fur; she then licks it off)

Household cleaning products

Iron with a dangling cord

Knives and scissors left out on counters or tabletops

Little stuff on the floor (pins, nails, coins, game pieces, marbles, buttons)

Metal cleaner

Mildew remover

Mothballs (the fumes cause liver damage, so use cedar in closets instead)

Office supplies (paper clips, rubber bands and staples)

Onions (cause anemia)

Paper shredders (cats can hit the on button and touch the shredder opening. Some people who work from home keep a document shredder on the setting "Auto Feed," but make sure yours is always in the off position unless you are actively using it.)

Pepto-Bismol and other anti-diarrhea medications

Plastic rings from plastic bottles (cats love to bat them around, but they will also chew and swallow them)

Reclining chairs (can trap a cat inside, so look carefully before retracting the chair)

Roach and ant sprays and powders (roach baits are safe)

Room deodorizers and sprays (painful to a cat's sensitive nose)
Secondhand smoke (The fur traps smoke particles; the cat licks her fur)
Silica gel packets (in pills, shoes and bags to keep out humidity)
Toilet bowl cleaners (cannot be used if your cat drinks from the bowl)
Yarn, string and ribbon (when swallowed damages the intestines)

Poisonous Plants

African violet	Mosaic plant	Rhododendron
Azaleas	Norfolk Island pine	Rubber plant
Begonia	Oleander	Schefflera
Calla lily	Peace lily	Spider plant
Cast-iron plant	Peperomia	Swedish ivy
Cycad	Piggyback plant	Succulents
Dieffenbachia	Pink polka-dot plant	Ti plant
Easter lilies, daylilies	Philodendron	Tomato plants
Ferns	Ponytail plant	Wild mushrooms
Ficus	Pothos	
Grape ivy	Prayer plant	

A WORD ABOUT ELECTRICAL AND PHONE CORDS

Until you get a kitten you probably won't notice how many phone cords and electrical cords there are dangling throughout your house, but once you decide to get a kitten, you had better get those cords out of the way. All cats like to play with cords, but kittens are especially vulnerable because they chew things, and if your kitten chews an electrical cord she can get burned and/or cause a fire. The other danger is that she can tug on a cord above her and pull down on top of herself whatever is attached to the cord, whether it's a lamp, a hair dryer or an iron.

The cords on window blinds and drapes are especially dangerous for kittens. There's the risk that she could get tangled in one of those cords and get trapped or strangled. Make sure that all window cords are rolled up and taped or secured with a hook.

Some of the worst tangles of wires in a house are behind desks for computers or behind entertainment systems with multiple components—in those situations you want to gather all the

 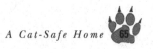

cords into a bunch and secure them inside the plastic tubing designed for baby-proofing or office organization. If you don't want to buy tubing made just for cord coverage, you can use inexpensive PVC tubing from a hardware or home improvement store and then make a lengthwise cut so you can insert all the cords inside the tube. Another option is to run the cords along the baseboard and nail them in place with wire brads designed for that purpose; if there's a rug, you can tuck the cords underneath it.

GARBAGE CANS AND WASTEBASKETS

Your kitchen garbage can should either have a step-on pop-up lid or be inside an under-counter cabinet equipped with a child safety latch. You don't want a cat tipping it over or ingesting any of the contents. If anything in your garbage has a strong, cat-attractive odor, such as chicken or fish bones, the safest thing is to take it to an outside garbage bin.

Your bathroom wastebasket needs to be kept in an under-sink cabinet with a secure lid because many of the things you throw out, such as dental floss or razors, might interest your cat but also pose a danger for her.

TOILET SEATS

The water in the toilet can be mesmerizing to some cats. If a grown cat falls into a toilet, she *might* be able to get out, but a kitten certainly will not be able to, so keep the lid closed on any toilet in your house. Also, do not use automatic toilet bowl cleaners because there's always the chance that a toilet lid will be left open and a curious cat will dip down in there for a drink—and drinking blue water is *not* good for her.

KITCHEN COUNTERS

Anything that touches food in your kitchen becomes interesting to your cat, who has a very good nose for odors. But that means that any knives, scissors or skewers you've used for meat or something else delicious need to be put behind a closed dishwasher door or washed right away. Otherwise your cat could jump up to investigate, land on a knife or lick it and cut herself. She may also try to eat anything that's got a good flavor on it, like a sponge or paper towel left around after wiping up juices, so everything needs to be thrown away or cleaned right after use. (Sorry, but no more leaving a sinkful of dirty dishes until the morning.)

HOT PANS ON THE STOVE

You need to get in the habit of putting any cooking pan into cold water after using it, otherwise the cooking odor could tempt your cat to jump up and burn herself. If this should happen, call your vet or local veterinary emergency facility while you take care of the first order of business: cooling down your cat. You can soak towels in ice water and wrap the cat in them or squirt alcohol directly on her skin, where it evaporates quickly while cooling the skin. But no matter what you try to do, you want to do it while on your way to the vet, which is where your cat needs to be so the doctor can evaluate and treat her.

HIDING PLACES CAN BE DANGEROUS

Before you bring a kitten home you need to look at the rooms in your home from a cat's-eye view. No kidding—you need to get down on your hands and knees and see what your kitten will see. Some places she may choose to go into, and others she may be busy exploring when someone shuts her inside. Always check drawers and closets if you don't find your cat in plain view.

One of the first things a kitten may do in a new place is to look for the smallest, most hidden space and get herself wedged in there. An adult cat who is feeling disoriented or scared may do the same thing when you first adopt her and bring her home. Not only do you want to be able to find your cat, but you also want to avoid having her stuck or panicked in a spot from which she can't extricate herself.

What follows is a quick checklist of places to look for a wayward cat: These are also some of the "mechanical places" (dryers, car engines) you should check for a hiding cat before turning them on. Expect anything and everything: My editor, Erin, a veteran cat-lover, was hostess to a friend's 25-pound cat who got "lost" at her house by smashing himself flat behind a row of books. Any door left open even a little is an invitation to a cat to find her way in—so even if you can't imagine any logical reason why a cat would want to go somewhere, just assume that her curiosity knows no bounds.

CHECKLIST OF COMMON HIDING PLACES

Closets
Inside boxes or shoes
Drawers (inside or behind, so use caution in closing)
Cabinets (especially with audio/video equipment)
Refrigerator (behind or inside it)
Suitcases
Bags (paper, cloth, leather)
Pile of laundry
Dryer
Dishwasher
Behind sofa
Behind bookcase

A NOTE ABOUT REFRIGERATORS

Kittens are notoriously curious about what's behind a refrigerator, where it is dark and warm. She may be trying to hide or follow an insect that flies back there, but the point is that it's such a pain to get at the back of your fridge that you need to make it inaccessible in the first place. You will want to find the least unattractive way to block off or fill up the voids at either side of the refrigerator if it's not a built-in. You can tape a strip of cardboard on the side(s), or something more attractive or permanent if you are motivated (the same goes for the sofa or bookcases). As

 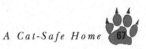

for the inside of the fridge, anytime you open that door when the kitten is nearby, she may want to see what's inside and can jump in without your even knowing it. So it's important for you to develop the habit of always checking before you close the refrigerator.

KEEP DRYER AND WASHER DOORS SHUT

Cats will explore anywhere, and a dryer makes a nice cozy place to nap but a very bad place to be once a machine turns on. Don't turn on the washer or dryer until you've looked *and felt* to make sure the cat isn't in there.

The Danger of Household Visitors

You would probably never think that relatives, friends and other visitors could pose a danger to your cat, but they certainly can. People who aren't themselves cat owners (or people who have cats but never had a chance to learn what you will now know) can unknowingly put your cat in jeopardy. The very first thing that visitors do—before they even consciously do anything—is rattle the resident cat with their very presence. Newcomers, especially overnight guests, disrupt the normal routine of a household just by being there, and cats depend on a normal, predictable routine. Service people who come to do work on your house, visiting children and anyone else who comes in can disturb a cat's routine, opening and closing doors or windows through which a cat might dash if she was sufficiently rattled.

As you will see, many of the hazards listed could apply to you and possibly others in your household as well as to occasional visitors.

OPENING OUTSIDE DOORS

The most worrisome thing visitors can do is to accidentally let your indoor cat out the door. If your indoor cat has never shown interest in going outside when you go out, you're lucky. Many people have to make a habit of guarding the doorway with their foot or body to block the cat from trying to escape. However, the confusion and commotion that visitors bring can stress or frighten a cat enough to make her bolt out the door, even if she usually wouldn't. And if you have one of those just-give-me-a-chance-and-I'm-outta-here kind of cats who is always ready to make a break for freedom, newcomers to the household may inadvertently give the cat that chance she's been waiting for.

OPENING WINDOWS

It may not occur to a visitor that leaving a window open will give a curious cat a place to fall out—and if you are on a higher floor in an apartment building, the fall may be substantial. Most people don't know that cats do fall out of windows regularly and can get hurt or die doing so, despite their ability to land on their feet. A cat may chase a fly or moth right out that window, but just the thrill of adventure alone is enough to entice a kitty out on the windowsill. A cat can squeeze through even the smallest space, so leaving a window open "only a little" may still pose the danger of jumping or falling. The safest thing you can do is to put screens on all your windows and leave them on year-round. An open window in a cat-safe house should never be a possible exit, only a place for a cat to get some fresh air.

OPENING DRAWERS AND INSIDE DOORS

Both you and your visitors should pay attention to whether your cat shows any interest in a drawer or closet you open, because later she can get trapped in these places if you shut the drawer or door behind her. This is especially true of the refrigerator, where cats have suffocated because someone closed the fridge door without seeing the cat go in.

LOOK WHERE YOU SIT OR WALK

It may sound unlikely to you, but people do sit down on cats; they also step on them or trip over them. This happens much more than you might imagine, so even if you feel foolish, tell your guests to be on the lookout.

HOUSEHOLD REPAIR PEOPLE

Depending on your cat's personality and the nature of the work you are having done, you might want to put the cat into a room that is off-limits to humans. Put a note on the door to that effect.

Dangers During Remodeling

If you are having construction done on your home, it poses special dangers and stresses to your cat. Although some people would suggest that you send your cat away to a willing friend's house or to a cattery to be boarded, we know that being sent away can be highly stressful to a cat, so it's better to try to find a way to keep her safe and sequestered at home during construction.

There are a number of predictable problems that can arise during remodeling, including situational hazards such as toxic fumes or construction debris and disturbances to the cat's environment that may make her want to escape. What follows are some safety suggestions that should keep your cat comfortable while you make your home more comfortable for you.

 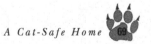

Construction Safety Tips

- Create a cat sanctuary by setting aside a room that is away from the construction activity. Put the cat's tree or scratching post, litter box and bed in the room.
- Lock the door from the outside (but with the key in the lock for emergencies) and put a sign on the door for workers and others: "Cat-Safe Room—Do Not Enter."
- Use a solid-sided crate or cage to isolate the cat if the construction disturbance is going to be brief. (A cat feels safer if not exposed on all sides in a wire-sided cage.)
- Before letting the cat out at the end of the workday, first make sure that the day's construction has left no new way for the cat to escape.
- Before letting the cat out, either close off the area under construction or go through it carefully, picking up any small, hazardous construction materials that a cat could step on or ingest.
- Before letting the cat walk around, make sure there are no containers of toxic materials or spillage that the cat might walk through and then lick off herself, ingesting poison.

Special Holiday and Party Dangers

CHRISTMAS

Christmas is a hazardous holiday for a cat, offering her many enticements that are fraught with danger. There should be a big blinking red light above the tree itself to indicate the multitude of ways that it is dangerous to a cat. There are many other ways that cats can get into trouble exploring their environment on Christmas. (All the advice here also relates to Easter, Hanukkah, Thanksgiving, birthdays or any other occasions when gifts and decorations come out.) Holidays mean lots of activity, guests who may pat or grab the cat and spook her and foods out in the open that are not cat safe.

Cat-Proofing the Christmas Tree

- An average-size cat can knock over even a large tree, so make sure you get a heavy, sturdy base (not one of those rickety green metal pans on spindly legs).
- Pick a tree with a wide, sturdy trunk to avoid the danger of a top-heavy tree that is vulnerable to tipping over.
- You can even put a small eyebolt (a closed metal circle that screws into wood or a wall) from your hardware store into the wall behind the tree and then tie a length

of strong, transparent fishing line around the trunk and through the eyebolt to secure the tree to the wall.

- Bring the tree into the house several days before you intend to start decorating it. Leave the tree unadorned for a couple of days so you can see what the cat may be plotting. If you catch her chewing on the pine needles, you can stop her by clapping your hands together (the universal gesture to a cat to cease and desist).

- If she starts to climb the tree, do the same thing—clap as you approach her, using your clapping hands as the deterrent that will drive her away.

- The water that collects in the reservoir is dangerous for cats because it is a landing place for any pine sap that might drip down. Sap is toxic to cats, as is any product you might put in the water to extend the life of the tree. So you will need some sort of netting over the reservoir that will allow you to add water but prevent your cat from reaching it.

- The tree lights are dangerous if chewed, so each strand should be sprayed with a bitter solution meant to discourage chewing.

- The piece of electric cord that goes from the tree to the wall is especially vulnerable, so cover it with an electric-cord tube meant to hide all the desk wires in an office or even just an empty cardboard paper towel tube. (No one will notice it behind the tree.)

- Twinkling tree lights attract cats, so try to get the nonblinking ones. (They are easier on people's nerves, too.)

- Always unplug the lights when you go out so that your cat doesn't find some way to get her little fangs around the cord and get shocked.

- Tinsel is not worth the jeopardy—the way it moves and shines is enticing to a cat and encourages climbing. Also, tinsel often falls off and can be deadly if a cat ingests it.

- Don't use tree ornaments that can break. There is always the chance that a cat will bat one off the tree, so use only those that will survive a fall. If you must hang breakable ornaments, hang them way up high out of the cat's reach.

- Ornament hooks should also be avoided because they don't hold the ornaments securely and can be a hazard. Instead, use the green twist-tie material sold to stake plants in the garden—or the ones that come with plastic bags.

- The long ribbons from packages are also potentially dangerous because a kitten may chew on one and wind up swallowing it; stick to pre-tied bows. And make sure all wrappings wind up in the trash after gifts are opened.

HALLOWEEN

Halloween can be especially dangerous for a cat because there are sick individuals in our society who want to use cats for cruel, twisted rituals that range from torture to killing on this holiday. Black cats are in special danger because of their historical connection to Halloween. This is such

a problem that some animal shelters will not allow anyone to adopt a black cat during the entire month of October.

During the day and night of Halloween, the best thing you can do for your cat is to keep her shut away in a part of your house far from all the commotion. Put her litter box and her favorite bed or perch in there and put on some soothing music. Your cat will not appreciate children running around in costumes, all wound up on Halloween candy! Cats also will not do well with the doorbell ringing and all sorts of dressed-up strangers carrying bags. For that matter, keep an eye out for Halloween candy (especially chocolate, which is particularly bad for cats) before and after the big day.

Environmental Dangers

THE DANGER OF EXTREME HEAT

Hyperthermia (overheating, also known as heat exhaustion) can be dangerous for a cat's health because a cat's system does not handle the heat well.

✦ Causes of Overheating

Being confined to an overheated area without a cool space or access to water is the main cause of a cat becoming overheated. In hot, humid weather, cats are especially prone to heat exhaustion and dehydration. In very hot weather cats can get overheated if they spend hours outside or if they fall asleep in a garage or get inside a parked car (even if the car is not in full sun). Other causes of hyperthermia are stress, fever (from infection, or a reaction to medication or vaccination), metabolic imbalances in the thyroid or as a result of having seizures.

Be especially careful during warm months of the year or if you live in a climate where it is always hot. Heat exhaustion is a debilitating disorder that can easily progress to the point of becoming *heatstroke*, which is potentially fatal when it reaches the point of multiple organ failure. You can tell if your cat is suffering from hyperthermia because she will be breathing rapidly and with some difficulty, her mouth will stay open, her eyes may seem glassy and she may even pass out. The full list of possible symptoms is below.

Signs of Heat Exhaustion

- Rapid panting
- Muscle weakness
- Staggering
- Rapid heartbeat
- Fainting
- Tremors
- Vomiting

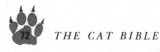

A cat experiencing heat exhaustion must be cooled down immediately or heatstroke, which can kill her, is likely to occur. When a cat reaches the stage of heatstroke her panting will become increasingly fast and labored. On a very hot day, especially if it's humid, the cat will be taking in large quantities of hot air that is hotter than her own normal body temperature (which ranges from 100.4 to 102.5°F). If hyperthermia is not relieved and a cat's body temperature reaches 105°F or higher, cell damage will start, resulting in liver, kidney and gastrointestinal dysfunction, reduced oxygen in the blood and subsequent destruction of muscle tissue, impaired brain function and heart failure. This is probably as much warning as you need to understand that you *cannot* allow your cat to get overheated. Some cats are at higher risk for hyperthermia than others.

CATS WITH HIGHER RISK OF HEATSTROKE

Obese cats
Older cats with age-related conditions such as heart disease
Densely coated breeds (Himalayans, Persians) that cannot dissipate heat
Brachycephalic breeds (short noses, flat faces) that may lack enough space in nasal
passages to cool the air passing through them

If you think your cat may be suffering from heatstroke, it is a true medical emergency (that phrase you hear on outgoing doctors' and veterinarians' office message tapes really applies here). Contact your vet's office to make sure a doctor is available, or contact a veterinary emergency clinic and make plans to transport your cat immediately. Every minute counts, so while you are making the call or arranging transportation, you must begin following the steps below to begin cooling your cat. However, *do not delay immediate transport to a veterinary facility,* so that the staff can examine your cat and administer the necessary care, including IV fluids.

If you are all alone, then getting the cat to professional care is your number one priority. At the very least, you can grab a bottle of room-temperature water (not cold from the refrigerator) to pour on the cat's head and belly, just to get started on cooling her down on the way. If you have help, you can do some of the emergency measures below at the same time you are preparing to leave and during transport.

WHAT TO DO IN CASE OF HEATSTROKE

❑ Do *not* try to soak the cat in cold water—and certainly not in icy water, which would be too much of a shock to her system.
❑ Move the cat to the coolest place possible—an air-conditioned room or air-conditioned car or, failing that, a room with a ceiling fan or a portable fan.
❑ Use a cool, very wet cloth to wipe the cat down. With a long-haired cat, part the hair so you get the cooling water down to the skin.
❑ Use an ice pack (or a bag of frozen vegetables) wrapped in a pillow case on top of the cat's head and against her inner thighs—large blood vessels pass through there.

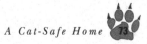

With the steps above, you will aggressively lower your cat's body temperature. However, you must monitor her temperature if you continue these steps for any length of time before reaching a vet. You don't want to plunge her temperature down dangerously low and cause *hypothermia* (see below). Use a "fast read" automatic thermometer with a lubricant and follow instructions on "How to Take a Temperature" in the medical chapter. A helpful instructional video on taking your cat's temperature from the Cornell Feline Health Center (associated with the Cornell Veterinary College) is available online at www.felinevideos.vet.cornell.edu.

If your thermometer shows your cat's temperature is cooling down to a normal range (100.4 to 102.5°F), then stop your aggressive cooling because the danger point for hyperthermia has passed.

EXTREME COLD

Hypothermia, as you might have guessed, is what happens when a cat gets too cold. This can happen when a cat spends a long time outside in frigid weather; it can also come from a serious disease. A kitten can also easily get chilled because she has minimal fat stores for insulation. Lowered body temperature can also occur when a cat gets hurt (especially with a blow to the head)—the next thing that can happen is that she can go into shock.

You can rewarm her by putting some towels in the dryer and wrapping her up in them while taking her to the vet to be evaluated. Just as with people, do not rub a cat anywhere you suspect frostbite since the friction can damage her skin.

THE DANGER OF BRIGHT SUNLIGHT

Just as with people, too much direct sunlight can cause skin cancer in cats. In the same way that fair-skinned people are in the most jeopardy from the sun, white or lightly pigmented cats are most at risk for skin cancer—even if it is just their nose or ears that are white. If your cat is indoors-only and you live in a hot climate with large windows where she likes to hang out in sunny spots during the prime hours of sunlight (between 11 A.M. and 2 P.M., when the ultraviolet rays are most potent), you might want to consider putting a coating on your windows with a UV filter. A filter will decrease a cat's risk of getting skin cancer with the added benefit of keeping your house cooler, thereby lowering your energy costs.

If you have or plan to have a cat who is outdoors most of the time, it is not a good idea for her to lie in the baking sun for extended periods of time. In so far as you can alter her habits, try to keep her out of the sun during those crucial hours.

Your New Cat's Homecoming

A NEW-CAT "SAFE ROOM"

An adult cat entering your home needs to have a room to herself where she can mentally and physically adjust to her new environment. Change is threatening and stressful for cats, so giving your new cat a "welcome room" is a kind and thoughtful way to help her transition into your family. A cat needs to feel safe and at ease in her new home, and it takes some cats longer than

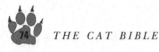

others to make this transition. You can never go wrong by giving your cat a secure, quiet room to get her bearings.

An adult cat doesn't need to be confined to a bathroom, nor do you have to remove furnishings to accommodate her. However, if the room you choose does not have furniture she can hide behind or underneath, then you need to put out a couple of cardboard boxes, lined with a towel or small blanket or a worn sweatshirt of yours. You can cut a door in the boxes large enough for her to get into the box and feel safe. You can make one of the boxes extra cozy so that it doubles as a bed for her, or you can buy her a bed (more on those in the next chapter).

Be sure that the food and water are far from the litter box and that you provide her with a satisfying scratching post. If you have the space and resources, it's also great to buy or create a climbing retreat for her to jump up onto.

USING COMFORT ZONE FELIWAY TO SMOOTH THE WAY

Pheromones are chemicals that cats produce through their facial scent glands, which is why cats rub their cheeks against things: to leave their individual scent. A cat marks her territory with these pheromones, creating a calming effect for her while leaving a "calling card" to other cats who pass by. There is a synthetic version of these feline facial pheromones called Comfort Zone Feliway, which comes as a spray as well as a diffuser that plugs into an electrical socket and is dispersed in the air of the room. The product was originally developed to prevent urine marking, since a cat is less likely to mark where there is facial marking, but it has also been used for a long time as a calming agent, since research has shown that spraying objects with Comfort Zone Feliway in the cat's environment has a positive effect in anxiety-producing situations. Whether your cat is moving to a new house or into a cage at the vet clinic, this product can help calm her and accustom her to new places or objects by making them seem familiar to her.

Spraying the corners and legs of furniture in the cat's safe room makes the room less alien and more inviting to her. As she ventures out of her safe room into the rest of the house you can make her transition smoother by spraying prominent objects throughout your home. "Prominent" means any surface that a cat might naturally rub her cheeks against—not a flat surface such as a wall or the back of a sofa, but rather the corners of low tables, chair legs, door frames, and so on. You can also plug in a Feliway diffuser several hours before bringing in the cat, which will calm and comfort her by making the environment seem familiar.

Feliway comes with instructions you should read and keep so that you have a clear sense of how to best use the product. The main thing to keep in mind is that you are trying to mimic what a cat would do with her own facial pheromones, duplicating where and how she would rub objects.

There is no need to use Feliway with a kitten because they do not begin facial marking until they are older, nor do they mark with urine at an early age.

TIPS FOR USING FELIWAY

Spray about 4 inches away from the object.
Spray about 8 inches up from the ground, where a cat's cheeks would reach.
Use one squirt only—do not saturate.

Spray only objects—never the cat.

Spray each spot once or twice a day for a month.

You can stop spraying anywhere the cat rubs her cheeks.

Do not spray near the litter box (a cat would never rub there).

WHEN WILL SHE BE READY TO COME OUT OF HER SAFE ROOM?

Trust your cat to let you know she is ready to start exploring the house. A cat who still hides when you come into her safe room or who isn't eating yet still has some adjusting to do. It will be a good sign that she feels at home when she has settled in her own daily routine of eating, drinking water, using the litter box and moving freely around the safe room. The cat needs to be curious and relaxed about you, so go into her room, bring food, clean the litter box and let her be the one who approaches you.

Once you reach this point, you can open the door to the safe room and let her explore further *at her own pace*. Don't force her to come out or carry her out—let her take it one step at a time. Most cats like to move slowly in finding their way in a new environment, so just follow her lead and things should go well.

A NEW-KITTEN SAFE ROOM

Even with every possible safeguard, young kittens will still find a way to get themselves into trouble. One of the best things you can do for a small kitty is to create a safe room that you can put her in when you go out. This will keep her out of trouble, and it also lays a good foundation for the boundaries you are going to set for her—such as not jumping up on the kitchen table or staying away from other places in the house that you decide to put off limits.

By putting a satisfying scratching post or cat tree in your kitten's safe room, she'll come to learn quickly what it's for and become accustomed to using it (rather than your furniture). Put her litter box at one end of the safe room, away from the scratching post and her eating area, so that her elimination area will be clearly separate, reinforcing the natural instinct to do her business away from her living area. When a kitten has the run of an entire apartment or house, there are too many options and places to experiment for all her needs and she may get confused. With a safe room, the choices are narrowed down to the correct ones, building habits of a lifetime.

◆ Setting Up a Safe Room

A bathroom is the best bet for a kitten safe room: It is an easy room to make safe because there is nothing to ruin and it's quick to clean. However, you do need to remove *all* the human elements from the room, which means putting away towels, bath rugs and bathmats, as well as draping the shower curtain up on the rod. You will want to take the toilet paper off the spool (unraveling it is a kitten favorite) and take any personal products (including the soap and soap dish) out of the tub or shower and put them away in a closet or up on a high shelf in the shower. If you have a stall shower, keep the door shut.

If you decide to stash things in an under-sink cabinet, make sure to kitten-proof it with a baby-proof latch. Many cats use their paws in a raccoon-like way and can be surprisingly adept at opening or maneuvering things. Be especially careful with medications or ointments of any kind, keeping them all up high in a closed cabinet. And the toilet lid *must* be down or the room is not safe for a kitten. Water is interesting to cats; all it takes is one misstep off the edge of the slippery toilet seat and that kitty can drown.

✦ Making the Room Fun

Now that you've taken every last thing out of this bathroom, you need to put something back in to keep the kitten amused and happy. So you will want to buy or create a number of kitten toys and amusements to put in the room (more on what those can be in the next chapter). Each time you leave home, you will put the kitty in her room and leave two new, different toys for her, taking back the two toys from the previous time she was in there. Cats get bored having the same toy all the time, so by rotating the toys, you always leave her something fresh and intriguing. If you can create or buy some sort of climbing tower (more on that in the next chapter) to put in her safe room, it will go a long way toward keeping her amused and burning off energy while you're out.

Put a cardboard box into the room because cats love to have places to hide; it's just in their nature. Turn a box upside down and cut a hole large enough for her to go in and out, like it's her personal cave. Inside the box, put a towel or, even better, one of your old sweaters or a sweatshirt, worn and not washed, so the cat can become familiar and comfortable with your scent.

At the opposite end of the room from where you put the litter box, you will need to put a comfy bed for her and a bowl of fresh water. No food bowl is necessary since free-feeding dry food is unhealthy (more on this in the nutrition chapter). In the chapter on litter boxes you'll learn more than you've ever thought you needed to know about where cats relieve themselves and the importance of keeping the two aspects of a cat's digestive system—"food in" and "food out"—as far apart as possible. Litter box problems are at the top of many cat owners' gripe lists, so it is important to help your new kitten develop and maintain good elimination habits throughout her lifetime.

✦ When Can the Kitten Have Freedom?

As soon as the kitten is using the litter box consistently and has "bonded" with her scratching post, you can increase her territory beyond the kitten-safe bathroom. Depending on the layout and size of your home, this may mean adding a room or two at a time or it may mean adding the whole rest of your home all at once if it's an apartment. You want to try to keep her litter box where it has been so that she knows precisely where to go when the urge comes over her. If you move the litter box at the same time that you give her a bigger space to explore, you may be asking for trouble—you want good litter box habits right from the beginning. Adding more litter boxes is a good idea and avoids mistakes.

Please keep in mind that whatever spaces in your house you add to your kitten's territory, they must all be just as safe for her as that little bathroom was. Kitten-proof every area in your home that she will enter, and then let her at it.

 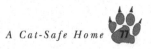

The Controversy of Indoor Versus Outdoor

There are two big moral issues that surround having a cat. The first is the problem that everyone agrees on: the goal of having all cats neutered to reduce the enormous cat population and avoid having to euthanize so many healthy cats. The other big question, and the one we're going to address here, is whether you should ever allow a cat to go outdoors. Fewer people agree about whether cats should be confined indoors for their entire lives. As you will see below, there are numerous parts of this equation.

WHAT EXACTLY IS THE PROBLEM?

The indoor/outdoor controversy has become such a heated topic that cat advocates at shelters and rescue organizations often require that people adopting a cat promise to keep her inside at all times. Breeders of cats often have the same requirement of those buying their kittens. And these people aren't just asking for a verbal promise that a cat will stay indoors: Buyers and adopters are often asked to sign a contract stipulating that they will never let the cat outside.

Although I fully respect and appreciate the reasoning behind the theory of indoors-only, I have to admit that in my own experience and in practical terms, there seem to be some cats who are happy only if they have the freedom to go outside. The true nature of these cats seems to be fulfilled when they have outdoor privileges. Of course, not all "outdoors" is equal or even comparable: a rural setting has none of the same safety issues as a crowded community in suburbia. The problem I see with the never-outdoors argument is that everybody has a different lifestyle. The issues that affect a cat's safety are quite different in remote areas or farmlands than they are in cities or densely populated areas. Realistically, most people probably live in populated communities (whether urban or suburban) where there are many cars and very little territory where a cat has the opportunity to explore or hunt safely. It should be obvious that a cat allowed outdoors in those circumstances is in great jeopardy.

SO WHAT IS A PERSON TO DO?

If you are in that minority who live out in the true country, with many acres of land far from a busy road, and coyotes do not roam your area, then it may seem kind of ludicrous *not* to let your cat enjoy the world outdoors. However, the professional guardians of cats—those in the world of humane societies and shelters—take a strong stand for all cats staying strictly indoors, without exception. These devoted animal protectors know the statistics, which are certainly compelling: a well-looked-after indoor cat can live to age 20, but if that same cat is allowed outdoors, the average life span is 7 years. But it is really tempting for a cat lover who lives near fields or woods to offer his cat the chance to go outdoors and experience the world, exercising her natural physical abilities to run and hunt. Perhaps it is unrealistic or irresponsible for those people to indulge what could be viewed as a "romantic" idea of a cat's natural pleasure in being her true self. Personally, I have often been torn between no-risk pragmatism and watching my cat's apparent delight in stalking and pouncing on everything from a blowing leaf to a darting mouse. It is not simply a question of a longer, safer life but also the cat's quality of life.

HOW MUCH DANGER IS THERE *REALLY*?

The main reason for the indoor-only movement is that cats are killed at an appalling rate when allowed outside—cars hit most of them, dogs attack some, and coyotes and other wild animals kill others. Cats can ingest poisons put out for rodents, and diseases and illnesses they pick up from unvaccinated cats can sicken them enough to kill them. I can attest to this tragic consequence personally since several of my cats lived with me in southern California, where coyotes are bold, wily and hungry predators who will come right to the door in broad daylight in populated areas, looking for small dogs or cats to eat. They will even come in pairs or threes and go after big dogs if they discern that a dog is weak, old or otherwise physically vulnerable. And when I adopted or found cats who had an unstoppable drive to get outside, it wasn't long before they disappeared, and I fear that coyotes were the cause of their demise.

IS THERE A TRUE "OUTDOOR CAT"?

I think the question of whether you decide to keep a cat exclusively indoors—or even whether you are able to do so—depends at least in part on whether that cat ever had freedom to go outdoors and how much it mattered to her. A cat who is determined to get outside will find a way—all it takes is a split second for her to dash through an open door, even one that is opened only a crack. One moment of inattentiveness on your part and she is gone. I have had this happen myself with a cat or two, and in my experience there are certain cats who pine to get outside, sitting near a window or door, waiting for the opportunity to escape. There is no hard and fast rule about which cat will try to escape: I imagine it's about their individual personality. It may be that some cats, once they've tasted the great outdoors, cannot get it out of their mind, while others are fully content to stay inside for the rest of their lives with the nice climate and delicious food you provide, displaying no desire to live by their wits for even an afternoon. Maybe it's a little like the difference in people: those who crave a chance to go adventure camping with Outward Bound and those who think "roughing it" means a hotel without room service.

THE EMOTIONAL NEEDS OF AN INDOOR CAT

A cat who lives exclusively indoors has needs that people all too often disregard. All cats have an instinctive drive to explore the territory around them, patrolling and looking for hunting prospects. A cat is born with a naturally strong drive to explore her environment and to prey on small creatures—these are the fundamental drives that rev her engine. These two instinctive behaviors require a lot of concentration and effort, so cats who are free to roam outside naturally burn off mental and physical energy. These activities excite and stimulate a cat in the most appropriate way, followed by the pleasurable relaxation when the adrenaline from hunting wears off. An outdoor cat who lives in the country and can roam and hunt and return to a cozy house afterward is a deeply content animal. We have to find ways for indoor cats to express these drives indoors.

◆ Create Variety in Her Life

If your cat is going to live entirely inside, then you need to offer stimulating situations and objects to keep her mentally sharp and emotionally content. Indoor cats need to experience as many people and situations as possible, so that they don't become overly sensitive to new events.

✦ Overly Sensitive Indoor Cats

If a cat is naturally reticent or cautious and also lives inside without much stimulation, she can become overreactive to things in her environment. Even the smell of your shoes, when you return from being out in the world, can be interesting to an understimulated cat.

The best way to avoid the possibility of your cat becoming unused to change around her is to provide change all the time. The more things that your cat can see, smell and experience, the better chance that she won't have a meltdown when people come to visit or you bring new objects into the home. In the next chapter, on stuff for cats, there are suggestions about stimulating toys and how to use them play with your cat.

✦ Overly Dependent Cats

An indoor cat can become so tightly bonded to the people she lives with that she really suffers when they go out. One way to guard against this is to offer as many stimulating elements in the cat's life as possible, and follow the suggestions about ways to avoid or remedy separation anxiety in the chapter on emotions.

SOME CATS ARE BETTER AT BEING INDOORS

Some breeds of cats are more suited to a less active, less stimulating lifestyle—which means they make better indoor cats. The kind of cat you choose should be determined by how well the cat makes the transition to indoor living or accepts it from kittenhood.

Whether you have a small apartment or a large house makes a big difference in the environment for a cat. For example, energetic breeds such as Siamese and Burmese, which bond closely with people, will probably not do well if they are expected to spend time alone in a smaller apartment. Basically, you could say that these breeds are unsuited to small quarters, although at the same time you have to consider how much solitary time this type of cat would have to endure, because that would be equally relevant in determining whether they could be content living in a small apartment if it also meant frequent human companionship.

Older cats may be more suited to an entirely indoor life, so if you are getting a cat for the first time and can only provide an indoor life in a somewhat limited space, the ideal cat for you may be an older one with less drive to explore and hunt.

OCCASIONAL OUTDOOR JAUNTS

Indoor cats who are allowed outside only sometimes—for example, if they go with you to a country house on weekends—can suffer from the frustration of experiencing freedom and then being confined again. Some cats can make this jarring transition without problems but for others the shift from being cooped up to being let loose in the wild outdoors is just too much. Or, I should say, it's having to return inside after experiencing freedom that is too much to ask.

A cat who is having trouble adjusting to this transition will show the typical signs of feline stress and distress, which you can read more about in the chapter on emotions. Stressed behavior includes things such as overgrooming and licking to the point of removing hair, causing skin sores and so on.

Also, it can be dangerous to offer the occasional outdoor jaunt to indoor cats, since they tend to be "soft" and don't understand the physical demands and jeopardy of being outdoors. They can get confused and wander off or become frightened and flee in a panic, making them targets for tougher animals.

PROVIDING A SAFE OUTDOOR ENCLOSURE

In the next chapter you can read about different kinds of window boxes and patio enclosures you can buy or make to give your cat the benefits of being outside without the danger of complete freedom.

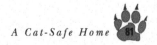

Chapter 4

STUFF FOR YOUR CAT

This is a chapter stuffed with stuff that your cat might like . . . definitely needs . . . and will probably turn up her nose at. Some of the things you'll learn about here may surprise you (such as the best material and shape for food and water bowls), and some of the things may make you scratch your head, but there are a few core elements of a cat's equipment (such as a scratching post, for example) that are important for you to know about to help make life with your cat harmonious.

The chapter is organized alphabetically, so you can go right to what you need to know. However, I'd suggest glancing at other topics along the way, since there are things you would do well to find out about that your cat will really appreciate. (For the pithiest description of how fussy cats can be about what you buy for them—beds, in particular—go back to the Introduction and see what Celia Sack of Noe Valley Pet Company had to say on this topic.)

Beds

Beds can be a tough call because each cat is so particular about where she'll sleep and how it should feel. I have yet to hear anyone disagree that all cats love to sleep in a box full of sweaters, preferably yours. But no matter how much a cat might like this arrangement, and even if you had enough sweaters to go around, I can imagine that you might not want the box-of-old-sweaters look as part of your décor.

CUP BEDS AND BEDS WITH HOODS

Cats seem to love the cozy sensation of a bed that surrounds them with high sides or with a "roof." Cats with short hair especially seem to appreciate the extra warmth and security of this type of bed. These beds have names such as Cozy Cup and are made of foam with a cover that is usually fake shearling on the inside where the cat sleeps, with some kind of nylon material on the outside of the cup. These covers have elasticized edges and they come off for laundering, but the downside (especially if you are the impatient type, like me) is that they can be challenging to put back on after washing—it is tricky to pull the elasticized cover over the foam and get it to conform to the shape again.

SHEARLING MATS

All cats seem to love the pet mats made from fake shearling, which is soft and cozy, launders easily and doesn't take that long to dry. This is the same kind of material that the interior of the cup bed is made from. If you have to take your cat anywhere in her carrier box, you'll be doing her a favor if you put in her mat from home. It will make her carrier more comfortable and it may make her feel less agitated and more secure because she'll have something familiar in there with her. Mats made of faux shearling come in various sizes and thicknesses. You can get them through most catalogues, at any pet store or online at sites such as KV Vet Supply (www.kvvet.com), Drs. Foster & Smith (www.drsfosterandsmith.com) or www.dog.com.

CATNAPPER

This product, made by a company called Flexi-Mat, is a window seat hammock, so it is a bed and window seat at the same time. It can fit any windowsill and it can be installed permanently with screws, or temporarily by using Velcro, and it holds up to 35 pounds. It is washable, but if you put a shearling mat in it, the cat may enjoy it more, and you can wash just the mat. It costs less than $50 and can be ordered directly at 800-338-7392.

SLEEP RIGHT THERMAL CAT CUSHION

This product was designed for kittens who need extra warmth, but older feline citizens will probably appreciate it, too. It is made of fake shearling and uses neither batteries nor electricity—its heat-reflective surface directs the cat or kitten's own body heat back at the animal. It is carried at PetSmart and costs under $20. More information is available from the company that makes it, at www.bramton.com or 800-272-6336.

Bowls for Food and Water

The shape of the bowl is important because a deep, narrow bowl is really uncomfortable for a cat. A bowl of this shape can crowd or crush a cat's whiskers, soil the hair on a long-haired cat's face, and cause problems for flat-nosed breeds such as Persians or Himalayans. Cats generally do best with both food and water bowls that are wide and shallow.

Plastic bowls are practical because they are inexpensive and lightweight. Most cat bowls are

made from plastic, but serious cat people know that it's better to use ceramic or metal. Plastic causes allergies for many cats, who lose hair on their chin, get acne or even develop sores on their chins. Plastic can also be unsanitary because the small scratches on the plastic surface can harbor bacteria, especially with the superficial cleaning we tend to give our pets' bowls. Those same scratches can be uncomfortable for a cat's rough but very sensitive tongue when she is eating. Another problem with plastic bowls is that because they are so lightweight, they don't stay in one place while she is eating, and the poor cat may have to chase her bowl around the room.

Stainless steel is a traditional favorite because it is unbreakable and easy to clean. However, stainless bowls are lightweight and need some kind of holder to keep them in place while a cat is eating. Some stainless bowls have a rubber rim to keep the bowl in place while kitty is eating—you just have to remember to slide the rubber off periodically and give it a good scrub.

Ceramic and glass are also good materials for cat bowls, because they are heavy enough to stay put while a cat is eating, but because they are breakable they may need to be replaced. Also, cracks and chips on the rim of a ceramic dish can be irritating to a cat's tongue and also are a place for bacteria to grow that can irritate your cat's chin and tongue.

Double bowls look like they'd be a good idea, but they are not. If you thought you would use the double dish to put out dinner for two cats, think again: cats like space to eat, not to be crowded up against another cat. A double bowl can actually cause problems between two otherwise friendly cats who simply cannot tolerate being on top of each other to eat. You'll learn more about multi-cat households in that chapter, but it is well known that cats need space when they are eating. If you were thinking of using a double bowl for one cat's dry food and water, think again about that: The food falls into the water and makes it unappealing.

Carriers

Your cat must get used to being in a carrier because there are frequently situations when she needs to be transported, whether to the vet, to the groomer, or in an emergency evacuation situation. The only safe way to transport a cat is in a carrier made for that purpose—you may imagine your cat would be happier being carried, but once you leave the safety of your home, all it takes is one startling moment and she is out of your arms and gone, maybe forever. So a carrier is a must—as is getting your cat comfortable with it. Here are a number of styles or kinds of carriers, a checklist of things to consider, and some tips on ways to make a carrier more welcoming.

CHOOSING A CARRIER

The kind of carrier you need depends somewhat on your lifestyle and what that carrier will be used for. If you only intend to take the cat a short distance to a vet or groomer, then a basic plastic carrier is all you need. But if you plan on traveling or taking longer trips in a car, then it makes sense to get a carrier that is roomier, with comfort in mind. If you want to take your cat on board an airplane with you, you'll need one that can fit under the seat in front of you. Each airline has different rules, so you need to check with them about specifics.

A *basic plastic carrier* is the typical hard-sided plastic cage with a metal grate for a door in front.

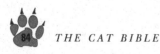

These carriers are the ones approved for use in an airline baggage compartment and also are the type of carrier good for use in a car for travel. Hard sides are the most comfortable for most cats, because soft-sided carriers can collapse on your cat when you set the bag down. Imagine how distressing it would be if you were in a tent that folded down on top of you, added to the other stresses a cat is dealing with just leaving home.

A *cat tote bag* is more of a fashion statement, like the kind of bag that some people tote their little dogs around in. Totes have handles, like a giant purse; the cat gets in on top, between the handles. They have a mesh panel at one or both ends and some have zippers. Most people put these handles over their shoulders, which means the cat is transported close to their side. This can be reassuring for the cat, but it also means she is right there in the middle of whatever the person is doing. Depending on the cat's personality, this can be fun and interesting or it can be sheer misery.

A *carrier/bed* is a nice bed made of a basket fitted with a pillow. When you want to use it to transport your cat, you snap on a mesh lid with a handle and off you go. This is truly a carrier that you can leave around the house and let the cat get completely comfortable with, and then use for travel when needed.

WHAT TO LOOK FOR IN A CARRIER

It has to fit the cat. This means she has to be able to lie down, stand up straight, and turn around. However, you don't want a lot of extra room that will allow her to slip and slide around when the carrier is lifted and moved. A useful rule of thumb is that a carrier should be no more than one and a half times the size of your cat—or, said another way, the length of your cat, plus half as long.

Bigger is not better. A cat feels safest when she can brace herself against the sides of a carrier, which is not possible if it is too large.

What size should you buy? Medium is the appropriate size for almost all cats. If you are buying a carrier for a kitten, rather than buying a small one that she will outgrow, you can buy the medium size and cut out a small cardboard box to fit inside, with a towel wrapped around it so that it fits snugly into the carrier. Very few cats—other than a Maine Coon—are big enough to require a large size.

Certainly *do not* buy a two-cat carrier—they are big, bulky and not user-friendly, neither for you, nor for the two cats who will be slipping and sliding against one another in there as you struggle to lift the carrier and walk with it.

A top- and front-opening carrier is easiest. If you choose a carrier with a top opening—or where the whole top half lifts off—it allows you to place the cat in from above (instead of having to shove her into a door from behind) and you can lift her out from above, too. A top opening also allows the vet the option of checking the cat out right in the carrier, which for some cats makes them less stressed. And no matter how you get your cat out of the carrier, you should never just tip it and have her tumble out—you'd think it would be unnecessary advice, but you'd be surprised how many people do this without thinking of the effect on the kitty.

Are there ventilation holes at both ends? The carrier needs air flow, so cross ventilation is the best way to be sure of it.

Should you get a top that is transparent or open mesh? This would be a good option for a bold and secure cat who likes to be able to look out. Other cats might feel too exposed and threatened, so

you have to know your cat's temperament before making that call. Of course, you can always drape something on top of an open-topped carrier, but that is sort of awkward. They say that cats who suffer from motion sickness do better with a see-through top, but again, this depends on the individual. See if you might borrow a friend's carrier to test it out before making your decision and investment.

Make sure the carrier is well-constructed. Run your hand inside to be sure there aren't any sharp edges or protrusions. Check out the hinges and handles and whatever other hardware might be on it to see if it fits together well and seems to be of decent quality. Check the latches; open and close the door. To see how it handles, take a small bag of pet food off the shelf in the store and put it inside to see how the carrier feels with weight in it.

Is it comfortable for you? Although the cat's comfort and safety come first, the handle also has to fit your hand well and be well-balanced with weight in it.

INTRODUCING YOUR CAT TO THE CARRIER

The most important part of the cat-carrier relationship is how you introduce your cat to the carrier and how you first use it with her. Many cats are freaked out about their carriers because the only association they have is being stuffed into it and whisked off to the vet's office. To avoid having this happen to your cat, here is a checklist of ways to get your cat comfortable with her carrier:

WAYS TO MAKE THE CARRIER APPEALING

1. If possible, start when the cat is young so that she doesn't develop a negative association with the carrier. If she is older when you get her, proceed as if this is her first encounter with it. Even if she already has a bad feeling about carriers, you are going to change that by treating the carrier as not something to dread, but something positive.

2. You want to make the carrier seem like a normal part of the landscape, maybe even something special, not something scary. Leave the carrier out in a room where your cat spends time, placing a really comfortable small pillow, blanket or folded up towel, a small catnip toy, and a favorite food treat inside. A cat's curiosity being what it is, she cat will surely come sniffing around and be delighted to find those surprises inside.

3. Leave it out like that for at least one or two days a week so that it becomes something familiar but also a special amusement. Make sure the door is propped open and that the carrier is backed up against a wall or a piece of furniture so that there is no chance it will tip over if the cat gets inside and shifts around in there.

4. You want to get the cat used to different things happening with the carrier. So once in a while close the door on the carrier and leave the room for a quarter of an hour. Then come back and open the door, propping it open so the cat has the sense that she can come and go at will. Another time, close the door after the cat goes in, pick up the carrier, and walk it around for a bit. Then set it down, open the door, and offer the cat a treat. On a different occasion you can take the carrier for a drive in the car, even just around the block, and when you return home, set the carrier down, open the door, and offer a special treat. Do all of this as though it's no big deal: the cat will pick up on your low-key emotions and will follow your lead.

GETTING A RELUCTANT CAT INTO HER CARRIER

If your cat already runs for the hills when the carrier comes out, you may not be able to change her mind about it, but you may be able to get her in there more smoothly.

Remember that you want to succeed on your first attempt because if the cat "wins" the first round and escapes, each successive attempt to get her in is going to become more like hand-to-hand combat.

Retrieve the carrier from wherever you stow it, but don't let the cat see it. Just put it somewhere with easy access for you.

Next, get a thick towel and wrap it around your cat, making sure her feet are well wrapped so she can't try to claw her way out. Cats who don't want to be placed in a carrier will reach out and push against the carrier with their feet to avoid being placed inside.

Once she's "toweled," put her in the carrier all wrapped up and close the door quickly. You don't want to take any chance that she could get out. Don't worry about the towel—she will unwrap herself inside the carrier.

If your cat has issues with the carrier but doesn't despise the carrier so much that she requires a towel, then you need to get her in there gently and swiftly and immediately shut the door so there is no chance she can take off. It's a timing thing: Put her into the carrier front feet first and as you are lowering her hind end down, close the carrier. Your own hand will probably still be in the carrier but that's okay. What you're trying to prevent is the cat's mad dash for freedom, and by keeping your hand there as a safeguard, you can shut the door on your hand and then slowly withdraw it, tucking any part of the cat's anatomy into the carrier with that hand as it leaves.

Catnip

Catnip is an herb in the mint family and it contains a volatile oil with a scent that has a euphoric effect on some cats, making them "high on life." A substance called *nepatalactone,* found in the leaves and stems of catnip, is thought to produce these bouts of ecstasy. Several varieties of this plant grow wild in dry, fairly infertile places. All types of catnip create a feeling of well-being and lower inhibition in most cats, who will rub, run, lick, jump, chew and roll in it. It is believed that even the great wild cats, from cougars to lions, get a kick out of catnip.

Some catnip producers claim health benefits for their product and claim it is an important source of vitamins. While catnip may be vitamin-rich, there is disagreement about the amount and kind of vitamins it contains. Those who are skeptical point out that no cat could eat enough of the herb to get any measurable amount of vitamins.

WHAT IS THE "CATNIP EFFECT"?

The "catnip effect" is similar to the effect that an aphrodisiac (or even an illicit drug like Ecstasy) might have for a human. Catnip is a hallucinogen that lowers a cat's inhibitions and puts her in an altered state for about fifteen minutes. The catnip effect can also involve rubbing against things, leaping, purring and rolling around on the floor. Cats may roll in catnip, lick it or eat it—and while eating it is harmless, its effect is only achieved by smelling the herb.

NOT ALL CATS REACT TO CATNIP

Only 2 out of 3 cats are affected by this herb. The ability to appreciate catnip stems from an inherited gene. The response to the plant is absent in one-third of all cats, making them immune to its charms and pleasures. Maine Coon cats are especially fond of it, while Siamese, Burmese and Himalayans are least affected by it since these breeds originated in areas where catnip does not naturally grow.

ADULT CATS ONLY, PLEASE

Only adult cats should be offered catnip since it has no effect on kittens. A cat needs to inhale catnip to get any effect because it functions through the olfactory nerves. The reason kittens do not react to catnip is because before the age of 3 months, a kitten's olfactory senses have not yet reached maturity. Six months is the youngest age at which you should offer the herb to a kitten. Also, kittens do not need any extra stimulation since they are already full of beans.

CAUTIONS ABOUT CATNIP

If you have a multi-cat household and have never offered catnip to a particular cat, you might want to try it when the cat is alone to test its effect on her. One drawback to catnip is that some cats react to it with aggression toward other cats. There are males who go from playing to aggression in a heartbeat. You don't want to offer it to a cat of either sex who shows aggression because catnip will cause the animal to lose her inhibitions, which may escalate the aggressive behavior.

Don't offer catnip more than once a week. Cat handlers agree that although it is a safe, non-addictive substance that you could theoretically give your cat every day, the problem is that with frequent exposure a cat becomes immune to its effects.

Do not leave catnip-filled toys around the house or you will be ruining the pleasure for your cat. If she is exposed to the herb all the time, its pleasurable effects will be lost on her because of the immunity that occurs with constant exposure. But don't worry: If you have done this in error, just put the toys away for a while. When you offer her a new catnip goody a week later, her response will be restored.

WHERE TO GET GOOD CATNIP

You can buy catnip-filled toys, dried catnip ground up or in leaf form, or you can grow your own herb.

◆ Store-Bought Toys with Catnip

Toys you buy with catnip are the least desirable way to offer catnip to your cat. Often they have been packaged for a long time and the catnip's effectiveness may be diminished. They rarely contain good-quality catnip and they may not even use real catnip. Also, toys often contain the stems of the catnip plant, which are sharp and can hurt your cat if she tries to munch on them, which is something cats often do with catnip.

◆ Loose Catnip

Once again, quality is everything. Read the package to be sure that it says only "leaves and blossoms"—the better brands include nothing but. You don't want any stems. Supermarkets have the lowest quality (just like with pet foods)—pet supply stores and cat specialty stores are a better bet.

◆ Growing Your Own

You can buy catnip wherever seeds are sold in your area, and grow your own plants by following the instructions on the packet. The catnip plant spreads everywhere, so you'll need to keep it trimmed back, grow it in a big pot outside, or even keep it inside on a windowsill. Also, since it will attract loose cats in the neighborhood, you want to grow it where they cannot get to it. Don't let the plant flower or you'll get fewer, less potent leaves; pinch off the top flowering buds of the plant as they appear. When it's time to harvest the plants, cut them at the base, tie them into bunches the size of a big handful, and then hang them upside down in a dry, dark place. When they are fully dry the leaves will be brown and shriveled; carefully pull them off, taking care not to crush them or you will release and waste the oils, which have the valuable aroma; throw away the stems. (Don't the instructions sound a little like a 1970's handbook for marijuana growing?)

◆ Storing Catnip

How you store catnip is important, too. If the catnip comes in a bag, put it into a tightly sealed, airtight container and make sure you store it where your cat cannot get to it.

To keep catnip fresh, store it in the freezer, either in small airtight containers or in tightly closed, small freezer bags with all the air pushed out to prevent ice crystals from forming. This system allows you to take out just one portion at a time. Let it come to room temperature and then crush it before you offer it to your pussycat.

HOW TO GIVE CATNIP

◆ Release the Oils First

If you are using loose catnip, rub it between your palms in order to release the oils before sprinkling it on the landing of your cat's climbing structure or just putting it down on a paper plate for her to roll in. A less messy way to give it is to put a handful of catnip into the toe of a small sock and tie off the sock. Roll the sock around in your hands to release the oils into the enclosed space before putting it down.

◆ Make Your Own Toys

Another fun way to offer catnip is to buy a couple of those little mouse toys made of real fur and park them in an airtight canister of catnip. When you remove the mouse and give it to your cat it will be infused with the catnip essence, ready to cause a sensation.

You can find catnip in various forms at all pet stores, but you can also go right to the source. Felix Katnip Tree Company (206-547-0042), 11504 320th Avenue N.E., Carnation, WA 98012, sells Felix Fine Ground Catnip, their own Katnip Tree, and other products.

PetGuard (800-874-3221), P.O. Box 728, Orange Park, FL 32073 will send a catalogue with a wide range of products, including catnip.

Claws and Nail Caps

A cat who scratches furniture is a big problem—you can read all about this in Chapter 6, on behavior. Sometimes a cat cannot be convinced to scratch only on a post. Declawing, also covered in the behavior chapter, is a barbaric procedure that you would never choose for a cat you love. But destructive scratching is an undeniable problem, too.

Soft Claws nail caps to the rescue! This product was developed as an alternative to declawing and consists of glue-on caps that fit over a cat's nails. They come in colors, for the festive-minded owner, or in a natural shade. Cats of all ages tolerate them very well; they come with simple instructions and you can apply them yourself. They are safe and last from four to six weeks before they have to be replaced. All pet stores carry them and your vet may have them as well. Call 800-989-2542 or go to www.softclaws.com for more information.

Cleaning Products

Having a cat in the household may require a bit of extra housework to keep things tidy. This first section is about household cleaning products that are safe or not for your cat, followed by a section of products for cleaning up your cat's accidents. The issue about cleaning products is that cats may be in jeopardy around many of the chemical-laden products in your home because they will lick off anything that touches them or that they step in. Therefore, whenever possible, avoid using strong chemicals: instead, use cleaners that are as "green" as possible. You will also be reducing your family's exposure to harsh chemicals and putting less pollutants into the environment—so you're helping your cat and doing everyone a favor!

PRECAUTIONS

◆ **Rinse, Rinse, Rinse!**
No matter what cleaning products you decide to use, the best safeguard for your cat is to meticulously rinse the area afterward so that she cannot step in any chemical residue and then lick it off.

◆ **Chemical Cleaners are the Most Dangerous**
Ingredients such as phenol and its derivatives, including creosote, naphthol and wood tar, are in some of the popular brands of cleaning agents and they are particularly toxic to cats. If they ingest

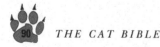

this kind of chemical cleaner it can kill them. Check labels carefully; throw out products you have that contain them and avoid buying anything with those ingredients. Some are even harmful if just inhaled. A cat down at floor level is often right where many chemical solutions have been placed.

◆ Chlorine Is a Common and Dangerous Ingredient
Most household bleach contains chlorine and while it is a good disinfectant for household surfaces, it can cause all kinds of physical misery to a cat who breathes or licks it.

◆ Drain and Toilet Bowl Cleaners are Irritants
There are corrosive acids or alkalis in these products. Contact with them can irritate or damage skin and eyes, as stated on the warnings on the packages.

CAT-FRIENDLY HOUSECLEANING PRODUCTS

◆ Stabilized Chlorine Dioxide
This is different from chlorine bleach. It is an odorless disinfectant that destroys bacteria, viruses and fungi without generating toxic by-products or harming cells.

◆ Baking Soda, Vinegar and Lemon Juice
These products are considered natural cleaners. While they are definitely more cat-friendly than the chemical cleaners out there, they are still not totally benign. For example, baking soda is a salt, which can cause a chemical imbalance in a cat who licks it up; it can also react negatively with stomach acid.

◆ Borax
Borax is a natural mineral that you can use to clean and disinfect. It is safe for cats if used as directed, but it can pose a problem if used in excess and can even be fatal if a cat ingests even a small quantity.

◆ "Green" Cleaners
Environmentally friendly cleaning products are made from plant extracts and are basically safe to use around animals. Simple Green and Seventh Generation are well-known brands.

STAIN AND ODOR REMOVAL PRODUCTS
A number of products are made specifically for cleaning cat stains and removing their odor. Enzymatic cleaners, such as Nature's Miracle Just for Cats Stain & Odor Remover, does not only what the name suggests, but also breaks down the chemical marker that a cat leaves behind with her urine. This is the trigger that brings a cat back to urinate on the same spot again, so eliminating it goes a long way toward breaking a potentially vicious cycle.

There are some less well known enzymatic odor removers that completely remove urine odor. Zero Odor is a pump spray that works through molecular bonding, causing odor molecules to

become inert. It is nontoxic and safe to use around pets, and it can be used on any surface. For $30 you get two 22-ounce bottles and a DVD with behavioral tips (800-526-2967). X-O is an organic, biodegradable odor remover originally used for human hospital settings and which just recently joined the pet market. Go to www.TheCatBible.com or www.xocorp.com (800-442-9696) to find out how to get a free sample or purchase it.

Enzymatic cleaners pose no threat to a cat, which is comforting since they are the recommended way to clean up urine marking. Some experts question whether after treatment a cat can *still* smell the urine and will mark there again. It may be a question of finding an effective product, like those mentioned above.

◆ Removing the Carpet

There will still be times when a carpet has sustained so many markings that the only way to get rid of the smell is to get rid of the carpet. However, don't assume that your work is done; urine usually soaks through to the pad beneath and sometimes even the underlying flooring has been contaminated, too. To avoid more out-of-litter-box experiences in the future on your new floor coverings, look at the chapters on behavior and the litter box so that you can better understand and manage the situation.

Collars and ID Tags

A collar is the first sign that a cat has a loving home and if your cat is an outdoor wanderer or an indoor-only cat who got outside in a mad, impulsive dash, it is the only tangible connection to you. Your chances of being reunited with your kitty hinge on whether she is wearing a collar. All cat collars should be "breakaway," with an elasticized area that allows the collar to slip over a cat's head or break apart if she gets hooked on something and pulls back.

FITTING A COLLAR

If you can fit two fingers underneath the collar, it's loose enough to pull over the cat's head in case she gets stuck somewhere. You should check the fit on a kitten every week, since she is growing fast and a collar that was loose enough one week may be uncomfortably tight the next.

AN ID TAG IS YOUR BEST BET

Your cat's collar needs an ID tag, making it possible for the people who find her to bring you back together. The information that matters most on an ID tag isn't your cat's nickname or even your address—it's the telephone numbers where you can be reached. If you can include your home and cell phone numbers with area code(s), you'll improve the likelihood of having your cat returned.

Because ID tags often fall off, order at least one extra tag so that if your cat loses her tag, you won't have to wait weeks for a replacement. In addition to an ID tag, for built-in insurance you can get a nylon collar that has your phone number stitched into it. Some pet stores have them for order; otherwise order online from many Internet pet sites.

If you move, be sure to change your contact information on a tag and don't let the cat out until she's wearing your new phone and address.

An indoor cat's tag should identify her as an indoor cat so that the people who find her will realize she is not used to being outside and won't be able to find her way home.

MICROCHIPS

Microchips are a nice new technology but they are unknown to most people. Most anybody who finds a cat will look for a collar first thing, but only animal-savvy people will know that a cat could be microchipped, with a pellet the size of a grain of rice having been painlessly injected underneath the skin on the top of her neck. Do not depend on a microchip to bring your cat home since people who find her will just assume she's a lost or abandoned cat, not knowing that a vet or shelter can scan for a microchip.

Another problem with ID chips is that different companies make them and only a scanner from the company that made it can detect the chip. So before you have a chip placed, call your local shelter and find out what brand of scanner is in use in your area.

Deterrents

There are several things your cat may do that you would like her to stop doing—and there are products out there to help you get your point across.

Designed primarily to teach kittens to keep away from forbidden areas, SSSCat Automated Cat Deterrent comes in an aerosol can with a motion sensor and emits a blast of air. The spray can be adjusted to any angle or direction and can be used anywhere—doors, tables, countertops. When the device senses movement it gives off a soft warning beep, followed by a shot of unscented, pressurized air. It works on batteries and costs around $50, with pressurized refills at $15. It is available at all big chain pet stores; for more information contact Premier Pet Products, 888-640-8840 or www.premier.com.

Sticky Paws are nontoxic, transparent strips designed to keep cats off places you don't want them, such as furniture, plants or countertops. The strips are made of a sticky, acrylic-based material that will not harm upholstered furniture; however, you cannot use them on wood and painted surfaces, leather, vinyl or wallpaper. The tacky surface is repellent to cats, who hate it as soon as they touch it. The strips need to be replaced monthly to retain their tackiness. Sticky Paws strips for plants are crisscrossed on top of the pot edge to keep your cat from digging in the plant, while still allowing you to water it. They are available at most pet stores. Visit their Web site, www.stickypaws.com.

Doors for Cats

Depending on where you live, how safe the outdoors is for your cat and whether you even want to let your cat go outdoors, there are various models of cat doors to choose from. You will need to decide which of your doors would be best for your cat to use and then choose a pet door style designed to work with that door type. If you don't have another cat who is already using the door, then follow the guidelines below to get your cat comfortable with the door.

Teaching your cat to use the door is easier than you might think since all you're doing is encouraging her to try it, then making sure the process goes smoothly and does not frighten her. The first step is to secure the flap wide open so the cat can come and go freely through the opening. Use food, a catnip toy, or a dangle-at-the-end-of-a-stick toy to encourage her to come through the opening. You want to do this only a few times before lowering the flap, as described below, because otherwise it may appear like a trick to the cat.

Once she knows where the door is and has gone in and out a few times, you'll have to fiddle with taping up the flap just enough so that she can see through to the other side. Next she has to learn to push against the flap to gain entry. Use a food treat of high value to the cat—something that is really delicious to your cat but not usually on her menu, such as meat baby food on a small spoon—which you can put through the door opening so she will follow it.

There is no foolproof way to go through this process because every brand of door is somewhat different, with magnets of varying strengths that hold the flap shut, and a flap itself that can be heavier or lighter and looser. Your cat's individual personality and size also come into play when she is learning how to manipulate the flap: a brave, bold cat will have a vastly different experience and learning curve than a timid, shy kitten.

Watching other cats is the best and simplest way for your cat to learn to use a door. You don't have to go through any of the above "door activities" if you have another cat who is already using the door. Cats learn by example and will be following the other cat in and out in no time. If you only have one cat or if you've never had a cat door before, it might be feasible for you to take your cat(s) to the house of a friend whose cat already uses a door, but only if the cats are compatible. Unless your cat is super-friendly and relaxed and your friend's cat is like-minded, however, you're probably best off dealing with your own cat on your own turf.

MAGNETIC COLLAR DOORS

These doors only open when they detect a transmitter on an animal's collar. These collars are designed both to make it easier for a timid or small cat to use, since they do not have to push the flap open, and to prevent another animal—whether a wild raccoon or just another cat—from being able to enter through the cat door.

Depending on where you live, this lockout feature can be valuable, especially if your cat would not be able to go outside safely without it. However, a magnetic collar is bulky and can be cumbersome and heavy for a smaller cat to wear all the time. The best way to decide whether this product is appropriate for your cat is to weigh the pros and cons above.

Furniture for Cats

CAT TREES

The climbing/playing/napping towers sold for cats are often called "cat condos," but I'll call them "cat trees." They are not just silliness or a waste of money. Indoor cats desperately need mental and physical stimulation and things to tickle their curiosity. A cat tree helps to fulfill this need by providing different climbing levels, hidden spaces and scratching opportunities. If you have an overweight cat, the stimulation of the tree will help her shed some pounds. And if you have more than one cat, the pleasure and use of the tree is multiplied many times over as they interact in its spaces.

A cat tree may take up a sizeable space in your home, and a well-designed and well-made one can cost quite a bit, too, but you may think more kindly of it when you realize that it meets some of your cat's most basic instincts—to climb, to hide, to scratch, and to perch.

QUALITIES TO LOOK FOR IN A CAT TREE

- ❏ Soft surfaces make it more appealing, which is why most are carpet-covered.
- ❏ The more nooks and crannies, the better.
- ❏ Sisal-covered posts link one level with another and serve as built-in scratching posts.
- ❏ The tree should be as tall as possible because cats love height, but make sure it's stable.
- ❏ To judge stability in a store, pull down on the top level as if you were a cat jumping from one level to another. Make sure the tree does not wobble if you try to simulate your cat scratching or any other activity.
- ❏ Your cat should be able to get easily from one level to another. Look at the steps and jumping angles and see if they accommodate how your cat gets around.
- ❏ Consider your cat's age. Kittens need shorter distances so they won't fall; older cats need ramps between levels. Multiple cats need a more elaborate tree—or even two trees.
- ❏ Distances between levels should be no more than 18 inches apart.
- ❏ For stability, the largest components should be at the bottom and the base should be very heavy.
- ❏ With a single-post cat tree, the components (beds, tunnels, perches) should not stick out too far from the center post or it can topple when the cat gets on top.
- ❏ Multiple posts at the corners of the base with the components mounted on them are more stable.
- ❏ Perches and landings are more secure if fastened to posts in at least two places. If there's only one point of attachment, make sure it is very firm and strong.
- ❏ Make sure that the carpeting and sisal are well secured—especially if you have a very active cat.
- ❏ Choose a tree with parts that are easy to replace in case components wear out.

◆ Ensuring Success with Your Cat Tree

Your cat may be eager to try the new tree and need no coaxing from you, but some cats aren't so quick to try out something new and strange. Some of the manufacturers of cat trees put catnip underneath the carpeting to lure reluctant cats onto it in the beginning. You can do the same thing: Use catnip spray on the tree or sprinkle it on landings and perches.

Where you put the tree has a lot to do with whether your cat will take to it—she's not going to rush to use a tree that is tucked away in a dark corner or in an unused room. Put the tree close by

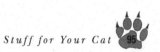

household activity—and near a window, too, so your cat can look out from all the new perches and there's a greater the chance she will get your money's worth!

Do not put a litter box anywhere near the tree—and do not put food or water bowls near it, either. Cats are "programmed" by nature to keep separate areas for playing, eating and eliminating; if you put all of them in one place, at the very least you will have a cat who goes outside her litter box. Furthermore, she may avoid the costly and complex tree you have just knocked yourself out to provide. So keep this play area away from the cat's functional areas.

Declawed cats can use a tree just fine. They can climb and jump and get some of the physical pleasures that declawing may have taken from them.

◆ Where to Get a Great Cat Tree

Many Web sites offer cat furniture, but some products were standouts, according to *Cat Watch*, the magazine of Cornell University's veterinary school, which offers an ongoing wealth of information. Subscribe at www.catwatchnewsletter.com.

- ❐ At www.catsplay.com you can get custom cat furniture to fit in with your decorating style, even color-coordinated with your home.
- ❐ The Feline Furniture Company's site, www.felinefurniture.com, has pieces that are made for kittens and smaller cats but can grow with the cat.
- ❐ A high-end selection of durable trees with environmentally friendly features can be found at www.all-cat-furniture.com.
- ❐ The Felix Katnip Tree Company (206-547-0042, www.felixkatniptreecompany.com) sells loose catnip and their own Katnip Tree, but it does not come with instructions for assembly and apparently people tend not to assemble it correctly. If you decide to order one, request assembly instructions.
- ❐ "The Cat Loft," an imaginative climbing, hanging-out arrangement, can be found at www.iroquoisinnovations.com.

WINDOW PERCHES

There is an economical, easy-to-install window perch called Deluxe Window Seat that is made by the Omega Paw company and sold for about $25 at many pet stores (call 800-222-8269 to find a retailer near you). All you have to do is install two bolts into the windowsill for a molded plastic perch to fit into.

If you put a bird bath, a bird feeder, a squirrel feeder or any combination of them outside the window with her perch on it, your cat will be mentally occupied for hours a day, plotting murderous thoughts. While it might seem cruel to taunt your cat with this theatrical adventure when she can't go outside, you'll discover that cats can also be happy just *dreaming* about swallowing Tweety Bird.

Grass Gardens

Cats love to munch on grass, and if you give them some of their very own, they're less likely to chow down on your house plants (Chapter 6, on behavior issues, has tips on how to protect your indoor plants from cat attacks). You can plant a grazing garden for your cat using the kits they sell in pet stores, or you can make your own. Your local hardware store may have the ingredients you need to grow some grass; you can also go to a big store such as Kmart (where Martha Stewart has some nifty seedling starter kits that would work well for cat grass). Get a small bag of starter potting soil and some seeds. Oat, rye, barley, wheat and bluegrass are all safe and good for cats. You can also grow catnip and catmint from seeds or seedlings, if you have the luck of finding them near you.

Use a fairly shallow container so the cat can crouch beside it and munch to her heart's content. Since the grass garden is part of your home, make it attractive with a pretty container if you're in the mood to go beyond utilitarian. Think outside the box, so to speak—use a ceramic or a glass baking dish that fits into a basket. You can also use a low basket to hold and hide several of the little biodegradable seedling pots themselves, which will look much nicer than just the functional containers themselves. It's easy to let your house be overtaken by "cat environmental enhancements," so anything that you can do to keep it from looking as though a cat decorated it is a step in the right direction.

Grooming Products

The more you groom your cat, the less cat hair there will be everywhere else. Chapter 9 is devoted entirely to the topic of grooming, but here I will just mention some of the best grooming products to get the job done efficiently and comfortably, for you and for your cat.

JW Pet Company makes fabulous brushes. I was visiting a friend who had a JW Easy Groom with Smart Grip brush for her cat. I tried it on my dog Jazzy, who has always hated being brushed and has a thick double coat from her Collie side. With the JW brush, she loved every minute of it—it was the first time she had stood still to be groomed. When I studied the brush I could see why they are so pleasant for the animal: They have round tips on every metal prong of the brush, so with each stroke you massage rather than scrape. The brushes are also great from the user's perspective because of the nonslip, hand-fitting handle and a curved head that lets you reach into those hard-to-get-to places. They also keep hold of the hair you are brushing out, rather than letting it fly all over the place. Best of all, these brushes are well under $10 and are available in most pet stores. If you need help finding them, call JW at 800-407-7826.

Zoom Groom is a soft rubber brush with thick, comblike rubber teeth. It resembles a curry-comb for a horse in that you use it in a circular motion to massage the skin, loosening dead hair. You can use another brush (such as the JW above) to brush and catch the loosened hair, or you can use the Zoom Groom in a brushlike downwards stroke and collect most of the loosened hair that way. The loose hair gets well caught in the teeth and is easy to lift out. The Zoom Groom is long-lasting and can be cleaned or disinfected. It is found at almost every pet store. For further information visit www.kongcompany.com.

 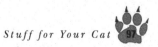

The Speedy Groom brush is a double-sided brush that lets you bathe your cat without the time and stress of an actual bath. It consists of layers of moistened cloths soaked in a solution of vitamin E and aloe. You brush your cat with it and as the unscented cloths get dirty, you peel them away, throwing loose hair away with the dirt. The ribbed handle is easy to grip even when damp. The price is very fair—under $4 for the brush and the same price for a refill of 14 grooming cloths—and it is sold at most of the pet stores. The brush is made by Hartz, so you can find out more at 800-275-1414 or www.hartz.com.

GROOMING TIPS FOR PEOPLE

Cat hair around your house is an inevitable by-product of sharing your life with a cat. No matter how meticulously you bathe and groom your cat, there is still going to be some hair on your furniture and clothes. Here are some suggestions for keeping that flying cat hair under control.

- ❑ To clean hair off a cat tree, use the cat's hair brush to scrape it all into a pile, then vacuum with a carpet attachment.
- ❑ Use a damp kitchen sponge or dampened rubber gloves to get hair off clothing. They roll hair up and you can rinse them off.
- ❑ A soot and dirt removal sponge from a pet store can be used dry, is inexpensive, and can be washed.
- ❑ Sticky rollers or masking tape are time-tested ways to remove pet hair.
- ❑ Set your clothes dryer on air fluff and put a pair of pantyhose or nylon netting in with the clothes, which will grab hold of the hairs.
- ❑ Add up to a cup of white vinegar to the your laundry wash cycle to keep hair from sticking to clothes. The vinegar also acts as a fabric softener.

Harnesses and Leashes

There is a section on leash training and taking walks with your cat in Chapter 14, so you can see all the considerations that go into it. If you decide that your cat is a good candidate for walking, then here are some tips for buying the necessary equipment for safe and comfortable walks.

The first thing to buy is a harness, which is necessary because most cats won't tolerate any pressure on their neck from a leash attached to their collar. Also, since most cats wear breakaway collars, the collar would come apart with the least pressure from the leash. The difference is that when you attach a leash to it, a harness distributes the pressure from the leash, spreading it out across the cat's chest. Most cats do not have a bad reaction to the sensation of pressure from the harness. Premier recently designed a well-fitting harness and special cat leash that is available at most stores that carry their Gentle Leader for dogs.

Buy the harness in person from a store where you can bring your cat in her carrier, or one that will allow you to take the harness home to try it and return it for another size if need be. Size isn't something you can guesstimate because each cat's body has its own particular build and will work with some brands of harness better than others.

- ❏ *Make sure the harness is made especially for cats.* There is no dog harness—however small—that is going to fit a cat securely and comfortably.
- ❏ *Choose a harness that's a little too big rather than too small.* You're better off with one that is a little too big so that you can make adjustments as needed. A harness should fit snugly—it is about right if you can slip two fingers underneath any strap.
- ❏ *Make sure you have adjusted it correctly.* If you are unsure about the fit even after following the instructions, do not take the risk of using an ill-fitting harness and your cat getting loose. Before you take your cat for a walk, ask someone in the store who knows that brand of harness to demonstrate and then practice with it yourself.
- ❏ *Make doubly sure your cat cannot escape from the harness.* Spend as much time as you need in the safe room before you and your cat set foot out your front door. The lightweight figure-eight harnesses that are readily available may be too easy for your cat to wriggle out of.
- ❏ *Make sure the harness is easy to put on.* A harness is one of those items you should not buy on-line or from a catalogue because the only way to know how it works is to try it in person. Choose one that closes with plastic connectors that click together, not buckles you have to do up. Also, the closures should be on the cat's back or sides, not underneath the belly or chest where you can't see what you're doing.
- ❏ *Try the harness before you buy it.* Any nice pet store will let you do that—and some even have a stuffed animal or a very obliging store cat you can practice putting it on before you go home. When the time comes to try it out on your cat, you don't want to rattle her by fumbling and being impatient yourself.
- ❏ *The younger you start a kitten wearing a harness, the easier it's going to be for both of you.* So the sooner you start, the better.

Patios and Fences

PATIO ENCLOSURES

Patio enclosures are an option only for people who live in a house with a yard. If you rent the house you live in, you may think it's not worth the trouble and expense to make an "addition," but some of these products may work as a nonpermanent addition. Or if you're really handy, you might be able to modify them to make them easily removable to give your cat a special safe patio of her own.

◆ Options for Those Without a House

You may not have a patio because you are an apartment dweller, but that doesn't mean your cat can't have her own window patio. These units fit into your window like an air conditioner and give your cat a space to watch the world go by. At the end of this section there is a list of companies that make patio enclosures; some make window patios, too.

✦ Different Ways to Make a Cat Enclosure

Depending on the weather where you live, it can be fairly easy to build an enclosed patio or deck for your cat or to alter an existing patio to make it cat-safe. You can do it yourself with your own materials, use a ready-made kit from a company like Purr . . . fect Fence (see chart on the next page) or hire someone to do the work and build you a screened porch. For cold-weather climates, there are prefabricated screened porches that have glass inserts to exchange for the screens in winter. If you're handy, you can build an outdoor cat pen sort of like a rabbit hutch: a simple wood-framed structure built against a wall of your house or garage, with wire mesh attached on the outside of the wooden frame to form the outside walls of the enclosure.

✦ Where to Put the Cat Patio

The location of a cat patio depends on the climate in your area. People who live in northern climates will want to situate a cat patio facing south to take advantage of the sun and maximize the number of days the patio will be comfortable for cats. People who live in hot climates will want to do just the opposite; to avoid exposing their cats to additional heat from the sun, they should choose a north-facing part of the house, preferably with some natural shade from trees or the house itself.

✦ Cat Enclosures Need Shelves

Cats like to get up high, so to make the cat patio user-friendly, you'll want to make shelves and platforms. This will allow your cat to jump up and look out. If you have multiple cats, the shelves will give them places where they can get away from each other. By including shelves, you maximize the cat's ability to use the space and it also means the patio doesn't have to be especially deep because the cats can enjoy the world from those perches.

✦ Provide Ramps to Get Up to Those Platforms

Shelves and high perches in the enclosure will be even more appealing to your cat if there is a fun way for her to get up there. Use tree branches, logs or wooden planks to link the shelves with each other or the ground. Climbing is a natural part of your cat's repertoire, so you will double her pleasure by giving her climbing surfaces, too.

✦ Install Some High-Definition Cat TV

The only thing more fun for a cat than her very own outdoor space is having a bird feeder right outside it where she can watch her fine-feathered friends come and go. The Knox County Humane Society in Maine refers to the bird feeders outside their volunteer-built cat patios as "cat TVs" and they call the tropical fish tank (securely covered) inside another of their indoor/outdoor cat pens "kitty Internet."

✦ Don't Shut Yourself Out

Don't forget to include some sort of entrance for yourself onto the patio so you can clean and repair whenever necessary. A cat flap that leads from your house directly out onto the cat patio makes life a lot simpler when space is limited because you don't have to provide a water bowl and litter box out in the enclosure. You will need to include those items if the cat has no access from the patio right back into the house. Even if there is a cat flap, it would be nice to put water and a litter box on the patio for the cat's convenience—although always at separate ends of the space.

An outdoor patio is also a great place to grow kitty grass in clay pots so that the cat can just help herself when she's in the mood.

ADDING A CAT FENCE TOPPER

If your yard is already fenced, you can add a topper of plastic mesh that is designed to keep cats from getting out over the top. You attach poles with metal brackets to an existing fence. Plastic mesh extends from one pole to the next, angled in from the top of the fence: Think of prison movies you have seen with the barbed-wire wall topper that extends around the prison grounds to keep anyone from going up and over. While the intention of keeping the inmates in is similar in both situations, obviously the plastic mesh cat fence isn't quite so intimidating as the prison barbed wire!

Several companies (see below) sell the components you will need to install these kitty barriers, which is apparently quite easy to do. They say all you need is a ladder, a screwdriver and a drill. However, whether you are handy or not, before you can consider whether the cat fence is a good option for you, you must already have a strong, secure, tall fence, either chain link or wood, from which the poles and mesh will extend, or you must be willing to build one.

If you do have a sturdy fence around your property, you should walk every inch of it from a cat's point of view to see where a cat might be able to escape: holes underneath fencing that a cat could squeeze through, rotting or broken areas of a wood fence or a gate that a cat could squeeze through. Repair and block any potential escape routes before you install the cat fencing so you won't have to worry. Purr . . . fect Fence (see below) has a slanted fence topper built into their simple design, which anyone can install, and supplies the fence itself.

The Humane Society of the United States in Washington, D.C., has compiled a list of companies that sell specialty cat fences, enclosures and runs. The Humane Society does not endorse these companies, but they have done us all a favor by creating this list, which ultimately keeps cats out of harm's way while giving them a good quality of life.

Where to Find Cat Fences and Runs

Cat Fence-In, 888-738-9099, www.catfencein.com

Affordable Cat Fence, www.catfence.com

C&D Pet Products Cat Enclosure Kit, 888-554-7387, www.cdpets.com

Just 4 Cats Outdoor Safety Enclosure Plans, www.just4cats.com

The Kitty View, 877-548-8988, www.kittyview.com

Purr . . . fect Fence, 888-280-4066, www.purrfectfence.com

Do-It-Yourself Cat Fence (from Alley Cat Allies), www.feralcat.com

The Cat Veranda is a window-mounted observation cube. It is a small open-air patio about the size of a window air conditioner. It is available at 800-732-2677 or www.petsafe.net.

Ramps

Senior cats move more slowly and stiffly as arthritis curtails their jumping and running. Several different ramps and platforms are available to assist an older or compromised cat with climbing onto his cat tree or window perch, or onto your couch or bed.

The Green Duck ramp is one of the best. Affordable and lightweight, it is made of carpet-covered wood panels and works at almost any angle. When opened all the way, this ramp measures 12 inches wide and 44 inches long, with a lip at the end that rests on top of the furniture. Because it folds and weighs only 10 pounds, it's great for travel and can easily be stored when you're not using it.

Restraints

Some cats need to be restrained when receiving medical attention, having their claws trimmed, or being bathed. For frequent maintenance tasks such as nail trimming, follow the instructions in the grooming chapter to make it a relaxed, positive experience.

RESTRAINT BAGS

These are polyester mesh bags (like the ones to launder delicate things) that you put a cat in to keep her from being able to scratch or escape while being bathed or treated medically. You drape the open bag across her back and close the collar, making sure that the strap is secure and tight enough to keep her from wiggling out. Secure the hook inside the zipper and zip it shut, being careful not to pinch any part of the cat. A model with zippers in the front and back is best, depending on why you need the cat restrained.

Klaw Kontrol is considered one of the best-designed and easiest to use restraint systems and is sold as a four-piece set, including a coated nylon restraint bag, a muzzle, and straps to make carrying it easier. It sells for around $40 from Bachman Associates at 650-557-1507 or www.klaw-kontrol.com.

MUZZLES

Cat bites are dangerous, causing more problems that a dog bite. A cat's bite has a greater chance of becoming infected and is usually medicated more aggressively by doctors treating these wounds in people. Using a muzzle is a great short-term solution to accomplish a quick task that the cat would otherwise not permit.

OmniPet Adjustable Muzzle can be found at www.omnipet.com and 800-442-5522. The Quick Muzzle is also very good and can be found at www.fourflags.com and is easy to use and reliable.

Scratching Posts

One of the most serious problems that people have with their cats is that they scratch the furniture. This problem can become so serious that people resort to mutilating their cat by declawing her, giving the cat away, or just abandoning her. There has to be a better solution, which is to have the right scratching post in the right place and give your cat positive reinforcement to do the right thing. For more on understanding and dealing with the "scratching problem," you can read the chapter on behavior issues, but as far as buying equipment goes, you *must* provide at least one fantastic post for your cat to scratch if you want her to choose that over your furniture. A scratching post needs to be rough to the touch: sisal rope covering it is optimal. The Felix Katnip Tree and some others have sisal-covered scratching posts built into their design.

Cats scratch not just to sharpen their claws and remove the dead sheath, but to stretch their back and whole body, which is something they want to do when waking up in the morning or after a nap. So make sure a good scratching post is somewhere readily available so your cat can get right to her post (and not your sofa) when she wakes up.

Some cats will willingly use a small, disposable two-sided corrugated cardboard scratching board; some cats will use a cork board made for scratching, but both tend to slide around and ultimately don't give your cat the stretch she craves.

The Ultimate Scratching Post is expensive ($70 plus shipping) but a lot less than it would cost to re-cover furniture. The post is made of sisal and is nearly 3 feet tall, with a 16-inch base that not even a Maine Coon Cat can push around. It also has a 7-inch-square landing perch for smaller cats and kittens. Assembly is quick and easy, it's nice looking, and despite sounding large it actually doesn't use much space. You can order directly from the manufacturer at www.esmartcat .com or from the Drs. Foster & Smith catalogue www.drsfosterandsmith.com or call 800-381-7179.

MAKING YOUR OWN POST

If you're the handy type, you can bang together your own scratching post but you should probably take a look at a quality commercial post to get a good idea of what it needs to look like. The main requirements are that it be very stable and covered in rough material. Since wrapping a post in thick sisal rope is not particularly easy in a home workshop, you can use a piece of carpet with a rough backside and affix it to the post with the backing toward the cat. Ironically, the main problem with most commercial scratching posts is that they use the soft side of carpet facing the cat, and a cat wants to scratch on something rough, with texture she can dig her claws into. If you have already bought a scratching post made in this incorrect way, you can remedy the situation by stapling or nailing another piece of carpet wrong-side-out around the soft one that's already there.

WHERE SHOULD YOU PUT THE POST?

There are a few options for where you can place the post to get the most possible use, effectively curtailing scratching anywhere else in the house. One good place is in a corner with the base

 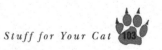

wedged in against the two walls so it can't move around when the cat scratches against it. But if there is a particular piece of furniture that the cat likes to stretch and scratch on, you should put the scratching post very close to that furniture so that when she goes to the forbidden area out of habit, the new post will become the surface she prefers to scratch.

TEACHING YOUR CAT TO USE HER POST

If your cat doesn't immediately go to the post out of curiosity, then you will need to encourage her to go there. When she is nearby, go over to the scratching post and run your fingertips down it, making purring noises. If your cat doesn't go right to the post, lay it on its side and place her on top. Don't place her feet up on the post or grab her legs and try to manipulate her limbs—cats hate that and you'll only give her a bad first impression. Instead, stroke her firmly down her back while she is on the post. Most cats will dig their claws into the post as an expression of pleasure, which is what you want. Continue to run your fingernails down the post, followed by a firm stroke down the cat's back; keep doing this so that the pleasure of your stroking gives her a positive association to the post.

Sprinkle catnip powder on the post once a week to encourage your cat to use it, and then follow the encouragement instructions above every day for about a week. The pleasure your encouragement gives her will help her develop a lifelong, positive habit of using the post.

Toys and Playtime

Although this chapter is about "stuff and things," I thought it would be helpful to tell you how to use the toys and amusements to get the most out of them.

HOW AND WHY CATS PLAY

✦ Kittens Need to *Learn* How to Play

Kittens aren't born knowing how to play—they have to learn the skills. Those who don't have the opportunity to play with littermates at a critical age may never really learn how. While in some places it is common to take kittens away from their mother at six weeks old, there are experts who say this is a mistake that will have lifelong repercussions; a kitten has to stay with her litter to become fully socialized. Research has shown that the age when a kitten develops her most important play skills is eleven weeks—this is when playfulness among kittens is at its highest level. Studies have shown that kittens who stay with their mother and littermates until twelve weeks will be more flexible and sociable later in life. If your cat does not respond to the typical signals that cats give each other when they want to play, it means that she probably was not exposed to games as a youngster.

Take it easy on kittens when playing. It can take as little as five minutes for a kitten to be satisfied with playing, and then she might crash. Never wake a kitten up to play—she needs her rest. And don't play with her to the point of collapse—five minutes of fun, then naptime.

Don't let a kitten bite your fingers or toes. What may seem funny at first can become a downright

pain if you allow your cat to chew on your digits. Cats have sharp teeth and can get wound up enough to give you a serious bite that is painful or breaks the skin—so never let this habit begin.

Kittens who live alone can often be observed playing with imaginary friends, using the same body language as they would with a live kitten playmate. Sometimes this "hallucination" of playing with imaginary friends can continue on into adulthood.

◆ Adult House Cats Play More than Feral Cats Do

Experts believe this is because we keep our cats in a kitten-like environment. For many of us, play is a sign of happiness, and so we encourage any animal we live with to play because it makes us happy. Playing seems to make cats content, too, even though it isn't something they would naturally continue into adulthood on their own.

◆ Cats Follow Movement

They'll chase sunbeams on the floor, shadows on a wall or a curtain blowing in a breeze. Some tests show that cats prefer to play in dim light, which is probably because they are naturally nighttime predators and that's when their instincts are most tuned in. So when you want to play with your cat, turn the lights low and see if she responds more enthusiastically.

◆ Cats Get Bored by the Same Old Thing

Anything that is around all the time and readily accessible loses interest. Variety and the element of surprise are big motivators for cats, so leave out just a few toys at a time and rotate them to keep it interesting.

INTERACTIVE PLAYING WITH YOUR CAT

Playing is as important to the health and happiness of your cat as food. She needs to play for stress relief, for physical and mental stimulation, to keep weight off and to make a bond you.

◆ Some Good Kitty Games

Fetch. Some purebred cats are known to be especially keen on playing fetch, but many cats can learn to enjoy this doglike game with their people. Many cats are dedicated fetchers and seem to favor bedtime as the time they most like to play.

Hide and Seek. Cats like to stalk a partially hidden object. They like to be able to hide, spring out and attack, and then retreat to hide and start all over again. The watch/wait/pounce game is endlessly entertaining to most cats. Here is one way to play this game: Lead your cat to a doorway by wiggling a dangle toy, which you'll read more about later in this section. Get on the opposite side of the door from the cat and close it almost all the way. Take that toy-on-a-string and wiggle it under the door or through the slight opening. Begin slowly, then wiggle it more quickly. Move the toy around in any way that engages your cat's interest. Dangle it just out of her reach, but as with any game, let her win every so often to keep her engaged and make it more gratifying.

"Bait" Under the Covers. Another kind of hide-and-seek is to take a big piece of crumpled-up paper—or any cat toy—and move it around under your bedcovers with a dangle stick or just with your hand. Wiggle around whatever you have under the blanket, then let it come out for a moment, then put it back under the blanket again. You could even wiggle your toes around under there and she would happily pounce, but the problem with doing that is there will be many times you do *not* want your feet "hunted" under the blankets, so don't start the habit now. You can also do this under a blanket or big towel on the floor and leave your bed out of it. All this baiting is great fun for a cat and will drive her happily crazy.

Stair Banisters. Many cats enjoy playing on a staircase, batting at whatever you entice them with on the other side of the staircase spindles.

Laundry Baskets. A laundry basket—or any open container—is a great place for a cat to crouch down and be able to spring out at any dangle toy you might have outside.

Paper Bags. These can be more exciting than the fanciest cat condo tower. Just leave a paper grocery bag or shopping bag on its side, fold over the top edges of the bag to form a cuff so the bag stays open, and your cat will find her way in. She will discover that she can hide in the bag and pounce on a toy that you jiggle around or a ball of crumpled paper you toss outside the opening. Change the places where you put the bag, which makes it more exciting for the cat. *Warning:* If you use a paper bag with handles, cut them off before letting the cat play because otherwise she can get her head caught in there.

Cardboard Box. Cats love a cardboard box—they find it irresistible. Lay a cardboard box on its side on the floor, either empty or with shredded newspaper inside. You can seal the box and cut a hole in one side, or tear off one flap and tape down the others so that the opening remains relatively small and the interior of the box is dark and cozy. Only bring the box out a few times a week or it will get old for the cat, as will anything else that she always has access to.

Soap Bubbles. If ever there was an easy and cheap way to entertain your cat, this is it: a jar of bubbles. Blow some bubbles and see whether your cat is one of those who love to bat at them or chase them.

Flashlight or Laser Pointer. Most cats are fascinated by a light beam from a flashlight or laser pointer that shines on the wall or across the floor. Cats will chase a reflection wherever you send it, so make sure you play with a laser pointer away from obstacles that the cat might collide with (a kitten following a laser beam is so intently focused on it that she can crash into furniture or even the wall). *Warning:* Do not let children play with a laser pointer around cats unless they are supervised. A laser shined directly into a cat's eye (or a human one, for that matter) can cause permanent damage or even blindness.

A Second Cat. If you have the time and space, a second cat is the best play toy you could ever give your cat. The two can run, hide and wrestle with each other.

◆ Tips for Playing Successfully

Cats Get Easily Bored by Their Toys. Put the cat's toys away after each playtime so that they seem fresh and new when you take them out next time.

Watch Out for Dangerous Objects. Curious kittens and cats will play with anything they find on the floor, tabletop or underneath the bed. This means that dental floss, ponytail bands, string, rubber bands and other stringlike objects can wind up down your kitty's throat. Keep them out of reach.

Let Your Cat Decide How Long You'll Play. Most cats only stay engaged for about 5 minutes, although they can enjoy several short play sessions. Once a cat doesn't want to play anymore, it's over—you will have to find something else to entertain yourself. Don't force the issue or you may aggravate her to the point where she becomes aggressive.

Early Morning and Late Evening Are Favorite Playtimes. Probably because they are nocturnal hunters, cats prefer to play at these times and they also prefer dim light. It's often hard to engage a cat in play in the middle of the day, even if that's most convenient or appealing to you.

Let the Kitty Win. You may not realize that while playing is fun for a cat, winning is even more fun. So when you are playing hide-and-seek or dangle games, remember to give your cat a chance to seize the toy every so often.

Two Play Sessions a Day, Minimum. Planning for play sessions is a good idea because most people's lives get so busy that a cat's playtime is easily forgotten. A play session with your cat needs to be only 5 to 10 minutes. At least 2 play sessions a day is a good idea for most cats' physical and emotional well-being. Sadly, not many cats get this playtime since few people know how much cats need it. This does not mean you have to give your cat 100 percent of your attention when you're playing with her—you can talk on the phone or watch television while playing, so long as you can see her out of the corner of your eye to keep it interesting for her.

A "Favorite Game" Ritual Is Special. Even though most of the advice that follows is about making play creative, inventive and surprising, there is also a place for a tried-and-true game the cat can count on. When you discover your cat's favorite game or toy, set that aside as her play ritual, and use it at a certain time of day, in the same area of your house, with the same toy in a similar fashion each time. Cats love predictability and routine, so having a toy or game that falls into that category is a highly pleasurable treat. A bonus is that if you have someone cat-sit, you can teach the sitter the ritual game and it will make the cat more comfortable with her.

TOYS FOR YOU AND YOUR CAT

If you are like most people, toys that you can play with together are the best investment you can make in your cat's recreational future. There are many wonderful toys out there to make play

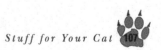

more challenging for her and easier for you, and there are also so many toys you can make with everyday items around the house. So take your pick from the listings below and have a party with your kitty. When creating or buying a toy keep in mind that a cat will gravitate to a toy that conforms to a size they would interact with in nature: the true prey of a cat is small and lightweight, whether it is a bird or rodent.

Cats love playing with people so much that some will drag their toys around, bringing them to you to play with them. Some cats even play fetch.

◆ Lure on a Fishing Pole

Several well-known toys involve a birdlike lure that dangles off the end of a pole. Everybody's all-time favorite toy in this category is Da Bird, which makes a birdlike sound with its wings when you make it fly through the air. Another lure toy is the Bamboo CatFisher Rod and Reel, which is a 2-foot collapsible rod-and-reel toy. The Dragonfly is just what the name implies: a dragonfly at the end of a long, flexible wire so thin you can barely see anything but the lifelike insect at the tip. This toy is a little pricier because each one is made by hand, but the pleasure both you and your cat will get from it makes it worth the investment. The Cat Dancer is a simple and inexpensive toy that gives hours of pleasure—it's just a long wire with paper rods at the end that bounce and jerk like an insect when you move it. It's great for really athletic cats who like to leap and bounce, especially those who routinely hunt flies in the house. The Cat Charmer is a snakelike toy made by the same company. The Swizzle Teaser is another popular lure toy that makes a slinky movement on the ground. It has a feather tail that is detachable, which means sometimes your cat may actually snatch it and catch it. The Kitty Tease is a string attached to a pole with a bit of denim dangling at the end (if ever there was a toy you could re-create yourself, this has to be it), and it is a good, low-key choice for a cat who needs coaxing to come out of her shell and play. Purrfect Wispy Close-Up Toy™ has 10 inches of peacock feathers on an acrylic wand. Available at www.catconnection.com or 866-386-6369. Play-N-Squeak Fishing Pole has an imitation fur catnip mouse that clips onto a fishing line. Call 800-565-2695 or www.ourpets.com.

The Bamboo CatFisher Mouse Mitt is a soft canvas glove you wear that has four detachable catnip-scented toys that dangle from your fingers. This toy is also supposed to teach kittens not to bite your fingers. A unique interactive toy is the Quickdraw McPaw, which is a little feather at the tip of a soft plastic tube with a hook that allows you to draw the feather back up into the tube. If a cat is fearful or older and slower, this is a toy she can enjoy without much physical exertion.

These kinds of toys are universally loved by cats and people because they allow a cat to simulate real stalking and pouncing while giving people the added bonus of enjoying the sight of their cat in action. There's no reason why you can't make your own versions by taking a child's fishing rod or a long thin rod like a garden bamboo stake and then attaching a cat toy such as a little furry mouse (which you could tie by the tail) to the tip with string.

Here are some tips for playing well with lure toys. (See also "Tips for Playing with Your Kitten" in Chapter 6.)

Think of yourself as the director/choreographer. You need to have a sense of drama when playing with your cat. For example, start the chase slowly, with the prey "creeping" around a corner—and when the cat goes after it, find a place where the prey can "hide," giving the cat time to come up with a game plan. Have the prey come from the side of the cat and then dash for safety. Be unpredictable. Think like a hunted, frightened little creature and make the lure *be* that critter.

Don't make the chase impossible. Make it a challenge, but have the lure stay within reasonable limits of speed and height. If it all moves so fast that the cat doesn't have a snowball's chance in hell of winning . . . well maybe she'll shrug and give up. Keep things just beyond her reach, enticing her.

Don't run her ragged. The point of playing isn't to exhaust your cat or have her panting. This is meant not as a way to wear your cat out but as a way to engage her, to use her mind as much as her body, and do it with you.

Don't just stop in the middle. Let the game come to a crescendo, like a great opera, and then slowly wind down. Don't just build your cat up to a frenzy and then look at your watch and stop cold. The game needs to have a natural progression and then a resolution, as a real hunt would. Have the lure sputter to a standstill, then let the cat bat it with her paw and push it back into life. Finally, let the cat win at the very end. It is a just reward for all the work you will have put her through—and good for her self-confidence, too.

Mix it up. Change the toys you play with and the way they move so the cat doesn't know exactly what to expect.

Make realistic movements. People can make the mistake of jerking the lure too quickly when the movement should be as realistic as possible: a quick darting motion and then stillness. Birds, mice, fish, rabbits and bugs are just some of the prey that fascinate cats—and you want to imitate those creatures when using the lure. Real prey tends to move just a little and then freeze, so drag the lure quickly across the floor but then stop. Then advance it a little bit more, and stop again. Make an erratic motion, like a real animal's movements.

Prey never runs toward *a cat.* Don't insult your cat's intelligence by having the lure go in the direction of the cat—your actions need to make logical sense. Even the world's dumbest mouse knows better than that.

Get the cat's attention. Wave the lure slowly in front of her: Once you have her eyes on it, move it away from her. You can almost hypnotize a cat this way.

Chase and pounce. Keep the lure just out in front of the cat, which should entice her to pounce on it. Keep it just ahead of her if you can.

Let the cat win. It's only fair that for all the times that you have made the lure evade your cat's attempts to get it, you should let her win. Let her pounce on that lure and show it who is boss.

Once she gets the prey, the game is over. Once the cat has had a chance to attack the lure, you should put it away for another day, which will keep the toy fresh and interesting for the cat next time. Since she can't eat her "prey," which would be the natural thing to do, give the cat a tasty treat as an alternative to finish off the game. You can also time your play before the cat's dinnertime and make that her reward.

◆ Wind-up or Battery-Powered Toys

These are available wherever cat toys are sold, and can be great fun for a cat—and great fun for you to watch. The Hartz Cat Attack is a motorized critter that skitters all over the place with your cat in hot pursuit. As with any cat toy, use it sparingly because cats get bored quickly and you

 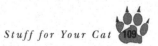

don't want to turn them off any one outlet for their natural instincts. The Zig-N-Zag ball moves unpredictably as the cat rolls it, with the cat being the propulsion for it. Play-N-Squeak is a furry catnip mouse that makes realistic chirping noises when touched (via a lifetime battery inside). Play-N-Treat is a toy into which you put dry cat food or other kitty treats. The cat has to manipulate it to release the food, which can keep a cat mentally and physically engaged for hours.

• Toys for Solo Play

Keep in mind that playing alone means bringing life to a "dead" prey—so these need to be lightweight so that when the cat bats at them, they do "come to life."

Kitty Hoots Crackler is a catnip-filled soft toy that makes a crackly sound, a noise cats love, when touched.

Smarty Kat FlutterBalls are small faux-leopard fleece balls with detachable feathers held on with Velcro. Cats love to drag them around as their "captured" prey. Bamboo CatFisher Bobber is a stationary weighted bobber that dangles a catnip-filled toy from a spring steel coil. It gives kittens something to swat at and play with when they're home alone. It always returns to an upright position no matter what the cat does with it.

• Catnip-Filled Toys

Everything you need to know about catnip itself is earlier in this chapter. You can hide your cat's weekly catnip toy around the house for her to find and it's a big thrill for her, but only do it once in a while. The SmartyKat Refillable Catnip Toy is a plush toy with a pouch you fill with catnip; it comes with a refill, but use it with your own fresh catnip each week and it will be good for years to come.

• Visual Entertainment

TV & Radio. Watch your cat's reaction to various television shows and see if she seems to show interest in a particular kind of show. Nature shows on the Discovery Channel and National Geographic Channel have images and sounds that many cats respond to.

Television Draping. Some cats can create playtime for themselves by getting on top of a television and looking down at the screen from above. The television is hot, which cats crave, and if she swishes her tail or moves her paws in front of the screen she can enjoy the reflection.

Videos and CDs. You can buy videos and CDs that have images and sounds especially geared to cats: There are birds, squirrels and other animals running around, as well as other cats. These videos are made especially to stimulate the mind of indoor cats and especially cats who spend most of their time alone.

Bird Feeders as "Cat TV." If you live anywhere that you can put up a bird feeder, go right out and do so. A bird feeder outside a cat's window (or her outdoor patio) gives her hours and hours of stimulating entertainment as she plots how to get at those birdies.

Fish tanks as "Kitty Internet." If you have the room and energy to get a small fish tank—10 to 20 gallons is plenty—and stock it with fish, you will be giving your cat hours a day of riveting entertainment as she tries to figure out how to get in there. When you buy the tank, tell the salesperson that you need a cat-proof tank and she will sell you the necessary safeguards to make sure the cat can't get into the tank.

✦ Hidden Treats

Each time you go out of the house, pick two new places to leave a little tasty morsel (a piece of cheese, a piece of cat treat) for your cat to find. Your cat's powerful sense of smell will lead her to your hiding places, which you have to change all the time. Underneath furniture and on top of high shelves are some of the places that cats like, so look at your potential hiding places through catlike eyes. When you get home, make sure you check to see whether your cat found those treats so they don't become a "science experiment" under the couch.

✦ Some of the Best Toys in Life Are Free

There are so many everyday items that cats love to play with that the list can go on and on. While fancy toys may be fun to buy, and some are fun for you to share with your cat, she may have even more fun with some of the items below:

Plastic neck rings from plastic milk containers
Empty cardboard boxes
Empty paper grocery bags (on their side, cuff folded over, without handles)
Cardboard toilet paper and paper towel tubes
Clear plastic safety rims around the lids of dairy product containers such as cottage cheese
Drinking straws
Empty plastic film containers
Plastic tops from water or soda bottles
Wine corks
Nuts in the shell
Seashells
Ping-Pong balls
Feathers from a large bird (seagull, peacock, wild turkey, crow)
Pipe cleaners
Small vegetables: a Brussels sprout, string bean, baby carrot or grape
Balled-up paper from a glossy magazine page
12-pack soda box with one end cut off and a toy thrown inside
Cotton swabs
Medium-size button tied to a piece of string, dragged underneath a throw rug

✦ Toys to Avoid

There are just a few toys and games that can be dangerous, as you will see in the chart below, although in the case of lure toys they should only be available to your cat when you are present.

 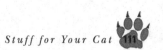

To explain the danger of aluminum foil balls: People will reuse aluminum foil that had food in it and form it into a ball. The smell can be delicious to the cat, who will want to chew on the foil, but if swallowed, aluminum foil is dangerous. For this reason, don't even get into the habit of using a foil ball as a toy since at some point someone will unknowingly use a piece of food-contaminated foil and there will be trouble.

DANGEROUS TOYS

Aluminum foil balls
Plastic bags—they make a great crinkly noise but can cause suffocation
Ribbon, string, dental floss or rubber bands—easy to swallow, causing intestinal damage
Lure toys on a string or wire—put away when human not playing
Toy tied to doorknob—never do this because your cat can get caught in the string

Chapter 5

YOUR CAT'S EMOTIONS

We like to feel we know our cats so well and have a special understanding of them, yet we are often baffled by their behavior. Truth be told, we are often clueless about what our cats are thinking and feeling. Some aspects of the cat psyche are understood scientifically, but relatively few topics related to cats have been the subject of controlled studies. Cat lovers have gathered knowledge by putting a great deal of faith in their own intuition and observations. This seat-of-the-pants approach to unlocking the mysteries of a cat's mind has brought people a workable cohabitation with cats, but we are still a long way from truly comprehending what makes cats tick. This chapter will reveal some fundamentals about the feline psyche that may help you to better understand your own cat and cohabit more harmoniously.

Tens of millions of people have lived side by side with tens of millions of cats for a very long time—4,000 years is the generally accepted length of time that we can trace our relationship with them. However, cats never became as fully domesticated as dogs, nor did we ever develop a hierarchical relationship where we became the "masters" of cats. As time has progressed, people seem to have more desire to really understand these gorgeous creatures—to get under their skin and into their minds.

There are natural remedies for many of the emotions and behaviors you'll read about here at www.spiritessence.com.

Cats Are Natural Loners

Cats have lived as solitary hunters for most of their ancestry. Early cats in the wild didn't depend on any other creature for their comfort and survival—not their own kind, not humankind. So what we may interpret as "aloofness" or "indifference" is really just self-sufficiency—a self-reliance that has been in their genes and stood them in good stead for centuries. Cats are programmed to rely on their own skills and judgment, never depending on a leader or a group to help them make decisions. Cats do not look to us for supervision or permission, they don't turn to us for affirmation, nor do they accept training, by and large.

Cats accept the improvements that we make in their lives but they do not accept that we should have any control over them. People can give safety, sustenance, and comfort to a cat, but both sides know that she could walk out tomorrow and find her own way if it came to that. The underlying independence that keeps a balance of power between people and their cats is the source of our fascination and frustration with our feline family members. But it's really helpful to keep in mind that you need to accept your cat as she is—and for who she is.

Does Your Cat Love You?

There are people who claim that cats *use* people, they do not *love* them except for what they can provide. To my ears, that cynical viewpoint is fueled by a basic misunderstanding of what makes cats tick and how they express themselves. There are a number of unique ways that cats express affection to other cats and to people, which you might not necessarily identify as love because they can't be measured by the yardstick of how people display emotion. What follows are some of the ways your cat can show she loves you.

TUMMY DISPLAY

Your cat may greet you by lying down with all four feet in the air, showing you her stomach. Between kittens and cats this is an invitation to play: The standing cat jumps on the prone one and they may growl and tumble in a make-believe wrestling match. A kitten does this with her littermates to invite contact and initiate play. When a cat shows her belly as a greeting to a person, it shows she's relaxed and without qualms about showing vulnerability. Although some cats will accept their belly being rubbed, this behavior is not intended to solicit contact so much as to demonstrate acceptance and trust of you.

WEAVING THROUGH YOUR LEGS

This affectionate behavior originates with a kitten's greeting to her mother. Kittens greet their mother with their tails upright, which they then wrap around her rear end so that she will lie down and they can nurse. As a kitten matures, she will continue to rub against friendly cats—and humans—to place her scent on them. Cats' tails carry their unique personal scent from their anal glands, so when a cat rubs her tail against another cat or you, she is marking you with her own scent. People often think that this display of affection means their cat wants both affection and food. However, it is primarily the emotional response that a cat is seeking. Recent studies have shown that one reason for the alarming rate of obesity in cats is that people misinterpret their cats' attempts to make an emotional connection as being a plea for food—and eventually the cat herself is "trained" by her person's response to expect food when she rubs against his legs.

RUBBING HER HEAD ON YOU

Cats use the scent glands on their heads and around their mouths to deposit the facial pheromones in those glands on objects that protrude in their territory. Rubbing shows positive emotion and seems to be comforting to a cat, too. Some of the usual areas they mark are doorways, chairs, bed frames, table legs—and your legs. Rubbing is friendly, social behavior and many times cats who share a home will rub against each other's heads in passing, as a way to reinforce their familiar scents. If your cat rubs her head against your face—which is called "bunting"—it is a gesture of familial love. Rubbing on her mother's chin and nose was a bunting behavior your cat did when she was a kitten, seeking to nurse from her mother. Rubbing may be accompanied by purring, and if she gets even more carried away she may open her lips while bunting and drool.

SHOWING HER BOTTOM

Your cat may come to you and turn around, her tail raised, as if offering you her behind—which is exactly what she is doing. This behavior is related to the one above because it is about offering to identify herself with the smell of her anal glands. Another theory is that this "butt display" harks back to when she was a kitten and her mother cat groomed her bottom. In either case, you can take it as a sign of closeness and perhaps a sign that you remind her of her mother cat. It is a compliment and sign of connectedness and if you give your cat a scratch at the base of her tail, it will be a nice gesture in return.

KNEADING

When your cat is resting on your lap and massages your legs with her paws, it's called kneading (it's also referred to as "making biscuits" or "milk treading"). This is a sure sign that your cat is really content. She may be feeling the way she did in her mother's nest, when she kneaded and massaged her mother to make the milk flow faster. Now this is her way of expressing her affection to you, showing that she feels safe and content.

If a cat gets carried away with kneading, it can get tiresome, especially if she also digs her claws in. But resist the temptation to push her off or chastise her in any way, which could confuse her and damage the bond between you two. Kneading is a powerful expression of trust and affection and should be treated and accepted as such.

DROOLING

Some cats drool while they purr, signalling their contentment when you are stroking them. If your cat is one who drools copiously, take it as a compliment because it means your petting is so pleasurable that the cat has forgotten to swallow. You can relieve some of the drooling by touching your cat's nose or the side of her mouth with your fingertip, which will remind her to swallow that saliva.

LICKING

Licking is a grooming behavior in cats, so if your kitty licks you, it means she views you as one of the family. Cats only groom other cats they know and like and consider to be family members.

HEAD BUMPING

Cats will acknowledge each other with a bump of heads. It is a greeting between cats who are friendly, so if your cat does this to you, it means she views you as a family member. She's also marking you with scent from her facial glands.

Does Your Cat Have ESP?

There are cat enthusiasts who are convinced that cats can pick up their people's thoughts, just as they believe they do with other cats. People who live closely with their cats may begin to notice that the cat's personality, energy level, physical condition, and emotions seem to mirror their own. For example, it's not a stretch of the imagination to see that if you are emotionally strung out or preoccupied, your cat will pick this up and may display some of the same feelings. If you are grieving a loss, your cat can seem to share some of the emotions. If you have been aware of these emotional resemblances, you can be pretty sure it's not just your imagination: Your cat *is* tuned in to you. Those who have experienced this "mirroring" by their cats see it as a profound expression of their cat's attachment and love for them.

There are those who go a step further and say there is an extrasensory phenomenon in which cats seem to know in advance that their person is coming home and begin to display anticipatory behavior about 15 to 30 minutes before the person walks in the door. At least one study was done in England to replicate this behavior, and those observing were amazed that even if the person varied her schedule in what time she came home, and varied the conveyance by which she returned, the cat seemed to know every time that the return home was imminent. This study confirmed the belief in a cat's extrasensory ability to "just know" her person was coming—but if not by the clock, nor by the sound of a familiar car engine, then how does she do it?

Nobody knows how a cat picks up this signal or information, but the scientific studies were carefully constructed and showed that there is specific anticipatory, alert behavior in cats during the 30 minutes before their people arrive home. Scientists are at a loss to explain it, but more than a few cat aficionados are convinced that this is an example of how we can share thoughts telepathically with our cats.

Cats Who Chat

Some breeds of cat, generally the Orientals, are just naturally more talkative. However, if your cat has generally been quiet and starts chatting up a storm, there are several possible reasons. The first thing you want to rule out is a physical problem, since a cat who is sick or in pain may vocalize to express her discomfort and elicit your help. If your cat is older and a trip to the vet uncovers no physical explanation for the sudden talkativeness, it may be that she is disoriented and having "senior moments" when she is confused and needy. This condition of senior cats is known as cognitive dysfunction and is equivalent to senility in people. Your vet can help you determine if this is what is bothering your cat and what measures you might take to alleviate the symptoms.

Anxiety and stress can also stimulate a cat to speak up. See the chart at the end of this chapter about what causes stress in cats. If there is any commotion or change of a physical or emotional nature in the household, a cat may express her feelings about it by speaking up. Giving her extra attention and special times to be quiet may soothe and reassure her.

Another reason your cat may be chatty is because you have encouraged her to be—perhaps without realizing it. If your cat has meowed at you and gotten any sort of reply, then when she next meows and you do *not* reply, you encourage her to meow more or more loudly. Once she has done this a few times, it probably annoys you, so you give her a big (perhaps cranky) reply—but nonetheless she gets a response. If her meowing gets her different levels of response from you at different times—sometimes you reply quickly, sometimes loudly, sometimes not at all if you don't hear her—that erratic response (called "intermittent reward" in animal-training lingo) actually teaches her to be more persistent and loud than if you answered her every single time.

The fix for this chattiness—should it be behavior you want to end—is not to talk back to her, ever. You can talk to her, but not in direct answer to her meowing, unless you want to maintain this interspecies dialogue throughout her life. In general, if you ignore her talking, it should stop because her behavior is not being reinforced. However, if ignoring her does not diminish her talkativeness—and your vet has ruled out a medical issue—then you need to consider your cat's overall frame of mind and whether she is experiencing a high level of stress or anxiety that you might be able to relieve.

Chattering is a strange noise that cats make when they see potential prey—it is a rapid clicking of their teeth with a high-pitched whining sound to go with it—and it probably signals an abundance of adrenaline, a rush of excitement anticipating the hunt. Some experts surmise that this chattering sound is an automatic response by the cat as she contemplates her prey because if she were to capture it, she would deliver a deadly bite, severing the other animal's spinal cord. So the chattering may be an automatic physical preparation to hunt and kill. What is of interest is that cats will never make this chattering sound when they are observing the *human* animal—which should be of some small comfort to us.

Scaredy Cats: The Fear Factor

Cats have fears and phobias, neuroses and compulsions and can experience a lot of stress in their daily lives. This section explains the things that can disturb your cat and suggests possible solutions to these emotional issues and sensitivities. Unless you understand and support your cat through these issues, there is the chance that they can develop into complicated problems, so you would do well to make the effort.

The phrases "scaredy cat" and "fraidy cat" come directly from the general truth that cats *are* a fearful species. Fear is probably the emotional weakness most common to cats, and it can range from timidity and cautiousness all the way to extreme anxiety, in which a cat spends a large part of her time hiding. Instead of thinking of this characteristic in a negative light, another way to describe this inborn aspect of cats is to look at it from a more objective perspective and call it hypervigilance, or an extreme awareness of potential danger. Some people find cats to be nervous creatures, but I think it depends on the individual. There is no doubt that the tendency toward fear, alertness and being on their toes has allowed this small, vulnerable species (who had to hunt to survive, putting them in even more jeopardy) to thrive, essentially unchanged, for thousands of years.

FEAR OF THE UNKNOWN

Most cats dread what they don't know, which is often any unfamiliar sound, sight or person. Cats love things that are familiar to them; they may even embrace them *because* they are familiar. So you can use a cat's comfort level with anything that is predictable to help overcome her fears. You can transform the feared object/sound/person into something familiar through slow, repeated exposure to it until, before long, it might actually become a familiar favorite.

WHAT MAKES AN INDIVIDUAL CAT MORE FEARFUL?

Cats who suffer the most from fear of new things—or loud noises—tend to be cats who lack the spontaneous curiosity that is natural to their species. Generally, fearful cats are not outgoing; they will make a bond to their primary person or people but will run from new people (see below).

SOME CATS ARE GENETICALLY PREDISPOSED TO BE FEARFUL

Twenty-five percent of cats have a gene for fearfulness that their parents have passed on to them. Added to that predisposition you have a crucial period of development in early kittenhood, from 2 to 7 weeks of age, when kittens learn feline social skills and how to interact with their siblings. The earliest weeks are also when a kitten learns what it is to be handled by people. If a kitten grows up without being touched by human hands, and sees people infrequently if at all, that kitten is more likely to become a frightened, skittish cat. One of the main reasons kittens should be handled briefly but frequently from their earliest days is so that people become a natural, welcome part of their world.

WAYS TO SOOTHE A SCAREDY CAT

✦ Music Feeds a Cat's Soul

Playing classical or soft jazz music for your cat is both an excellent way to keep her company when you're out of the house and wonderful "medicine" to soothe the soul of an anxious cat. The therapeutic benefits of music are well known for people—lowering heart rate and blood pressure while raising spirits—and music seems to have a similar positive effect on cats.

Certain musical vibrations and frequencies are similar to those in purring—tonalities that are thought to promote healing and emotional well-being. Individual cats have their own preferences for types of music—play anything from country music to chamber music for your cat while you are around and see if you can tell which styles appeal most to her. But no matter what you decide to leave on when you go out, any music will probably have a positive effect on a tense or timid cat.

✦ Desensitizing a Fearful Cat to Household Appliances

Almost anything that frightens a cat can be turned around by exposing her to it at a distance, in small increments, until she becomes less and less reactive to it. For example, the common household sound of the vacuum cleaner is a source of considerable fear for many cats, who run and hide when you turn on the vacuum.

If you want to change this, begin by turning on the vacuum behind a closed door in a room as far as possible from where the cat hangs out. Now go hang out with your cat and create a positive association to accompany that distant vacuum cleaner noise: play with her and feed her tasty morsels. This is called *redirection.* On subsequent days, move the vacuum closer, but still not near enough to elicit a fear response; turn it on while you once again make a positive experience for your cat. At some point, your cat will be ready for you to bring the vacuum into whatever room or hallway is closest to her cat tree or wherever she generally hangs out. Muffle the sound of the vacuum with a quilt wrapped around it (taking care not to block inflow or outlet of air so you don't wreck your vacuum) and turn it on.

The point isn't to make *you* into a neurotic vacuum freak. You don't have to actually vacuum with the vacuum cleaner—this exercise is just about the scary sound of it. Leave the machine on and go play with your kitty, both of you ignoring the muffled sound of the roaring monster in the adjacent room. Your cat may reach the point where the vacuum monster is tamed: The kitty may still look concerned and may give the machine a wide berth, but at least she's no longer heading to hide in the hills.

✦ Ways to Touch Your Scaredy Cat

Some cats are so fearful—usually because of early bad experiences with people (or such neglect that they have had no contact with people)—that directly patting them is too stressful. But by slowly and surely making contact with them in other ways, you can turn a frightened, timid cat into a more confident one who will come to enjoy your friendship and touch.

Use Your Voice to "Pat" Her. Don't underestimate the power of a soothing, warm, gentle voice to help a cat come out of her shell. Anything kind or loving you say will convey your intent and be generally reassuring. Cats also enjoy listening to a person singing a song or even humming, so take advantage of this chance to sing outside the shower to a willing audience.

Use a Long-Handled Brush to Stroke Her. You know those bath brushes with the long handle that are supposed to let you scrub your own back in the tub? Well, an even better use for one is as a gentle brush for your cat—the soft bristles of the brush are pleasurable for her (perhaps reminding her of her mother's rough tongue), but the beauty of it is that the long handle gives you enough distance that the scaredy cat won't feel overwhelmed by your proximity. Good spots to brush are under the chin and cheeks and on the shoulders and chest. Think of the brush head as your hand and make smooth, firm strokes, always going with the direction of the hair. Your cat is sure to be purring in no time.

Keep It Short. Edgy cats can only tolerate a limited amount of interaction, so plan your touch sessions to last no more than 4 or 5 minutes. After that amount of time, the cat may "max out" and become agitated.

Don't Expect Purring. It may take a fearful cat quite a while to be physically relaxed enough to purr. All in good time.

Let Your Cat Choose the Spot. Watch and see where your fearful cat most likes to hang out and do your stroking and bonding there. It's best to be in a location where she feels comfortable—especially since she's a cat who already feels *un*comfortable going into this. Whether it's on a cat tree, in a cozy bed or on a thick rug, wherever your cat can relax the most is where you should go to give her the attention she'll come to love.

Fear of New People

Cats have varying degrees of fear toward visitors. Some cats simply are not social by their nature and keep to themselves when strangers are around, while others seem to freak out just because strangers are there. Cats like this cannot tolerate the presence of visitors at all and will run and hide for hours. A cat who may otherwise seem well adjusted and calm can go right over the edge when a new person enters the scene.

REASONS FOR THE FEAR

Every visitor-phobic cat has her own reasons for her reaction. One possibility, as mentioned above, is that when the cat was young she was not exposed to people or to their comings and goings. Another possibility is that something frightening happened the first time that guests arrived at your house (an incident that you may not remember but that your cat will never be able to forget, given the long memory and grudge holding that cats are capable of). If those original visitors were frightening to your cat, she could have been left with a permanent phobia of the arrival of strangers.

"UNDOING" STRANGER FEAR

◆ Do You Really Need to "Fix" the Phobia?

Before we go into the ways to countercondition stranger anxiety in a cat, I think it's worthwhile to take a moment to ask the question that people often overlook: Is it really worth it to your cat to have to overcome her own terror? From the animal's point of view, it's not a bad idea to stop and consider whether it is worth the emotional toll it will take on the cat (and the considerable effort required by you) to try to reverse her natural inclination. To some degree, the answer depends on whether you have a very social lifestyle and a home in which people are constantly coming and going, so that your poor kitty is constantly on the run and hiding out.

Even if you do have an active household, whether or not your cat needs to be taught to accept strangers depends in large part on whether *you* place a value on having a cat who is relaxed and

can enjoy company. A fearful cat might learn to *tolerate* visitors but would probably never relax and enjoy them. Does it really improve a cat's quality of life to try to overcome fear and panic about new people when running away solves the problem from your cat's perspective? You may think you are doing your kitty a favor by helping her to achieve socialization and overcome her fearfulness, but look at it from the cat's perspective before embarking on a "kitty makeover." Stop and ask yourself the question: "Will my cat be better off for this, given what it will cost her to go through it?"

◆ Ways to Cure Visitor Phobia

There are a number of ways to help your cat overcome stranger anxiety, and they all start with the idea of trying to slowly acclimate your fearful cat to the arrival of newcomers. Most plans to help a cat overcome fears and phobias hinge on the concept of desensitization, which means slowly, repeatedly, and from a distance presenting your cat with the frightening stimulus until it frightens her less or not at all.

Those who undertake the desensitization of cats with stranger phobia suggest that the first step is restraining the cat—she must not be able to flee from what frightens her. This means putting a harness and leash on her (if she will tolerate it) or confining her to a carrier so that when the doorbell rings she cannot take off to hide. If you are using a carrier, put it in the room where guests will congregate and then the cat will eventually realize that these newcomers mean her no harm—at least in theory. The idea is to repeat this scenario many times, enlisting as many family members and strangers as possible, until the cat calms down and accepts that she has to deal with visitors as a part of life.

The desensitization process gains momentum as days or weeks pass and you ask visitors to sit near the carrier where the cat is confined, and sit closer each time, eventually giving them tasty bits of food to offer to the cat through the cage door. The behaviorists who set out this plan also suggest keeping food from the cat for 12 hours before visitors arrive, so that she will be eager to accept any morsels they offer her. At this point I part company with the whole enterprise because it seems like you would be forcing your cat to jump through burning hoops just so Aunt Millie can stroke her. My personal reaction to this is that if your cat enjoys you and the house in an unvisited state, then give her a break and let her hide from company if she wants. (Honestly, don't you sometimes feel like doing that, too?)

You could also try getting her used to strangers with a less rigorous desensitization, using your own low-key version. If your cat doesn't like visitors, but neither does she run like a hunted beast when someone rings the doorbell, you might be able to ask a friend to come over and approach her slowly at a distance. Give your friend some high-value treats (that is trainer-talk for something that's *really* delicious to your cat and not usually on her menu, such as chicken). As long as she remains calm, your friend should toss out a yummy treat. Moving slowly, he may even get a little closer to her. The next time this friend visits, he will get increasingly close to your cat, dispensing treats in her direction as long as she remains calm. The first greeting might be at 3 yards away and the next time half that, if the cat can handle it. If your cat shows signs of fear, such as pupils getting wider and ears flattening on her head, have your friend back off. He's going to have to decrease the distance between them more slowly. With a slow-and-steady-wins-the-race approach,

 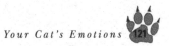

you may be able to change her mind—but it may not work with just any visitor; it may turn out that your cat will only accept this one friend.

◆ Solving Intense Fear of a New Person

A new person may enter your life of whom your cat is extremely fearful, to the point of biting or scratching if the person makes any advances on her. This is called fear-induced aggression, and if the cat directs it at someone who is going to be a regular part of your life (let's say a roommate or a fiancée) then you obviously have to do something about it.

Use Play to Reduce Aggression. If your cat cannot stand your new spouse or partner, have the new person (NP) engage the cat in a play session—any of the interactive toys mentioned in Chapter 4 will work beautifully for this. By playing with the NP, the cat can build trust at a comfortable distance: The cat feels emotionally safe and your partner can feel physically safe that the "attack cat" isn't going to pounce at any moment. Through playing with the NP, the cat begins to associate that person with something fun and positive.

If your cat is especially fearful and timid, then play should include lots of hiding places. Depending on how much furniture you have (chairs and sofas and their pillows are the best hiding places of all), you can create some temporary hiding places for the cat before beginning the play session with the NP. The fearful cat will be more willing to play—and will have a better positive association—if you pile up some sofa cushions in the middle of the room or put out a cardboard box on its side and a couple of handleless paper bags with a cuff to keep them open. Now the cat can play and have somewhere to bail out if her anxiety starts to climb.

Put the New Person in Charge of the Cat. Another way to change the cat's reaction is by turning the NP into the only human who will meet the cat's needs. This is only a temporary arrangement, but even so, it may be difficult for you to stick to. However, it will yield the result you want, which is for the cat to accept, and perhaps even like, your NP (this probably is only worth the effort if the NP is going to be an important or permanent part of your life).

The sequence of steps that follows will only change your cat's attitude to the NP if two things happen: (1) you remain committed to giving your cat *not a drop* of attention and (2) the NP gives the cat food and attention but *stops immediately* if the cat gets aggressive.

CHANGING YOUR CAT'S MIND ABOUT A NEW PERSON

- ❏ You must stop feeding or paying attention to the cat.
- ❏ The NP will take over feeding the cat.
- ❏ Any attention has to come from the NP.
- ❏ You have to completely ignore the cat: no looking at her, no talking to her, no touching her. Don't allow her on your lap, on your bed or even next to you. The cat will reject the NP's attention if she's still receiving any at all from you.
- ❏ The NP can offer special treats (meat, cheese, baby food on a spoon).
- ❏ If the cat is calm, the NP should stroke her.

❑ If there is any aggressive reaction (hissing, growling, biting, scratching), the NP should get up and walk away without reprimanding the cat.

❑ No physical punishments—they only make things worse.

❑ The NP should stand up and walk away to show that affection has to be on his terms.

Life Is Stressful for All Cats

I am not being facetious when I say that cats cope with more stress than most of us have ever imagined. Behind those wide unblinking eyes, beneath that regal exterior, pounds a little heart overwrought with worries. Cats are fearful and hypervigilant by nature—they notice everything, with eyes, ears and nose that are constantly taking in a barrage of information, not all of which they can even process.

Before humans came along to incorporate cats into their barnyards and eventually into their parlors, surviving in nature could not have been a picnic for cats. Yet somehow, when I see how many human-related events upset them, I have to think that going back to the olden days would be bucolic, when their only worries were finding enough mice to gobble, a trickle of water and a warm place to sleep. There were always a few predators, of course, but how much more complicated is life now for cats, spent around noisy, nerve-jangling machines and entwined with humans and all their intense emotions.

Big Causes of Cat Stress

- Move to a new house
- Structural renovations in a house
- Arrival of a new baby or an adult
- A new cat or other animal
- Loss of family member, cat or human
- Environmental disasters /emergencies (flood, fire, displacement)
- Hospitalization or boarding

Smaller Causes of Cat Stress

- Loneliness, lack of human contact
- Redecorating (new furniture, paint)
- Litter boxes (new litter brand, not cleaned, too close to food, no privacy)
- Children (of all ages)
- Multi-cat territorial disputes
- Illness
- Repeated loud noises
- Change in food
- Rough handling, abuse, punishment

 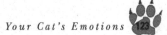

- Change in household routine (people's schedule changes)
- Sighting unfamiliar cat outdoors
- Lack of hiding places
- Confinement with no exit
- Overcrowding—too many cats for the size of the house
- Living with cat-hating family member
- Raised voices/tension/anger between humans
- Divorce
- Holidays or big parties

MOVING TO A NEW HOUSE

Moving to a new house is stressful for people as well as cats, which means that your cat not only has to deal with her own fears and worries but has to cope with your emotional upheaval, too. It may help you to remain more calm and centered if you realize that your state of mind—and the extent to which you are running around double-time before and during the move—has an impact on your cat.

Keep in mind that the thing cats like most is familiarity and routine, and the thing they like least is the disruption of that routine—which means that moving is probably a cat's biggest nightmare. Besides staying as calm and collected as you can, here are some other ways to help your poor kitty get through moving.

◆ Spray Comfort Zone Feliway Beforehand

When you are getting ready to move, there will be boxes coming and going. To the cat, these boxes represent alien objects invading her space. Although boxes are otherwise a source of fun to cats, having a lot of strange-smelling boxes coming into the house can be stressful. You can solve this problem by spraying Comfort Zone Feliway (see Chapter 3, "Your New Cat's Homecoming") on the corners of the boxes *before* you bring them inside, to transform them into pleasant, unthreatening-smelling arrivals.

◆ Create a Safe Room in Both Houses

If possible, have a room in your current house that the cat can be comfortable in, with her cat tree and, if possible, a piece of furniture she enjoys. Try to pack up this room last—that way, despite all the commotion in other parts of the house, one area will remain that is a sanctuary for the cat. Then create another safe room in the new house—again with a piece of furniture the cat knows and likes to hang out on, and her cat tree as well. Once more, the room will be an oasis of calm for the cat amidst the activity of moving in.

You can spray Feliway on the corners of furniture or other objects that have been brought to the new house because they will have been touched by strangers and their odor will be altered. Feliway will restore the pleasant association the cat had with that furniture or even her own cat tree if it has been touched by unfamiliar people.

◆ **Create Pleasant Associations with the New House**

Although you may be exhausted and overwhelmed yourself by the move, take a few minutes to play with your cat in the safe room. Although your initial reaction to this advice might be, "*What?* You want me to *play* when I have fifty boxes to pack and unpack?" you may get some benefit from it, too. Taking a break from the moving madness will probably do you good, while helping to create a good feeling about the new abode for your cat and reaffirming your bond to her.

Separation Anxiety Syndrome (SAS)

People are not really aware of how much their cats can suffer from being separated from them, but it is a common source of misery for many cats. People are not conscious of SAS in cats for several reasons. First, there is the assumption that cats are independent and could live without us anyway. Second, the feline display of separation anxiety is subtle or convoluted, unlike in dogs, who express their dismay at being separated by barking and whining enough to rile the neighbors. Separation anxiety in cats is not always immediately obvious, but it can be the cause of self-destructive grooming and some of the more difficult cat behavior problems: spraying, scratching and eliminating outside the litter box (often on their person's bed or other personally scented area).

Most people have experienced the angry response their cat can have when left home alone: Not only has there been destructiveness, but when the person gets home the cat will turn her back and clearly ignore then. If you doubt that cats are social creatures (and therefore are distressed by being left alone), just notice how often your cat will eat nothing until you come around, and then run to her bowl and start eating, inspired by your company and happy for it. This should be an indicator to all of us that we matter much more to our cats than they let on. Therefore, it falls on us not to take our poor cats' stoicism for granted, and not to assume that just because they are willing to spend all day—or even *days*—alone, they don't get lonely and pay an emotional price for it.

AVOID BREEDS PRONE TO SEPARATION ANXIETY

If you know that your work and social life will keep you out of the house a great deal, then plan ahead so that you don't set yourself—and your kitty—up for failure. Avoid getting any of the following Oriental breeds because they are prone to experiencing separation anxiety, with the Siamese at the top of the list: Abyssinian, Balinese, Bengal, Burmese, Cornish and Devon Rex, Havana Brown, Sphynx and Tonkinese. These cats require human company—they cannot tolerate being ignored when you are home, and certainly not when you slip out without mentioning it.

SIGNS OF SEPARATION ANXIETY

House soiling
Destructive behavior
Excessive grooming
Hiding

 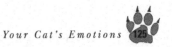

Loss of appetite
Increased vocalization

DEALING WITH SEPARATION ANXIETY

Once a cat has developed profound separation anxiety it is unlikely that you'll have much luck changing her attitude, but if your cat is just showing the first signs of SAS, there are some modifications to her environment that might help relieve that anxiety. Making the cat's environment at home as stimulating and pleasant as possible gives you the best chance of taking the sting out of being left alone.

- ❐ Rotate a couple of toys every few days so there is always a new one to investigate.
- ❐ Get a great cat tree and put it near a window so that the cat has lots of interesting things to look at.
- ❐ Once a week sprinkle catnip somewhere new—on a landing of the cat tree, on a furry toy mouse—but not more often than that or it will lose its punch.
- ❐ Put some high-quality kibble in one of those hidden-treat toys (a Rubik's cube for animals) so the cat will have to find it and then figure out how to get the treats out of there.
- ❐ Put a box and a paper bag on their sides in unexpected places so your cat has the fun of discovering new hiding places.
- ❐ Leave on music and a television channel with pleasant chatty shows.
- ❐ Put in a video made just for pets left at home; these have images of other cats and prey animals intended to amuse and stimulate animals at home.
- ❐ Ask a friend or neighbor to drop in during the day when you're gone and hang out with your cat, even if it's only for a few minutes.
- ❐ Get a companion cat or dog so that your cat has another creature to commiserate with about being left home when you are out having all the fun (and you can come home to *two* little faces staring at you accusingly). If you get two littermates, there's a good chance they will be great playmates, accustomed to relying on each other for fun and games.

WHAT ABOUT MEDICATION FOR ANXIETY?

There are situations in which a cat's SAS is so intense that no amount of human understanding and support is going to turn things around. In cases such as these there is a place for using medication to stop the downward emotional spiral. The drug most frequently used is the tranquilizer Valium (generic name diazepam), although some vets may want to use the antidepressants Elavil (amitriptyline), Prozac (fluoxetine) or BuSpar (buspirone).

Personally, I have to admit that I cannot see how a cat benefits from a chemical tranquilizer such as Valium, which requires blood tests while taking it and which has to be discontinued fairly quickly for health reasons. However, if your cat isn't making much progress in becoming sociable, you may want to talk to your vet about giving her a mild sedative. Valium or antianxiety drugs can sometimes help get a cat over the hump at the beginning of desensitization (meaning her sheer panic when she is forced to stay in the same room with the object of her terror). However, since the cat can develop a dependence on these drugs, they can only be used in the short term and you would have to withdraw her from the medication fairly soon.

Comfort Zone Feliway (discussed in depth in Chapter 3) is a synthetic version of a cat's natural facial pheromones, the ones she rubs all over wherever she goes as a way to mark her territory and fill it with a familiar scent. Feliway was developed to counteract the anxiety that drives cats to do destructive things such as urine marking and scratching, and it is available from most vets and in pet stores. It comes as a diffuser that plugs in or as a room spray and seems to work magically for many cats, settling them down and dissolving their angst. It does not work for all cats, so you can only hope that your cat is not one of those who is oblivious to the calming odor.

Flower Essences are a completely natural product, distilled from plants, and are often quite successful in helping cats through emotional situations. They are also an affordable option compared to Feliway, which is expensive. Bach Flower Remedies were developed by Dr. Edward Bach, who came up with 37 different formulas. For cats, the ones that count are Rescue Remedy (a de-stress formula used by people, too) and Spirit Essence's Hyper Helper or Obsession Remedy. You can go to www.bachcentre.com or www.spiritessence.com and learn more about these substances.

Although some people recommend putting a few drops of the essences into your cat's water bowl, it's often nearly impossible to see your cat drinking at all. Instead, rub a couple of drops of the oil on the inside of the cat's ear and it will travel into her system.

CLINGINESS AND STRESS

One symptom of a cat feeling stressed is that she may stick to you like glue, following you wherever you go. She may also look agitated, seem unable to settle down, and when you go out may become distressed enough to vocalize about it, even if she is normally not a chatty cat. Some cats become so overwrought that when their person leaves the house they will do anything to try to follow, including scratching or biting at the door, marking with urine, or other aberrant behavior. Sometimes a cat this distraught will urinate on the absent person's clothes, bed or favorite place to sit.

If your cat is following you everywhere, displaying what is often referred to as "shadowing" or "Velcro" behavior, be aware that this is a sure sign that she is feeling stressed and probably is suffering from separation anxiety.

Tips for Living with an Anxious Cat

- Stay relaxed yourself—she can pick up on your stress level.
- Don't actively try to get her to face something new.
- Try to stick to a routine—it is comforting and reassuring.
- Don't force her to be in a room with you or anyone else.
- Let her choose how close she gets to anyone.
- Let her have hiding places where she won't be disturbed.
- Use lure toys to encourage play and playfulness.
- Let her set the pace for all interactions.

 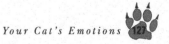

Things Cats Do Under Emotional Stress

There are as many diverse cat behaviors that indicate emotional stress as there are potentially stressful events, as you can see from the lists above. Apparently, life is harder for our cats than we ever realized. What follows are some of the odd behaviors cats engage in to relieve stress—many of which can be self-destructive and require your intervention. Of course if there's any way you can determine what is stressing your kitty and reduce or eliminate it, that will go a long way to helping her to relax and take a deep breath.

OVERGROOMING

Because we are used to seeing cats groom themselves frequently, it's easy to overlook normal grooming that has mushroomed into constant, obsessive, self-destructive licking. Often, we don't see what has changed in our cat's behavior until we see the hair is gone from a bald patch where she has licked it clean, or licked to the point of making a sore on her skin. Cats who express their emotional upset by overgrooming will often continue to the point of licking away entire patches of hair and even causing lesions on the underlying skin. If their licking goes far enough to break the skin's surface, infection can occur.

This behavior is most frequently seen in high-strung breeds such as the Siamese, but it can happen to any cat. In fact, obsessive grooming is common enough that there are nicknames for cats who do it to themselves—they are sometimes referred to as "self-barbers" or "fur mowers." It seems that for these animals, the licking relieves their stress and even puts them into a "relaxation zone." Then what can happen is that some of these cats actually enjoy being in that self-induced relaxed frame of mind, and their habit of overgrooming will continue even when they are *not* stressed—perhaps because they are bored and the relaxed state is an appealing alternative.

◆ Causes of Overgrooming

Sometimes the reason for obsessive licking is only physical—the cat has painful matting or irritating parasites—but most often licking has a psychological source. Finding the reason is fundamental to turning the cat around emotionally. There are a few theories you can test out. When a cat overgrooms only occasionally, it may have to do with a lack of stimulation in her environment and the need for more outlets. A good start to providing a fix for that is to engage the cat in interactive physical and mental play with you (see "Toys and Playtime" in Chapter 4).

On the other hand, if a cat is overgrooming frequently, she simply may not be able to deal with whatever stress she perceives around her. Her issues may be triggered by tension or friction in the human part of the equation—or, if she lives in a multi-cat arrangement, she could be having problems within her feline social group. She may have issues with one other cat or, if you have more than two cats, it may be that group living just does not agree with her personality and she can soothe herself only by overgrooming.

Try to determine the cause of your cat's excessive grooming behavior by making a change in her living conditions to see if her grooming behavior changes. If the layout of your home permits it, isolate her for at least a couple of weeks. Give her a quiet room with her own litter pan and food and water bowls (far from her toilet area, of course). Keep a radio tuned to a nice classical or jazz station. Everyone in the household should pay the cat as many visits as possible; you want to keep her "fed" emotionally and for her to experience her isolation as something positive, not that she has been ostracized. A sensitive cat may even experience this experimental isolation as another stressor and she could continue or even escalate the overgrooming, at least during her initial adjustment to being alone.

◆ Psychogenic Alopecia

Psychogenic alopecia is a neurotic behavior in which a cat pulls out her hair as a reaction to stressful elements in her environment. As with overgrooming, pulling her hair out apparently serves to relieve that anxiety in some odd way. Alopecia is seen most often in those purebred cats that are considered high-strung, such as the Siamese, Burmese, Abyssinian and Himalayan. The remedy for this kind of alopecia is to try to identify the stressful element in the cat's life and reduce it—and to give her extra time and affection to reassure her.

However, there is also a physical—not psychological—condition, feline endocrine alopecia, in which a cat loses hair over a part of her body without scratching or other signs of irritation. You should see your vet to distinguish between the two, because the doctor can determine which version of the condition it is. With endocrine alopecia, he can use hormones to restore the cat's fur, although there is controversy about this treatment and he may wish to explore other methods of treatment.

ANOREXIA

When a cat loses her appetite or stops eating, it is a telltale sign that she is not well. If this lasts more than one day, she definitely needs to see the vet. It isn't just physical problems that cause cats to stop eating: Sometimes emotional problems or stress can cause anorexia. Your cat could stressed by any of the reasons on the charts in this chapter (see "Life Is Stressful for Cats," earlier in this chapter), but one predictable reason is grief over the loss of another cat who shared her life. Grief can cause loss of appetite in people, too.

A perfect example of how stress can cause anorexia in cats is that when they are hospitalized they often stop eating—whether because they don't like being in a cage, or can't deal with the sights and sounds of all the other dogs and cats in the facility, or due to the change in their food, bedding and litter.

◆ Anorexia Is Dangerous

Cats cannot go long periods without eating—it is dangerous for their health and can even be life-threatening. Going without food is even more dangerous for overweight or obese cats because they can die from fatty liver disease without consistent nutrition.

A cat should not go more than two days without food. This is the rule of thumb for when to take your cat to the vet to rule out any physical problems. See the vet *right away* if two days have passed without food intake. This is yet another reason that people must not leave their cats home alone without someone to drop in on them, give them attention and monitor whether they are eating and drinking their usual amounts.

◆ What You Can Do About Emotional Anorexia

If your vet determines that there is no physical, medical explanation for your cat's refusal to eat, then the first thing to do is try to encourage your cat to take in some food. Your involvement in her food preparation and her eating habits is probably what will make the difference in inspiring her to eat.

◆ Does She Not Like to Eat Alone?

Some cats really love to have company while they eat—so much so that if they are all alone they don't even want to eat. You may have noticed that if you are gone all day or away overnight, you may return to find that your cat has barely eaten—but runs for her food bowl the moment you return. If your cat is like this and is showing signs of being anorexic, then dine with her. Escort your cat to her food bowl, or call her and talk to her encouragingly as you go to put it down. Then continue chatting to her and stroke her back while she eats.

◆ Make Her Food More Delicious

❐ If your cat isn't already on canned food, then switch her to it now.

❐ Put some of the super-flavorful water (not oil) from a can of tuna (for humans) on her food to give it a taste boost.

❐ Put some teaspoons of meat baby food on top of the cat's food.

❐ Her food may taste more appealing if it is slightly warm—a few moments in the microwave is enough.

EATING WOOL AND OTHER FABRICS (PICA)

Wool chewing, sucking and eating is one of the complex behaviors called *pica*, which means the ingestion of nonfood items. Some cats will eat mouthfuls of wool—and sometimes other fabrics on surfaces as diverse as furniture, carpets, drapes, shower curtains, electrical cords, pantyhose, bedding or clothing (especially made of wool). Many of these cats prefer the worn clothing, bedding or towels that have been used by the people in their life.

Wool is the fabric of choice for some of these cats; it may be either the smell or feel of the wool that attracts them. However, most fabric-eating cats are much less discerning. They don't even confine themselves to natural fibers and will venture right out into the vast smorgasbord of synthetics, too.

◆ Which Breeds of Cats Do This and Why?

It was once believed that wool eating was a distinct quirk of Siamese cats, and later other Orientals like Burmese, but eventually people realized that the habit was not limited to any breed at all. However, it does seem that the cats who do it are especially sensitive and also highly attached to their humans, since it often happens when the people leave, and so it seems to be an expression of separation anxiety. Although no one knows for certain what drives a cat to do this, some surmise that it stems from too-early weaning and is a form of oral satisfaction, which fills a kittenish need for suckling—or else it could be genetic predisposition, anxiety or boredom.

People who have observed fabric-eaters say that when they go about their task it is with total absorption, as if nothing else exists around them. Sometimes the animal seems almost catatonic. People have reported that once these cats get going, nothing can deter them: making a loud startling noise or using a squirt bottle of water will elicit almost no reaction. The cat pays no attention to your attempts to distract and stop her, and if interrupted she goes right back to eating. Pica often continues throughout the cat's entire lifetime.

◆ How Do They Do It?
Cats start the process by grasping a mouthful of fabric with their front teeth and canines. They then transfer that mouthful to their back teeth, powerful molars that can pulverize the cloth. Some of them can take in a disturbing amount of material this way. The good news is that most of the time the material goes right through their digestive system and causes no physical harm, although there are cases where cats have gotten intestinal blockages that were life-threatening or fatal.

◆ What to Do About Fabric Eating
Although the solution to most pet problems is to remove opportunity from the animal's environment (as in not leaving food on counters), it is a lot harder to remove fabric, which is pretty much all over the house. However, if your cat exclusively chews wool, you are in luck, because it's quite easy to eliminate that from her grasp by stashing away sweaters and blankets.

Although there are some other deterrents listed in the chart below, most behaviorists have found that one way to stop a cat from eating fabric is to ensure that she has the feeling of a full stomach all the time. There are those who think the feeling of emptiness may contribute to the disorder and that the cat is seeking the comforting feeling of a full belly, even though fabric eaters have good appetites and eat a normal amount of food at mealtimes. There has been success in just leaving dry food out at all times, in addition to regular meals. However, since free-feeding any food is so bad for any cat's health, please try this for only a short time if you absolutely must.

SOLUTIONS TO FABRIC EATING

- ❑ Remove as much of the fabric from the cat's surroundings as possible—which may mean confining the kitty to a fabric-free area such as the kitchen.
- ❑ Remove access for several weeks to her favorite fabric.
- ❑ Cats who eat fabric only when the humans leave them—and are very clingy when the people are around—need their dependence to be reduced.
- ❑ Interrupting the cat during her eating trance by startling him with noise or water may work—or it may force her to eat fabric secretly, where you can't see her.
- ❑ You may be able to change your cat's taste for fabrics by treating "bait" pieces with bad-tasting oils such as eucalyptus or menthol (not hot spices since, surprisingly, some cats learn to *enjoy* tastes like chili, Tabasco or pepper).

 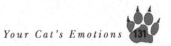

Grief Over Losing a Person or Animal

Cats can grieve and go through mourning when they lose a human or animal companion. When the family structure is disrupted, animals can react as much as people do: Cats can cry, lose their appetite, sleep too much, develop insomnia or become withdrawn and moody. Cats can have profound attachments that cause deep reactions when those relationships are lost. Researchers at big veterinary colleges such as Cornell spend time and resources teaching people to recognize that animals share the same neurochemistry that allows humans to feel happiness or sadness.

CATS CAN FORM DEEP ATTACHMENTS

For a long time it was believed that cats were loners who needed no other creature in their lives—at times we have even perceived cats as antisocial beings. While some cats may be content living a solitary life, many others form profound attachments to other cats and people. When that bond is broken, the cat who survives can go through a grieving process as real as any human's. And just as with people, that pain will lessen with the passage of time.

GRIEVING IS AN INDIVIDUAL PROCESS

Just as people have different ways of expressing sadness over a lost loved one, so are cats individual in how they go through the grief. Keep an eye on your cat right after she loses a member of the household to see whether she is suffering from any of the following typical reactions to grief.

SYMPTOMS OF GRIEF

- ❑ Sleep disturbances
- ❑ Changes in eating patterns
- ❑ Disinterest in playing
- ❑ Housetraining mistakes
- ❑ Excessive howling, meowing or other vocalization
- ❑ Loss of appetite including refusal to eat
- ❑ Repeatedly returning to locations where lost companion used to spend time
- ❑ Sitting silently, staring at the wall or out the window
- ❑ Running away

Ways to Help a Grief-Struck Cat

- Keep routines such as feeding and grooming.
- Spend as much time with the cat as you can.
- Have friends the cat knows pay visits and make a fuss over her.
- Give her something with the scent of the lost person or animal.
- Keep her company at mealtimes and make her meals extra tasty.
- Do *not* get another cat—at least until your cat has completely rebounded.

GRIEF COUNSELING FOR CATS—TELEPHONE PET LOSS SUPPORT

Chicago Veterinary Medical College, 630-603-3994
Colorado State University, 970-491-4143
Cornell University, 607-253-3932
Grief Recovery Hotline, 800-445-4808
Iowa State University, 888-478-7574
Michigan State University, 517-432-2696
Ohio State University, 614-292-1823
Pet Grief Support Service (Arizona), 602-995-5885
Tufts University, 508-839-7966
University of California at Davis, 800-565-1526, 530-752-4200
University of Florida, 800-798-6196, 352-392-4700
University of Illinois, 877-394-2273, 217-333-2760
University of Minnesota, 612-624-4747
University of Pennsylvania, 215-898-4529
Virginia-Maryland Regional College of Veterinary Medicine, 540-231-8038
Washington State University, 509-335-5704

PET LOSS GRIEF COUNSELING ON THE WEB

American Veterinary Medical Association, www.avma.org (they have grief counseling under "Goodbye My Friend")
Animal Love and Loss Network, www.alln.org (an organization of pet loss counselors)
Delta Society, 425-226-7357, www.deltasociety.org (has information about counselors and links to support groups)

 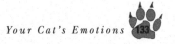

Chapter 6

UNDERSTANDING YOUR CAT'S BEHAVIOR

This chapter is organized alphabetically around those natural cat behaviors that can be confusing and can potentially cause grief to the human inhabitants of the house. Most of the feline behavior in this section is perfectly normal and predictable—which means that if it bothers us, *we* are the ones who must change our point of view and make accommodations for those things our cats do that we dislike or which just plain annoy us. As long as we're all clear that the adaptation has to come from the human side of the equation, then harmony and understanding (sorry if that sounds like a corny 1970s pop tune) will ultimately prevail.

That isn't to say that unusual cats or peculiar situations that fall outside the normal curve shouldn't be dealt with accordingly. However, the cat behaviors that seem to offend people most seem to be natural functions or instincts—scratching, aggression, marking and litter box issues. So it would seem that understanding the motivations behind cat behavior is the key to making things more harmonious.

As for litter box issues, that topic gets its very own chapter because it is so heavy with misunderstandings, yet fixable problems, which cause people to give up on their cats for lack of information. Litter box "failures" are the cause of so many good cats being abandoned to shelters where they may be euthanized, creating heartache for the people who once loved them. So it's worth dedicating a chapter solely to changing this trend.

Many of the issues in this chapter can be addressed with the natural remedies at www.spiritessence.com.

Aggression (In All Its Forms)

Aggression is a negative word: It is loaded with value judgment. When the word *aggressive* is used to describe something or someone, it predisposes the listener to dislike and distrust that thing or person. For animals, however, aggression is a natural, normal, healthy, appropriate behavior or reaction. In cats, aggressiveness can be about self-protection or defense, or it can be offensive—often for the very same reasons. It can also be about play or sex. Cats are small and vulnerable creatures, and if they did not have aggression as part of their arsenal, it is doubtful whether they would have survived for so many millennia. The sections that follow describe the kinds of aggression you can expect to see in your cat and help you see what is normal and what may fall outside those boundaries.

Animal behaviorists have divided aggression in cats into about ten types, which may seem irrelevant to you if you have just been clawed or bitten. However, if you are *not* a direct recipient of a cat's aggressive behavior, then it is interesting to understand what is going on and why, especially if you have multiple cats. After the chart you will find a further description of those types of aggression that may need further explanation.

TYPES OF AGGRESSION IN CATS

Fear aggression: a cat attacks when frightened

Food aggression: a cat attacks to protect her own food or take another's food

Inbred aggression: the result of poor breeding by people without the knowledge to make good choices in breeding pairs

Maternal aggression: a mama cat defends her young

Paternal aggression: an unneutered cat (a tom) kills kittens sired by another male

Play aggression: mostly exhibited by kittens and adolescents while playing

Prey aggression: a cat stalks or kills another creature

Redirected aggression: a cat cannot get at the object of her fury, so she lashes out at a "bystander"

Sexual aggression: between a male and female in heat

Territorial/status aggression: a cat uses force and/or intimidation to control others and get what she wants

FOOD AGGRESSION

Cats have been known to attack to protect their food resources, or in order to steal food from another cat. Food guarding and aggression are generally an issue only in multi-cat homes. If your cat was a stray, she may have had to fight for meals or go hungry much of the time, and if she spent time at a shelter, she may have encountered a similar competition for food. Living in close quarters with another cat in your home may trigger that response in cats with those backgrounds.

FOOD AGGRESSION CAN BE AN EXPRESSION OF DOMINANCE BETWEEN CATS

If one cat is clearly dominant, there will be no problem—the subordinate cat accepts his place, the dominant one makes clear her supremacy and the dominant one always eats first. It is only when two cats who are about equal in the pecking order have not determined who is on a higher rung that aggression erupts over food, resulting in nasty fights. Feeding time becomes a contest to see who can top whom, rather than a pleasurable experience.

✦ Things You Can Do to Avoid Food Aggression
The easiest fix for this problem is to give the cats separate feeding areas at different locations in the kitchen. Have two food dishes and two water dishes—the safety net of the distance between them may be all it takes for the aggressive cat to show no signs of her problem.

✦ If the Problem Is Between a Cat and Dog
Since dogs love the extreme smelliness of cat food, both canned and dry, your dog will probably make every possible attempt to help himself to the cat's yummy food. This can irritate your cat no end. But the solution is easy as pie: Elevate the cat's food dish, placing it up on a counter, and the mutt will have to make do with his own food.

✦ For Severe Food Aggression
If your cat really wigs out when another cat comes near her food bowl, rather than putting the nonaggressive cat in such an uncomfortable position, the easiest thing to do is to feed the cats in different rooms. The aggressive cat will eat more comfortably if she doesn't have to fret that someone else is going to get her food, and the cat who is the victim of the aggression is going to be eternally grateful to you.

INBRED AGGRESSION
A cat who is unpredictably aggressive may just be "wired" wrong. This type of aggressive behavior can only be blamed on or explained by the cat's own biological makeup. The cat may lash out at the slightest provocation—for example, when she is startled, when someone comes too close or when a person reaches out to pat her. Aggression can be passed on in the genes, and since aggression is obviously not a desirable attribute in a cat (despite the "Beware the Attack Cat" signs you may have seen for sale), clearly no breeder would knowingly want to perpetuate this tendency passed on by the parent(s). A consultation with your vet should help you determine if this is truly inbred aggression or if it is caused by something else, such as a medical condition.

If your cat is a purebred and you got her from a breeder, then you have a legitimate claim with the breeder, depending on what age the cat was when you become aware of the aggression. There is no hard and fast rule on what that age might be, but using common sense you wouldn't expect a breeder to honor your claim in a cat who has reached adulthood or her first birthday. Depending on how serious the problem is, a good breeder should offer to exchange your kitten or cat. At the very least he should remove her parents from his breeding program until he can discover which of them is responsible for this unfortunate trait.

REDIRECTED AGGRESSION
This usually happens with indoor cats, generally because they have access to a window and see an unfamiliar cat outside whom they cannot get to. The adrenaline that flows when your cat sees an

intruder and the frustration she feels at not being able to go deal with it can cause an outburst of aggression directed at the next creature who comes along. This poor victim generally has no idea what triggered the attack and may retaliate or not, depending on her personality and also the underlying hierarchy with the attacking cat. (There may be times when you need to rebuild the self-confidence and self-worth of the cat who has been attacked, which you can do at least in part by spending extra time playing with her.)

Watch your cat. Start paying attention to whether your cat is behaving oddly when she looks out any window, and then see what she is reacting to. If there is a stray or a neighbor's outdoor cat out there, you want to block your cat's visual access to her. You don't want your cat's redirected attacks to become a habit, so you have to be on alert as to what is triggering the attacks. Such aggression can also be redirected at people or at a family dog.

Potentially, an ongoing problem may result from these moments of frustrated rage, setting up a negative dynamic between two cats where the victim becomes terrified of the aggressor, who may have developed a habit of "beating up" on the victim cat. You may have to separate the cats into different areas of your house until the two are settled down again. At that point, allow the cats back together in the area where the attack happened so it can become a neutral zone.

General Tips for Dealing with Aggression

- ❐ See the vet to rule out possible underlying medical/physical causes.
- ❐ Learn your cat's individual body language and be alert for warning signs.
- ❐ Avoid situations that triggered the aggression previously.
- ❐ Spend time sitting in the room where the cat tree is or where it's most likely that fights might take place so you can be there to intervene.
- ❐ If you are there when aggression begins, turn it into a play session instead.
- ❐ Interrupt aggression with an unemotional reaction: Clap your hands or throw a shake can, but don't make it about your disapproval.
- ❐ Use the least amount of aversion technique (spray bottle, splashing a glass of water) needed to get the desired results.
- ❐ Create distinct "safety zones" where each cat has food, water and a litter box and can avoid the other cat(s).
- ❐ Consider reducing the number of cats you have in the household.
- ❐ Discuss drug therapy with your vet and, if appropriate, use the smallest possible dose for the shortest possible time, combined with behavior modification.

AGGRESSION TOWARD PEOPLE

It is not considered normal for cats to be aggressive toward people—especially if they aren't provoked. However, that doesn't take into consideration the fact that for many cats, too much affection *can* be a provocation—to which they respond by aggressively lashing out. This negative behavior from a cat is something that almost everyone has experienced at some time, when a cat they are touching turns on them unexpectedly. Since this is a common occurrence, you need to be prepared for it, understand why it happens and plan ways to avoid provoking it in your cat.

Keep in mind that cats are independent animals who, if they were living on their own without people, would rarely have physical contact with other cats or other animals (including the human animal). Cats are natural loners, and other than to mate or fight, they do not normally have physical contact—which means they will be in a heightened state when touched.

◆ Biting Aggression During Petting

Biting is the most common form of cat aggression toward people, and it is a kind of communication: Your cat is telling you to back off. However, it is pretty unpleasant to be petting your cat and suddenly receive a hard bite when you thought she was friendly and enjoying herself. Being bitten in this situation can be especially disturbing because it seems to come out of the blue: Your cat is next to you, purring as you pet her, when without warning she reaches back and bites you hard. Did you do something wrong? Is your cat suddenly "possessed"?

Cats bite because of a basic incompatibility between human and cat: We like to pet a whole lot longer than they like to be petted. There is a too-much-of-a-good-thing aspect of giving affection to any cat—the animal reaches a saturation point when she just can't take any more. The bite is meant to let you know when that moment has arrived. Cats are not naturally sociable animals—they are intended to live a solitary life, and we interfere with that by making them part of our "family." Although many cats adore physical affection, they aren't naturally programmed for it, so when we pour on the affection it seems to cause, in essence, a short circuit in their brains.

◆ Petting Aggression

Petting generally creates similar problems to the biting behavior discussed above, but there are some other twists and turns worth noting here.

Physical affection toward a cat that elicits an aggressive reaction from her is sometimes called the "petting and biting syndrome." It varies from cat to cat, but basically the cat attacks (with teeth and/or claws) the person who is caressing her. This can happen when a person has been stroking her only briefly, or in other cases after prolonged stroking, but the reaction is sudden and severe, with teeth, claws, and sometimes a powerful backward kick. Following such an attack, a cat will usually put some distance between herself and you, and then will settle in to groom herself as a way to calm herself down.

The "scratch and bite" response is something you may be creating in your cat if you stimulate her physically more than she can handle. If you pet a cat too intensely or for too long, she may have an eventual meltdown and turn on you because you have stimulated her past the point where she can process it or control herself. This can be true of a cat you have adopted who came from a situation where she was neglected and craving affection—but then when you give it to her she is overwhelmed. It's too much of a good thing, too "rich" for her system, and she lashes out without understanding why.

What Causes Petting Aggression? One theory is that the cat is in a kitten-like frame of mind when accepting your physical attentions and so she allows herself to be coddled. But then all of a sudden her brain switches gears to the adult, independent side of her personality, which rebels against being held or confined in any way, even against being stroked on your lap. And so she lashes out to assert her independence.

Another theory is that a cat's personality type has a lot to do with it. Whether or not a cat becomes hyperaroused from affectionate contact may be a reflection of her underlying nature. Think of cats as being generally divided into two personality types, warm and cool. There is rarely, if ever, an aggression problem with warm cats, who demonstrate a need to spend time with people and to experience physical affection from them. It is logical that when a warm cat's desire for contact is the greatest, she is highly unlikely to respond negatively to human affection. Conversely, cool cats may be all right with contact that they initiate and can terminate at will, but they may reject advances from a person who tries to pat or play with them.

You May Need a Check-up at the Vet. If you think your cat may be hurting somewhere—inside or out—you should let the vet have a look at her. If you realize that your cat bites you every time you touch a certain area, this could be a pain response and you need to get it checked out.

Watch Where You Are Petting. Some cats have especially sensitive zones on their bodies where they really dislike being touched. The neck, stomach and rump are common areas of supersensitivity, and touching them can result in a bite to tell you off.

One problem is misunderstanding a rollover with the belly exposed. Not knowing what your cat is communicating when she shows her belly—and mistakenly thinking she wants you to touch her stomach—can elicit a vicious response. When a cat rolls over and shows her belly, it may seem to you like a sign of submission or vulnerability and an invitation to rub her there. That is what it generally means in a dog and some cats. But, in some cases the "rollover self-defense" is a position cats take when fighting; a cat on the defensive will roll on her back with all claws exposed, as if to dare a more aggressive cat to "come and get me." If the aggressor does continue, the cat on her back will grab the standing cat and pull her down to bite her head, using her back claws to rake the advancing cat's belly. This defensive position, which is converted to an offensive purpose, is a great weapon for cats—but it's one that we can trigger if we try to play with a cat's supersoft belly fur when she is in this rollover position.

Which Cats Are More Prone to Biting? *Unneutered cats* can stand only limited petting, perhaps because if they have lived outdoors the only physical contact they have had with other cats has been during mating. Sexual intercourse is very unpleasant for a female cat: The male bites her on the back of the neck, holds her there, and then copulates with his barbed penis, causing significant pain (hence those chilling screams you hear from city cats in alleyways at night). (So much for the uninformed people who think that a female cat "wants" or "needs" to have a litter.)

Any cat who has lived outdoors and has had to deal with inter-cat physical issues will have a lower tolerance for being stroked. *Insecure cats* are also prone to cutting short a love-fest with a "don't-love-me-so-much bite."

Cats who roughhoused with their littermates or with people as kittens tend to continue that behavior into adulthood and transfer it to biting as a part of normal interaction.

Watch for Signs of Pending Aggression. A cat's body language will signal to you how she is feeling about your show of physical affection. Keep an eye on your cat's body language as you are petting her. If you see her tail whipping back and forth, especially the tip, or if she growls or makes a biting motion in the air, recognize these warning signs that she is about to lash out, and take your hands off her immediately. If her ears flatten back or you can feel her body become tense, the same thing applies—back off fast.

Bite Warning Signs

- A direct stare
- Eyes squinting, narrowed
- Ears point flat back against her head
- Growling
- Tail swishing, especially the tip
- Tense body position, rigid
- Leans away from you
- Mouthing your hand or arm

What to Do to Avoid Getting Hurt. If you see any of the reactions above—and definitely if you see two or more of them—stand up so that the cat falls gently to the floor. Do *not* try to lift her down while she's in a state of arousal or she may bite your hands. Leave the cat alone for a while until she has gathered herself and is her normal self again.

What to Do if You're Bitten. Even if you are startled or hurt, do not punish your cat in any way. Hitting a cat will just make her more likely to bite you the next time you initiate contact. Screaming or yelling at her will probably just make her more agitated. And do not pull away when she bites—that will hurt you much worse, tearing the skin. Instead, relax your hand or arm completely and do not resist or try to pull away when she bites. If your cat does bite you, leave the room and shut the door, to give her a kind of time-out.

TERRITORIAL/STATUS AGGRESSION

A dominant cat in a multi-cat home may show you some of the same aggressive behavior she displays to the other cats to maintain her position in the hierarchy. This behavior can include

blocking your path by lying across doorways, staring directly at you, mouthing (where she puts her teeth on you without applying pressure) or actually biting you when you try to lift her.

Ways to Avoid Triggering Biting

- Neuter your cat before she reaches maturity.
- Handle and groom your cat frequently and from a young age if possible.
- Groom with the same guidelines as for petting: Keep it short and sweet.
- Give your cat her own space—don't be constantly physical with her.
- Let your cat come to you for affection, not the other way around.
- Keep petting sessions really short—no more than 1 minute.
- Try to stop petting while the cat is still eager for more.
- Try giving a good treat (such as chicken) after a petting session.
- Try desensitization: no petting at all for a few days, then make it very brief when the cat initiates contact, and gradually increase the length of petting sessions.

Ways to Deal With a Cat's Aggression Toward People

- Learn when your cat tends to react aggressively so you can avoid those circumstances.
- Limit the amount of time you spend caressing or playing with your cat, and the number of times you engage her. If she does attack you, try to figure out how long you were caressing her before she lost it, and next time stop short of that amount of time.
- Leave your cat wanting more.
- Don't touch the sensitive spots on your cat—her belly and hind legs. A cat's back and head are the least sensitive areas, generally speaking.
- Be prepared with a squirt bottle or water pistol when you see your cat stalking you!
- Clap your hands and say "No!" sharply to interrupt what she was going to do to you.

Climbing on People and Drapes

CLIMBING ON PEOPLE

This is most often a kitten behavior, with little claws digging into your leg as the kitten tries to climb on you. There are at least three reasons this could be happening: She may want something from you, such as food or attention; she may have been taken away from her litter too young and not had the opportunity to learn appropriate social skills; or she may have a dominant personality that has not been held in check.

♦ How to Stop a Climbing Kitten

When she is still young you can cure her of this obnoxious habit by grasping her by the scruff of her neck and pulling her off you. Hold her up by the scruff and say "No!" firmly, then put her down and walk away, ignoring her.

♦ How to Stop a Climbing Cat

You cannot use the scruff-of-the-neck method with a grown cat because she may react aggressively and bite or scratch you. Usually only kittens will accept being lifted by the back of their necks because it was only recently that their mothers did the same thing. When an adult cat climbs on you, you want to make it a very unpleasant experience by saying "No!" and whirling around as fast as you can, or by jumping up and down to dislodge her. The cat will fall off or be thrown off by the force of your movements, and it will only take one or two of these energetic jostlings on your part to cure a cat of using you as a climbing post.

CLIMBING ON DRAPERIES

Many cats view draperies as their own exercise equipment. This climbing habit usually starts when they are kittens. A kitten may fling herself at the drapes, climb up to the top and then enjoy the view from up there. In fact, the primary reason that cats climb anything is because they like to be up high to look down on things. Also, if a kitten does not have enough stimulation in her environment to burn off her energy, then she's going to engage in escapades such as drape climbing.

Solving this problem requires a double-barreled technique: You want to make climbing unpleasant and you want to provide interesting alternatives. Cats climb draperies from the bottom up, so to deter drapery-launching you can tie a knot in the bottom of the drapes, or you could change to shorter drapes or to a different kind of window treatment entirely. You can also put double-sided tape such as Sticky Paws on the floor beneath the drapes, where your cat won't want to step on it. In addition, keep a squirt bottle of water in a strategic location in the room with drapes so that when your cat does try to launch herself and you're nearby, you can squirt her as you say "No!" This should make her jump off the drapes and she should be wet enough to not have any desire to get back up there.

The second part of the solution is to provide a really interesting alternative to drapery climbing, in the form of a nice, tall, sturdy cat tree (see "Furniture for Cats" in Chapter 4). If you have 2 cats, a fun tree will occupy them endlessly, and if you have only 1 cat, you will want to engage her in some interactive games using the tree (see "Toys and Playtime" also in Chapter 4) to burn off excess energy and engage her mind.

Crazy Kitten Behavior

There is nothing wrong with your wild, energetic kitten—she's just being a normal kitten, doing nutty things and propelling herself like a whirling dervish, only to collapse 5 minutes later and fall fast asleep. Many things that kittens naturally do can be maddening to people, but you need to understand that these are not "problems" to solve or behavior to be corrected; the kitten will outgrow them. Right now they are an important part of a kitten's development, so you don't even want to think in terms of stopping the behavior. But just because all kittens do these things doesn't mean you have to let your kitten run the show and take over your house. You may want to limit her to one room or only let her out of that room when you'll be around to supervise her.

There are two kinds of play behavior in kittens—social play with others and individual play with an object. Social play with other kittens happens primarily between 4 and 16 weeks of age and includes rolling around, biting, pouncing and pawing, along with chasing and stalking each other. In what is called "object play," a kitten will bite, chase, catch, bat and carry objects; this play resembles hunting behavior and gives her exercise. Social play with her littermates teaches a kitten to curb her teeth and claws and she learns how much bite pressure she can use. The chart below lists behaviors kittens use when playing with each other that can be frustrating and uncomfortable for people.

One rule to remember in guiding your kitten to grow up well is to praise her for doing what you want and to clap your hands to startle her for doing something you don't like. Other than that, ignore the bad and reward the good.

Annoying Kitten Play Behavior

- Biting people's hands
- Kicking at people who pet them on the belly
- Attacking the legs of people who pass them
- Getting into anything with an open door: closet, drawers, refrigerator, washing machine
- Attacking other older pets (who may have been sleeping at the time)

All this behavior is normal and healthy for a kitten—in fact, if your kitten does *not* exhibit all or most of these behaviors, you should have her checked out by your vet to make sure there's nothing physically wrong with her.

Tips for Playing with Your Kitten

- Keep her confined to rooms that are kitten-proofed.
- Get a good cat tree with scratching posts built in.
- Get great kitten toys and rotate them 2 at a time.
- Plan at least 2 interactive playtimes daily.
- Reward good behavior and ignore bad (or clap your hands to stop it).
- You can keep your kitten permanently occupied by getting a second kitten.

Chewing or Licking Odd Things

Cats have an acute sense of smell, and when something has an intriguing smell they want to taste it—even something as apparently unappealing as a plastic grocery bag. Plastic bags bring into the house with them the odor of where they have been or what they have had in them—which in the case of a grocery bag could be many different things. Even the bags themselves might have an intriguing odor, from the volatile chemicals that are used to make flexible plastics such as those shopping bags.

Some of the other items that cats lick and which seem less than appetizing to us are things such as photographic film, photos and electric cords. Cats' appetites for these things are quite individual because what appeals to one cat may hold no interest for others. Licking poses no danger, generally speaking, but obviously it would be a serious problem if a cat licked a plastic bag and then proceeded to eat it, since it would obstruct her digestive tract.

When a cat is chewing something bizarre such as a plastic bag there are a couple of things to determine whether this is a sign of an underlying problem. If the cat is simply curious about the plastic bag, she will check it out and then drop it, and that's acceptable curiosity. But if she constantly chews and sucks on many different items and for long periods of time, the question is whether this represents an obsessive-compulsive disorder. The other concern is whether the craving to chew and lick comes from a dietary craving for something missing in her food. Although researchers have not been able to identify a vitamin deficiency in cats who lick and chew (which might have been an explanation for the desire to taste strange items), you have nothing to lose by planting some kitty grass for her so she has something really satisfying and nutritious to nibble on instead.

Food Play

Some cats have peculiar habits at the table, so to speak: They will scratch all around their food bowl as if trying to hide or bury it. Although no one can be sure what triggers this behavior, there are a few possible answers.

SAVING FOR A RAINY DAY

Many large wild cats such as bobcats, lynxes and pumas will stash their food when there is a plentiful supply of prey around. These cats will also hide food when they have made a big kill they cannot finish eating. They will cover their extra with leaves, soil, grass or whatever might be available.

Domestic cats who stash their food this way have been observed digging it back up at a later time. This is a pretty interesting example of what is called "evolutionary adaptive behavior," whereby a domestic animal repeats instinctive habits based on needs of her ancestors that are no longer valid.

SHE DOESN'T LIKE THE FOOD

The other possible reason for trying to hide or cover food is that your cat is treating it like feces, covering it in the same way because she does not like it. If your cat has not had much appetite or shows little interest in the food you are serving, you had better consider changing the menu. There is a list of quality canned foods in Chapter 10.

Masturbation (by Neutered Males)

People are often perplexed to find their neutered male cat rigorously humping some inanimate object in their house—especially since they were probably not expecting any sexual behavior from him at all. But neutered cats can still get satisfaction from masturbating—this will be obvious if you ever see a male cat's glazed expression as he executes pelvic thrusts and then walks away to lick himself when he has finished. No matter how disconcerting this masturbation can be when it is performed on a piece of your clothing or a stuffed animal, it can be truly distressing when your cat acts out his sex drive on your leg or arm.

Some vets suggest that mounting and masturbating are seasonal behaviors that correspond to the times of year when females typically come into heat, which is late winter through summer. The more likely explanation is that your cat had a high sex drive before he was neutered, leaving him with the drive to have sex but the inability to execute. Whatever the trigger, if you want to keep this from happening, it may help to amuse and tire your cat so that he doesn't have a lot of pent-up energy to displace.

Scratching: The Biggest Problem

Nearly half of all people with cats claim they have a problem with their cats scratching their furniture and other belongings. What people often fail to realize is that scratching is as natural and important to a cat as breathing—it is part of her essence, her "cat-ness." So while scratching is a source of irritation and expense to people whose furniture is getting trashed, it's essential to understand that your cat does not scratch your furniture to spite you. She scratches because she *needs* to scratch, and she makes do with what she discovers in her environment—and once she has chosen a target for scratching, it becomes imbued with her scent and therefore is doubly appealing.

But since *all* cats scratch, you can't help but wonder why *all* people don't complain about it. How do the households that don't complain perceive their cats' scratching? How do they deal with it? Do they understand their cats' need to scratch and thus provide appropriately for it?

THE REASONS FOR SCRATCHING ARE NUMEROUS

The drive to scratch is inborn in a cat and it serves several functions, both physical and emotional. It is so important to understand these hard-wired instincts because it will make you more sympathetic and tolerant of your cat's strong need to scratch, and it will also help you provide the right kind of scratching post to meet this drive.

1. Scratching removes the dead outer sheath of a cat's claws by raking down the long, rough surface of her nail to reveal new growth beneath. The claws are formed in overlapping layers, like an onion, so "sharpening" her claws really means removing the outer layers to expose the new nail beneath it.

2. Scratching marks a cat's territory.

3. Scratching is an emotional outlet—a way to expel frustration, excitement or disappointment.

4. Scratching allows a cat to stretch out her spine, her back and shoulder muscles, especially upon awakening from a nap.

5. Many cats like to scratch while they are waiting for dinner and then again after they have eaten.

TEACHING A CAT TO USE THE POST

Note: When I refer to a "post" throughout this section, it can mean either a part of a top-notch cat tree (as described in the chapter on "stuff") or a free-standing post with all the ideal qualities described earlier.

Cats get attached to the territorial marker they create with their scratching, and the odor they leave on the scratched area brings them back to it. For this reason, you should be involved in choosing where that initial scratching takes place when your cat first arrives at your home so that she becomes attached to the wonderful cat tree and/or scratching post that you have provided for her. Even if you have already had your cat for some time before learning the importance of a desirable cat post, you are not out of luck. Later in this section I outline ways to retrain your cat to stay off your furniture and use the post you will have (perhaps belatedly) bought.

◆ Don't Hide the Post Somewhere Out of the Way
You want the post to be near the frequented area of your house so that your cat can jump right up and use it when the mood strikes her—first thing in the morning or after a nap, before or after meals, when she sees something outside the window (a bird, another cat) or when she has an interchange with another cat in the family that fires her up. If the post or cat tree is visible, your hope is that she will be more likely to go to it instead of to the chenille-covered chair that's in the same room.

◆ Do Not Put Your Cat's Paws on the Post
It's natural to think that if we just place our cat's paws on the post, she will get it—but this can actually backfire because cats do not like to be forced to do things, nor do they like to have their tender feet messed with. So rather than trying to force your cat's paws, you want to make the post fun and intriguing so that she'll want to use it on her own.

◆ Make It a Game

Dangle a lure toy right next to the post, so that when your cat reaches out for the lure she will feel the texture of the post. Scratch the post yourself with your nails or something that will create a raspy scratching sound, like a fork. Sometimes just hearing that noise will entice a cat to try it herself.

◆ If Your Cat Doesn't Have Any Interest in the Post

Although most cats like tall objects they can climb on, your cat may not be so inclined, which may be why a scratching post does not seem inviting to her. In this case, lay the post on its side and dangle the lure toy all around it so the cat has to touch the post. (If you have a wonderful cat tree with a scratching post built into it, it will be a bit more trouble to lay on its side, but this is simply a way to get your cat comfortable with the texture, after which it can go back to a normal upright position.) When your cat paws at the lure toy and jumps on the post, she will then discover the attractive texture and begin to give it a good digging with her claws.

◆ How to Tell If the Post Is in the Right Place

You'll know you have picked a good place for the post and that it is being used if you see your cat's crescent-shaped nail sheaths at the bottom of the post where she has shed them.

KITTENS AND SCRATCHING

◆ Place the Post in the Middle of Things

A kitten's post needs to be central to the area she inhabits so that she cannot miss it. This way, when the urge to scratch comes over her, the post is right there. If your kitten has the run of the whole house, then depending on the size of your house, you would do well to invest in at least one other post so that when she is off playing somewhere and the need to scratch or stretch comes over her, she'll have no trouble finding a post and then remembering what it's for. It's like potty training and having litter boxes readily visible and accessible: If a youngster has to search from room to room for what she needs, she may just do whatever she needs to do before she reaches that object. Make it easy for her and you'll build habits that should last a lifetime.

◆ Start a Kitten out Early with a Scratching Post

If you offer your kitten an appealing cat tree with one or more good scratching posts and she deposits her scent on it early on, then she is much less likely to scratch anywhere else. An ounce of prevention is so much easier than trying to break an ingrained habit once she has dug her nails into various pieces of furniture.

◆ Teaching a Kitten to Use a Post

This is actually pretty easy since kittens express a strong drive to get to the top of things, to climb to the highest possible point. You will notice this with a kitten who tries to climb on you or the

 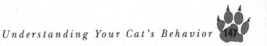

drapes—and this mountaineering phase *will* pass, by the way. But in the meantime, encourage her to climb that scratching post. Its main appeal at this stage may be as a tall object to climb, but it won't be long before your kitten's instinct to scratch will kick in, and by that time she'll already be bonded to the post. Teach your kitten to use the post just as you would a grown cat. With a kitten, you want to regularly create games around the scratching post to remind her that it exists and make it especially appealing.

MULTI-CAT HOMES AND SCRATCHING POSTS

If you have more than one cat, you will probably need more than one scratching post. One cat will often lay claim to a post as her own, and if she is a dominant or territorial cat, she may keep the other cat(s) off, forcing them to scratch in places you do not want. This does not always happen, but since it can happen without your necessarily being aware of it, it is better to be safe than sorry and have posts or cat trees in multiple locations.

RETRAINING A FURNITURE SCRATCHER

♦ Don't Try to Scare the Cat

Some people believe you should scare a cat away from furniture she has been scratching by doing things such as taping balloons to the furniture (they will supposedly pop if she accidentally scratches them) or squirting her with a water gun. This methodology is a poor one for a couple of reasons. First of all, given the fact that cats are naturally fearful creatures—along with the saying "once scared, twice shy"—it seems like a crummy idea to frighten your cat on purpose, because you will only succeed in making her afraid of you. The other reason that creating aversion through fear is a pointless pursuit is because the most effective way to train a cat (in other words, to convince her to do what you want by letting *her* make the decision) is to give her a substitute behavior. So ultimately, you don't want to stop her from scratching, especially since scratching is a vital part of her nature. Instead, you want her to scratch only in the places you are providing for that purpose. The same principle is used to teach a human baby not to touch certain things: You don't make a big drama about it or yank the object away. Instead, you "switch and bait," handing the baby something else that is safe and pleasurable so she doesn't even notice you've removed the forbidden object.

♦ Substitute Another Object to Scratch

Let's say your sofa or a favorite chair is the object the cat has been scratching. You need to make it suddenly unappealing. If she only scratches certain parts of the furniture, you can cover those areas with Sticky Paws, a product that is harmless to fabrics but makes the surface unappealing to cats. For a larger area, first cover the piece of furniture with a big sheet or drop cloth that you tuck in all around and tape down at the base (this is a temporary measure, not a redecorating tip). A bedsheet is best because you want the surface to be really smooth and therefore unappealing to your cat when she tries to dig her claws in as she did before. Now move that couch or chair out of the way to make enough room for a really appealing scratching post that will take its place, for a while anyway.

◆ Keep the Furniture Covered for a While

Ideally, your cat will saunter over to engage in some of her habitual furniture mauling, and lo and behold, her favorite piece of furniture is all covered up. But wait! In its place she finds a delightful cat tree and/or scratching post to use instead—much more satisfying for her claws and maybe even perfumed with catnip as a little bonus. Add to that a few little games played with you around the post, and chances are she will be thinking, "Who needs that old couch anyway?" Keep the furniture covered until your cat has been using the post regularly and is not making any attempts to get at the furniture under the covering.

◆ Gradually Move the Post to Its Permanent Spot

Although you can slowly shift the post to a place that's less intrusive for you, it should still remain in the general neighborhood as a visual reminder when the scratching urge comes over her.

SCRATCHING DOORWAYS OR ROOM ENTRANCES

Some cats scratch the entrance to rooms and especially the front door, to leave their mark—this behavior has nothing to do with sharpening their claws. For these scratchers, put a post next to the "incorrect" scratch target—the door trim, let's say—and cover that door jamb or doorway with Sticky Paws. Make sure that humans in the household know where this transparent tape has been applied so they do not lean on it and diminish its stickiness.

If there is no room near the doorway for a scratching post, you have two options. One is to use a sisal scratch pad that is designed to hang off doorknobs. The other is to get a flat scratch pad (or make one) with the back side of a piece of carpet and attach it to the wall next to the marked doorway.

HORIZONTAL SCRATCHERS

Some cats prefer to stretch out lengthwise rather than reaching up above themselves in order to scratch. If you see your cat scratching doormats, rugs, or the top of furniture, then you know she prefers flat, horizontal scratching surfaces and a tall post will not satisfy her.

There are two choices of flat scratching pads you can buy—a disposable cardboard scratcher that can be flipped over and used on both sides before you replace it (kittens love this one) or a flat pad covered with sisal rope made by the Felix Katnip company, which is similar to the first-rate cat tree they make. And of course you can make your own flat pad quite easily by covering a piece of wood with carpet, nailed down so that the backing is on the top.

Some cats like flat *and* high, so you can give them a smorgasbord of different angles and planes in their scratching equipment. There is even a wide scratch pad that is on an angle, which satisfies a cat who "goes both ways" in her choice of scratch object.

WHEN TO DISCARD AN OLD SCRATCHING POST

Never throw away an old post. A cat loves familiarity and never more so than with her post, which is rich with her marks and smells, and pleasing to her eye because she knows it so well—think of the proverbial man of the house and his attachment to the tattered old Barcalounger in front of the TV. A cat may not even accept a new replacement. You can re-cover the old post with sisal and upside-down carpeting, and/or get a new post that's as similar as possible and put it next to the old one. If the cat starts using the new post, great—you now have the option of dumping the old one. But because it's not alot of extra trouble to re-cover the old post, it seems wrong not to hold on to a beloved object.

PLASTIC NAIL CAPS

Given what we know about the importance of scratching to a cat, the idea of gluing plastic caps over her nails to put them out of the picture has to make you think twice. But Soft Paws (as the leading brand is called—see Chapter 4) may be a great solution for people who have tried behavior modification (a fancy word for all the scratching post advice above) unsuccessfully and are at their wit's end with their cat's destructiveness.

Soft Paws need to be applied by your vet, at the least the first time or two, since your cat may need to be restrained. Also, you can watch how your vet applies the permanent glue, although it isn't really permanent because the caps fall off within a month or two. Since nails are growing all the time, your vet will have to remove whichever caps have not fallen off (or been chewed off by your cat) and replace them with a fresh set. However, once applied, you can't just forget about the caps—you need to check them pretty much every day, since cats are clever at pulling them off. If even one or two come off, a cat can still do a lot of scratching damage with the nails that are now liberated.

These plastic nail covers can be neutral-colored, but they also come in a wide range of colors that look like nail polish. Claw caps are not an entirely comfortable prospect for your cat because she cannot fully retract her claws with the nails on. Also, it must cause her some psychic discomfort to be denied the natural pleasure of scratching and stretching. But if your only alternatives are to declaw the cat or give her away, then Soft Paws is a great resource.

Chapter 7

THE LITTER BOX
AND SPRAYING

Are you surprised that the lowly litter box merits an entire chapter? Would you be surprised to learn that probably the greatest complaint people have about cats is that they do not use the litter box consistently? Many thousands of cats are tossed out on the street every year—or relinquished to shelters where they will surely die—because they soil in the house instead of using the litter box that has been provided. But does anyone stop to wonder if the problem stems from a problem with the *litter box* and not the cat? Perhaps we may be at fault for the kind of box or litter we provide, where we put it and how often we scoop it.

For me, the biggest surprise of all was the discovery that people who share their homes with cats—newcomers or veterans—do not really have a clear picture of what makes for a successful litter box arrangement. I was abashed to learn that I was as ignorant as the next person about the right way to handle litter. I had no idea that there was more to it than putting down a litter pan, filling it up with litter, and taking out the icky bits when you saw them. In fact, there is much more to it, and those specifics are what make the difference between successful litter box compliance and a cat who is not dependable about where she relieves herself.

People who care for cats have never really been told the basic rules about how to set up a cat's litter box or care for it properly. Even the most cat-loving, lifelong multi-cat owner may not know some of the ways to make a cat comfortable in using a litter box. If you are a devoted cat person, you may be extremely observant, having spent a lifetime getting inside the mind of your kitties, empathizing with their habits and quirks. If that is the case, then you may have figured out some of the suggestions in this section on your own. But even so, you might read this chapter just to give yourself a pat (or a paw) on the back so you can see whether what you figured out by your own instincts and observation turns out to be part of generalized instructions.

Litter box avoidance is high on the list of problems people have with their cats—to such an extent that it is a common reason that people abandon their cats forever. So I'd say the topic definitely deserves some serious attention. You may be one of the lucky few whose cat never eliminates outside the box, but you are in the minority. Or it could be that you just don't know! Your cat may be eliminating randomly in places you haven't even thought to look: She could be making secret deposits under beds, in forgotten corners, or even on rugs in little-used rooms. However, many people know all too well that their cats have urinated on carpets, curtains, beds and furniture—but they have no idea how to turn things around. Once your cat goes down that road, watch out, because it is hard to make a U-turn back to the box. It's also a pretty rancid smell to come home to: Regardless of how efficiently you try to clean it, cat urine is a pungent and stubborn stain and odor. Having a cat who doesn't reliably use the litter box is only good if you're antisocial, since it's a sure way to discourage people from wanting to pay your home a visit.

Another litter box issue that this chapter will address is cats who get to the box but eliminate just outside it. This problem is usually easily fixed since it tends to be due to errors in the way that humans have prepared and tended the litter box. Nonetheless, I would like to share the sweet comment on this topic made by my dear friend Jill, who has been a lifelong shepherdess of an eclectic and ever-changing bunch of cats. She claimed never to have had litter box problems, but then again she has often lived in remote locations where it was safe for the cats to live partially outdoors. "You mean you've never even had the problem where they pee just *outside* the box?" I asked. "Oh, *that*," she replied gaily. "I just consider that an honest miss." I thought that was exceedingly generous of her—but for the rest of us who are not so forgiving, this chapter should help resolve our cats' litter box issues, "honest misses" or any other kind.

To begin with, the how and where of your cat's litter box is extremely important. The checklist below gives an overview of the individual topics you'll find in this chapter. To ensure a successful relationship between your cat and litter box, you will need to satisfy every one of the items below, which are covered in this chapter.

Checklist of Litter Box Issues and Equipment

- Correct size box (length and height)
- Number of boxes
- Proper location for boxes
- Appropriate litter type
- Correct scoop type and container or hook for it
- Container or bags for soiled litter
- Dust pan or hand vacuum for spilled litter
- Frequency of scooping
- Washing the box (frequency and "how to")
- Enzymatic cleaner for "misses" (honest or not!)

Why Cats Go Outside the Box

You're about to learn everything there is to know about litter boxes and why your cat may not be using hers consistently. This can be maddening, but leave no stone unturned: Something has caused your cat's aversion to the box and you need to get her back on track.

Reasons for Going "Outside the Box"

Rule out medical condition (see below)

Dirty box
Poor location of box
Box is covered or too small
Unappealing litter material
Sudden change in litter or box location
Too few boxes for number of cats
Unappealing cleanser used on box
Move to new house or renovation/construction
Disharmony with other pet(s)
Arrival of another cat in the household
Addition of new family member (spouse, stepchild, baby, grandmother, dog)
Senior cat issues (discomfort getting into box; senility)
General anxiety and fear
Change in food or feeding schedule
Change in owner's schedule; person home less
Previous bad litter box experience (attacked by another cat midstream)
Box is (or was) frighteningly close to a washing machine or furnace
Negative association: pain during urination due to urinary condition

RULE OUT MEDICAL REASONS

Before you knock yourself out trying to figure out which emotional or situational explanation might explain the problem, the first thing you want to do with a cat who urinates outside of the box is to get her to the vet for tests to rule out any physical illness. Cats are prone to problems with their urinary systems, which can cause unusual elimination behavior. If a cat has lower urinary tract disease problems, she could have urgency, burning, leaking, inability to void her bladder completely and/or pain—any of which could drive her away from the litter box. Once you have established her urinary health, you can aim at improving the litter box situation at your house.

Kinds of Litter Boxes

BASIC TYPES

◆ Covered Litter Boxes

This box is designed to please people—and it rarely appeals to cats. These are litter boxes that have a high (but often not high enough) lid that fits over the bottom litter pan, forming a tall, rectangular plastic box with an opening at one end for the cat to climb in. You may think that a covered box makes it more private and tranquil for a cat to relieve herself, but that is not looking at it from a cat's perspective. We humans prefer to do our "business" by shutting ourselves into a small room to use the toilet. We assume that a cat wants something like this, but it is not in a cat's nature to be hidden in a litter box with a cover. A cat does not want to have to crawl up into a small opening and down into the litter, which means she is trapped there while relieving herself. There is only one door in and she can't even see what's going on outside while she's doing her business, and fears being suddenly intruded upon.

Not only that, but for a larger cat, the walls of a covered litter box reduce the amount of space she has to turn and squat without pushing up against the sides of the box or the top; if she is a cat who doesn't squat low when relieving herself, the top of the box can interfere with her head, too. Plus, because people cannot constantly see the litter itself, it is too easy to forget to scoop it frequently enough. Because there is no air circulation, the stench and fumes of the trapped urine and feces burn your eyes when you finally lift off that roof. Just imagine what it's been like for the poor kitty, with a much more sensitive sense of smell—having to enter that *pissoir*! So there are cats who *will* use covered boxes, albeit not very comfortably, and other cats who will go just about anywhere else—only to be blamed for being a "bad cat" who doesn't use the "nice big box."

Covered boxes are popular because they work for *people*. They are people-friendly because you don't have to watch a cat doing her business, or smell it, or look at the remains of it, or even clean it up promptly, since out of sight is out of mind. As a bonus, there's less cleanup for you since litter can't spill over the side after an energetic digger covers her waste. But once you see it from a cat's point of view, you'll have to agree that these boxes are a good deal for you but a lousy one for the cat.

◆ Plastic Rectangular Boxes

Now that you know that covered boxes are for the birds, so to speak, you can toss out the lid and then see whether the bottom part of the box fits the size requirements below. It is not necessary to buy a designated litter box from a pet store—plastic storage boxes made by Sterilite make great litter boxes because they are inexpensive and come in many lengths and heights. Companies such as Rubbermaid also make lidded under-bed storage boxes that are low and rectangular, but it seems that the plastic used by Sterilite is easier to scrape off and clean.

◆ A Square Plastic Dish Pan

These can make excellent litter boxes because the sides are high, which keeps in kicked-up litter, and the square shape fits into smaller locations, like next to the toilet in the bathroom.

PICKING THE RIGHT SIZE BOX

There are two considerations when deciding the right size box for your cat: the height of the sides and the overall length.

✦ Height of the Sides

For an average cat: The sides of the box can be about 6 inches high, low enough to pop over easily, but high enough to contain the litter when the cat covers up after herself.

For kittens: The box should be small with low sides so it is easy for the little kitty to get up and over.

For seniors: The box should be large with low sides, because arthritis can make it difficult or painful to step over a side of any height.

For an energetic litter scratcher: Taller sides will keep more of the litter inside.

✦ Overall Length and Width of the Box

Length: A box should be twice as long as the cat herself—at an absolute minimum, 1½ times her length. You don't want your cat to step into a box barely her own length and have to scrunch herself smaller just to fit in there while doing her business.

Width: The box should be one cat-length wide, as wide as the cat is long.

Overall space inside: Make sure there is enough room for the cat to eliminate in a couple of areas and still have a clean place to put her paws. If the space is so small that a single deposit in the box uses up a lot of the litter surface, she will be discouraged from wanting to step back in there and use it again.

A WORD ABOUT PLASTIC LINERS

One thing all cat experts agree upon is that you should never line the litter box before putting in the litter. They all agree the plastic sheets sold as litter box liners are a disaster. The cat invariably tears a hole in that liner when scratching, and then urine flows underneath the liner and stays there in a smelly puddle where the litter does not reach to absorb it. Or else the liner wrinkles up just enough to trap wet litter and prevent you from scooping it; it breeds germs and a foul smell.

Some folks will advise you to put your entire clean litter box inside a tall kitchen garbage bag and fold it back over the box so that when it comes time to empty the litter you can simply pull the bag off and dump all the litter at the same time. The basic problems with plastic liners are magnified with the garbage bag because you have even more wrinkly plastic sheeting beneath the litter itself, meaning more chances for a cat to tear through it and let urine seep beneath, and more folds in the plastic where soiled litter can accumulate and smell. What makes the big garbage bag idea so poor is that on top of these issues, many cats will not even step into a litter box surrounded on all sides by the shiny wrinkled plastic garbage bag. (Maybe this is the reason a garbage bag as a liner makes cleanup easier: The cat won't step in the box, so she never soils it.)

Putting sheets of newspaper at the bottom of the litter pan, underneath the litter, is also a bad idea because the newspaper gets soggy and the contents of the box becomes a smelly, unscoopable mess.

The Litter That Goes in the Box

The kind of litter you provide can make a difference to some cats, and the litter itself is often at the heart of many litter box problems. Choosing a litter can be confusing, with new products coming out all the time, so how can you know which one is best for your cat? It's easy: Let your cat tell you. Experiment by trying a couple of brands to see which one your cat goes to most readily. Litter matters so much because unless your cat accepts the brand you are using, she will go elsewhere to do her business. This is called "litter box aversion" and it is a problem you want to avoid at all costs.

FLUSHABLE OR NOT?

Flushing litter into a septic tank can cause problems, so even litters that claim to be flushable probably should not be. Regardless of the claims made by the litter companies, it doesn't seem logical that your plumbing was intended to dispose of pounds and pounds of claylike sand. If you want to try flushable litter, first call your builder or the manufacturer of your toilet to see whether the plumbing or the septic system can handle cat litter. You might also want to contact your local building department to find out what the local rules are in your area before you flush that handle.

NO LITTLE DEODORIZING GRAINS PLEASE!

Most cats cannot stand the odor of the blue or green pellets in some brands of litter. Once again, that piney smell is something that might appeal to a person, but it has just the opposite effect on a cat. Even *people* don't like fake pine odor so much—like the sickeningly sweet pine smell in car air fresheners.

TWO CATEGORIES OF LITTER

Litter can be divided into two categories. Clay is the original, old-fashioned material that was once the only choice—and it can be further divided into "clumping" and "non-clumping."

Newer, non-clay litters have been developed and they are more efficient, absorbent and non-dusty.

✦ Clay Litters

The most common litter is made from Fuller's earth, which is a dry clay substance that forms lumps when wet. This conventional kind of litter is not biodegradable and it can be very dusty, which is unhealthy for the cat or anyone in the house. When you pour it into the litter box or when the cat scratches it, dust flies around. If you decide to use this kind of litter, then at least pick the least dusty one you can find.

Finer-Grained Clay Granules. This is a good choice for indoor cats, whose pads are not toughened up by outdoor living. Heavier-grained litter can actually be uncomfortable on tender feet, and if your cat seems reluctant to use this litter or is soiling outside the box, this could be why. Switching to a finer granule may solve the problem.

Clumping Versus Non-Clumping Clay Litter. *Clumping litters* are formulated to make clumps around moisture so that only the soiled litter has to be removed, and it comes out in a ball. This means quicker, more efficient cleanup for you, since you don't need to entirely empty the litter box and replace it as often. However, even with clumping litter, if lumps aren't scooped out quite regularly, the cat will scratch the clump the next time she uses the box, distributing the soiled material around the box.

Another problem with clumping litter is that it can stick to a cat's paws and then be tracked around. With this kind of litter, it is recommended that you empty the litter box entirely once a week and scrub it clean, especially if you have a multi-cat home. Clumping litter cannot be flushed. A small controversy about "clumping litter" is the unproven claim that it can be dangerous to cats because they could swallow some of it while grooming themselves, and the clumping litter could swell in the cat's stomach. No studies have ever been done about this, but the concern floats around, so if you have questions about possible jeopardy with clumping litters, you might want to discuss it with your vet to see if he has any opinion about this subject.

Non-clumping litter is more like gravel, which does not stick to paws as easily and get tracked around. However, all of it has to be thrown out each time you clean the litter box. And when you first pour it, it can be dusty, so avoid breathing in while you're pouring and keep the cat at a distance until the dust settles.

◆ Non-Clay Litters
When you see below how many alternatives there are to those big heavy bags of old-fashioned litter, you may be surprised.

Sand. This is very attractive to some cats, which can be a problem if your cat goes outdoors because she may get used to this feeling underfoot and decide to do her business in a children's sandbox or a neighbor's flowerbed. You can use sand in a litter box, but to avoid risk of disease it should be the sterilized kind of sand that pet shops carry for fish tanks; kittens, in particular, cannot risk any diseases.

Pelleted Wood Chips. This is a product made to be used as cat litter that is lighter, so it's easier to bring home and to empty out of the litter box. This quality can make it attractive to people with limited strength or physical problems that prevent them from lifting and carrying anything heavy.

Pine Litter. These plant-based litters are made from a natural pine, chemical-free base. Three popular brands are Feline Pine (800-749-7463), www.felinepine.com, ExquisiCat Pine Litter and Good Mews Cat Litter (888-877-7665), www.stutzmanenvironmental.com/goodmews.htm. This kind of litter is flushable and biodegradable, making cleanup a much less onerous job. Pine litter has a natural scent that reduces odor, it is not dusty and it does not stick to a cat's feet.

Wheat-Based Litter. Swheat Scoop Cat Litter (800-794-3287), www.swheatscoop.com, is made from wheat and is also biodegradable and flushable. It is unscented, and the wheat enzymes are apparently natural odor absorbers.

Corn-Based Litter. World's Best Cat Litter is made from whole-kernel corn. According to the manufacturer, it is biodegradable and flushable, even for septic systems. It is fragrance-free and has natural odor control qualities. Verbasis is another flushable, corn-based product with a lavender fragrance added—which may be a problem for cats who are very sensitive to odors.

Recycled Paper Litter. Cell-Sorb Plus Bedding & Litter and Yesterday's News are two of the litters made from recycled paper; they can be flushed and are biodegradable. Cell-Sorb Plus has natural gypsum added to it for additional odor control.

Crystals, Silica Gel and Pearls Litters. A few of the brands offering crystals (actually silica gel) that quickly absorb moisture and trap odor are Arm & Hammer Crystal Blend, EverClean Crystals, ExquisiCat Crystals, and Tidy Cat Crystals. The manufacturers of these dust-free, clumping litters suggest that you scoop the clumps daily but only need to throw out and replace the whole litter box contents once a month. Harvest Ventures Tracks-Less Litter Pearls are supposed to eliminate tracking because the pearls absorb moisture and trap the odor inside. The manufacturer claims this nonclumping product does not need daily scooping—instead, you replace the entire boxful once a month.

♦ **Specialty Litters**

Odorlockers Litter. Lower urinary tract infections can quickly become life-threatening blockages in a cat, but it's almost impossible to see one of the important clues to this problem, blood in the urine, because the amount of blood is so slight. Now there is a litter with blood-detecting granules, which come in a small packet that you stir into the litter. If the white granules come into contact with blood in the urine or stool, they turn blue—giving you an early warning so that you can contact your vet right away, before the condition escalates. The product is available at most pet stores, or visit their Web site, www.odorlockers.com, or call 888-223-8199 for more information.

Health Alert Blood Detection Granules. This product has the same function as the one above: as an early warning system for blood in the urine, which you might not otherwise see.

Dr. Elsey's Cat Attract Cat Litter. For cats or kittens just learning to use a litter box, this product has an herbal-blend scent that the manufacturer claims attracts cats to the box. This scoopable, dust-free litter can be used to train a kitten or to retrain a cat who has been soiling outside the box.

FINDING THE LITTER YOUR CAT PREFERS

The answer to which litter you choose will depend on your cat's personality, habits and preferences. You can tell that a litter is not to her liking by observing some of the signs below. The biggest clue is if your cat is not using the box; you can assume that if you have followed the guidelines in this chapter for litter box size, type and location, and if you are keeping it clean, then the cat must be avoiding the box because of the texture of the litter in it.

Telltale Signs of Litter Dislike

- She puts only two feet in the box, perching the other two on the edge.
- She shakes her feet when she steps out.
- She scratches and digs next to or near the box.
- She doesn't dig or cover the waste.
- She eliminates just outside the box.

✦ Conduct a Test

If you think that your cat may not like the texture of the litter you're using, but you aren't sure, you can do a simple test. Get a second litter box (the Sterilite storage boxes mentioned earlier are under $10) and put it side by side with the current box. If you are already using an old-fashioned clay litter, put one of the crystal or pine types in the second box next to it. You'll know the cat's preference based on whichever box she chooses.

✦ Try Different Sizes of Boxes While You're Testing

As long as you're experimenting with your cat's preferences in litter type, see if you can also narrow down which size or shape of box she prefers, too. The more elements you have in your favor with the litter box, the greater your chances are that your cat will reliably use it. After you find out which litter she likes best, put that litter into two different-shaped boxes (bigger or smaller, higher or lower sides) and see which one she chooses most often.

✦ Multi-Cat Home

If you have more than one cat, it is likely that your cats will have different litter preferences. Since you need to have multiple boxes anyway, who not fill them with different materials to cover all the bases?

CHANGING THE BRAND OF LITTER

If you decide to change the brand or type of litter your cat is using—either because you suspect she doesn't like the current one or because you are interested in trying one of the other materials—do it slowly. As with everything else in a cat's life, she will not like a sudden change in the texture beneath her paws; the difference in the feeling of the litter can be uncomfortable enough to make her step back out of the box she was just about to use. If the texture or odor of new litter is different, a cat can be confused enough to doubt whether this is her box and she should use it as she always has.

The safest way to make a change in litter is to gradually add the new material over the period of a week, slowly increasing the amount of the new kind while decreasing the previous brand.

Setting Up, Positioning, and Cleaning the Litter Box

The proper way to prepare and offer the litter box is one of the most neglected aspects of cat care. Most people tend to think that being generous with litter is good, that the cat likes the nice deep footing, and that a thicker layer will absorb more. (Certainly the manufacturers of litter would never want to change your mind on that.) But people have the incorrect idea that a box brimming with litter means they can go longer without having to scoop it. If you go for days without putting a scoop into that pile of stinky litter, your cat will go looking for a better option.

FILLING THE BOX

◆ Start with Baking Soda
Cat experts seem to agree about two elements of litter box preparation: using baking soda as an odor controller and using only a small amount of litter. There are litters marketed with baking soda already in them, but they may also have scents or other elements that you do not want, so it's better to manage the baking soda yourself. Before putting litter in the box, sprinkle baking soda generously on the bottom of the box; alternatively, you can mix it in with the litter. And you don't need to buy a boatload of small boxes of baking soda; large boxes of baking soda for laundry use are sold in supermarkets and big box stores.

◆ No More Than Two Inches of Litter
Perhaps the greatest revelation about successful litter box preparation is that all of the cat experts advocate using *very little litter* as the best way to ensure that a cat is committed to using her box. After a sprinkling of baking soda, you need to put as little as ½ *inch* of litter, and certainly no more than 2 inches in depth. This is quite a different picture than most peoples' litter boxes right now, which may have two or three times that much litter piled up in them. Reducing to this level of litter, you will find that it is easier for you to scoop and remove the soiled litter. This means odor will be less offensive and the more frequent cleaning will make the box more appealing to the cat.

◆ Remember This About the Smelliest Litter Boxes
The litter boxes that stink worst are the ones piled with pounds of litter. This means urine has been able to seep through all of it and there's not one grain that isn't contaminated with urine. So if your litter box stinks, the rule of thumb is to use *less* litter and scoop *more often*. It's as simple as that.

WHERE TO PUT THE LITTER BOX
It may seem logical to you to stash the litter box as far out of sight as possible—after all, it's not exactly pretty. But if it's too far out of sight, a younger or older cat may not remember exactly where it is or may not be able to hold it until she gets there.

♦ A Quiet Place

Cats like a secluded, quiet place to relieve themselves, so if your cat is physically well and able to get to an out-of-the-way box with no problem, then an infrequently used room is a good spot. Being out of the hubbub will give even a timid, insecure cat confidence to do her business.

♦ A Bathroom Near the Toilet

A bathroom makes sense because then all toilet functions in the multi-species family are happening in the same location. Many people put the litter box inside the bathtub because it seems easier to clean up spilled litter there than elsewhere.

Putting the box on the wall on the far side of the toilet is a quiet, out-of-the-way location, and a place that you will be aware of every time you use the bathroom. This gives you the easy opportunity to scoop the box since you are in there anyway. Because space is usually limited in a bathroom, you might want to use the square dishpan size of plastic box here, since it takes up the least room and also has those high sides that keep in the kicked-up litter.

♦ In Multiple Locations if You Have Multiple Cats

There is a pecking order among cats who cohabit, and that hierarchy can come into play when it comes to whose litter box is whose and who will be allowed to use it. Cats do "claim" a litter box as their own or make it clear that it is off-limits to a certain other cat. You can eliminate this intimidation as a source of distress and litter box avoidance by having litter boxes in various locations throughout the house—at the very least, one box on every floor of a multilevel house.

♦ Locations Not to Put the Litter Box

A cat is vulnerable when she is hunched down in a box of litter and she knows it, so she is less likely to feel comfortable and confident using a box in a high-traffic area of your house. If you have multiple cats, this is even more true because a cat always needs to feel she can escape in a pinch.

Near the Food or Water. Cats will not eat where they eliminate and vice versa; it's a rule they are born knowing. If you are pressed for space, then at a minimum the food and litter box must be on opposite ends of the room.

Near a Dog's Bed or Dog Door. A cat would never use a litter box with a dog staring right at her. (Wouldn't *you* want some privacy from another species?)

In a Room Where Children Play or Make a Commotion. Who wants to run the risk of being bombarded while trying to evacuate their bowels?

In a Heavily Trafficked Area. Avoid rooms that are used often, as well as busy routes between rooms for people or other pets. If there is too much activity near a litter box, or a perceived threat, a cat may not use the litter box at all.

 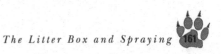

On Top of Carpeting. A cat may confuse the feel of the carpet with litter, or she may use the carpet as an alternative if she thinks the box isn't clean enough. If there is wall-to-wall carpeting where you want to put the box, place a sheet of clear, hard plastic (available at office stores or home improvement stores for use underneath desk chairs) underneath it.

In a Laundry Room. Many people think this is ideal because the floor is washable and not much else goes on in there, but many cats get startled by the sudden noises of a washer or dryer. Being frightened once, right when they are getting down to business, is a deterrent to using that box again for a more sensitive or fearful cat.

In a Basement Near a Furnace. The noise of the furnace coming to life can scare the dickens out of a cat, who would never dare awaken that monster again by going in the box. And the inaccessibility of the basement—having to negotiate a closed door or a flight of stairs on the way down—is often a deterrent, too, especially if it is cold, damp and dark.

In a Corner. A litter box in a corner can make a cat feel trapped because there is only one way in and out. This is especially true if you live with multiple cats, because a lower-ranking cat does not want to be cornered in the box if another cat should want to use it.

USING MORE THAN ONE LITTER BOX

There are several reasons that multiple boxes may be needed.

✦ Multiple Cats

The formula for determining how many litter boxes to put out is that there should be at least one box for each cat in the household plus an extra box "for the house." The boxes should be placed in various locations and should never be right near one another, in order to accommodate different personalities and habits of your cats. In addition, use a different kind of litter in at least one of the boxes so that if a cat has an aversion to the main litter, she will have the option to go somewhere more appealing to her.

✦ Your Cat Needs a Separate "Poop" Box

There are a few cats who will not do both functions in the same box. There is no consensus on what motivates this quirk, but the fact remains that it's a fastidiousness some cats have. You may find this out the hard way, but all it takes to cure your cat of eliminating outside the box is to give her a second litter box for solid waste. Don't put the boxes right next to each other or otherwise she might think it's just one big oversized box. Put them near each other, with some room between, and all will be right with her world now that you've figured this out.

✦ Your Aging Cat Is Having "Senior Moments"

Older cats can have dotty moments when they seem senile, just as older people can, and at times a senior cat may not quite remember where the litter box is or be able to get there in time. You can make life easier on both of you by putting out multiple boxes.

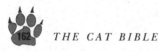

CLEANING THE LITTER: HOW TO DO IT AND HOW OFTEN

One thing is fairly certain: Most people don't scoop the litter often enough. Here are some general guidelines about box scooping and cleaning.

✦ What to Use to Scoop the Litter

Litter scoops with holes and slots of all sizes and materials are sold in pet stores, but they are actually not the optimal tool for good litter box cleaning. These scoops are intended to only remove the poop, which is not what causes the bad odor in litter boxes or makes them inhospitable to a cat. The real problem is urine, because it creates wet clumps of litter, which breed germs, smell bad and make a cat not want to set foot back in that box.

A big metal serving spoon with no holes or slits is the best scooper for completely removing those wet clumps of litter. This is why a shallow layer of litter is best: When the urine hits an inch or 2 of litter, it immediately forms a clump at the bottom of the box, rather than seeping and spreading throughout a pan thick with litter, where you can't remove all of it and it begins to smell. The big spoon will get the feces perfectly well, also.

Keep the metal spoon right next to the litter box, either hanging on a hook or nail or standing with the handle up in some sort of ceramic or other heavy container that won't tip over (an empty small clay flower pot, for example) with the head of the spoon hygienically out of the way, like a toilet brush.

✦ The Best Technique for Scooping

When you see a covered pile or a wet circle in the litter, tilt the box gently and slowly shake it so that all the dry litter falls away and you have just the wet clump waiting to be scooped with the spoon. Scrape up the wet lump, dispose of it as explained below, put the spoon scooper away, and shake the dry litter back so it forms an even layer in the pan. If you need to add a little more litter, now is the time. Keep a box of baking soda nearby to sprinkle below.

✦ How Often to Scoop

This varies to some degree with the type of litter material you've chosen, but in all cases the litter box should be cleaned at least once a day. Cats will be put off by a dirty box, which can actually drive them to eliminate elsewhere in the house or garden. Some aroma to the litter is necessary to reinforce the toilet function of the box. However, this association is especially important when teaching kittens (see below).

If humidity is high and you don't have air-conditioning, you will need to scoop more often because the litter won't dry out as well. If the box is in the bathroom where you take showers and steam up the room, the same high-humidity issues will apply.

If you have a job and are gone from home all day, it's a good idea to scoop the box first thing in the morning and then again when you get home in the evening. Those few seconds twice a day are all you need to keep a litter box fresh, odor-free and inviting to your cat. If you have multiple cats, you might want to scoop a third time at night so there's not so much cleanup to face in the morning.

 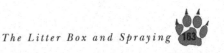

♦ What to Do with What You Scoop

Even if the litter box is in the bathroom, you cannot risk flushing the dirty litter down the toilet, no matter what promises the manufacturer makes on the bag. So you have a couple of viable options—the main point being that scooping out the litter should be a 5-second maneuver with no muss, no fuss.

Keep a Stash of Plastic Grocery Bags Right Near the Box. Each time you scoop, put the dirty litter directly into a bag and tie it off, then toss it in a small plastic garbage can you keep right next to the litter box. This allows you to keep the litter separate from the rest of the household garbage.

Keep a Plastic Container with Lid Next to the Box. Dispose of the dirty litter in the container. Once *that* container gets full, empty the contents into a plastic bag, tie it off, and toss it out.

CLEANING THE BOX ITSELF

If you use a sparing amount of litter and scoop the box frequently, you will only need to actually wash the whole box twice a month. "*Only* twice?" you say, as though it's a joke—because maybe you've never heard of having to wash the box at all, have you? You probably think that taking out the dirty litter is a big enough sacrifice—especially now that you've found out it should be done twice a day—and now I'm browbeating you about going a step further? Yup, that's correct: You *do* have to wash out the litter box, no doubt about that. You need to periodically clean off the residue of urine and feces that accumulates on the plastic—but it's not such a terrible task. All you need is a good quick swish with a bleach cleanser and hot water to banish any lingering odors and keep the box appealing to the cat and inoffensive to you, too.

♦ First Empty the Box

Dump out the litter remaining at the bottom of the box. If you have trouble lifting the box, an easy way to empty it is to lift one end and slip the opening of a plastic garbage bag (a tall kitchen bag will work, or an outdoor black garbage bag for a larger box). Then you can lift the other end of the box and slowly pour the leftover litter into the bag for disposal. However, the box should not be especially heavy no matter what size it is if you are following the suggestion of generally keeping much less litter in the box, only an inch or 2.

♦ Rinse the Box with Hot Water and Use Cleanser

Use your scooping spoon to scrape off anything that might be stuck, which also rinses off the spoon at the same time. The more hot water and cleanser, the better, to get off dirt and bacteria you can't see. If you want to use a long-handled scrub brush to clean the inside of the box, that's great; just make sure it is dedicated only to this task to avoid spreading the bacteria associated with a litter box.

♦ Use a Spray Chlorine Cleanser

Any commercial bathroom cleanser that has chlorine in it will do, or you can save money and make your own disinfectant spray. Fill a plastic spray bottle with a solution of 20 parts water to

1 part chlorine bleach. Make sure you squirt plenty of this solution into the box and on the scooping spoon, too.

◆ Rinse, Rinse, Rinse

You don't want *any* residue from the cleanser on the box because the odor could put off your cat and keep her from using the box. Chlorine is a very strong odor and cats have a highly sensitive sense of smell, so you want no chemical smell of any kind. You also don't want any chlorine residue on the box because a cat may lick her feet after going in there and ingest the chlorine.

Young Kittens and Litter

Even if you adopt a young kitten—between 6 and 16 weeks old—she will rarely have a problem using a litter box or tray. She doesn't need a mother to show her how to use a litter box; she just needs to be placed in it and the litter itself will inspire her to use it. Kittens naturally exhibit many of the behaviors associated with using a litter box; for example, scratching in loose material comes naturally to cats. A youngster will accept a litter box as her elimination destination, as long as you introduce her to it so that she knows where it is and she can get into it easily. If the kitty is really small, this may mean beginning with a small plastic storage container as a first litter box and then getting a larger one as the kitten grows. See information on the right size box for kittens earlier in this chapter.

If a kitten had a good mother who carried her away from the family nest to eliminate, the kitten will have learned from birth not to soil her sleeping area. For kittens who grow up in the same household as their mother, they also learn by watching their mother use the litter box, and they learn to associate it with that smell when watching her relieve herself. By the time a kitten reaches 6 weeks of age (which is when kittens naturally are weaned), she will be reliably using a litter box.

No matter where your kitten grew up, when a youngster joins your household you can get her on the right track simply by putting her in the litter pan before and after any significant activity: when she wakes up, after she's eaten and after she's been playing. It shouldn't take any time at all for her to make the association with a litter box and begin relieving herself in it.

GIVE HER MULTIPLE BOXES

Make sure you place several litter boxes in easily accessible locations. The more visible a box is, the greater the chance a kitty will make use of it. A young kitten can get distracted on the way to a litter box, she may not have the concept 100 percent locked in her brain yet or she may not be able to "hold it" all the way to a far-off box.

LEAVE A LITTLE ODOR IN THE BOX

Don't completely clean out the litter box while a kitten is young: She needs a little bit of smell from the previous use to keep her association with the box as her place to relieve herself. Leave a tiny bit of soiled litter behind when scooping, and in the early weeks you can forgo the bleach cleaning of the box. However, you also want to keep that litter box scooped frequently, at least twice a day, because if it becomes excessively soiled you can interfere with a kitten's bonding to the litter box.

Senior Cats and Litter Issues

Once a cat passes the age of 14 years you want to offer her as many litter boxes as possible to help ensure that she won't relieve herself anywhere else. An older cat may wet outside the box for several reasons, but with multiple boxes you give her more dignity by improving the odds that she'll remember where a box is and reach one in time to do her business. In this sense, there is a similarity between an older cat's needs and a young kitten's for litter boxes that are visible and easily accessible.

CONFUSION

An old-timer may be confused, especially upon awakening. She may have a dazed, senile kind of forgetfulness about where that one box is. For this reason, multiple boxes are recommended as a cat gets old and not quite so sharp.

WEAKNESS

An aging cat may be weak and not have the strength or motivation to make it all the way to a distant box.

ARTHRITIS

She may have painful arthritis that slows her down, preventing her from being able to reach a faraway box in time. A cat with arthritis may also have trouble getting up into the same litter box she has always used, so you may need to cut a lower entryway for her on one end of the box—or get a box with lower sides. The same physical limitations may make it hard for her to squat and aim correctly once she's inside the box.

Have You Ever Wondered About Toilet Training?

How would you feel if you never had to deal with a litter box again? You've been a trouper and read through this harrowing and exhausting section on the what, where and how of your cat's elimination needs, and I'll bet you thought at least once, "How come I can't just toilet-train the darn cat?" Well, apparently you can—at least according to an author who has written a whole book about it.

I've never tried this, and I only know one person who has—my editor, Jessica Sindler, who tried toilet-training the family cat, Chloe, when she was in sixth grade. It turned out that particular kitty could not give up the natural urge to dig, so when she got to the stage in the training where you completely remove the litter, Chloe just went on the floor! However, using the toilet has worked for some cats, so if you're game, there's a book called *How to Toilet-Train Your Cat: 21 Days to a Litter-Free Home,* by Paul Kunkel, that includes happy testimonials from cat owners who say it worked for them. I can't personally verify its methods, but I figure anyone who has 21 days to spare and a willing cat might just make fools of all of us hunched over the litter boxes we are slaves to.

Spraying: What's That All About, Anyway?

Spraying urine, also called marking, is a form of scent communication, in which a cat leaves scent markers to make a point, so to speak. Leaving a personal "message" through her scent glands or urine is one of the three basic ways that a cat expresses herself. The other ways that a cat can get her ideas across are vocalizing by using different "meow sounds," or using body language.

There are two kinds of scent markers. Pheromones are the "happy" marker. Pheromones come from the scent glands on her paws, head and cheeks, and a cat uses them to mark in a positive way. These glandular secretions are chemicals that provide unique information about each cat and are part of a complex communication system among cats. In the wild, pheromones serve many purposes, such as identifying members of a colony, marking territory, making sexual overtures, seeking information about unknown cats in the vicinity and testing the tendency toward aggression of other cats.

Urine is the other scent marker. Spraying urine is a natural behavior for a cat. She does it to mark territory, usually when she feels threatened or stressed. No matter how you feel about it, urine marking is not something that we should judge as being "bad." Spraying is a normal, natural form of communicating for a cat. Do not make the mistake of projecting human emotions or motivations onto her; your cat isn't doing this to be spiteful or get back at you. Spraying is a central part of the social structure cats use to communicate and is a normal feline reaction to specific situations. Unfortunately, it fits in really poorly with sharing a home with humans.

HOW SCENT MARKING IS DONE

◆ Marking with the Friendly Pheromones
A cat uses the glands in her cheeks to mark familiar territory that she considers her world. She rubs against objects in a familiar territory, leaving secretions of the scent glands on her face as a positive "message." It is a sign that she feels confident and secure. Depositing pheromones by rubbing her face along cabinets, against doorways, on chair and table legs—even on the people in her life—is a self-reassuring behavior that also has a calming effect on her.

Cats have scent glands on their paws, too, which is one of the reasons they scratch. Reaching up against a tree or other vertical landmark is an effective way to leave a calling card for other cats because it can be done at nose level, along with scratch marks to call attention to it. When you see dogs and cats studying marked areas with their noses, think of it as reading the Post-it Notes left by previous passers-by.

 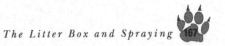

✦ Marking with Urine

Cats mark with urine for the opposite reason they mark with facial pheromones. Urine is used because the cat is threatened or stressed, usually in a multi-cat environment. Both males and females spray, generally around issues of territory. A high-ranking cat will spray in more than one location in the house to show how large her territory is and how important she is; a cat may spray when entering a new territory to announce her arrival and as a warning to others not to mess with her; an outdoor cat will often spray around the entire perimeter of her perceived domain.

✦ How the Cat Sprays

Urine spraying is a highly ritualized behavior. The first thing a cat will do is back up to the targeted object. Her tail quivers and twitches. She will knead the ground with her front paws or tread with her back paws. She may close her eyes and get an expression on her face that is almost like grinning. And then she will send a spray of urine out behind her and up against the chosen object. She will purposely spray at about nose height for another cat—the point of putting it precisely at that level is so that any passing cat cannot miss her mark.

✦ How Do Other Cats Get the Message?

Cats have a highly developed organ in the roof of their mouths called the *vomeronasal organ,* which allows them to detect social odors and sort them out. Sometimes when you watch a cat sniffing an object you can tell that it has been marked by another cat because you will see a sort of smiling or grimacing expression as the cat sniffs. This is referred to as the Flehmen reaction—the lips curl back as the cat sucks in air with the scent in it, running it past that special vomeronasal organ.

WHY DO CATS SCENT-MARK?

Cats will rub their foreheads and cheeks—and their tails, too—on other cats they live with and on their human companions. This is a form of social communication that connects the cats with each other, even though cats are not thought to be social, group-oriented creatures. Females who live in a multi-cat environment often rub each other as a greeting. Subordinate cats rub against the dominant cat in their group. Kittens rub against their mothers, which is a social survival behavior: It marks a kitten as belonging to her mother in case she gets separated, and it serve as reinforcement with a mother who might not be as committed to mothering as she should be.

In the wild, the only mutual rubbing that takes place is done by mating pairs of cats and by cubs living in the family group during the first few months. Domestic cats today, by contrast, rub against all of those they live with—cats, dogs, people—to create a group scent that connects them; it may also serve to automatically exclude any creature *not* wearing the perfume of the day. This is curious, however, since cats are decidedly not group animals by nature and this "group hug" doesn't really fit with their original instincts—which just goes to show how basic behaviors can evolve as the lifestyle of an animal changes over the years.

While we assume that cats rub on familiar cats and on people to put their own odor mark on them, some observers of cats wonder if the reason for rubbing against another cat may be different in some cases. What if a lower-ranking cat rubs not to anoint a more important cat with her own personal perfume but to receive the other animal's odor? In a group of cats with a hierarchy, if a lower-ranking cat acquires the odor of the top cat, it sends a message to any other group member that the lowlier cat is part of the in-crowd. It also is a reminder to the high-ranking cat that this cat may be lower on the social scale but has been "preapproved"—sort of like the stamp people get on their hand at the door once they have gained admission to an event.

SPRAYING TO COMMUNICATE

◆ Spraying Is a Different Issue from Peeing Outside the Box

Cats who urinate in places other than the litter box do so in a different way than cats who spray as a communication tool. A cat who urinates for any of the litter box avoidance issues discussed in the first part of this chapter just squats down and makes a puddle on a flat surface. This is entirely different from a cat who sprays to make a point. When a cat sprays, it is usually on an upright object; the cat remains standing and sprays the urine vertically behind her, which leaves a stream of urine rather than a pool of it.

◆ Spraying as "Feline Graffiti"

A good way to understand urine marking is to compare it to spray-painting graffiti on walls and subway cars, often done in neighborhoods where there are different gangs. Graffiti is used as a taunt to those who are in a rival group, and it is also a way to mark boundaries and claim territory.

◆ "Middening," or Leaving Feces

If you thought using urine as a way to communicate was disgusting, what do you think about leaving a solid marker? When a cat deposits feces to get a point across, it is called *middening*. In a free-roaming situation, this is something a confident cat might do: leave feces right on a boundary or path as a visual and olfactory marker. A cat living freely outdoors would usually do this in conjunction with spraying on the trees or bushes in the area.

WHY A CAT SPRAYS

Cats always have a reason for spraying, and once you know how to decipher the clues you may be able to alleviate the cause. Begin by collecting clues. Where is the cat spraying? When is it occurring? If the spray is underneath a window or on the wall across from it, it's possible that there is a strange cat appearing outside that window and causing your cat to make a territorial statement. Or if your cat is allowed outdoors and encounters a strange cat out there, upon her return your cat may feel compelled to spray her own territory for good measure.

If you've added a new cat to the household, that always shakes up the status quo; a resident cat is going to react, and it may be through spraying doorways or pathways.

Has a new baby or an older relative joined the household? Cats don't like change of any kind, and a shift in the family makeup can inspire spraying.

Have you bought new furniture, or even rearranged the furniture you have? A cat may feel inspired to mark anything new in her kingdom—and if the furniture has an unfamiliar smell, that is a good reason to spray it, too.

Have you been away from home, perhaps traveling? When you return, watch out where you put your suitcase, your briefcase or even your overcoat: Anything that brings new and strange odors into the house is fair game because a cat may feel compelled to spray it as an intrusive, alien arrival.

Spraying can be triggered both by objects that the cat "needs" to cover with her odor or as a generalized stress reaction to household change. One thing seems to be true, unfortunately: Almost anything and everything can be an inspiration for a cat to spray.

Reasons a Cat Might Spray

- Sighting of a strange cat outside
- Hierarchy issues with another cat or a dog
- Too many cats sharing a house
- Loss of a cat in a multi-cat household
- Loss of a human in the house—death, divorce, kid going to college
- Separation anxiety if bonded too closely to you
- New family member or pet arrives
- Reaching sexual maturity in unneutered males
- The cat's natural inclination—personality
- Scent of unknown cat on you or your clothing
- Move to new house or renovation
- Unknown human visitors
- Change in significant human's schedule
- Arrival of new furniture or other large objects

SPRAYING OR MARKING AS A PERSONAL MESSAGE TO YOU

◆ The Cat Marks on Your Bed

It is really upsetting to come home and find that your cat has urinated (or worse) on your bed. People often misunderstand the reason that a cat would choose their bed, so they assign evil motives to the cat's choice when what is actually motivating a cat is pure instinct. Your bed is a prime target because you lie on it for hours, building up a fragrant scent. Your cat does not anoint your bed to get back at you or to display anger. There are cat behaviorists who have come up with a surprising new theory about why cats urinate on their people's bed when the people are unavailable (either out of the house or fast asleep). Relieving herself on your bed actually feeds an emotional need for your cat. Apparently, the chemicals in urine seem to comfort a cat while she waits for her person. A cat who does this may also be looking for attention or food, but whichever the case, the odor of the urine appears to have a soothing quality. Fortunately, there is an easy fix for this particular problem: Shut your bedroom door when you are out or asleep. I just hope you figure out the logistics of this problem before the cat urinates all the way through to your mattress—because then you have a serious cleanup challenge on your hands.

◆ Separation Anxiety in Lonely Cats

A solitary cat who gets too closely bonded to you can become anxious when you leave her alone. However, cats do not exhibit what we might think of as classic signs of separation anxiety: They won't destroy objects in the house or take out their frustration on doors or other parts of the house itself. Instead, a lonely cat will stop eating, groom herself excessively or mark with urine. A cat suffering from separation anxiety not only will miss the box but will especially mark the personal property (such as the bed) of the person she is so closely bonded to.

FINDING THE URINE AND CLEANING IT UP

◆ Buy a Black Light

A black light, which emits ultraviolet light, is a good tool for any cat owner to have because it allows you to look all over your house for signs that a cat has been marking or eliminating in the wrong places. And you now know how to tell the difference between litter box avoidance, which is urinating on the floor, and spraying, which is done vertically against an upright surface. Nature's Miracle, the company that makes a urine stain remover, also makes a good black light (available at most pet stores) which will light up any urine stains in your house if you turn the other lights off and go on a hunt.

◆ Look Absolutely Everywhere for Sprayed Areas

To use the black light you have to remove all other light sources and then turn on the black light. Some areas where a cat has urinated are visible and smellable; others are well hidden and may be old and dried. But you have to clean and neutralize every single place any cat has ever urinated in your house to have any chance of putting an end to it.

◆ Don't Freak Out if the Black Light Shows Spots Everywhere

Black lights illuminate urine, but they also show the presence of any bodily fluids—so anywhere a cat had a bowel movement or threw up or even coughed up a hairball will shine under the black light. You're better off cleaning all of it, regardless of what it was, but don't just assume that everything you see is urine. The chart below gives you some ideas of locations that need to be investigated. I know, this probably isn't what you signed on for when you fell in love with that white kitty with the green eyes . . . but nonetheless, here we are.

The Litter Box and Spraying

Places to Check for Urine Stains

- Closets
- Under beds
- Furniture (front, back and sides) and the wall behind it
- Shoes and clothes (at bottom of closets)
- Doormats
- Baseboards and walls
- Doorways
- Behind doors
- Litter box areas (around the box, walls, entry to room)

CLEANUP TECHNIQUES

◆ Clean as You Find It or Mark It for Later

As you go around your house with the black light, if you don't find too many stains, you may want to treat them right then and there. However, if there are many stains, or if you'd rather check them all and then go back and attack them later, you can use the cleaning regimen below. Start by marking any stain that the black light illuminates by using masking tape on the outline of the stain. Use the tape like one of those television crime-scene body outlines, marking the exact boundaries of the stain as the black light shows it to you. Masking tape will stick anywhere and doesn't leave a mark when you take it off.

◆ Don't Use Normal Household Cleaners

Regular household cleaners or carpet cleaners will cover up the smell of the urine, but they won't mask the aroma enough for the sensitive nose of a cat. Also, some cleaners have ammonia in them, which is similar to the odor of urine and so should always be avoided.

◆ Urine-Neutralizing Products and How to Use Them

Buy a gallon container of Nature's Miracle, Simple Solution, X-O or any cleaning product that is enzymatic and will neutralize the odor, not just clean or mask it. You're going to need a large amount of this stuff to give all the stains a good going-over, so it's more economical to get the jumbo size and then transfer it into a manageable spray bottle. If urine has soaked through to the carpet padding or the floor below, keep in mind that it all needs to be treated. You have to remove all traces of urine and its odor or the cat will want to go back to that location for a repeat performance.

Follow instructions on the bottle, but generally these products require that you blot up as much of the urine as possible with paper towels and then spray liberally with the enzymatic cleaner. Leave the product on for about 5 minutes, then blot up the excess cleaner with paper towels or rags. Do not rub or you'll be working the urine deeper into the carpet fibers. Leave layers of paper toweling over the stain with a weight on top to soak up the remaining fluid, or set up a small fan to blow it dry.

◆ Figure Out Which Cat Is Spraying

To solve spraying in a multi-cat home, you need to figure out which cat is initiating the spraying. Unless you actually see the cat back up and spray something, there is a way you can "light up" an individual cat's urine to identify it as hers. First investigate the house with the black light so you can see what normal urine looks like. Then ask your veterinarian for some fluorescein capsules. These are filled with a nontoxic dye used for eye exams. Give this capsule to the cat you most suspect of being the sprayer and the dye will show up later in her urine. Turn on the black light and the fluorescein-stained urine will jump out at you. If you don't find any traces of lit-up urine, that means your suspect was *not* the sprayer. Now give a capsule to the next most likely culprit and so on, until you identify the perpetrator.

WAYS TO STOP SPRAYING

There are several things you can do right off the bat to lower the likelihood of spraying in your house. Your overall goal is to create a calmer, more secure environment for your cat so she doesn't have stress and anxiety. After you read this section, you will get to the real cure for the nightmare of spraying: a product called Comfort Zone Feliway. The philosophy behind using this product is based on the fact that cats do not urine-mark where they facially rub.

◆ Neuter and Spay All Cats

I hope this would already be the case, but if for some reason you have unneutered males or unspayed females, please make an appointment at the vet to correct that right away.

◆ Have Same-Sex Cats Only

There are studies that show that an all-male cat population will spray much less if there are no females around to inspire their territorial marking. Female cats will spray equally whichever the sex of their housemate cat.

◆ Introduce Environmental Change Very Slowly

Any physical changes to a cat's world can trigger anxiety-related marking. If you are going to get new furniture, consider getting one piece at a time. You can even cover the furniture with a cloth that you have first rubbed all over your cat (to pick up her scent) or sprayed with Comfort Zone Feliway (see below).

◆ Introduce New Household Members Slowly

Before bringing home a new baby, first "break the news" to your cat's olfactory system by bringing home items of clothing that the baby has already worn. Put a piece of the infant's unwashed clothing wherever your cat hangs out—on her climbing tree, on her bed—to get her accustomed to the baby's smell ahead of time so his actual arrival isn't such a shock.

◆ Reduce Conflict in a Multi-Cat Household

In a group that lives together, a lot of marking and spraying is directed at other cats. By reducing any potential issues over territory, food resources and litter boxes, you will lessen the need to spray and stake a claim. Have one litter box for each of your cats, plus one "for the house"; multiple food and water bowls help as well, all as far apart as possible.

◆ Close Curtains on Windows Where Strange Cats Walk Past

This is a pretty logical fix: If your cat cannot see another cat strolling past, she won't have the need to mark in response to it.

◆ Change the Cat's Association with the Area

Cats will not eliminate or spray where they eat or where they have marked with their "happy pheromones" from their facial glands, and you can make this work in your favor. This simple fix can be the most important thing you can do. Take your cat's food bowl and put it right over an area where she has been spraying (after you do the whole cleanup routine on it, obviously).

◆ Spray with Feliway

Read the section below to understand how spraying with this remarkable substance can help make your cat a happy camper and take her off the "naughty list" at the same time.

COMFORT ZONE FELIWAY

Comfort Zone Feliway is a spray that contains synthetic feline facial pheromones, meaning that some enterprising scientist has found a way to bottle the calming, happy-making chemical that cats produce when they contentedly rub their facial glands on surfaces in their environment. That smell relaxes a cat and puts her in a Zen-like state of mind; best of all, she would not dream of spraying where she smells facial pheromones.

◆ Each Cat Thinks Feliway Is Her Very Own Pheromones

The beauty of this product is that it can fool even that supersensitive kitty nose into thinking that she herself rubbed on those surfaces where she encounters Feliway. If a cat believes that she already facially rubbed on a location, she gets an immediate positive association and assumes it's a safe, relaxing place. By using this product, you can tap into your cat's instinctual system and turn a location with negative association into a positive, nurturing space.

Use Feliway along with behavioral modification techniques such as moving your cat's dinner dish to the area she soiled. You can also engage in play sessions with your cat in an area she soiled, which helps to transform its association for her.

◆ How to Use Feliway

First Clean the Area with Plain Water. The chemicals in Feliway can be neutralized by detergent or a specialized cleaning product, so just wash down the area with water and dry it.

Spray One Squirt of Feliway Twice a Day Over the Area the Cat Previously Sprayed. Since natural cat pheromones fade after 24 hours, by spraying Feliway twice a day you keep a consistently high level of pheromones in the air.

Don't Limit the Feliway to Sprayed Areas. Spray prominent objects in the areas where your cat spends the most time—and especially in those areas where you may have noticed she is not really relaxed.

Use Only a Quick Little Spray on Each Spot. Do not overspray.

Spray Twice a Day for 30 Days. The product is designed to flood the objects and environment with a positive association. After 30 days, evaluate your cat's response and decide whether to continue spraying twice a day for another 30 days or cut down to once a day. Your eventual goal should be to reduce to spraying the areas every other day and then finally 2 or 3 times a week. Don't rush it; slow and steady wins the race, and reordering your cat's perception and changing habits takes time.

Spray at a Cat's Nose Height. Direct the spray 8 inches up from the ground and about 4 inches away from the object.

Spray Table Legs, Chair Legs, the Corners of Furniture, and Doorways. Any nose-height vertical object should be given the Feliway treatment.

Create a Network of Calming Pheromones. Your goal is to spin a web of positive association over the cat so that if she feels anxious or agitated when she first enters a room and has the desire to spray, she will have changed her mind by the time she walks by all the vertical areas that smell of Feliway.

Comfort Zone Feliway also comes as a plug-in diffuser. The plug-in is especially useful if the spray-marked area is all in one room, but it can work wonders in any area where a cat has been feeling skittish or insecure.

MEDICATIONS FOR URINE MARKING

If you have tried every suggestion in this section and your cat is still spraying and marking, there is something else you can try: antidepressant medication. Urine marking is one of the conditions in cats where doctors often feel that the best thing to do is try pharmacological treatment. Studies show a 90 to 100 percent improvement in anxiety-driven urine marking in cats who took such medication. But of course the real solution is to address that underlying loneliness and boredom by giving the cat daily interactive play sessions. Relieve the cat's situation by finding a friend or a pet sitter who will come in during the day when you are at work.

Since one of the underlying causes for spraying is thought to be stress, veterinarians have also tried antianxiety drugs with varying degrees of success. When first taken, drugs such as diazepam and buspirone significantly reduce spraying in up to 75 percent of cats. However, when the cats are taken off the drugs, they go right back to spraying.

More recent studies have shown that fluoxetine and clomipramine are really effective, and cats are less likely to return to spraying when they are taken off these medications. Fluoxetine is a human antidepressant in the SSRI (selective serotonin reuptake inhibitor) family; clomipramine is a tricyclic antidepressant. Neither drug is licensed for use on cats in the United States, although clomipramine is in Australia. This means that if your vet would like to try antidepressants on your cat, the prescription will be "off-label"—he'll tell you that the drug has been shown to be effective but hasn't been licensed for this particular use, and you will sign a consent form. By the way, this is quite common in veterinary medicine because it is so costly to get a drug license for different uses that most drug companies do not apply for the animal use license.

Chapter 8

HUMANS AND CATS

In our cohabitation with cats, there are issues that can cause conflict and chaos. One of the reasons for the discord is that we don't really understand what makes a cat tick, and we sometimes lose sight of the fact that our cats are animals—animals who have to make quite a massive adjustment to live by our rules and within our walls. Your relationship with your cat will go more smoothly if you try to understand the true nature of the beast within. Respect and enjoy the fundamental truth that she is an *animal,* first and foremost. We often treat cats like children, friends or even dogs—but probably not often enough as *cats,* the unique and fascinating creatures they are.

One mistake we make in loving our pets so much is that we risk crossing a line and forgetting that cats are profoundly different from people: in their needs, in how they experience the world and interact in it and in their style of communication. It is important to learn to appreciate and understand these differences because it will allow us to fully enjoy the experience of interspecies living. By finding a way to cohabit in harmony, we can enjoy our differences as well as the aspects of sharing our lives with our cats that make us feel so intensely connected to them. It is selfish and at times even cruel to hold a cat to human standards of reasoning or behavior. Any companion animal has to fit into the lifestyle of her human and abide by humans' rules, but it is our responsibility to set it up right and make it work.

Unlike dogs, cats rarely feel the need to compete with the people in their lives to test who is in charge. Jockeying for the alpha role, the top spot, is really not an issue that is on the table between cats and humans. We function as a source of nourishment and comfort for our cats, who often fall into the (unnatural) role of being needy, dependent kittens with us. But there are other areas where we are less in synchrony with our cats than we would like. It helps to always keep in mind that cats are already subverting their true nature just by living with us. We are responsible for making any other adjustments and accommodations necessary for cats to fit in to our lifestyles. That's only fair, right?

This chapter covers many of the issues and problems that arise when humans share their homes with cats. The topics listed here are those areas where you may misunderstand what your cat is all about. What you need to do is to make her comfortable and also protect yourself. I hope that what you find here will help you enhance the relationship you have with your cat and reduce areas of conflict or misinterpretation.

Allergies

It may seem as though many people are allergic to cats (and dogs), but in truth it's only 15 percent of us, according to the Humane Society of the United States. One of the reasons that this issue matters to the HSUS, which is a nonprofit organization in Washington, D.C., protecting the welfare of all animals, is that despite loving their cats, people often abandon them when they cannot cope with their allergic reactions to their pets.

But if you or someone who shares your home is having allergic symptoms around a cat, take heart: There are a number of things you can do to reduce your symptoms. This advice is not just about keeping you (or other people who are allergic to cats) more comfortable; it's also about preserving your cat's place in your heart and home forever.

WHAT'S BEHIND ALLERGIES

◆ It Is Not Your Cat's Hair That Causes the Problem

A common misconception is that a cat's fur is what causes an allergic reaction. The real allergens are the secretions from oil glands in the animal's skin, dander (tiny dead skin particles that flake off) and the proteins in a cat's saliva. Saliva is a big factor, given that a cat spends up to half her waking hours grooming herself with her tongue—and you'll be coming into contact with that dried saliva, spread around all over her body.

◆ The Name of What You Are Allergic to Is Fel d 1

Fel d 1 is a protein produced by various parts of a cat's body, including the anal sacs, the salivary glands and the sebaceous (oil) glands of the skin. Fel d 1 is released into the environment on flecks of dander (dead skin cells) and microscopic particles and can remain there for *years*. So while sitting on a couch next to a cat may trigger your symptoms, since Fel d 1 is airborne it can be detected all over, even in places your kitty has never set foot—from public transportation to buildings, schools and offices.

◆ Symptoms of Being Allergic to a Cat

Symptoms an allergic person experiences include runny nose, itchy or watery eyes, coughing, shortness of breath, wheezing and hives. If you develop these symptoms when you are in close quarters with a cat or during actual contact, there is a good chance that you are allergic.

However, there are other possible reasons for these symptoms, so don't just assume it's because of the cat.

◆ There Are Other Environmental Elements You Could (Also) Be Allergic To

Before blaming your pet for your physical discomfort, you might want to have an allergist test you, not just for cats but also for other common allergens such as mold, dust, pollen, insects or cigarette smoke. I am personally allergic to horses, dogs and cats, too. However, the allergy shots I've gotten for years and years are concentrated on dust and mold because, as I'll explain in the next section, these are the underlying allergies really responsible for my runny nose and eyes.

◆ The "Rain Barrel" Effect

Allergies develop over time with repeated exposure, so you could start out without any allergic reaction to a beloved pet and get more symptoms or more severe reactions as time goes on. Allergic people can tolerate a certain level of allergen in their environment until they reach the threshold their body can tolerate. But just like a rain barrel that can only hold so much water before it overflows, if you add any more to that threshold level, you trigger the allergic symptoms. A person who is allergic to cats is often also allergic to common substances such as dust mites, pollens and mold, which contributes to the rain barrel effect. So you could be reacting to other allergens in your environment, not just to your cat, which means you may be able to live comfortably alongside your kitty by following the suggestions in the next section.

WAYS TO DEAL WITH ALLERGIES

◆ Medications Can Relieve Symptoms

Prescription and over-the-counter antihistamine pills can reduce or eliminate physical symptoms and there are eye drops and nose sprays to control symptoms locally. Just as people who are allergic to pollen use medications during allergy season, when pollens are most concentrated in the environment, you can use the medications when you are going to be in close proximity to a cat.

◆ Allergy Shots (Immunotherapy)

Allergy shots have been shown to reduce symptoms in 65 percent of people living with cats (much better than the 20 percent improvement for allergies with dogs). For some people, the symptoms practically disappear over time. These injections work the way vaccines do: Your body reacts to the injected allergen by developing an immunity or tolerance to the allergenic substance. These shots are a long-term commitment, given first weekly, then biweekly and eventually monthly in gradually increasing concentrations over a period of 3 to 5 years, with the allergic symptoms lessening all the time.

◆ Wash Your Hands and Face After You Have Cat Contact

This can be difficult to remember to do, but if you at least wash your hands after handling your cat or her things, then you won't be carrying the allergens around with you, and you won't be touching your face with allergen-covered hands.

◆ Use a Spray That Destroys Dander

There are several sprays that you can use on your cat to "digest" the dander and saliva proteins that accumulate on her skin before they dry up and are released into the air to bother you. Allerpet (made by Allerpet, Inc.) and Dander Free (Earth's Balance) are two that I have used with good results. I have to say that although I often foolishly forget to use them regularly on my pets, the spray definitely makes a difference in my symptoms when I do remember to apply them to the animals. Instructions are to spray or rub the cat, getting the product right down to the skin all over her, every other day for the first week, and then once a week thereafter for maintenance. While you're at it, you can also spray anywhere your cat spends a lot of time where dander can accumulate: carpets, cat trees, furniture, cat beds. The sprays are known as probiotic solutions, which contain friendly microbes that digest dead skin cells and other microbiotic waste matter on the cat's skin. These sprays contain no hazardous ingredients and can safely be used near a cat's eyes and ears.

WAYS TO MAKE YOUR CAT LESS ALLERGENIC

Spay or neuter your cat. Unspayed females and unneutered males produce more allergen.

Spray Allerpet or Dander Free regularly. Massage the product down onto your cat's skin, which is where the dander originates.

Rinse your cat twice a week in plain water. Rinse with water twice a week, which will remove the saliva from the cat's coat, along with loose dander. There are those who say the water should be distilled (distilled water is sold in big jugs in supermarkets), but that may not be practical for you—and honestly, I'm not sure what difference that would make. But if you want to use distilled water, warm it first and rinse the cat well with it. If not, use warm water in a sink, preferably one with a spray hose. Keep the spray head very close to the cat's body, where it will be less bothersome to her. She'll get used to being rinsed: Follow the suggestions about bathing in the grooming section of the book.

Bathe her every 2 weeks. In addition to rinsing with plain water, a shampoo twice a month can help remove even more of the saliva and dander residue. Use lukewarm water (too warm and it can be counterproductive) and a mild cat shampoo (some are even soap-free), which will condition her skin and hair while removing dander and saliva. Lots more information about bathing is in the grooming chapter.

Keep the number of cats in the house to a minimum. The more cats, the more allergen.

Light-colored cats are less allergenic. Who knows why, but apparently this is true.

WAYS TO MAKE YOUR ENVIRONMENT LESS ALLERGENIC

Reduce exposure to other respiratory irritants. The fewer allergens you are exposed to, the less your immune system gets riled up. Avoid areas with tobacco smoke. Smoke from candles burning in a room at home or on a restaurant table can cause an allergic reaction in some people. If you notice that you get itchy, watery eyes when candles are burning, you'll know this is true for you.

Keep cats out of the rooms where allergy sufferers spend the most time. If this is too restrictive, then make sure that you rigorously and regularly follow all the cleaning suggestions below for those rooms in particular.

Keep cats out of the bedroom and do not let cats sleep on your bed.

Keep closet doors closed.

If you are the allergic person, have someone else do the housecleaning. If there is no way around you being the "designated cleaner," then give yourself maximum protection against the allergens you'll be stirring up by cleaning. Open windows before you start cleaning, wear a filter mask, wear protective gloves and wash your hands, forearms and face after you finish. Better yet, jump in the shower to rinse everything off afterward.

Reduce floor coverings that trap allergens. Minimize or remove carpeting. If you must have carpet, use one that cleans most easily. If you need to keep carpeting in your house, you want carpeting that you can keep free of allergens relatively easily. These are the qualities that make carpet easy to clean: low pile height and density, fluorocarbon-coated fiber and high-denier filament.

Easy-to-clean, hard-surfaced floors are best. Linoleum, vinyl, stone, tile, bamboo or wood are all good.

Eliminate draperies or curtains. If you want to keep drapes, use easy-care materials that you can wash frequently and hang again with no trouble. Hanging cloth surfaces are a magnet for allergens, and you really cannot clean them while they are hanging. If you can handle the expense of sending them to the dry cleaner, that might be less work, but keep in mind that there is more than a monetary price to pay with dry cleaning: The fluids they use are toxic to the environment and cannot be entirely neutral for you, either.

Choose the most dust-free litter you can find. Some of the more modern litter materials are less dusty than the original clay litter (see the litter box chapter for more).

Use in-room or central air filters.

Replace or clean filters on furnaces and vacuums.

Replace upholstered furniture with slipcovered pieces. It helps to be able to remove and wash the coverings of furniture in rooms where the cat spends time. To deactivate Fel d 1 you need to wash them in hot water (130°F).

Get allergen-proof covers for mattress and pillows and wash them often.

WAYS TO SERIOUSLY CLEAN THE HOUSE

Wipe down furniture surfaces and walls weekly. Use furniture spray to help remove allergens from hard furniture surfaces. Using a damp disposable cleaning cloth, wet-wipe the walls. The allergens that cats produce—dander and saliva from self-grooming—become airborne when they are dry and have a stickiness that makes them adhere to the walls. If you are strictly against using disposable materials from an environmental standpoint, then use a cloth that you can rinse and wring out often during the cleaning process.

Wipe off the baseboards. The same sticky residue that attaches itself to the walls also collects on the baseboards. Regularly wipe down the area of the wall that meets the floor—and if you have baseboard heating that blows the air around, pay special attention to the wall area above the baseboard.

Use a vacuum with a HEPA filter. A central vacuum system is very effective, too. An ordinary vacuum will *not* remove Fel d 1 that is deeply embedded in carpet or upholstery and may actually stir up more of the allergens into the air.

 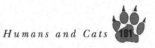

Vacuum as often as possible and follow with wet-mopping. The more often you clean, the fewer allergens there will be in the environment. A once-a-week vacuuming is not going to cut it if you really want to keep a house as nonallergenic as possible. Also, the more you vacuum up those particles, the less chance they have of getting embedded deep into materials and nooks and crannies around the house.

Wash your cat's bedding with hot water weekly. Identify where your cat sleeps or hangs out the most and put washable covers over those areas. If it's an actual cat bed, make sure it has a removable cover; on other areas the cat frequents, you need to keep towels which you can remove and wash in hot water (as noted above).

Ceiling fans are big dust collectors. Few people realize that the tops of ceiling fan blades are a prime location for dust and animal hair to settle—and then be blown around the room when the fan is turned on.

Problem Behaviors

This section alphabetically lists a handful of the irritating things that cats do, and how to put an end to these behaviors: begging, charging the door, counter surfing, demanding attention, nocturnal playing and stealing.

When you want to solve problems or change any behavior in a cat, there are three parts to making a successful change. First, you have to *understand the cause* of the behavior; second, you have to *change the environment;* and third, you have to *redirect* the behavior to something positive. Remember that you bear the responsibility for harmoniously cohabiting with your cat, and these situations that arise are very much in your hands to solve.

Begging at the Table

People often think of dogs as the biggest problem when it comes to begging at the table, but cats (and especially kittens) can also be terrible pests at the table, meowing and pawing you, standing on hind legs, jumping up on the table, rubbing all around your chair and jumping onto your lap, or squeezing behind you onto the chair you're sitting on. People often encourage begging by occasionally feeding cats from the table. I say "occasionally" for a reason: If a trainer really wants to ingrain a habit in any animal, intermittent rewards are the most powerful training tool they can use. By giving a reward only every so often, the animal will repeat the behavior more consistently and quickly than if she got a reward every single time. You get the point, right? When the checklist says "Never," it means precisely that; there can be no "just this once."

If you've followed the rules on the checklist below and your cat persists in trying to weasel food out of you, make it easy on both of you: Close her in another room when you are eating. How much simpler can it get?

Checklist to Discourage Begging

- Never feed anything in the kitchen while preparing a meal.
- Never feed anything from the table.
- Never feed from dishes used on the table.
- Never let her on the table, with food on it or not.
- Ignore her while you're at the table—don't give any attention, physical or verbal.
- Don't leave food on the table unattended—all it takes is one good bite to convince her to keep coming back for more.
- Feed the cat before you eat, if possible. If she's not hungry, she'll be less likely to beg.

Charging the Door

You certainly don't want your cat trying to fly out the door past you, either when you're leaving or returning home, but many cats lie in wait for these moments.

HOMECOMINGS

Most cats have an uncanny sense of time and routine, and if you follow any sort of schedule, you can be sure your cat knows what it is. This means you can pretty much expect your cat to be waiting inside by the door when you come home. To avoid having your cat come bounding toward you when you walk through the door—and perhaps go charging right out the door past you—the first step is to remove the doorway itself as the focus. Slip in the door and shut it quickly behind you, walking right past the cat. Then call her to you from a location at a little distance from the door, where you can engage in your greeting ritual. Instead of coming home and making a fuss over her at the door itself, start greeting her at this new "hello kitty" spot. With any luck, before long she will sit and wait for you there.

LEAVING HOME

To prevent your cat from dashing past you out the door when you're going out, redirect her attention to something more interesting, such as a toy you set in motion. Try one of the balls made for cats that have smaller balls or bells inside that bounce around when you roll the ball. There are also balls that you put kitty treats or bits of tasty dry food inside that a cat has to roll around to get the treats to fall out. These toys—or any others that your cat enjoys—should be rolled away from the door just as you are about to exit, to keep her attention on something else as you're leaving.

IF YOUR CAT ISN'T SO EASILY FOOLED

If your cat is too smart to be fooled by your attempts to distract her from dashing past you out the door, try to install a friend with a squirt gun or squirt bottle outside the door. Have your

friend standing at such an angle that he can see the cat but the cat doesn't see him, and then have him squirt her as she tries to slip out the door. The point of this is to startle the cat but leave her thinking that it is the door that did it to her, and that the door should be avoided in the future.

Counter Surfing

Cats like to jump up on kitchen counters for two reasons: they are nice high places, something cats love, and there may often be something tasty up on the counter. There are two ways you can discourage a cat from jumping up on the counter. The first is to make the counter really uncomfortable with a deterrent such as a strip of Sticky Paws that runs all along the top of the counter near the edge and on the edge facing out. Cats don't like to touch sticky surfaces, so when she leaps up and her paws touch the nasty sticky tape, she will jump right back off. Obviously you don't want to live with a sticky-taped counter forever, but generally it doesn't take more than a couple of unsuccessful tries to convince a cat not to go up there.

Some experts suggest squirting your cat with a squirt bottle when she tries to jump up, but this seems unrealistic to me since there are so many variables you have to control: You have to be there when the cat decides to jump; you need exquisite timing to do this at the exact moment she is about to jump; you have to hit her only on the rump with water; and she must not realize it came from you. I think that's asking a bit much, so remove yourself from the equation and let the Sticky Paws do the job.

The other way to keep your cat off the countertop is to avoid leaving unattended food that would smell or taste good to her. If you have occasions when you have food you want to leave out at room temperature, then pop it in your unheated oven or microwave for safekeeping (just don't forget it's there).

Demanding Attention

A cat who is an affection hog can be pretty irritating or she can be delightful, depending on your outlook. Cats like this seem to never leave you alone, interrupting you at the desk, in bed, at the table, even in the shower, demanding to be included in whatever you're doing and "complaining" bitterly if they are excluded.

It may seem unusual for a cat to want to be the center of attention and always close to you, since cats are generally independent creatures who remain somewhat aloof. However, needy or super-attached cats do exist.

WHAT MAKES A CAT CLINGY AND DEMANDING?

There are a number of possible reasons for your cat's dependence on you, some of which you may be able to alter.

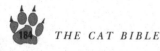

✦ You May Be Fostering "Codependence"

You may be creating a clingy cat if you constantly include her in your thoughts and activities while you are home—by talking to her, encouraging her to be on furniture with you, frequently calling her to you with treats and encouraging her to follow you from a room when you leave. When a cat begins to expect this level of interaction all the time you're in trouble unless it's what you want, too, and intend to continue to provide it.

✦ Your Cat May Be Sensitive

A cat can be demanding because she is more sensitive than other cats about being separated from a person she is attached to. Such a cat may have started out with a timid, insecure personality and your loving treatment has intensified that need for attention and reassurance.

✦ The Cat Had Too Much Contact When Young

If a cat received too much attention from people when she was a kitten, she came to expect this level of interaction as normal. Because her expectations are unrealistic, she may be grappling with the shock of having to spend many hours a day alone.

✦ The Cat Had Too Little Affection and Attention as a Kitten

If a kitten was neglected either by her mother or by the humans who raised her, she may wind up trying to make up for lost time.

✦ Some Cats Are More Interactive and Demanding by Nature

In addition to cats who are inherently insecure, there are others, such as the Siamese, who are naturally interactive.

✦ If a Cat Gets Attention by Demanding It, She Will Keep It Up

If you give in to your cat's entreaties to constantly touch or play with her, it will only intensify her needy behavior and she will surely keep on doing it.

✦ If a Cat Is Bored, She May Become a Pest

A cat who is understimulated may nag at you because she has nothing to do and a lot of pent-up energy.

✦ Emotional or Physical Discomfort Can Make a Cat Clingy

If a cat has any physical problem, it can make her clingy; the same is true if she is under stress. Since cats rarely display pain, if your cat's personality changes to being more needy, it could be worth a visit to the vet to rule out any possible medical problem.

✦ Insecurity or Fear Can Explain a Demanding Cat

A cat who is fearful and edgy may be like this is because she needs reassurance that everything is fine. In human terms she might be considered paranoid or a worrywart.

WHAT YOU CAN DO TO MAKE IT BETTER

◆ Change the Cat's Daily Activities to Encourage Independence

If you normally spend a lot of time keeping your cat company when she eats and/or you play with her frequently during the day, change these routines. Let her eat and play on her own with a toy she can bat around so she develops some independence.

◆ Provide Items to Help Her Develop Independence

If she doesn't have a great cat tree, maybe now is a time to get one. Rub catnip in a couple of places on it and watch what happens.

◆ Get a Companion Cat

If your cat is stuck to you like glue because she is lonely and fearful, another cat could help solve the problem. A four-legged companion could be just the thing to keep her company and overcome her doubts and fears.

Nocturnal Playing

Cats are the original night owls: They come alive as it gets dark. Cats naturally become more active after dusk, when the light is fading. Muted illumination is the light in which a cat's eyes work most efficiently for hunting, so even though cats have been domesticated for generations and their food comes out of a can, their internal clocks are still set for nocturnal activity. It is normal for a cat to take naps during the day (hence the word *catnap*) and then become active when the sun goes down, especially young cats and cats who lack stimulation during the daytime. In addition, because you may be out for most of the day, the time when you come home often coincides with darkness falling, which gives your cat even more reason to perk up. This might not be a problem if you fully understand how important it is to satisfy your cat's basic needs for play, hunting, mental stimulation, affection and food (in no particular order).

There's another problem with feline night owls, which goes beyond their need to be engaged with you at dusk: They want to tap-dance on your head while you're sleeping. The solution some people come up with is to shut their cat out of the bedroom, but that's not really a satisfying solution because you feel bad for the cat's sorrowful meowing and scratching on the other side of the door—and sorry for yourself for having to listen to it.

SATISFY YOUR CAT'S NATURAL BASIC NEEDS

The nicest way to "cure" a cat of late-night playfulness is to create a scenario for her in the evening that will satisfy her basic nature and allow her—and you—to slumber peacefully afterward. The basic routine she would follow in the wild would be to hunt, eat her prey, groom herself and rest afterward. You need to re-create an evening along the lines of that natural cycle so that you can tire her out at the end of every day.

◆ First, Play with Your Cat

Using a lure or other interactive cat toy that simulates prey, play with her at some point during the evening and then again right before you turn in. This takes care of the hunting portion of her natural cycle.

◆ Next, Feed Your Cat

Save a portion of her daily food allowance to give her last thing at night, after you tire her out playing. Don't feed her a greater quantity than you did before, but divide up her food so that this becomes a third meal of the day. This should be the absolutely last thing you do when you are ready to brush your teeth. This satisfies the eat-her-prey part of her natural wiring.

◆ Now She'll Groom Herself

You may have noticed that your cat always grooms carefully after eating. That is what she will do now (thank goodness it doesn't take any further involvement from you). The feline habit of thorough self-cleaning after eating goes back to life in the wild, where cats need to meticulously clean off every speck of the animal they just consumed because that scent might attract other predators who would go after the tasty-smelling cat herself. This fulfills her hard-wired drive to groom herself scrupulously.

◆ Finally, Sweet Dreams

Having satisfied her other basic nighttime needs, your cat can now put her head on the pillow with a sigh, having fulfilled her natural destiny. Her nocturnal cycle is complete—now you can get a good night's sleep, too.

WHAT IF YOUR CAT STILL WON'T SETTLE DOWN?

If you have gone through the steps above and your cat is still ready for some action and is just generally being a pain in the neck, fill up one of those balls that the cat has to bat around to get treats out of (available at any pet store) and roll it out into another room. If your cat has this big a night owl problem and she has a favorite toy (such as a catnip mouse or the treat ball), then withhold that toy all day and only give it to her last thing at night so that she can knock herself out with it.

Stealing

You may think you have a criminal cat—a compulsive thief who goes around the house taking your stuff—and wonder how you went wrong in raising her. Don't worry, she's not really a delinquent, just a curious gal. Cats who take things do so out of a love for novelty—a strong curiosity about anything new and unusual that comes into their world. I only use the word *steal* for fun, and it really isn't fair because cats have no sense of right or wrong or even ownership. Everything is fair game.

TAKING THINGS IS FUN AND EXCITING FOR A CAT

A cat may pick up something she's batted off a desk or counter and sneak away with it. Her basic nature is to hunt for something and then, when she snags it, to find a quiet corner and investigate her catch. Food can be intriguing because it has an alluring smell, but there are also many other objects that can catch a cat's fancy. However, if you have a cat who steals, you cannot leave food out on a counter or table or anywhere unmonitored, even for a moment. It's not just that you don't want to lose your food to your cat or that it makes a mess of everything when she takes it off your plate or the counter; it's also because there are numerous things that shouldn't go down a cat's gullet in the first place.

WATCH OUT FOR FABRIC HOARDERS

Some cats are fond of chewing on particular kinds of fabric and will take the pieces away with them. Two of the popular materials that cats swipe are wool and knitted clothing. Some cats will gather up enough of their favorite fabric to fashion themselves a heap of it to sleep on. If your cat has a favorite fabric, make sure you don't leave out *anything* made from it around the house. Close all drawers and closet doors and put laundry baskets out of her reach. Otherwise her curiosity may turn into an obsession, your things will get ruined and your cat may swallow some of it and really do herself harm.

KEEP HER OCCUPIED

You need to stimulate a cat who borrows things around the house. She has a strong drive to do more, see more and play with what she finds. Is she the kind of cat who can't wait to check out your paper grocery bags the minute you bring them inside? Then give her a thrill: Ask for paper bags at the market and as soon as you empty them of groceries, fold back the opening of the bag into a cuff that stays open when you lay it on its side. Remember to remove the handles so she doesn't get caught in them. Put a couple of bags on the floor like that and see what fun your cat has playing in and around them. To engage her mind and tucker her out you can also try using a lure or interactive toy.

The Human Kind:
Babies

Cats pose no jeopardy to babies, so just forget that ludicrous old wives' tale about cats sucking the breath out of a baby. There is a not a scintilla of truth to this myth; it's just a silly superstition that evolved. However, you do need to prepare your cat for the arrival of a new baby.

PREPARING YOUR CAT FOR THE LITTLE NEWCOMER

Cats don't just dislike change; they *hate* it. A baby does not just change the number of people living in your house but throws an entire household on its ear. Furniture moves, new equipment arrives, routines are thrown out the window, there are new noises and smells and a troop of visitors—from a cat's point of view, nothing could be worse. The arrival of a baby puts a cat at risk of being discombobulated and displaced.

Cats do best when they have a predictable routine, but when a baby is expected, a cat has a lot to contend with, including changes in where her food and water dishes are, when dinner is served, where her litter box(es) are. The kindest way to soften the blow for your cat is to introduce her to all the elements of life with a baby slowly, in small increments and well before the baby's arrival. A great tool is a CD of baby noises to prepare the cat for these unusual sounds (see p. 191).

THE CAT'S PERSONALITY CAN MAKE A DIFFERENCE

If you have a shy or timid cat, you want to give her extra time to prepare for the newcomer. Give her a chance to see and smell the baby's things before the baby gets there. Let your cat explore the nursery on her own, or if she has an especially cautious or fearful personality, carry her in to give her a sense of security and then take her around to examine the baby's clothing, diaper pail, equipment, toys and so on.

Some fearful cats will slink around in a kind of furtive, nervous way during the adjustment period. Do not misinterpret this as a reflection of the cat's "attitude" about a baby or ascribe any human-type feelings or motives to a cat such as anger, resentment or jealousy. This behavior is simply the way your naturally reticent cat is reacting to changes in her environment. A cat may try to be "invisible" or furtive while she adjusts to the upheaval in her life and her territory is redefined.

A confident, extroverted cat, on the other hand, may slide right into life with the new baby as if it's no big deal. Cats with high self-esteem may seem a little concerned at first, but often they settle back into their routine in no time. Some highly independent cats will go on about their business without a noticeable reaction to the new baby—they are just fine as long as their mealtimes or other basic feline needs are maintained as they were before.

PREPARE THE NURSERY A LITTLE AT A TIME

Fix up the baby's room in stages if it is logistically possible. Try to have painting, furniture, carpet and drapes done one at a time, so that the cat doesn't have to cope with a barrage of new decorating sights and smells all at once. Of course, it depends somewhat on your cat's temperament and how much she generally reacts to change and new stimuli. For a highly reactive, sensitive cat, a gradual adjustment really can make a difference, so let her walk around in the nursery and get used to it at her own pace.

Once she has taken stock of the newly redone room itself, let the cat explore the baby's things in her room by putting the equipment out before the baby gets there. A stroller, a carrier, swings, a rocking chair—whatever things you plan to use for your baby should be available for the cat's inspection.

MAKE THE CRIB OFF-LIMITS BEFORE THE BABY COMES HOME

Many cat experts suggest that the most important part of getting a cat comfortable with the whole event of a new baby—while setting boundaries for the cat at the same time—is to set up the crib as soon as possible and then make it off-limits to the cat. A cat should never ever get into a crib because cats are constantly stepping in and out of a litter box and they carry the remnants of

 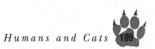

what they have stepped in on their paws. Regardless of how well you keep it clean, nonetheless, it is a litter box. Later in this chapter, you will see that there are a number of illnesses and parasites that cats can pass to people. Even if you are initially opposed to excluding your cat from the crib, you'll probably change your mind when you learn what a cat can pass on to a baby by sharing her bed. To keep your cat healthy and your baby safe, your cat should live exclusively indoors and have yearly vet exams—or twice yearly as she gets older.

You need to make that crib the least hospitable surface in your house using the same methods you would to make other surfaces in the house highly disagreeable to a cat (more on that in Chapter 6).

By their very nature, cats love a high, cozy perch, so to discourage the cat from jumping up in the crib, scratching against it and other unwanted behaviors, put Sticky Paws tape on the legs, edges and even the crib bars to make it unpleasant for the cat to touch the crib. If the cat still shows interest in the crib even when it is covered with Sticky Paws, then fill the crib (before the baby occupies it, of course) with empty soda cans, empty water bottles, beach balls or anything similar that will move and make noise if she somehow manages to jump in there. Probably the simplest thing to do is to buy a crib tent, available online or at most baby stores. It fits over the top of the crib and makes it impenetrable.

CLOSE THE DOOR TO THE BABY'S ROOM

This is a good habit to get into right away so that the nursery is off-limits to the cat. Once the baby arrives, the cat should never have the opportunity to go into the nursery without you.

If for some reason you don't want to keep the nursery door shut, you can install a tall baby gate that the cat cannot jump over. You could even put a temporary screen door on the baby's nursery that can be latched shut. Both of these options allow the cat to see what's going on inside the nursery without being able to go in. If it's important to you to visually include the cat even while physically excluding her, then it may be worth it to you to go to that trouble—as long as you recognize that you will be doing what feels right to *you*, since a cat can live quite well without knowing every little thing that goes on in the nursery.

GET YOUR CAT USED TO LESS OF YOUR ATTENTION

If you are someone who spends a great deal of time one-on-one with your cat and you worry that after the baby comes your cat will think she is being replaced or rejected, there are ways to prepare her for the upcoming shift in your attention. You will need to get your cat used to the idea that she may no longer be front and center in your world. Once the baby enters your home, there will be times when your cat wants you to pay attention to her and you are going to need to ignore her. To some cats this is no big deal, but to a cat who has enjoyed a close bond with you—especially really interactive Oriental breeds—this "brush-off" is something you should practice before the baby enters the picture.

A cat usually prefers to be the one to initiate affection and cuddling, and your cat has probably trained you quite well to respond in the way she wants. You will need to reverse things so that *you* become the initiator of affection, dispensing it on your terms, rather than passively reacting to your cat's demands.

However, you don't want your cat to become stressed because you rebuff or reject her when you're with the baby. Practice giving her less attention before the baby comes to give her a taste of what the new arrangement will be like. The main difference is that she won't be in charge of demanding affection anymore: She'll have to let you make decisions about when and how much interaction you will have with her.

Although some part of you may want to shower your cat with love and attention before the baby comes, don't do it. You may think you are being kind, but actually it would be cruel: The emotional transition for the cat will be much harder if you increase her affection quotient only to cut it way back after the baby comes. Let her get used to seeing a little less of you while you are expecting the baby—nothing dramatic, just a smaller response or a less immediate one from you. You've already shown your cat how easily you can be trained: Your cat speaks, you speak back; she speaks twice, you offer cuddles or fresh food or open the door to the garden. Now you need to change that communication flow so that *you* invite the cat into your lap and *you* call the cat for breakfast, acclimating her to how it is going to be from now on.

But this does not mean that everyone in the household has to follow your lead. In fact, it would actually be great if you can encourage other family members to do just the opposite of your "affection rationing." During this transition period, the more people who acknowledge your cat, whether physically or verbally, the less chance she will be offended down the road by your strange decision to go off and have a two-legged baby.

FIRST INTRODUCTIONS TO THE BABY'S PRESENCE

◆ Introduce the Cat to the Sounds of a Baby

There are going to be a lot of peculiar noises that your cat will hear once the baby arrives: musical mobiles, lullabies or other music, squeaking toys, rattles—and don't forget the startling, piercing sounds of the baby himself. You can buy CD recordings of baby sounds (like www.sounds of baby.com) that you can play for your cat so infant noises become as normal to her as the noise of the dishwasher or TV.

◆ The Smells of the Baby's Things Are Novel, Too

With a baby come powders, lotions, oils, baby wipes and diaper cream (plus formula if you are not breast-feeding), all of which are unlike anything the cat's sensitive nose will have encountered before. Rub some of these things on your own skin in the months or weeks before your due date so that the cat becomes accustomed to the odors before the little angel actually arrives. The powerful smell of dirty diapers is another assault on a cat's supersensitive nose, so once the baby comes you need to put dirty diapers in closed plastic bags and store them in a closed container to minimize the chance that the cat will be inspired to spray in response to these odors.

◆ The Smell of the Baby Himself

This is another surprise for the cat that you can accustom her to ahead of time. When the baby is born, take a piece of clothing the baby has worn or a blanket he was wrapped in (*unwashed* is the

point, of course) and let the cat sniff that before you actually bring the real little person home. This gives the cat yet another layer of familiarity and comfort with the newcomer. Some people put the baby's blanket near the cat's dinner dish or on her favorite bed or perch, to get the cat even more accustomed to the baby's personal fragrance.

FIRST INTRODUCTION TO THE BABY

Some cats are more curious about infants than others, but after the initial adjustment period, usually a baby does not have much of an impact on the cat's life, and most cats ignore small infants after the early meetings. Once a cat gets used to the new sights, smells and sounds, as well as to however the household routine has changed, she will go on her merry way.

✦ Make It a Positive Experience

For the first meeting and all the other early encounters between cat and baby, have some tasty tidbits (such as cooked chicken) ready to give your cat. In a calm and affectionate way, praise your cat during the meet-and-greets and then give the treat when your cat is acting appropriately. The reason for this is to create a positive association for the cat: The baby is a good thing for the cat; the baby causes good things to happen.

✦ The First Face-to-Face Meeting of Baby and Cat

Keep it simple and straightforward. Hold the baby and let your cat sniff the infant. Don't be surprised or worried if your cat shows a heightened curiosity—that's natural for a cat being exposed to anything new and interesting. It's no cause for worry.

✦ Let Someone Else Hold the Baby

If the cat's greatest emotional attachment is to the baby's mother or father, then for the first cat-baby meetings let someone other than that parent hold the baby while the parent makes a big, affectionate fuss over the cat. (This does not contradict the advice that you should withhold extra attention in the weeks and months before the baby is born. In that case, the issue was behavior on your part that led your cat to expect a certain level of interaction all the time. Instead, this advice has to do with a special occasion when the people who matter most to the cat should give extra cuddling to ensure a positive experience when your cat is being introduced to the baby.)

THE CRAWLING-AGE BABY

Once a baby can crawl, she will be quite another story for your pussycat to live with. A baby who is on the move will probably invade a cat's special escape spaces (behind and under furniture, etc.), and a crawling baby might also motor right over a cat—or at least give her a rude awakening if the cat is dozing when the baby comes upon her.

Once a baby can crawl and then toddle, a cat needs a safe place where she can escape from those prying little hands. The safest escape destinations for a cat are up high, with an elevated spot in every room out of the young child's reach. The cat's safe place can be as simple as a windowsill, a shelf emptied of books or doodads, or a counter, desk or table that the cat can easily access. A sturdy cat tree that a child cannot topple or is taught is off-limits can be the best retreat of all.

NEVER LEAVE A CAT ALONE WITH A CHILD

This advice applies for all young children: newborns, toddlers and any little one up to preschool age. A child cannot understand a cat's experience of the world any more than a cat can really grasp what that strange-looking and oddly behaving little human is all about. Cats can be nice pets for children but only after the children are old enough to learn to touch gently and never to pull, poke or chase.

URINE SPRAYING IN REACTION TO A BABY

Some cats may pee in the house before or after the baby arrives. Often a cat will spray on something connected to the baby, such as a crib blanket. Do not take this to "mean" anything, and do not assign human emotions and motivations such as jealousy or competitiveness to the cat; this marking does not symbolize any "feelings" the cat has about the baby. People worry that spraying is a personal statement from their cat, but that is because they do not understand the instinctive reasons that motivate a cat to spray in the house.

If your cat is timid or particularly attached to you, she may be more likely to spray on or around the new baby things. However, spraying is really an instinctive reaction to something foreign coming into the house. Cats spray not out of emotion but rather to cover the unfamiliar baby odors in the house and/or to mark new objects as part of her territory.

The urination may also be a sign that the cat is agitated. Read the section about spraying in Chapter 7 on litter boxes to understand more about this common behavior, which can be a sign of stress or disorientation.

KITTY RULES FOR KIDS

◆ Take Nothing for Granted

Just because your cat tolerated the child or your child handled himself well with the cat one time, there is still a good chance that one of them could react differently the next time. You need to stay close by and monitor any reactions to keep both of them safe.

◆ Feliway to the Rescue (Again)

If you doubt whether your cat is comfortable with your child, you can spray Comfort Zone Feliway on the child's shoes, socks and pant legs.

◆ Teach a Child How to "Be a Cat"

If your child is old enough to understand the concept of seeing things from another point of view, then "play cat" with him so he can experience what it feels like to be a cat. Get down on all fours with your child and put your faces really near the ground. Explain that this is where the - kitten or cat sees the world from. Getting that perspective can help a child understand how scary the world can seem to a small animal. Then use your imagination to create your own pretend-you're-a-cat games. For example, you could have your child remain in the cat position while you jump or run past (as the child might do), and explain how this can startle a cat.

◆ Explain Kitty Body Language to Your Child
There are a number of physical warning signs that your cat will give when she wants a person to stop touching her, or when she is resting and does not want to be approached. These are described in Chapter 2. You can teach your child to "read" your cat's body language by explaining some of these common feline physical communications.

◆ All Cat Play Should Be on the Floor
It is safer for the child and more secure for the cat if there is a household rule that the child has to be down on the floor if he wants to play with the cat. This eliminates the hazard of a child trying to get up on a cat tree to get at the cat, or trying to pick the cat up and take her somewhere. By initiating a floor rule, you teach the child respect for the cat's space and her body itself.

◆ Teach Your Child How to Touch a Cat
At the earliest possible age, start showing your child how to stroke a cat. You might want to use a stuffed animal to demonstrate and practice on. Hold your child's hand and guide it very lightly along the cat's back. Show him the difference between desirable stroking and ways *not* to touch a cat, such as patting (which can get too thump-thump-ish with children), hitting or grabbing a fistful of hair.

◆ Show Your Child Your Cat's Special Places to Be Stroked
Guide his hand under her chin, between her ears, and at the base of her tail, where it joins her body. Point out how your cat raises up her hind end, or purrs and leans against him, to show how happy he is making her.

◆ The Belly Is a Vulnerable and Sensitive Place on a Cat
Many cats dislike having their bellies rubbed, at least until they feel really secure with the person doing it. Alternatively, a cat may accept her tummy being touched for a brief moment and then will react with teeth and claws to end it. In either case, it poses a risk for a child, and so the belly should be an off-limits area.

◆ Touch with One Hand Only
By teaching your child to use only one hand when playing with a cat, it means that he cannot hang on to the cat and hold her against her will. It also means that if he follows the rule, he will be unable to pick the cat up.

◆ Children Should Not Lift a Cat
There is no reason for a child to be allowed to pick up a cat. A child may be too small or uncoordinated to pick up a cat securely. We've all seen children holding a cat by the armpits while

the long-suffering kitty dangles precariously. There is no need for a cat's tolerance to be tested this way.

◆ Do Not Hold a Cat Who Wants to Leave

Children can learn early that when a cat wants to walk away or jump down she has to be free to do so, or in the struggle to hold on to her they may get hurt. Point out to your child that the cat loves him and will always come back; she just needs some "alone time."

◆ Repeat These Exercises Many Times

Don't think your work is done just because you've shown your child once how to handle himself around the cat. Do not assume that he understands and will remember how to do it the next time. As with any learning process, it will take time and many repetitions.

◆ Don't Leave a Preschooler Alone with a Cat

There is no way to anticipate the odd ideas a young child can come up with in discovering ways to explore the cat's world. It's best to be around to steer his imagination in the right direction.

◆ There Should Be Off-Limits Cat Zones

The Litter Tray Can Look Like a Fun Sandbox to a Child. Litter boxes should be off-limits to children. If your child is too young to understand this rule, then you have to make the litter box inaccessible and put it somewhere a little kid cannot get to it.

A Cat Tree or Scratching Post Can Be Dangerous for Toddlers and Small Children. A child might try to pull himself up onto it and tip the whole thing over on himself. Your cat also needs a safe space where she won't be hassled.

The Cat Bed Is for the Cat Only. If your cat sleeps on a bed, she has to trust that she will be able to snooze there in peace and not have to keep half an eye open for surprise interruptions.

The Cat's Dinner Bowl. A child needs to learn respect for the cat's dinner hour and to give her peace and privacy when she is eating. If your child doesn't fully understand this, you can play cat with him and show him what it feels like being crowded when eating, or having someone mess around with his food dish.

Diseases Passed from Cats to People

Zoonoses is the peculiar word for diseases that animals can give to humans. Fortunately, there are not many illnesses that fall into this category and they occur rarely, but it's worth knowing about the ones that do exist.

RABIES

This is the most well known of the illnesses that various animals (not just cats) can give to people. Rabies is passed through infected saliva, so a cat can only get it in the first place if she is bitten by a wild animal such as a raccoon, fox or bat that has rabies. The likelihood of this happening to your cat is pretty slim, depending on the wildlife where you live, and the chance is pretty much zero if she is an indoor cat since she would be unlikely to encounter any of these rabid creatures in your living room. Theoretically, a cat could also be bitten by a rabid dog, but even if you have an outdoor cat who could encounter a loose, rabid dog, it seems equally unlikely that she'd allow a dog to get close enough to bite her.

INTESTINAL ROUNDWORMS

These parasites can be passed to us by cats who have eliminated in the soil around your house. If you have a garden and any cats have access to it, they may have used it to relieve themselves, so avoid direct skin contact with moist, potentially contaminated soil. If you aren't sure of contamination, wear rubberized gardening gloves and wash your hands thoroughly with very warm water after gardening. The best way to avoid getting roundworms is to have the vet check your cat's feces periodically for signs of the parasite's eggs. Careful personal hygiene will protect your family's health, so make a point of always washing your hands well after cleaning the litter box or handling the cat.

RINGWORM

Ringworm is not a worm but a fungal skin infection that is highly contagious. You can get ringworm from being in contact with an infected cat, or even by gardening outside where your cat or others are allowed because there may be microscopic ringworm spores in the soil outside. Therefore, a cat allowed outside has a greater chance of passing the disease to you. Do not allow an affected cat to sleep on your bed or lie on your clothes, since the infection can be picked up from sheets or clothing.

Children are especially prone to developing ringworm, so try to instill the habit in your kids—and everyone else in your family—of always washing their hands after brushing, stroking or holding the cat. (Frequent hand washing also goes a long way toward preventing contagious illnesses such as colds in your family.)

Your cat may not even have any outward signs of contamination, but if you have a red, itchy, raised, inflamed sore on your skin, you should suspect ringworm and go to your doctor for treatment. You also need to take your cat to the vet, who can cure her of the fungus in 2 to 3 weeks. Ask your vet about a medication called Fel-O-Vax MC-1 that both prevents and treats ringworm.

CAT SCRATCH FEVER

Cat scratch fever (also known as cat scratch disease) is caused by a bacteria that some cats—but more likely kittens—have in their mouths and underneath their claws. It can be a serious illness for a person, and younger people are more likely to be affected by it. A person who catches it can have a number of serious symptoms, including fever, swollen lymph nodes and loss of appetite. What begins as a skin wound will turn crusty in a few days and swell like an infected insect bite or abscess. Since this disease can then spread to the person's internal organs, it's important to get immediate medical care and have a blood test to determine whether your symptoms are from cat scratch fever.

TOXOPLASMOSIS

One of the better-known illnesses that people can theoretically get from cats is toxoplasmosis. There is a general awareness of this because pregnant women are cautioned not to clean their cat's litter box. Although people who get infected usually show nothing more than mild flulike symptoms, there is serious jeopardy during pregnancy because the growing fetus is vulnerable to this disease. Pregnant women are cautioned to both wear rubber gloves and wash their hands after scooping the cat's box.

◆ What Is the Disease?

The organism that causes toxoplasmosis passes its eggs in a cat's feces. The cat herself does not seem ill, but people can pick up the disease from stroking a cat who may have the microscopic eggs on her fur. However, there is no chance that an indoor cat can get it, and it is highly unlikely that anything but a true country cat could contract the disease. In order for a cat to get toxoplasmosis, she has to kill and eat a forest rodent who has it, which would leave microscopic eggs in her stool.

◆ Raw Meat Is the True Risk

Ironically, there is no more than a minuscule chance of a person contracting toxoplasmosis from cat feces. However, touching or consuming raw meat actually does pose a risk. This is why pregnant women are warned to eat their meat well cooked. If a person even touches raw meat and then does not wash her hands before touching vegetables or lettuce that will be eaten raw, she can get toxoplasmosis.

◆ How to Know if Your Cat Has Toxoplasmosis

For all people living with cats, the safest thing to do is get your cat tested for toxoplasmosis. If she does not have it, you can keep her healthy and safe by not feeding raw food to your cat and not allowing her outdoors to kill and eat birds and rodents, which carry toxoplasmosis. It would not be a bad idea to have everyone in your household adopt the habit of washing their hands after every physical encounter with your cat.

STAYING HEALTHY WITH YOUR CAT

The American Association of Feline Practitioners (AAFP), veterinarians who specialize in cats, have issued guidelines to reduce anyone's chances of catching a cat-borne infection or illness. These are the major points from their recommendations:

- ❑ Make regular vet visits with fecal samples; discuss deworming and vaccination needs.
- ❑ Vaccinate your cat against rabies.
- ❑ Ask your vet about Fel-O-Vax MC-1 for ringworm.
- ❑ Ask your vet about flea and tick control medicines.
- ❑ Take your cat to the vet without delay if she seems unwell.
- ❑ Handle a sick cat as little as possible, or wear disposable gloves and wash hands afterward.
- ❑ Do not handle stray cats.
- ❑ Keep cats indoors to eliminate risk of contact with fleas, ticks, other animals and their droppings.
- ❑ Feed only cooked or commercially processed cat food.
- ❑ Do not share food utensils with the cat.
- ❑ Don't let cat lick your face.
- ❑ Do not allow cats to drink from the toilet.
- ❑ Don't engage in rough play or teasing that could elicit scratching or biting from your cat.
- ❑ Forbid biting and scratching. Contact an animal behavior specialist or vet if you cannot stop it completely.
- ❑ Clip or cap your cat's claws to reduce the risk of being scratched.
- ❑ If you are bitten or scratched enough to break the skin, get medical attention right away.
- ❑ Scoop the litter box at least once a day.
- ❑ Wash the litter box regularly with hot water and bleach (and rinse well).
- ❑ Cover your child's sandbox to keep cats from using it as a litter box.
- ❑ Avoid touching the litter box if you are pregnant or have a weakened immune system.

Meeting a New Person

Some cats are super-friendly and happy to meet your friends, house guests, roommates or new partner. But other cats are reticent about new people and can be unhappy and unsettled if someone new enters your life.

TAKE IT SLOWLY

If you have a new spouse or partner moving in, the more slowly you move new things into the house, the easier it will be for a cat to adjust. If it's going to be a big move, bring a few carloads or boxes of the new person's stuff beforehand to give your cat a chance to adjust gradually.

If your cat was allowed in the bedroom before and you want to exclude her now that you have a partner, start shutting her out of the bedroom as soon as possible, before the new mate actually moves in. This gives the cat a chance to adjust to changes one piece at a time.

IF THE CAT DOES NOT LIKE SOMEONE

If you have a close friend or an intimate partner and your cat does not take to him at all, Comfort Zone Feliway to the rescue! During the getting-to-know-you phase, have your significant other spray his shoes, socks and lower pants legs with Feliway. This will make the new person smell familiar and appealing.

◆ Read Feline Negative Body Language

There are several clues a cat can give about her displeasure with someone, but unfortunately we haven't been given an "owner's manual" about our cat to give us guidelines.

If a cat rubs her head and cheeks on a person, that is a good sign. But if she rubs her facial gland and then immediately backs up and stares, do not try to pat that cat—you could get bitten or scratched.

If a cat backs up and stares at you, don't try to close the distance between you. A stare is never a friendly gesture, and backing up to put distance between the cat and someone is a direct challenge.

Do not reach out or try to pat a cat who is displaying hostile body language. You can easily get nailed.

◆ Follow Feline Etiquette

Cats Do Not Like Being Stared At. Cats stare at their prey when they are hunting, so they don't like it done to them. If your new living companion is not familiar with cat behavior, then explain that to him, so he will avoid direct eye contact.

Looking Away Is Actually Good Cat Etiquette. Instead of looking right at the cat, have the new person turn his head sideways and glance indirectly. And when the new person *does* look at the cat, he should give the cat a long slow blink, which is the feline way of saying hello. You will see how much a cat appreciates a new person blinking at her: She will probably give a blink back in return, a good sign that communications are open.

Cats Are Most at Ease if They Are Not Approached. A cat will be relaxed and make contact sooner if a new person keeps to himself and allows the cat to go to him. A new person should not approach the cat or try to pick her up—that's way too uppity at this point. If the new person stays still and basically ignores the cat, the kitty will go to that person eventually. This explains why cats so often go to the person in a group who likes them the least and pays them no mind at all—because that is most appealing and comfortable for a cat.

When the Cat Does Come Over, Ignore Her. Let her sniff the new person and his belongings.

Avoid Loud Voices, Quick Movements and Big Gestures. All these can be threatening to a cat, at least in the beginning. Try to keep it toned down.

Stick Out a Finger for Her to Sniff. This allows her to become familiar with the new person before he reaches to pat her.

If the new person will be living with you and handling the cat, you need to set very clear boundaries about what can be done—and what cannot. Here are some guidelines for the new person:

Do not ever be the one to punish or reprimand the cat. It's not your job.

Don't try to lift or shoo the cat off furniture. You'll make an enemy that way.

Spend time using interactive toys so the cat can come to know you better and share a positive experience with you.

Feed the cat meals for a positive association, but leave the eating area if the cat seems uneasy. On the other hand, many cats really enjoy company while they eat, and some even appreciate being stroked down the back while they are chowing down, so watch the cat's reactions and behave accordingly.

Petting Problems

It's a funny thing about petting cats—many of them will only tolerate a limited amount of affectionate stroking before reacting badly. To understand a cat's true nature, it helps to look to the wild, where cats are not generally contact animals. Unlike most other mammals, for whom physical proximity is natural, adult cats are aloof and spend very little time actually touching another creature. Some individual cats can only tolerate a brief amount of physical closeness; even with their own species, they only have physical contact with another cat to mate, play or fight. Although there are many cats who love being petted and held, many others are just are not wired to snuggle and cuddle with people; it is not instinctual for them.

Pay close attention to the physical clues your cat gives you about how much touching she wants, and respect how much time alone and personal space she needs. She will trust you not to invade that space and eventually may learn to be more comfortable with physical affection.

Even if you are a cat's most beloved person, one day you may be quietly stroking her and find yourself shocked to be on the receiving end of a nasty bite or scratch. The first time this happened to me—with Florence, a lovely big fluffy white cat we inherited with a house we bought—I thought something was terribly wrong with her. "No wonder those people wanted to sell this house," I thought. "It was the only way to get away from this crazed cat!" But of course I was dead wrong. Florence was a sweetie pie, one of those stretch-out-lengthwise-on-your-chest-when-you-lie-down kind of cats, and plenty affectionate—but it had to be on her terms. I knew nothing at the time about the "switch" that can go off in cats when they reach a limit on physical contact and just cannot tolerate a moment longer of that stimulation.

Chapter 6, on understanding your cat's behavior, goes into this issue of a cat's personal limits for tolerating physical stimulation. Have a look back at that section and then rethink the way you interact with your cat. You cannot simply sit beside the average cat while reading a book, continuously stroking her from head to tail, because you run the risk that at some point she will go into sensory overload and tell you to knock it off by running away or by biting or scratching you. This reaction does not come completely out of the blue, although at the time it may seem unprovoked and even vicious. Your cat probably gave you some subtle signals that she'd had enough of that lovey-dovey stuff—but if you don't know what body language to look for, then that cranky bite takes you totally by surprise.

Your Last Will and Taking Care of Your Cat

You may not want to think about it, but what will happen to your cat if you pass away first? This may seem like a depressing or stressful topic, but by facing it now you extend a most loving and generous gesture to your cat. Only 20 percent of people with pets make provisions for them in their wills, yet it is a fairly simple thing to do. Writing a will that considers your cat's welfare and future will eliminate any worries you might have about what will happen to her if you should die before she does. Without any legal documentation of your wishes regarding your cat, she would be passed on to an heir like a piece of property. Therefore, if your family members are not ideal future caregivers for your cat, make sure you identify a friend who is.

The easiest way to provide for the cat is to add a provision to your will that gives the chosen person ownership of your pet. With just a few words you can protect your cat's welfare in case you can't be there to do that.

ASK A FRIEND OR RELATIVE

The first step is to ask a close friend who loves cats—or at least loves yours—if he would be willing to give your cat a home if anything should happen to you. But just asking is not enough. You need to invite this person to spend plenty of time with your cat(s) so that he realizes the full extent of what his responsibility will become. Just to be prudent, ask a backup caretaker should the first person turn out to be unable.

CARRY A WALLET CARD

Once you choose a caretaker, it would be prudent if you put a card in your wallet labeled "*My Pets: In Case of Emergency*" and include your chosen caretaker's name and phone number, along with your vet's name, phone number and address.

CONSULT WITH AN ATTORNEY

To be certain that your wishes are carried out, you can have an estate attorney draft a will or an amendment to your existing will that leaves your cat to a friend or relative. No matter how simple you think an issue is, a will can complicate everything unless it is spelled out perfectly, so you may want to hire an estate attorney to give you peace of mind.

You can also establish a trust for your pet. Pet trusts were first legalized in the state of California and are now recognized in 24 states. These trusts can be minutely detailed about how you want your beloved kitty looked after, right down to the brand of cat food she should get. However, although you can give ownership of your cat along with funds to look after her, the court can reduce any amount if it appears to be excessive. An estate attorney will know if you are in one of the states where it is not legal to leave money directly to your cat, in which case you have to give the money in trust to the friend or relative who will take in the cat.

GET THE HUMANE SOCIETY OF THE UNITED STATES WILL PLANNER

The HSUS has a great packet of information to help you plan for your pet's care if something should happen to you. The kit of information includes a 6-page fact sheet with sample phrases for an attorney to use when including directions for the care of your cat in a living will or trust. The kit also contains stickers to alert emergency personnel that your cats and other pets are inside the house and an alert card for your wallet in case something happens to you and your pets are home alone. For a copy of this kit contact HSUS at 202-542-1100 or visit www.hsus.org.

IF THERE IS NO ONE TO STEP IN

If you have no relatives or friends who can look after your cat, there are retirement homes for pets that offer long-term care for a fee or donation. Two of them in New York State are the Golden Years Retirement Home at Bide-a-Wee (www.bideawee.org) and Pet Estates (www.petestates.com). Contact them for information about other facilities that might be nearer to you.

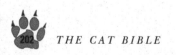

Chapter 9

GROOMING

Brushing Your Cat

You may wonder why you even have to think about grooming an animal who spends a good portion of her waking hours doing that very thing for herself. But there *are* a number of good reasons why your cat will benefit if you brush her regularly.

❑ Long-haired cats need the most help keeping their coats in tip-top condition, but even short-haired cats benefit from strokes from your brush.

❑ Outdoor cats naturally shed twice a year, in preparation for winter and for summer, since they are exposed to the outdoors and the natural changes in the light and temperature. A completely indoor cat does not have major sheddings twice a year because she lives in artificial light and a more consistent year-round temperature, so she sheds moderately but continuously. In either case, shedding creates a lot of excess hair for the cat to lick and swallow. Without grooming help, especially at these times, your cat can wind up with uncomfortable hairballs from all that swallowed hair.

❑ A cat experiencing stress, even a small dose of it, will shed automatically as a response. Since we know how long the list is of stress factors for cats, this can happen quite frequently and your cat will need some extra brushing help from you. So if you know that your cat has recently been in a stressful situation—your absence, going to the vet, household visitors and so on—then jump right in with some extra brush strokes.

❑ By grooming your cat you are conducting a health check at the same time. You will be able to feel any lumps, sores or ticks and see ear mites or fleas. This gives you a chance to correct these problems before they cause medical problems or physical discomfort.

❑ If someone in your household suffers from allergies, you can make things easier on them by grooming your cat regularly with Allerpet or Dander Free to reduce dander.

❑ By getting your cat used to being frequently handled all over her body, you will accustom her to being touched by strangers, such as her veterinarian, the pet sitter or your friends. It is especially useful to make her easier to handle for when you have to give her medication.

START YOUNG

If you have a kitten, the sooner you start getting her used to being brushed, bathed and having her nails cut, the easier it will be on both of you down the road. If a kitten is accustomed to standing for brushing and the sensation of the brush and her nails being exposed, then there is no trauma or drama about it. If you have a grown cat who has not had a good foundation in being groomed, it will be an ongoing effort to get her to relax and maybe even one day enjoy the pampering. Follow the tips below to make grooming a positive experience.

⬩ Keep It Short and Sweet

Don't make grooming sessions too long with a cat. It is far better to groom half of your cat in one session and the rest later on or on another day. Each cat is different, but if your cat can tolerate only so much petting, then grooming is not going to be her favorite pastime. Respect your cat's patience level and don't push your luck. And think of each grooming session as a chance to re-inforce her positive perception of the experience.

⬩ Be Gentle

Think of your cat's skin as delicate chiffon silk. Don't be in a rush. Choose a quiet time when both of you can enjoy grooming as a special time for closeness. Pulling or scraping with a grooming tool is truly painful. If you hurt her, she will dread being groomed and run for the hills when she sees that brush and rubber mat coming out.

Have a look at the suggestions under "Where and How to Groom" later in this section to develop brushing techniques that are pleasant for your cat.

⬩ Watch Your Cat's Body Language

If your cat's tail swishes or is in motion at all, that's your signal to end the beauty session. When your cat is getting fed up, she will discharge some of that tension in her tail.

⬩ Take It Easy on Her Tail

Cats are particularly sensitive about their tails and generally do not like having them touched. Keep that in mind when you are grooming the tail, especially of a long-haired cat, so that you can move swiftly and extra gently when brushing it.

EQUIPMENT YOU NEED FOR GROOMING

There are some basic tools that anyone with a cat needs, and some slightly different ones for different types of coats, but overall it's a pretty short, easy list.

Rubber bath mat with suction cups. You can place this on whichever table or counter you use to groom the cat. You'll also want to attach it to the bottom of the sink or bathtub when you bathe her.

A human nail clipper. The average small people's nail clipper is easiest for most people to maneuver and gives the best cut. Nail clippers for dogs are out of the question, and the "guillotine" style of clipper sold for both dogs and cats lend themselves to cutting too much.

A slicker brush. This is a handled brush with rows of wire bristles that can actually be painful on a cat's skin. You should test a slicker brush for yourself by running it down your own arm—press on it and see what it feels like. JW Pet Company makes a wonderful slicker brush with a ball on the end of each metal bristle so they don't dig into the cat's skin the way thin wire bristles can do. These brushes have really comfortable ergonomic handles, and they are inexpensive, too. JW also makes a brush with rubber spikes instead of metal ones. After using one of these brushes for the first time on my cats Bert and Ernie, I tossed out the old-fashioned prickly wire slicker brushes.

A Zoom Groom. This molded rubber oval-shaped brush has thick rubber nubs that act as "bristles." Zoom Groom comes in a variety of sizes and works wonderfully to extract and hold on to the hair of long-haired cats. It's a great massage tool for short-haired cats, too, loosening their dead hair.

A grooming glove. This is an optional grooming tool but a useful one. It is shaped like an oven mitt and has a rubberized area with nubs on the palm area so that you can stroke the cat, pick up dead hairs and stimulate the skin. This is a great piece of equipment if you have a cat who hates being groomed because it helps acclimate her to being touched without a harsh grooming tool; it is also a nice tool you can use to finish your grooming session and clean off any leftover debris.

A sprayer attachment for the sink. If you plan to bathe your cat in the kitchen or laundry sink and already have a built-in sprayer attachment, that's fine. But if not, you'll want to buy a rubber hose to slip over the faucet. You'll need the same kind of hose if you intend to wash your cat in the bathtub, unless you have a tub with a built-in sprayer. However, as you will note in the bathing instructions that follow, you don't want to use a spray head; you want a nozzle that water will flow out of without squirting. You can easily modify most attachments by removing the spray head.

Shampoo for cats. You never want to use human shampoo on cats, not even the fanciest product, because the pH of the shampoo is different; human shampoo strips the essential oils from a cat's coat (surprisingly, if you don't have cat shampoo and are forced to bathe your cat, you are better off using dish detergent than human shampoo). Pick a hypoallergenic non-soap shampoo made for cats with no additives like lanolin or conditioners, which coat the hair follicles and attract dirt.

Ask your vet to suggest a suitable shampoo. Be extra careful when selecting a product for a kitten, and remember never to use a product intended for dogs. Some groomers like to use liquid pure castile soap, which is usually available in the cosmetics section of health food stores.

A shining rag for the end. When you finish grooming your cat, firmly rub a piece of velvet or a soft chamois cloth firmly in the direction your cat's hair grows, to bring out the shine in her coat.

SPECIAL GROOMING NEEDS OF LONG-HAIRED CATS

A long-haired cat has to put up with an awful lot of grooming because she needs to be brushed practically every day to prevent her fine hair from getting tangled into mats. Every time you groom a cat with long hair—whether or not she has matting problems—make it a calm, affectionate experience and give her special treats for being such a good sport.

✦ Removing Matted Hair

Mats are painful for a cat because they pull on her skin like a too-tight braid. They are also painful when you try to remove them, and the only way to accomplish this is patiently and gently.

To remove matted hair, first sprinkle cornstarch on the mat—or squirt it with a spray cat-hair detangler—and work the mat out with a brush or comb, brushing gently from the skin toward the end of the hair. To help her tolerate the brushing, you can put a little bit of meat baby food or cat food on the finger of your other hand and let the cat lick it while you try to ease out the mat with a brush. If she gets upset, give it a break. Try for just a minute or two at a time, and stop if you don't make any progress reducing the size of the mat.

If the mat cannot be brushed out and is not too close to the skin, use blunt-tipped animal hair scissors to cut it out. But if it *is* close to the skin, experts caution that you should never attempt to cut it out yourself. It is too easy to cut the cat's skin and do some real harm. You're going to have to take the cat to a professional groomer. If the mats are really bad, talk to your vet about shaving the mats out while your cat is sedated. This should be incentive enough to keep up regular brushing in the future. (If you do have to sedate the cat to remove mats, you may want to ask the vet whether your cat's teeth should be cleaned at the same time.)

A Resco-brand coarse grooming comb is another tool you'll need to comb through long fur. *Do not buy the cheap combs in pet stores* because poor-quality combs can tangle hair. Find a pet store that carries Resco, which makes professional-quality instruments. The combs come in three sizes, but "coarse" is good for all long-haired cats. Start combing at the base of the tail and lift the hair a section at a time, combing underneath until you make your way up to the head and neck. This may require several grooming sessions if your cat loses patience.

✦ Tear Stain Remover

Long-haired cats, especially white ones, can get tear stains on the fur near the corners of their eyes. You can buy a tear stain remover solution from any pet store to help eliminate these stains. If tearing is excessive, consult your veterinarian.

SPECIAL GROOMING NEEDS OF HAIRLESS CATS

Hairless cats actually get dirty more quickly and need to be groomed more often than those with hair because their skin gets greasy. Use a soft human baby brush. For Sphynx cats (who are covered in a fine down), you need a rubber currycomb to massage her skin in circular motions to remove the loose down and release the oils on her skin. Hairless cats need frequent baths, as often as once a week. For touch-ups in between bath times, you can use unscented baby wipes, which gently remove the surface grease.

IF YOUR CAT HATES GROOMING

Some cats just cannot stand to be brushed and fussed over. If you have tried everything you can think of to make grooming a pleasurable experience and your cat still gets all worked up and fights you, you should consider using a product called a cat muzzle, which is made of soft material and slips over the cat's head. Ask about it in your pet store. It isn't like an anti-biting muzzle for dogs; it is more like the calming hood put over birds of prey before their handlers release them. Once on, it can have a totally calming effect on a cat, who will lie down on the grooming table and submit to being groomed.

WHERE AND HOW TO GROOM

Choose a table or counter that is a comfortable height for you. For many people this would be the kitchen counter, which is also usually in a well-lighted location. However, some behaviorists would advise against using any surface where the cat is not normally allowed to go since it sends a mixed message and contradicts the "no cats on kitchen surfaces" rule that most people like to set. It is better if you can find another spot to groom that is not normally off-limits to your cat, such as a bathroom countertop, a laundry room table or the top of the washer or dryer. But if you can't find an alternative surface, you'll still be putting down a rubber grooming mat that transforms the surface into another texture entirely, so you can make any location work for you.

Some people put down a towel for the cat to stand on while being groomed, but since a towel tends to slide around and bunch up if you are on a slick surface, you're better off using a rubber bathtub mat with suction cups. The mat won't slide and it will give her good footing, too, so she feels more secure.

Another option is to groom your cat on the floor. While no grooming mavens ever recommend it, I always groomed my cats by getting down on the floor with them. I'd put down a towel and invite them to stretch out and we both had an enjoyable time, for however long it lasted. It may not be the choice of a professional, but if you have no physical limitations that prevent you from getting down on the ground to brush your cat and clip her nails, I recommend getting down to the cat's level.

HOW TO USE THE SLICKER BRUSH

You might think it's wacky that someone has to tell you how to humanely use a wire brush on your cat, but doing it right can be the difference between a cat who enjoys being brushed and makes it a pleasure for you and one who fights you because it is miserable for her. The one essential trick is that you need to hold the handle of the brush low, close to the cat's body, almost in line with her back. If your knuckles are wrapped around the handle and touch her fur the whole time, you're doing it correctly. By brushing at this angle—with very little angle to the brush, actually—you avoid having the bristles dig into the cat's skin.

Try it on your own arm: Hold the brush low and close to your skin at your wrist and pull it up your arm toward your body. Your knuckles should graze your arm if you're doing it right. Now lift the handle so that the brush is at a right angle with the skin to feel how the teeth dig in when you use the incorrect angle. Unfortunately, that's often how people use a slicker brush, not knowing any better. Another habit you don't want to get into is using the brush the gentle way until the end of each stroke, when you tend to raise the handle up before breaking contact with the cat's fur and the head of the brush. Try that on your own arm and you'll see how lifting the handle at an angle digs the bristles in just as you finish the stroke—another painful experience for the cat. When you begin each brush stroke, take care not to just plunk the brush onto her body and then drag it; begin and end each stroke with kindness. Use that slicker brush delicately and you will have a better chance of having a content, well-groomed kitty.

Bathing Your Cat

Generally speaking, an average cat only needs a bath once or twice a year. However there are circumstances that require more frequent bathing. A cat with dandruff or other skin problems may need bathing every couple of weeks, and hairless cats need bathing every 7 to 10 days because of their oily skin. Also, if members of your household are allergic to cats, then frequent rinsing and bathing (twice a week for the rinsing and every week for the bathing) will make living with a cat much more pleasant for them.

PREPARATION FOR THE BATH

A successful bathing experience with a cat depends at least in part on having everything set up and thought out ahead of time. Even though you may feel sorry for your cat for having to go through this watery ordeal, it will help if you keep an upbeat attitude instead of a guilt-ridden one. Hold positive thoughts about how good the bath is for her and you will transmit an upbeat mind-set that the cat will pick up on.

Some people say it helps to visualize the bathing process before you begin; the way you see it unfolding is what you will make happen. You're going to soak the cat right down to her skin; then, starting from her neck and working toward her tail, you'll lather her with warm diluted shampoo; finally, you'll do a whole lot of rinsing before toweling her dry.

• Before You Start, Brush Her

If you have a long-haired cat, you must get rid of any tangles or mats before even one drop of water hits her or the tangles will tighten up and get much worse. Because detangling and brushing can take time and patience, plan to groom the cat over a period of hours, breaking it into several sessions throughout the day, before bathing her.

• Get Someone to Assist You

It is much easier to give a cat a bath if you have someone else to hold her gently. Of course you can do it alone, but it's a messier operation. With another person to hold the cat securely, you can concentrate on the lather and rinse aspects, and there's less chance of the cat getting spooked and trying to escape.

• Set Out Your Towels

Before you begin, put out a pile of old towels and/or a drying chamois (a synthetic material made for drying cats and dogs that absorbs many times its weight in liquid).

• Wear Clothes Ready to Be Soaked

Washing a cat can be a messy, splashy endeavor, so wear clothes that can take a beating.

• Set Out Your Shampoo and Acid Rinse

Get a plastic squeeze bottle, like the kind sold in kitchenware stores for dressings and sauces, and fill it with a mixture of half shampoo and half warm water. Then make your rinse water. This needs to be in a bigger container, such as a half-gallon plastic jug or juice container. Into it put 8 parts of warm water to 1 part plain distilled white vinegar or lemon juice. This rinse takes out all the shampoo residue and leaves the right pH balance for the coat and skin.

✦ Warm the Water and the Sink

Put the rubber mat in the sink or tub and run very warm water to take the chill out of the basin. Then lower the temperature so it is just pleasantly warm, and keep the water running the entire time. You want the temperature to be consistent when you use it, so as not to startle your cat. A cat's body temperature is slightly higher than ours, so you want the water nice and warm but not hot. Try it on your wrist; if it's comfortably warm, that's perfect.

GIVING THE BATH

✦ Saturate the Cat Down to Her Skin

Especially if your cat has oily or greasy skin, it may take some rubbing around to get her fur well soaked. Once you've got her coat wet through and through, leave the water running throughout the bath, with the flow of water directed away from her. Do not spray her directly with the hose; cats hate that. Instead, hold the open end of it in your palm and let the water run out of the hose and into your hand, and then onto the cat.

✦ Lather Her Up Starting at the Neck

Squeeze some of the diluted shampoo onto the cat's neck and then onto her shoulders and chest. Then work your way back, lathering under her armpits and on her belly and torso, saving her inner thighs and tail for last.

✦ Rinse and Rinse and Rinse

Rinsing the shampoo out is so important—the residue can irritate a cat's skin. After all the shampoo is out, rinse with a couple of containers of your acid rinse water, and then rinse again with clear water after that.

✦ Squeeze the Water Out, then Dry

Press the cat's tail and legs gently with a towel or your fingers to get out the excess water. Then use a series of dry towels to pat and squeeze her dry. Do not rub a cat to dry her, especially a long-haired cat whose fur will get knotted from a rubbing motion when it is wet.

✦ Dry Her in a Small, Warm Place

You may want to put the cat in a bathroom with the door closed and a heater on until she is totally dry. Some cats will tolerate a hair dryer on a low setting, but be careful not to burn her or overheat her. Air-drying in a warm place is safer and easier. If the cat is allowed to walk around when wet, her wet fur can pick up dirt.

Bath Rules

- Never spray a cat in the face or dump water on her head.
- Use a warm wet washcloth to clean her face.
- Don't spray the cat directly with the hose; run the water into your hand first.
- Speak to the cat in a gentle, calm way while you bathe and dry her, to soothe her and reduce stress.

Skin Problems

There are a lot of reasons a cat can develop skin problems and numerous categories under which skin problems can fall. You should not try to diagnose the problem yourself. Your vet needs to do tests to determine what is bothering your cat's skin and what treatment is going to work.

Types of Skin Problems

Parasitic—the most common, caused by fleas, lice, mites

Fungal—caused by infections such as ringworm and yeast

Neoplastic—skin cancer

Nutritional—caused by deficiency in the diet

Seborrheic—caused by overproduction of keratin, resulting in blackheads on chin and lips

Viral—caused by a virus; cats with FIV and FeLV are especially susceptible

Bacterial—occurs when a scrape, bite or scratch gets infected; can become an abscess (a pus-filled wound)

Hormonal—caused by thyroid or pancreas malfunction

Immunologic—caused by an allergic reaction to pollen or dust

DANDRUFF

A cat's coat says a lot about her health, so if your cat has dandruff, she should be checked out by the vet, who may want to do a blood test to check her thyroid and other regulatory systems for imbalance.

◆ Diet Can Lead to a Dandruff-Laden Coat

Some nutritionists believe that allowing a cat to free-feed on dry food, particularly low-quality kibble, is the cause of skin problems. The theory these nutritionists have is that if a cat is constantly

smelling food, her body is in a constant state of preparation for digestion, and this constant physical readiness for processing food slows down her metabolism. If the metabolic system is not being efficient, your cat's kidneys and digestive system are not functioning efficiently, and waste products wind up being excreted on the skin instead of through the organs designed for those tasks.

Assuming this theory has merit, the solution is to feed a quality protein meal twice a day, as described in the nutrition chapter, with an exercise/play session right before meals to encourage the body to excrete waste through the normal channels. These nutritionists suggest that the best way to improve your cat's skin condition is to phase out the kibble in a cat's diet and replace it with high-quality protein. They also suggest boosting the fiber in the diet by adding a pinch of bran or finely grated raw carrot or zucchini to the food. While there is no absolute proof to support this nutritional theory, if you have a cat with a dry, flaky, greasy coat, what have you got to lose by giving this diet a try?

◆ Bathe Every 2 to 4 Weeks

You need to wash your cat frequently to restore skin health if she has a lot of dandruff. The acid rinse after shampooing, described in the section on how to bathe your cat, can be particularly beneficial. Be sure to rinse several times with plain warm water also, to be sure there is no residue on your cat's fur when you're done.

FUR ISSUES

A cat may have four types of fur on her body. Three are true fur, and the fourth is the whiskers (technically called *vibrissae*). *Down fur* is the closest to the cat's skin—it is very fine and short and keeps her warm. The *awn hairs* form the middle layer of the fur and are bristly, and the top coat is called *guard hair*, which is longer and thicker than the other two inner layers, protecting them against wet and cold.

The texture and amount of fur on a cat depends on her breed. Some long-haired cats have guard hair 5 inches long, while short-haired cats may have 2-inch guard hairs. And then there are breeds such as the Cornish Rex, which have only down fur and curly whiskers.

◆ Hair Loss

There are a number of common reasons that a cat can lose her fur, including a condition called *alopecia*, which causes her to lose clumps of it. The first order of business is to have your vet examine the cat for any medical issues that could be compromising her coat. *Thyroid or other hormonal abnormalities* are the first thing vets will look for. Other causes can be *external parasites* (fleas, mites), *internal parasites* (tapeworms or roundworms), or *infection* (bacterial, viral or fungal). And then there are cats who are *allergic* to medications, foods or environmental elements such as grasses, molds, dust and mites.

◆ Reddish Tinge to the Fur

Red streaks can sometimes appear in a cat's coat that is not normally red. Some say this is a sign of a serious protein deficiency, but more commonly the streaks are blood deposited from the

cat's mouth when she is grooming herself (if she has dental disease or other oral problems), or the red streaks could be a sign of flea infestation since flea feces are basically digested blood. In any case, this warrants a visit to the vet to find out the reason and correct it.

◆ A Cat Who Grooms Too Much

It's probably time for a vet consultation if your cat licks, rubs or sucks her coat constantly. Overgrooming can cause all sorts of skin problems, from fur loss to skin irritation, sores and scabs. This behavior can be caused by anxiety (sort of like nail biting in people), in which case it is called *psychogenic licking*. Another reason can be that the cat licks to relieve internal pain from urinary problems or external discomfort from fleas or mites. Even when these physical problems have been solved, she may still continue this self-soothing behavior of frequent licking. Your vet will have some ideas about how to break this cycle, whether by using Comfort Zone Feliway in a spray or diffuser as a calming agent in the atmosphere or by prescribing a temporary antianxiety medication for your cat. In addition, please explore homeopathic remedies at www.spiritessence.com.

◆ A Cat Who Grooms Too Little

This is generally a sign of ill health in a cat, especially when it goes along with lethargy or lack of appetite. Other reasons that a cat might not be keeping herself tidy are because she is overweight or arthritic and cannot reach all areas of her body to groom, especially the hind end or belly. Alternately, a cat with a long, thick coat may simply need your assistance to get the job done well.

Nail Clipping

Even with a scratching post, which allows the nail sheaths to slough off, most cats need their nails trimmed once or twice a month so they will not get overgrown and cause pain or damage things they snag with their claws.

Cats do not generally like to have their feet handled, so a mild amount of resistance is normal when you first set out to trim her nails. However, if your cat panics and tries to escape, you should have a groomer, or better yet your vet's office, do the trimming so that no one gets hurt. You should ask to be present so that you can watch how they do it and learn the proper technique to do it yourself at home.

THE FORMULA FOR STRESS-FREE NAIL CLIPPING

The simplest advice there is about how to make your cat accept getting a manicure is to start young. Cats are especially sensitive about their feet, because before domestication the feet were essential to the way a cat hunted, climbed and defended herself. Once a kitten learns to trust you with her feet, you can make nail clipping a calm, pleasant experience and should not experience resistance from her.

If your cat is already an adult, please keep in mind the natural protective instinct cats have about their feet. It is stressful for them to have their feet handled, period. You need to get a cat used to this sensation very slowly—no rush, no timetable. Little by little, during daily grooming or just during petting, touch her toes with the lightest touch, and over time she will become desensitized to the feeling and accept it. Then you can move on to the next steps below.

◆ Start by Gently Touching Her Feet

First get your cat really relaxed by cuddling or stroking her in the way you know to be her favorite (if you haven't figured this out, it's the way you touch her that makes her purr the most or offer you that part of her body she likes you to touch). Then touch her feet, very gently pressing down on each of her toes, which extends the claws—just for a second on each toe, and just long enough to get the claw to peek out. Do this every day for a week.

◆ Study Her Claws

After a week, your cat should be relaxed when you play with her feet. Now you're going to start exposing her claws and leaving them out for a moment. The best way to get that claw to extend all the way out is not so much by squeezing the toe but by placing a finger underneath her paw, on the pad just beneath the claw, and pressing up. The claw will come right out.

The claw will be transparent or whitish with a very hooked curve on the tip. That curved white bit at the very end is all that you are going to be cutting. You'll see a pink center with a vein in it, which is called the quick. Be sure to avoid cutting the quick when clipping nails because it will hurt the cat and bleed quite a bit. Some cats have black nails that you cannot see through, so be sure that you clip just the curve of the tip to blunt the nail and avoid the quick.

◆ Touch the Nail Clipper on the Cat's Toes

Once your cat is comfortable with having her claws exposed briefly, touch her toes with the clipper, but don't cut anything yet. Just get her used to the feel of the clippers on her feet. Do this for 2 or 3 days.

◆ Cutting Your First Nail

Don't be nervous. There's no reason to be worried about hurting your cat because you are only cutting off the dead nail—you aren't going anywhere near that scary quick. You won't risk hurting (and thereby scaring) your cat if you avoid cutting close to the quick and you're only snipping off the very little curved bit at the tip. Begin by cutting a nail or two at a time so you can feel at ease and not strain your cat's tolerance level. A few hours later, clip another nail or two and give it a rest again. Do only a few nails at a time, going slowly and getting both of you accustomed. Think of nail cutting as blunting the tip, just snipping off a teeny bit. Your goal is that when the cat steps down on her foot, the new flat tip that you cut will be flat on the ground.

◆ If You Do Hit the Quick

Don't be alarmed if you take off a little too much. The nail does bleed quite a bit if you hit the vein. There are three ways to stop the bleeding: use a styptic pencil (sold for men who cut themselves shaving) that you dab onto the nail, have a box of cornstarch nearby so you can put a little

in the palm of your hand and dip the bleeding nail into it or use a soft bar of soap that you can press the nail into for the same effect.

Tooth Brushing

Yes, you heard correctly! Brushing your cat's teeth is actually one of the most important aspects of grooming because good teeth and gums go a long way toward keeping a cat comfortable and healthy as she ages. Gum disease in particular leads to a variety of health issues for cats (just as it does for people). When I say "tooth brushing," the real goal is health at the gum line, keeping that area plaque-free—very similar to dental issues in humans. When there is inflammation at the gum line there can be pain, infection and eventual loss of teeth.

START AT ANY AGE AND BRUSH AS OFTEN AS YOU CAN

This is the most realistic advice I can give because if your cat is 8 years old and has never had her teeth brushed before, it will be much more difficult (though better late than never). If you can brush every few days, that would be nice, but if all you can manage is several times a month, that's still better than not at all.

If you can, start the kitten young and develop the habit and routine for both of you. If your cat is older, do the best you can. If you get discouraged that you are doing too little too late, don't lose sight of the fact that it's a lot better than doing nothing.

HUMAN TOOTHPASTE IS BAD FOR CATS

Toothpaste for humans is really not good for a cat—a cat is bound to swallow anything you put in her mouth, and it can hurt her innards.

FIND A TOOTHPASTE SHE LIKES

There are several toothpaste brands made just for cats, so experiment to find one she really loves—she'll be more cooperative about having her teeth brushed. You can pass along your cat's rejected toothpastes to other friends with cats, which may inspire *them* to try tooth brushing on their felines.

USE A FINGERTIP TO SIMULATE A TOOTHBRUSH

Get your cat used to having your fingers in her mouth by putting a small amount of cat toothpaste on your finger and rubbing it gently up where the gum meets the tooth.

APPLY THE TOOTHPASTE

Use a piece of gauze wrapped around your index finger, a rubber-bristled fingertip brush or a small soft toothbrush made for children. Ideally you want to brush with a circular motion up at the gum line, but don't irritate your cat or frustrate yourself. The real value is getting the paste up on the gums where it can get to work on plaque, with or without the boost of the brush.

OTHER DENTAL HEALTH PRODUCTS

Several companies make disposable plaque-removing wipes that claim to fight gum disease. Kitty ToothWipes have baking soda in them and cost about $8 for 40 wipes.

Other forms of dental health products are Triple Pet brand Plaque Off Fresh Breath drops, which you can add to the cat's water bowl (Benedent Corp., 800-450-4977, www.benedent.com). Dental Treat Paste is meant to be given as a separate treat and is supposed to slow plaque formation (www.vetbasis.com, or at PetSmart 877-473-8762).

Chapter 10

NUTRITION

You are probably going to be very surprised by what you learn in this chapter. Most people have no idea that the food they are offering to their beloved kitties may be doing them harm.

The information you'll read here may strike you as revolutionary—it will cast doubt on the choices you have always accepted as the best way to feed your cat. Those food choices are what your veterinarian has probably also accepted, and therefore recommended to you. Veterinarians are doctors trained to diagnose and cure illness—education about nutrition and its part in wellness as well as its role in causing illness is as lacking in veterinary training as it is in the training of human doctors. Most vets have their hands full keeping up with the developments in the medical field and do not have the time—or maybe even the motivation—to learn more about cat nutrition and evaluate what is in those bags and cans. Please understand that I do not intend any disrespect toward vets in this chapter—but at the same time I urge you to take personal responsibility for doing your homework and changing what goes in your cat's bowl. This chapter is the homework, but don't think of it as an onerous task. Look at this as an opportunity to educate yourself and take a stand about what goes into your kitty's stomach.

You may have a variety of reactions to the information you'll read here—disbelief, anger, frustration and annoyance. You may be resistant to some of the ideas put forth in here, but that is natural. Changing habits is difficult, and changing your perspective can be even more difficult. Depending on your personality and how many years cats have been an important part of your life, you may be more or less willing to be open-minded. It is likely that the more devoted you are to your cats, the more you will view this information as a challenge to your knowledge or how much you care.

Cat-lovers are in a difficult predicament because we can be misled by clever marketing and often deceptive advertising into believing that a particular food is good for our cats. We might realize that those jugs of multicolored cat crunchies in the supermarket are a product, like dish soap, made for profit by a big company. However, why don't we stop to learn what the ingredients mean and question what is in that food? We need to take personal responsibility for informing ourselves and making nutritional choices that will ultimately keep our cats healthy for a long time—and very few of us do that.

We all know the saying "You are what you eat," and that is especially true for a cat, with her sensitive digestive system and urinary tract, so we cannot afford *not* to be vigilant in what we feed our animals. I am glad to take responsibility for opening your eyes to what those words on pet food bags really mean, and to explain how to pick a healthy food that is more appropriate for your cat. In all likelihood, that is not the food you are feeding her now.

Other people may be defensive or not accept the information you'll find in this chapter. If you choose to talk to your vet or other professionally minded acquaintances about what you read here, they may doubt what you say because it contradicts the common practice of free-feeding dry cat food. But stop and think about that negative reaction. These people never questioned what goes into commercial cat food, but now get defensive when those ingredients are called into question. The information in this chapter comes from a vast network of authors, holistic vets, professional journals and the cat food companies that make excellent-quality foods. I owe a special debt of thanks to Lynette and Jenny of the volunteer group at www.FelineOutreach.org, who are fantastic examples of Feline Foodies, devoted to educating others about the right foods for cats. All these people want better-quality food to keep cats healthier longer.

Keep in mind the beauty of a supply-and-demand economy. If enough consumers lodge a complaint about a pet food simply by not buying it, and instead they choose a brand with superior ingredients—they will ultimately improve the way all cat food is made. The power for change is in each and every person's hands because we have the power in our pocketbooks.

Some Basics About Feline Nutrition and Digestion

THE CAT'S DIGESTIVE SYSTEM

As an obligatory carnivore, cats must eat mostly meat. This means that the cat's gastrointestinal tract is shorter than a dog's or a human's. During the cat's evolution, the GI tract adapted to the main diet being meat—so the feline digestive system evolved to process high calorie meat proteins, with hardly any vegetation. This has resulted in a shorter feline intestine, and means that the cat's digestive system cannot process fibrous foods which usually have a prolonged digestion time. Feeding a high fiber food only makes this situation worse because it places an unnatural burden on the cat's system, causing weight gain and a reduction in the nutrients that the cat's system can absorb from the diet.

ANIMAL PROTEIN IS ESSENTIAL

A cat is almost entirely carnivorous by nature (also known as an "obligate carnivore") so foods that are made primarily of cereal grains pose a problem for felines. A cat needs a diet of protein and no more than 20 percent carbohydrates. A carb-heavy diet is ill-advised for a cat because it can lead to serious health issues: obesity, diabetes, digestive problems including serious consti-

pation and urinary tract problems (to which cats are prone in the first place). Carbohydrates are not natural to the cat's digestive system in anything but the smallest amounts—for example, the undigested grain and plant matter that would be in the stomachs of rodents or birds they would feed on if they were fending for themselves in nature.

CATS ARE NOT VEGETARIANS

Cats cannot be vegetarians; it's as simple as that. This is at least in part because they need a chemical called *taurine,* which their bodies can only get from meat, unlike people's or dogs' bodies, which can manufacture it themselves. In theory, a nonmeat diet could be a healthy option for dogs, but a vegetarian cat is a contradiction in terms. A cat cannot live on plant matter alone—at least not well, and not for long.

Because taurine is essential to a cat's survival, check what you are feeding. Canned food needs to have at least .05 percent taurine (although more is even better) and dry food should have at least .16 percent taurine. If you are a vegetarian or vegan who is determined to impose your personal nutritional choice onto your cat, then you need to be sure at the very least that she gets a taurine supplement from the vet. She cannot survive without it.

Even though you could create a vegetarian diet for a cat that would include added taurine, along with some of the other essential components of meat, why would you go to that trouble? (Do forgive me, please, for feeling the need to suggest that if you feel so strongly about having a vegetarian animal, bunnies make very nice pets.)

SENSE OF SMELL AND TASTE

Cats have a powerful sense of smell, with receptors so sophisticated that they can distinguish between the smells of different proteins and fats. If something smells good to a cat, she will eat it; if not, she probably won't. Cats cannot taste sweetness (which dogs can). So to encourage a cat to eat, a food must first appeal to her odor receptors, which is why very strong-smelling cat foods have been developed.

CATS DON'T NATURALLY DRINK WATER

Wild cats receive nearly all the fluids they need from the prey they eat—small rodents, lizards, birds, bugs—which usually have a moisture content of about 70 percent. What most people don't know is that cats do not like to drink water. Some may learn to do it because of their totally dry diets, but it doesn't come naturally. The theory is that today's cats are not water drinkers because historically they were dependent on their prey as the principal source of fluid. It is thought that this nutritional quirk remains as the result of cats first being domesticated in Egypt, which has a hot, dry climate and where water is scarce (hence those camels with handy humps for "refueling"). It is believed that the feline system evolved into one where survival did not depend on finding drinkable water; instead, cats had to depend on their prey for their fluid intake, deriving it from the blood and other internal fluids of small birds and rodents, which are about 70 percent moisture.

Today's cat who is given nothing but dry food becomes dehydrated, causing her urine to be highly concentrated. Healthy urine should be dilute, or "watered down," and so highly concentrated urine commonly leads to urinary tract problems for cats, such as the formation of crystals and stones. Problems such as constipation and intestinal blockage can also be traced back to a cat's natural disinclination to drink fluids.

In addition to the modern problem that cats do not get enough moisture in their food (i.e., no moisture at all in dry food) and the fact that drinking water does not come naturally to them, because of their acute sense of smell cats are especially sensitive to the odor and taste of their water. They are so picky about odor that if water doesn't smell right to them (if there is a chlorine or other chemical odor, or if another pet has taken a drink from the bowl), they won't touch it.

Getting Your Cat to Drink More Water

- Offer bottled water if your cat refuses tap water and shows a preference for a particular bottled variety; you may want to make the investment in bottled water for long-term health benefits.
- Buy distilled water in large jugs if bottled spring water is too costly.
- Water at room temperature appeals to some cats, especially prior strays who are used to drinking out of puddles or other standing water.
- Try a recirculating pet water fountain (sold in most pet stores). A little pump feeds water down a plastic slide into a bowl and recirculates it back up again. Some cats are enticed to drink by the moving water, though others are not fooled by the same old water going around.
- Avoid plastic bowls, which retain odors no matter how they are washed.
- Get a bowl big enough not to squash her whiskers when she puts her face in to drink.
- Do not keep the water bowl next to the food dish—many cats dislike this.
- Scrub out the water bowl every day and refill with fresh water.

HOW OFTEN SHOULD A CAT EAT?

Since cats are true carnivores, their diet should consist almost entirely of meat, which takes many hours to digest. A good meal once a day is ideal for a cat's natural cycle of digestion. Cats in the wild hunt at twilight, eat what they catch, and then sleep until dusk the next day. In a natural state, a cat's gut is set up to gorge on a meal (when she finds prey), then not eat again for many hours, in some cases even for days. This allows for proper and complete digestion of a meat-based diet and elimination of the by-products.

But we all know that our house-bound cats are obviously not wild animals and they are used to eating more frequently than once a day. Also, we would probably not be comfortable feeding a cat that infrequently—it may be feline nature to gorge and fast (like a lion in the jungle), but it's human nature to feel good about our pets having a nice full tummy.

Since cats are creatures who thrive on a predictable schedule, the healthiest solution for a

domestic cat is a twice-daily feeding schedule that allows her stomach to digest and empty itself completely. This encourages an efficient digestive process that will be ready for the next meal on an empty stomach. If your cat has been free-feeding (see below), do not worry about changing her routine. She will soon adjust, as long as there is a somewhat predictable schedule. If you will be gone the whole day, then feed her in the morning before you leave (never leaving the bowl down all day, for reasons you'll see below) and then feed the second meal whenever you get home. The number of hours between meals is not critical, and for a nocturnally lively cat, the later she eats, the more it encourages her to sleep and not bug you during the night, as long as you throw in a play session before bed.

HOW MUCH FOOD DOES A CAT NEED?

A cat's stomach—before it is filled and expands—is about the size of a quarter. There are different opinions on how to determine the quantity of food to give your cat, as well as the amount of time she needs to be allowed to finish eating. Some people say a cat needs about 3 ounces of food at each meal; other people calculate that an average 8-pound cat who is healthy and active should eat the equivalent of 8 mice a day, with each mouse calculated at being about 30 calories.

You may be confused by the amount of food recommended on the cans themselves, which may suggest feeding a can for every 6 to 8 pounds of body weight. In the case of a very large cat like a Maine Coon, this would mean an absurd quantity of food. The best way to determine the right quantity is to feed 6 to 8 ounces of food every day for an average-size cat of about 10 pounds, which means give two meals of one small can (3 ounces) at each meal.

There's another way to decide the right amount for your cat: Let her tell you herself, since many believe that a cat will self-regulate and eat as much as she needs at any one time. Rather than worrying about portion size, you can measure your cat's nutritional needs by feeding her twice a day and each time giving her 15 or 20 minutes to eat to her heart's content. Put down half a can at first and if she polishes that right off, then give her a few tablespoons more until she is satisfied and walks away.

HOW MUCH DOES A KITTEN NEED TO EAT?

Young cats need to eat more frequently because they have tiny stomachs, a fast metabolism that burns up fuel quickly and they are growing. Basically a kitten needs about twice as much food as an adult cat. Go to the end of this chapter for more information about when, what and how much to feed kittens.

HOW MUCH SHOULD A CAT WEIGH?

The ideal weight for a cat is hard to judge, since cats come in so many shapes and sizes. However, if your cat has a belly that hangs down and swings when she walks, you need to make plans to reduce her weight. Oftentimes this will mean simply removing all dry food and feeding canned or raw instead, which research shows is the best diet for every cat.

How do you avoid raising a fat cat? The sorry truth is that it takes hard work on the part of the humans to make a cat fat in the first place. Most cats would not get fat since they are not normally prone to overeating: They naturally eat just until they are full. However, if a cat's environment is understimulating and she doesn't have enough to do to occupy her body and mind, and on top of that she has a bowl of constantly available starchy kibble to snack on, it's happy hour at the Carbo-Bar, which puts her at risk of becoming obese. If your cat is healthy, she will not have occasion to become fat if she gets two meals a day of actual meat. The main problem with free-feeding kibble is that a cat eats and eats but never gets truly satisfied because the food lacks the nutrients her body requires and she is just gorging herself on carbohydrates.

I realize that this last bit of information is probably shocking to many people, but stick with me here. The whole sordid story of poor cat nutrition will unfold in this chapter, along with ways to get your cat on the right track.

WHERE TO FEED

Keep the cat's litter box far from her dining area. Also, keep the food bowls in a quiet spot, away from areas of high traffic or hubbub. If you have multiple cats, place their bowls at a pleasant distance from each other so there is no competition or fear of poaching. Set it up so that they can all eat in peace and harmony, which is best for digestion in any species.

Good and Bad Ingredients in Cat Foods

PRESERVATIVES AND OTHER CHEMICALS IN FOODS

Processed foods are as much a concern for animals as they are for people. They often contain poor-quality ingredients and are full of preservatives, which may harm pets. The labels on commercial products can be deceiving because pet food companies add large quantities of premixed vitamins and minerals to their products and each of the individual ingredients in these concoctions contains some kind of preservative. So while the label may not list preservatives and claim "no *added* preservatives," your cat will be eating chemicals in various ingredients added during the manufacturing process.

◆ BHA and BHT

These two preservatives have been considered toxic for decades, and were once in snack foods for humans, too. They are chemical antioxidants that keep the fatty contents of pet food from turning rancid. These chemicals have been linked to birth defects and liver and kidney damage. If a cat ingests them at every single meal, it has to take a toll. The value of BHA and BHT to pet food makers, who still routinely use them, is that once they are doused on kibble, the stuff can stay "fresh" for vast amounts of time.

◆ Ethoxyquin

This is another antioxidant preservative that was once added to most pet foods to keep them from going bad. It is now proven to be toxic to animals (*really* toxic—it is known to cause blindness, leukemia and cancer of the stomach, skin, spleen and liver in companion animals). It took a while, but finally many of the pet food companies bowed to consumer pressure and removed it from the foods, which now bear the proud claim "No added ethoxyquin." *Except this may be a de-*

ceptive claim, folks. Pet food companies can state they don't add ethoxyquin to the food at their plant, but that does not take into account that suppliers of the raw ingredients of the foods (the meat and fats) have already treated them with this deadly chemical *before* shipping them to the pet food company. There's no way of being certain which kibble is free of ethoxyquin; one solution would be to choose a product from one of the high-quality pet food companies that has not had to be on the defensive about their ingredients.

◆ Flavoring Agents
Artificial flavoring agents are also added to many commercial foods, and although they are tasty to cats, they are unhealthy for them—and actually toxic in large quantities. Flavored pet foods also contain preservatives and added dyes that turn the naturally grim, gray color of dry food into a bizarrely unnatural red color, but some marketing genius must have decided this is what people find appetizing when they go to purchase cat food.

◆ Kava, Comfrey and Pennyroyal Are Dubious Supplements
AAFCO (Association of American Feed Control Officials) has moved to ban these three ingredients in pet foods, on the basis that not enough is known about their safety and usefulness in a cat's diet. Dozens of other supplements in cat foods have not yet been proven safe or effective, but these three have recently been singled out.

FATS IN CAT FOOD
All commercial dry pet food has fat added to make it more enticing, whether mixed with the other ingredients or sprayed on the finished product at the end. Fats give off an intense odor that attracts cats, who are especially stimulated to eat by their sense of smell. However, you need to know that frequently the source of fat in pet foods is old cooking oil sold by restaurants to pet food companies when they can no longer use it in their kitchens. It is then added to your cat's food instead of being thrown out or used for industrial purposes.

PROTEIN IN CAT FOOD
In nature, the prey that a cat would eat consists mostly of muscle meat; about one-sixth is organ meats and some intestines and blood vessels (if we discount feathers or fur). The best fuel for a cat's digestive system is meaty raw food, but if you're not going to feed raw, you want to at least follow those proportions in the prepared food you choose. The highest-quality proteins are those that come from muscle meat (what we think of as the flesh of the animal) and organs, because these both have the right balance of amino acids to aid a cat's digestion, allowing her body to most efficiently utilize the protein source.

◆ Low-Quality Protein
Generally speaking, the protein quality in most commercially made pet foods is low. These ingredients have to be processed under high heat and often sprayed with chemicals afterward. A pet food manufacturer can also count feet, eyes and feathers as part of the total protein content of their

food, although the lower the quality of protein, the more processing it needs to pass even those low government standards. Besides being less nutritious, or even useless to your cat's system, which cannot assimilate them, low-quality protein is also a cause of alkaline urine, a leading cause of urinary problems in cats. The pH of a cat's urine is affected by diet, and urine with an acidic pH is the most desirable because it prevents the growth of germs that cause feline urologic syndrome (FUS).

◆ Meat By-products

If you think what you just heard about "meat" sources is nasty, you're really going to be disappointed when you find out about by-products, the other animal protein sources in cat food. By law, by-products can contain moldy, rancid or spoiled meat, as well as the tissue and muscle meat too full of cancer to be eaten by humans. Diseased tissue, hair, pus, decomposing carcasses and meat rejects from the slaughterhouse all go into those little cans in the supermarket. Dead, diseased and dying animals are fair game for pet food, as are "downer animals," the ones who cannot walk to the slaughter. These are referred to by the pet-food watchdog groups as the "4 D's."

Food Pets Die For, by Ann N. Martin, verifies the reports I had been hearing that thousands of pounds of euthanized pets from shelters are also put into pet food. Did any of us ever stop to wonder what they do with the hundreds of thousands of pounds of shelter animals killed every year? A shelter animal is put to death every few seconds in the United States: What happens to all those bodies? Or even when our own beloved cat or dog is put to sleep humanely by our own vet? A fee is paid and a truck comes to dispose of those bodies, and we're too emotionally involved to stop and ask what will happen to them. We've all avoided thinking about this. There are some crematoriums in clinics and shelters, but they occupy a lot of space and cost at least $100,000 for a small one, so few facilities can afford it. Trucks of meat of all kinds make deposits at the rendering plants across the country, much of which winds up in pet food.

Roadkill is also permissible in pet food. This may mean nothing to you if you live in an apartment building in a city, but anyone who lives in a rural area can attest that there are constantly deer, raccoons, possum and squirrels that are killed on the road and picked up for disposal. Did you ever stop to wonder where they take these carcasses?

These random protein ingredients must be sterilized with high heat, high pressure and chemicals, and sometimes irradiated so that they do not sicken your cat immediately. At this point, you must also be thinking about the long-term health consequences of filling your cat with these ingredients.

Dry Food Is Basically Disastrous for Cats

The single most serious problem in feline nutrition is that most cats are fed exclusively dry food (also called kibble), *which is not an appropriate food for a cat*. You must be thinking, "Everybody feeds their cats dry food, right?" Sure they do—because nobody told them otherwise and everybody else feeds it and always has. Topping off a bowl of kibble is great for *people*—it's quick, clean and easy for people to deliver. You can well imagine how happy the pet food industry is about

that unquestioning devotion on the part of their customers, who are people, of course—the ones with the wallets. I'm here to urge you to "think outside the bag." I'm here, as your cat's best friend, advocating for a good hard look at what is in those bags of food. I may have an uphill battle ahead of me with some of you who have been doling out dry food to your cats all their lives. But the best-kept secret in the pet world is that a diet of dry food is to blame for many of the serious health problems that plague domestic cats. Many cats can tolerate that diet for years, but eventually it will catch up with them and cause health issues.

DRY FOOD LEAVES CATS DEHYDRATED

With a moisture content of around 10 percent, dry food goes against the basic design of a cat's digestive system, since it is not instinctual for a cat to drink water. As mentioned earlier, a cat's natural dinner in the wild would have about a 70 percent moisture content, which is sufficient to hydrate a cat. But if kibble is the main food for a cat, it leaves her with urine that is too concentrated and contributes to various medical problems such as diabetes, urinary stones and other bladder problems.

DRY FOOD CAN CREATE A FINICKY EATER

If kibble is left out all the time, a cat is never fully hungry. This can become a reason that a cat refuses to eat.

DRY FOOD DOES *NOT* CLEAN A CAT'S TEETH

How did this bogus claim about dry food originate? The same myth is in circulation about dry dog food, that somehow it "cleans" an animal's teeth, but if you stop for a moment you'll see there is no logic to it. Cats crunch on dry kibble with the points of their teeth, the grinding surfaces. Oral problems are almost entirely centered on the gums and gum line (gingivitis), where kibble makes no contact. If someone told you that eating potato chips or pretzels cleaned your teeth, wouldn't you think that was pretty funny? Well, most dry cat food is about as nutritious as those human snack items—and about as valuable to dental health as they are, too.

LEAVING KIBBLE OUT TO FREE-FEED ONLY BENEFITS PEOPLE

People who have watched their cats crunching away at a feeding bowl throughout the day and night have come to believe that dry food and the method of having it always available must suit the feline digestive system. But the unfortunate truth is that free-feeding dry food is only good for *you*, because it is convenient—you don't have to go out of your way to provide your cat with a fresh meal twice a day. You assume your cat is content because she nibbles periodically and has lots of meat on her bones—but there's a lot more to the story.

Some feline nutritional experts believe that free-feeding kibble is actually detrimental to a cat's health. Regardless of what the food is, they say that constantly available food is unnatural for the feline digestive system. Their theory is that the smell of food triggers a cat's brain to prepare her to eat, and her blood flow will be redirected to the stomach in preparation for digestive duties (that won't even take place since it was only a sniff). Meanwhile, the organs that process waste are unable to function optimally. These organs of elimination are the kidneys, liver and pancreas, as well as the skin itself. The natural processes of elimination and detoxification are constantly interrupted by the smell of food, which can lead to problems with the skin, fur and other systems. The cat may ultimately gain weight, not just because of the high carbohydrate content of dry food, but also because her body isn't burning the fuel efficiently and her system cannot eliminate the wastes properly.

Having food constantly available can also affect the urinary system. Some studies have shown that simply *smelling* food can affect the pH of a cat's urine, causing it to become alkaline. Feline urologic syndrome is made worse by alkaline urine, whereas many urinary tract issues in cats are avoided or even cured by maintaining an acidic urinary pH.

Food and the Human Bond

Animal behaviorists suggest that you can enhance your bond with your cat by giving small tasty treats. When your cat rubs against your legs or when she "talks" to you, many people automatically "reply" by giving her a treat; the food has brought you together in a pleasurable way. However, the fallacy in this reasoning is to decipher your cat's rubbing against your legs as a request for food, when in fact it may be a display of affection, or boredom or pent-up energy needing an outlet. Sometimes cat lovers are people with "eating issues" who themselves have come to equate food with love. They will use food as a palliative, a "self-soother," and they will eat when they are anxious, depressed, lonely or frustrated. This is a *human* reaction to emotional stress or imbalance, but it is not the natural feline response to those emotions.

We make a serious mistake when we give food to our cats in response to any attempts they make to get our attention. As Freud once said about his own elaborate theories, "Sometimes a cigar is just a cigar." Sometimes when a cat rubs against you and meows it is just for the pleasure of being in contact with you. Don't be so quick to presume hunger pangs and automatically put down a dish for your cat, rather than taking a moment for an ear scratch. If you do this, in effect you are teaching your cat that when she wants to interact with the two-legged species, it has to be about food.

Leaving food out gives psychological comfort to people. For some cat people, leaving a heaping bowl of kibble so their cat "never has to go hungry" fulfills a deep psychological need in themselves. People often have no clue that their own psychological needs could be influencing their decisions about nourishing their cats. Some human psychologists say that providing an unlimited supply of food for our cats so that they never have to "do without" is a way of reassuring ourselves of the same thing. This may sound far-fetched, but don't dismiss it too quickly. Many people with eating issues are influenced by the connection that food equals love, and it is not inappropriate to think they might transfer this to their cats, which could certainly explain some of the obesity in household cats.

A sure indicator that there is truly a subconscious psychological component to free-feeding a cat is when a cat owner cannot bring himself to change feeding patterns even after learning that free-feeding kibble is unhealthy and that feeding wet food twice a day is best. If a person feels "bad" or "guilty" or "cruel" for taking away a cat's endless bowl of kibble, it might be worth looking at the situation from this psychological perspective.

You might wonder what motivates my little foray into human/pet psychology. It's all about the

cats—if I can help one person get unstuck and do the right thing nutritionally by her cat, then it's worth having to suffer through a little armchair Freud!

Changing Over to a Better Diet

The most efficient way to break a cat of the habit of free-feeding kibble is to do it cold turkey: Get rid of the always-available crunchies and replace them with two meals a day of protein-based food that you make or buy for your cat. You have several choices of methods to feed your cat: commercial food from a can, a raw dehydrated food to which you add water or raw poultry you prepare yourself or purchase already ground and supplemented. There are a number of Web sites for information about feeding cats properly, which are run basically as a public service by volunteers who care deeply about educating other cat lovers about proper nutrition, and giving them advice and support in that journey. The organization that I turn to for many questions is Feline Outreach (www.felineoutreach.org). I hope that when others take advantage of what Lynette, Jenny and their fellow volunteers have to offer they will also make a donation, as I have. Pet Grub (www.pet-grub.com) is a site with good information about raw feeding for those who want to learn more about that option; Anne at Cat Nutrition (www.catnutrition.org) is a wealth of information, and Dr. Lisa Pierson is a pioneer veterinarian in the field of correct cat feeding (www.catinfo.org) and has a professional consulting business.

SOME GOOD CANNED FOODS

There are a growing number of high-quality cat foods sold in pet food stores, with more companies joining the field all the time. Please go to the nutrition section of both www.TheCatBible.com and www.CatChatRadio.com for a constantly updated list, which I will maintain by adding as many fine foods as possible. Below is an alphabetical list of the better brands and the flavors that are recommended.

There are also some supermarket brands of canned cat food that can pass muster with the Feline Food Police (meaning those who volunteer for some of the organizations listed above). However, it is super important to buy ONLY the flavors that are recommended of any brand: As good as some versions of the food are, other flavors with corn syrup and corn in other forms are not healthy, and those with "gravy" should be avoided, too.

Please note that many of these foods contain beef, fish, "meat" (of unknown origin) or even a small amount of grains. Since poultry and rabbit are the most appropriate and digestible proteins for cats, some of these supermarket brands may therefore be inappropriate for cats with food allergies or gastrointestinal disorders. Fish should be fed sparingly, but can serve as an excellent tool for transitioning cats to canned food after a lifetime of "kibble addiction." Likewise, liver can be an "addictive" ingredient for cats, and therefore you should offer it sparingly or infrequently.

Fancy Feast has a line of "elegant medleys:" as a response to the popularity of high-end foods like Merrick and Wellness, Fancy Feast responded by adding unnecessary vegetables to their food. **Note:** Added vegetables should *not* be a reason to buy Merrick or Wellness. If any-

High-Quality Canned Foods

- AvoDerm
- By Nature
- California Natural
- Canine Caviar for Cats
- Eagle Pack
- Evo (the high end of Innova)
- Felidae (from the Canidae company)
- Innova
- Merrick

- Natural Balance
- Nature's Logic
- Nature's Variety Prairie
- Newman's Own
- PetGuard
- Solid Gold
- Timberwolf Organics
- Wellness
- Wysong

thing, you should be "tolerating" those vegetables and even fruit (really not advisable for cats) just to be assured of getting higher quality meat, without "meat" of unknown origin or "by-products."

Whiskas Savory Ground Pate—Chicken Dinner, Mealtime, Bits o' Beef, Turkey & Giblets (not the Whiskas in gravy—The savory ground pate is grain and vegetable free, and the "chicken & tuna" works well for transitioning cats to canned)

9-Lives—Chicken Dinner, Super Supper, Chicken and Beef Dinner, Chicken and Tuna Dinner, Turkey Dinner, Chicken and Seafood Dinner, Liver & Bacon Dinner, Prime Grill with Beef

Happy Tails—Chicken Dinner, Chicken & Tuna Dinner, Mixed Grill, Super Combo, Turkey & Giblets Dinner, Salmon Dinner (any of the flavors not in gravy)—This is Jewel's store brand (Jewel is a large grocery store chain in the Midwest).

Friskies—Supreme Supper, Mixed Grill, Country Style Dinner, Poultry Platter, Turkey & Giblets Dinner

Trader Joe's—Chicken, Turkey & Rice, Turkey & Giblets, Oceanfish, Salmon & Rice, Tongol Tuna & Shrimp, Tongol Tuna & Crab, Seafood Medley, Tuna Dinner—all excellent for transitioning cats to canned food. The chicken and turkey flavors are usually appropriate for regular feeding. Although the first three flavors contain grains, it is a small amount and seems tolerated by many cats with diabetes or gastrointestinal disorders.

Pro Plan—Adult Chicken & Liver Entrée, adult Turkey & Giblets Entrée

Fancy Feast Gourmet Feast—Almost all flavors in the gourmet feast line are low in carbohydrates (grain and vegetable free): Gourmet Chicken Feast, Gourmet Turkey & Giblets Feast, Tender Beef Feast, Tender Beef & Liver Feast, Savory Salmon Feast, Tender Chicken & Liver Feast, Beef & Chicken Feast, Chopped Grill Feast

Fancy Feast Flaked—Fish & Shrimp Feast (this is good for transition for a cat who needs fishiness to convince her about canned food)

RAW FOOD PROVIDERS

There are a number of small, privately run businesses supplying raw food for cats directly to people or pet stores. They are generally made of finely ground chicken meat, organs and bone with supplementation to make them a complete diet for a cat. Some of the better-known providers are Shelby at Feline's Pride (www.felinespride.com); the Connecticut-based, family-run Oma's Pride (www.omaspride.com); Wild Kitty Cat Food (www.wildkittycatfood.com); and Steve's Real Food (www.stevesrealfood.com). Check www.TheCatBible.com for more choices.

FREEZE-DRIED TREATS

When you want to give your pussycat a little something special—or you are trying to teach her a trick or coax her into doing something—it's always good to have a bit of tasty bribery handy. Commercially made cat treats are not made of ingredients that are compatible with a cat's digestive system. Your best bet is to keep a stash of freeze-dried goodies that are pure protein and can keep for a long time. Good choices for treats are Halo Liv-a-Littles (shop.halopets.com), Grandma Lucy's (www.grandmalucys.com/diner), Nature's Variety Prairie, Whole Life Products (www.wholelifepet.com/products) and Cherbey's Fish Jerky (www.cherbeys.com), which is dried human-grade tilapia filets, and while cats shouldn't have a steady diet of fish, they deserve a little taste once in a while.

CHECK FIRST WITH YOUR VET

Before starting a new diet, talk to your vet if you have any doubts about your cat's health and whether she can safely go a day or two where she might refuse the new food. Cats with cancer, diabetes, thyroid issues or kidney damage, or very old cats, cannot run the risk of going without food; your doctor will tell you if your cat is a good candidate for a diet switchover. The issue isn't whether your cat can benefit from the better diet, but how to make the transition to the new improved food without putting strain on her system during the switchover.

YOUR CAT MAY REJECT THE FOOD AT FIRST

Don't be surprised or discouraged if your cat refuses to touch the tasty "real" food you offer. Remember that cats are creatures of habit and will initially resist anything that smells, feels or looks different. But if you can have patience for 4 meals—2 meals for each of 2 days—your cat will almost certainly give in and try the new chow.

PUT ONLY A VERY LITTLE ON THE PLATE AT FIRST

Put just 1 tablespoon of the canned food onto a small plate. Even if your cat eats as little as a teaspoon, or even *half* a teaspoon, that is fine to start. If she eats a whole tablespoon and looks around eagerly for more, give her another tiny bit. You can keep refilling the plate in small increments as long as she is looking interested.

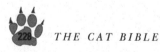

ONLY LEAVE THE FOOD DOWN FOR 30 MINUTES

After half an hour, you should take up the plate of food whether your cat has eaten it or not. If she hasn't eaten anything, do not get yourself into a panic. This just means she will be hungrier the next time, especially because she won't be snacking in between meals.

IF SHE DIDN'T TOUCH IT, PERK UP THE FLAVOR

If your cat rejected the first offering you made, then before you serve her a second meal at the end of the day, use a flavoring idea from the "Ways to Stimulate Appetite" section later in this chapter. Also, try a second brand of food with a different type of meat for the second offering of the day—and if she won't touch that, then try another brand. Right now you want to do whatever you can to get this ball rolling so she'll start eating. Cover the opened cat foods she rejected and refrigerate them so you can try them again within 3 days. Once she gets used to the unfamiliar soft texture of canned (or fresh) food, she might eat one of the brands she originally rejected.

WHEN YOUR CAT COMES TO YOU, DON'T MAKE IT ABOUT FOOD

If your cat comes to you for attention, do not assume it is about hunger and offer her a treat. Instead, give her affection, play a game with her or brush her. She will learn that there are no more random handouts of food and she won't expect food until her next meal. Also, playing stimulates appetite, so she'll be more motivated to eat.

IF SHE WON'T EAT AFTER 24 HOURS, GET CREATIVE

Some professionals say a healthy cat can go 2 days without food, while many say 24 hours is the maximum. Ask your own vet about this and then continue with this mission accordingly. Use an inexpensive brand of really stinky cat food to help your cat make this transition. If your cat totally rejects the first feedings you offer, and you have tried a flavor enhancer that made no difference, there is another way to make this transition. Mix a special treat food—shredded chicken or cooked salmon are surefire favorites—with the new, healthy meal to soften your cat's journey to the new food. (Under no circumstances should you use the dry food she's addicted to as enticement—that cannot even stay on your shelf.)

Make a small portion of 3 parts treat food and 1 part new food. If she will eat this and is looking around for more, give her a second helping (always a tiny amount) of this same mixture. Give this 3:1 ratio of food for 2 full days, or 4 servings.

Next make a mixture of equal amounts of treat food and canned. Give this for 2 days, always in really small portions, refilling when the cat looks around for more, and never leaving the dish down longer than 30 minutes.

For the final 2 days of the week, you'll be up to a ratio of 3 parts new food and 1 part treat food. If she'll eat that, then she's on her way.

Controversial Foods for Cats

THE QUESTIONS ABOUT FISH

Today's house cats have not evolved all that dramatically from their wild origins as large cats living in desert or jungle settings. Generally speaking, fish is not a natural part of a cat's diet in the wild. The strong association between cats and fish in our minds actually comes from cartoons and commercial cat food ads, since fish was originally used in cat food because it was a cheap, plentiful ingredient, whereas today fish has become primarily a costly luxury. Individual cats may like fish more or less, but as a species they have no special affinity for it.

◆ Fish and Magnesium

Some people are concerned about the amount of magnesium in fish, believing that it contributes to urinary crystals and eventually stones. While it is correct that fish (especially saltwater fish) is higher in magnesium than other kinds of protein, it is all relative. The magnesium content is measured per 100 grams of raw weight: Trout and catfish have lower magnesium levels (22 and 23 mg) than chicken thigh meat (24 mg), while chicken breast is exactly the same as mackerel (28 mg). Light meat turkey is 27 mg, dark meat is 22 mg, while salmon and cod are about 25 mg. Tuna jumps off the chart with an average of 50 mg of magnesium.

However, newer research has disproven that magnesium causes crystal formation. People often don't understand that two different kinds of crystals can form in a cat's urinary tract—struvite and calcium oxalate. Magnesium chloride acidifies the urine, which is exactly what you want to achieve in a cat who is prone to crystal formation, while magnesium oxide encourages a more alkaline urine, which is the ideal environment for struvite stones to form. In either case, just because a cat is fed a diet low in magnesium, this does not prevent crystals from forming—it is partly a genetic tendency.

◆ Tuna Has Become a Controversial Ingredient in Cats' Diets

Cats love the strong flavor of tuna, but it may not be a healthy food for them. Many nutritional advocates for cats say tuna should be avoided.

The Problems with Tuna

- It has a high concentration of mineral salts, which are bad for a cat's urinary system.
- The red part of the meat may contain toxins, especially mercury.
- It is high in polyunsaturated fats, which cats do not metabolize well.
- Canned tuna packed in vegetable oil robs the cat's body of vitamin E.
- Once a cat gets hooked on tuna, she may refuse any less intense-smelling food (and cats need variety in their food sources to avoid allergies and have a balanced diet).

MILK

The jury still seems to be out on whether milk is a wonderful or terrible cat food. Some say that milk upsets a cat's stomach and can cause diarrhea because she does not produce *lactase*, the digestive enzyme necessary to digest *lactose*, the sugar present in milk. Kittens are usually fine with milk, but it seems to be true that lactose intolerance develops with age and can cause digestive disturbance, gas and loose stool. However, there are cats who reach adulthood without experiencing any of those problems from milk, so it really depends on the individual—sort of like with people and milk products. It's your choice whether you want to try giving your cat a bit of milk from time to time to see how it goes down.

RAW DIETS

There is a controversial trend developing among a small but outspoken number of cat fanciers to feed raw meat and poultry to their pets. This new wave of nutritional philosophy has the enthusiastic backing of some breeders, holistic practitioners and just plain folks, who give passionate personal reports of the glowing difference they see in their pets' coats and general health after eating a raw diet.

Raw diets are not for everyone. One downside to this feeding practice is that a raw diet is deficient in calcium, phosphorus and other vitamins and minerals, which has to be supplemented, as it is in canned food. Also, there are concerns about the possible spread of disease because bacteria like salmonella in raw beef and chicken can be passed to human family members unless the most scrupulous hygienic standards are maintained in handling, refrigeration, preparation and cleanup.

One of the excellent places to learn about the reasoning behind raw feeding and to find guidance in how to do so safely is www.catnutrition.org. A veterinarian who is highly regarded by Feline Foodies is Dr. Lisa Pierson. She has her own Web site, www.catinfo.org, with much to offer.

Feeding Problems

LOSS OF APPETITE

You always want to rule out medical causes when a cat loses her appetite. Many illnesses—especially tooth pain and infection—can put a kitty off her food. Stress affects a cat's desire to eat. If your cat is nervous to begin with and on top of it is dealing with changes in her environment, it can put her off her food.

A cat does not eat the same amount every day. Weather-related factors such as temperature and barometric pressure can affect appetite. However, a cat should not go more than 24 hours without eating something.

- ❏ A change in where dinner is served
- ❏ The dish the food is offered in
- ❏ A new texture or flavor to the food
- ❏ Unfamiliar people around the house or a lot of coming and going
- ❏ A new animal in the household
- ❏ The recent loss of a person or animal in the family unit
- ❏ Unexpected or startling noises or intrusions near the eating area
- ❏ "Used food"—reoffering a cat previously offered food she left is not an option. Use it to flavor the dog's dinner. Think about this: Restaurants give leftovers in "doggy bags," not "kitty bags."

♦ Ways to Stimulate Appetite

Room-Temperature Food Is the Most Appealing. Think of food being at the temperature a cat would encounter in a bird or rodent she hunted. Cold food, directly from the fridge, is a turn-off.

Don't Try Anything New—or Do. Cats are creatures of habit, so if your cat tends to have appetite problems, you may find she eats best if you stick with familiar foods she already likes—what we would call "comfort food." On the other hand, some cats enjoy variety in their menu. For a cat like this, rotate different ingredients—frequent changes may make for more enthusiastic dining in the cat café.

Add Bits of Strong-Smelling Foods. Cats rely on their sense of smell, so foods with a strong odor can also inspire an appetite. You can use them alone or in combination, but since you're already dealing with a finicky puss, try just one at a time.

Try adding ¼ teaspoon of one of the following, sprinkled on top of her usual food: cooked liver, brewer's yeast, a small bit of sardine in tomato sauce (the oil isn't good for her), human baby food (lamb or creamed corn are the best flavors for a cat). You can also try a few drops of low-sodium tamari (soy sauce) to perk things up or add some Bragg's Liquid Amino Acids, found in health food stores.

Keep Your Cat Company. Some cats crave companionship during their meals and don't want to eat without your active attention, so try stroking your cat while she eats.

FINICKY EATERS

A picky eater isn't the same as a cat who once had a healthy appetite and then suddenly lost it over a short period of time. With a cat who is disinterested in her food, it may be that you have actually contributed to her reluctance to eat by feeding her from the table or by free-feeding kibble. One way to ensure that your cat learns to accept many odors, flavors and textures in her food is to feed her a wide variety of foods from the time she is a kitten (if you're lucky enough to get her when she's young, of course).

However, there may be other explanations for finicky eating that you should also consider. A good appetite and eagerness to eat are signs of health in any animal, and if these signs are absent, you need to consider what the cause may be, in consultation with your vet.

REASONS FOR BEING FINICKY

Medical causes: tooth pain, respiratory infection, kidney disease, diminished sense of smell (in older cats)

An unappealing bowl: make sure it's large enough, doesn't slide around, is not made of plastic and doesn't cause food to spill

Stress factors: any of the stressors in the behavior chapter, plus having to share a food bowl or eating area with a more dominant cat

Depression: recent loss of another animal or human in the household

Loneliness: she may feel alienated and want company while eating

Noisy area: move cat bowls away from high-traffic areas, children playing and the washing machine

RESISTANCE TO SWITCHING TO WET FOOD

Some cats become "kibble junkies" and turn their nose up at the delicious, nutritious healthy wet food you have gone to extra trouble and expense to provide for them. This can be entirely annoying to you, and make you wonder if you should just let the cat continue with dry food since she feels that strongly—but don't even think about it! Experiment with the remedies below and then phase them out after a day or two, by which point the cat may have stopped pouting and be digging into her new meal.

◆ Change Can Be Stressful

If your cat refuses to eat canned food, it may be a simple matter of a cat who dislikes change of any kind, and the new taste and texture of wet food may throw her off at first.

◆ Don't Let Her Go More Than 24 Hours Without Eating

If your cat is having a sit-down strike over the change in her diet, you need to do whatever you can to get her to eat even a little of it because a cat should not go more than a day without food.

◆ Try a Different Brand or Flavor

There are so many cat foods to choose from, and the first one you pick may not be to your cat's liking. Experiment with a few different ones until you hit upon one that she will try.

◆ Chunks in Gravy

This style of canned food often appeals to cats who are having trouble transitioning to wet food, and it can be a bridge to her new cuisine. Although this kind of canned food does not

have the optimal ingredients, it's still better than dry food if she'll try it. This type of food was the one in the huge food recall in March and April 2007.

◆ Grind Kibble as a Topping
Sometimes you can entice a cat to eat canned food by grinding a tablespoon of kibble to a powder and sprinkling it on top of the wet food. If the cat is dependent on the odor of her dry food, a few days of sprinkling may be what it takes to convince her.

◆ Chicken on Top
You can drop a few nuggets of fresh cooked chicken or freeze-dried chicken on top of the canned food. In the process of snatching that beloved chicken, your cat will get a few licks of the canned food beneath it and make a pleasant association.

◆ Bonito Flakes Save the Day
Cat lovers say that no cat can resist the allure of these dried tuna flakes, which you can sprinkle on top of her new canned food until she gets comfortable with it.

◆ Empty Bowl Panic Attack
Some cats panic when they find their food bowl empty, having always encountered a pile of kibble in there. Eventually your cat will realize that she's now nutritionally satisfied and has no need for a tub of dry food sitting around. But until she accepts that and an empty bowl agitates her; you can put a few small chunks of protein in your cat's bowl like Durango 95 percent chicken treats or Steve's Freeze-Dried Raw just to reassure her between meals that you are not going to let her starve to death.

ALLERGIES TO FOODS
If your cat has a food allergy, you will see a reaction anywhere from several minutes to several hours after she has eaten. The most common allergic reaction is severe, nonstop itching, although less dramatic skin problems such as dandruff can also signal a food allergy. There can also be gastrointestinal reactions such as gas, loose stool or diarrhea.

◆ The Most Common Allergenic Ingredients
Food sources that typically cause an allergic reaction are beef, milk, chicken, eggs, fish, soy, wheat and corn. But you should also consider that if your cat has been living on dry kibble, her allergies may not be due to any one food source—rather, she may be having a bad reaction to the chemicals in the food she has been eating. A cat may not necessarily show allergic symptoms right away—it can take months and even years before you can see the cumulative effects of these additives in the dry kibble she has been eating.

◆ Try a Hypoallergenic Diet as a Test
If you suspect your cat may have food allergies, one way to find out is to begin with a month-long hypoallergenic diet. You need to give your cat a diet free of artificial colors and preservatives to

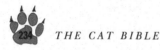

detoxify her system before testing individual ingredients. Lamb and rice are considered hypoallergenic ingredients by many people, although you cannot keep your cat on this diet indefinitely since any food fed exclusively in the long term may cause food allergies.

A lamb baby food for people will work for the experimental period. To get your cat accustomed to this food, put a little bit of it into her current food, increasing the amount every day until all she is getting is the lamb baby food. If her symptoms disappear on this hypoallergenic diet, which can take up to 12 weeks, then you can conclude that a food allergy was the cause of the symptoms.

Reintroduce ingredients one at a time for about 2 weeks each, beginning with the easy ones such as beef, fish and lamb. For each item, add only that ingredient during the 2-week period. If the symptoms recur, then you will know which ingredient is responsible and which foods to avoid. However, beef and fish are poor long-term ingredients anyway.

The second option is to switch to hypoallergenic foods regardless. Not everyone has the patience to live through months of concocting and waiting and watching. Since many allergies, especially skin problems, are related to the overall poor quality of ingredients in a cat's diet, not necessarily to just one ingredient, you may choose to bypass the whole food-detective exercise. There are a number of cat food companies making products with exotic ingredients such as rabbit and venison that a cat is unlikely to have ever eaten and therefore will not be allergic to at this point in time. Just as in the other experiment, you will discover whether problems were diet-related if they resolve themselves within 3 months of starting the new food.

What are good foods for this test? Pet food companies come out with new products all the time, so your best bet is to go to your local pet store to see what they carry or what they can order for you. Any of the companies making high-quality food will probably have a special line for allergy issues: By Nature, Merrick, Evo, Felidae, Newman's Own and Petguard are just a few of the excellent brands. Companies are constantly in flux, so I recommend checking my Web sites, www.TheCatBible.com and www.CatChatRadio.com, for an up-to-date list of fine quality brands of food.

Food-Related Dangers for Cats

PROPYLENE GLYCOL

The preservative propylene glycol was recently removed from cat food after it was found to damage their red blood cells.

SALMONELLA AND *E. COLI* IN RAW FOODS

These are two of the deadly bacteria often present in uncooked meats, so if you are giving your cat a raw diet you have to be very careful for her sake as well as for your family's. These pathogens can be passed from animals to humans—especially children—so people have to stay vigilant about where the food came from, where it was distributed and how it was stored before it came into your home.

PEOPLE FOOD

Any food packaged for people is inappropriate for cats. At the least, the amounts of ingredients will be incorrect for a cat, and at worst, they may be harmful to her. (So don't share your Stouffer's macaroni and cheese with your cat, and you probably shouldn't dip into her 9Lives yourself.)

CHOCOLATE

Chocolate is toxic to cats. A few ounces of high-quality chocolate can kill a cat. However, with rare exceptions, most of the so-called chocolate products you might have in your house contain very little true chocolate or cocoa powder. Except for the very fanciest chocolate makers and specialty bakeries, most of the confections sold today have flavorings and colorings but not enough true cocoa to pose any threat to your cat. However, products that contain only chocolate flavoring are still not an appropriate snack for her.

RAW EGG WHITES

The white of eggs contain an enzyme that destroys biotin, which is an essential vitamin in the B family, in a cat's body. It's okay to offer raw egg yolks (a heavenly treat for cats), but you'll have to separate them from the whites.

HIGH GRAIN CONTENT

Food with a high grain content and little protein can cause gas, a good reason to check the source and percentage of protein in a cat food.

Eating Houseplants

WHY DO CATS EAT PLANTS?

Why do cats have such an appetite for plants? We think it's because grass is a purgative that cats use to make themselves vomit, which may be an instinctive way to get hairballs out of their digestive system or to rid themselves of worms. Plants also satisfy a cat's natural craving for fiber and roughage, along with vitamins and minerals, so there are a variety of reasons for cats to be drawn to munching on your decorative greenery. Since a great number of houseplants are toxic to cats, we must protect our cats from their inborn desire to graze. Keep houseplants out of your cat's reach by making them inaccessible and/or unpleasant, as below.

KEEPING KITTIES OUT OF INDOOR PLANTS

- ❏ Hang plants from hooks or keep them up on stands the cat can't reach.
- ❏ Cover the dirt surface of the plant with pebbles (to deter digging or soiling).
- ❏ Spray the leaves with eucalyptus oil.
- ❏ Put Sticky Paws around the planter.
- ❏ Place plastic carpet runner (the kind with the points on the bottom) upside down in a circle around the pot.

GROW SPECIAL GRASSES FOR THE CAT INSTEAD

There are kitty grasses you can grow for your cat, which some cats really enjoy. They are much more enticing and digestible than houseplants and outdoor garden plants, a surprising number of which are toxic to cats (see the chart in Chapter 2 on preparing your house for a cat). You need to give your kitty the grass that is sold in pet stores just for this purpose. You may think that a cat eats what she needs and that her natural instincts should be trusted, but this is not always true, since her instincts are *not* telling her how deathly ill she can get from many growing things. So much for Mother Nature!

Understanding the Ingredients in Cat Food

It almost seems as though you need a special degree to read the labels on bags or cans of cat food—there are some words that you *think* you understand and others that you are certain you do not, and it's safe to say that it would generally be better for the big pet food companies if you do not understand. However, you have to make the effort for your kitty, so take extra time here to read about what all those similar-sounding words on the label really mean. Otherwise, you risk putting things into your cat's body that have no business being there—even if they have been manipulated into a pleasant-looking product that your cat eats eagerly. You can make healthy choices for your cat, but first you have to understand what you are up against: a multibillion-dollar pet food industry with the best advertising minds and public relations people that money can buy.

GENERAL RULES ABOUT READING A LABEL

Don't get too happy if a cat food says it complies with the Association of Animal Feed Control Officials (AAFCO) requirements "for all life stages." This organization is primarily focused on animals that will wind up on human dinner tables, and it sets woefully inadequate standards for pet foods. The standard feeding trial by which a pet food is deemed to get that AAFCO seal of approval is the following: If 6 of 8 cats do not *die* during the test period of 6 months, the food passes with flying colors, and the pet food company gets to put that seal on their entire line of food, regardless of the formula. In a nutshell, if a pet food manages to sustain life for *most* participants over the short haul, it gets the seal of approval. I think your cat deserves a bit more than that—don't you?

READ THE LABEL

To find a good commercial food, the first thing you need to do is read the label on the can. The foods to avoid are those with ingredients like corn gluten, corn meal, corn flour, rice or rice flour, white or sweet potatoes, carrots or any kind of fruit. Cats do not need vegetables, fruit and cereals, which are ingredients that sound appealing to people. They are not components of a natural or healthy diet for a cat. If a canned food doesn't have the carbohydrates listed above, then it will curb compulsive overeating, which many cats indulge in out of boredom or genuine hunger. Dry foods do not provide the satisfaction of eating something that is genuinely nourishing, so the cat keeps eating the empty calories because her appetite is never satisfied.

THE ORDER OF INGREDIENTS MEANS EVERYTHING

Pay most attention to the first three or four ingredients in cat food, since labels show the relative proportion of ingredients by listing the main ingredients first. However, you have to be on your toes when reading between the lines. Some companies will fiddle with the ingredient list by doing what is called "splitting." They divide one ingredient into several smaller categories on the label so that corn will appear in three different forms and therefore can be listed further down in the ingredients. Ideally, meat (preferably from a specified meat source) should be on top of the list, since cats are true carnivores, but the truth is that corn and wheat are often the predominant ingredients in lower-quality foods.

Here is an example of splitting in listing the order of ingredients on the label of one well-known cat food: *poultry by-product meal, ground yellow corn, wheat, corn gluten meal, soybean meal, brewer's rice.* By dividing corn into two categories, they are able to list the poultry by-product meal first, as though it is the main ingredient (which is nothing to be so proud of in any case, but still better than corn for a cat). However, if you add up all the grains, this "cat food" might be good for a cow or sheep but not for a carnivore like a cat, who needs nearly 100 percent protein.

Some of the Key Food Words to Know About

These are common words on cat food that you need to know:

Beef: This means what we think of as meat, and includes clean flesh from slaughtered cattle, the muscle and tongue, diaphragm, heart, esophagus, and any fat, skin, sinew, nerves and blood vessels.

Meat: This means beef, pork, sheep, horse and goat, but it can also include other unspecified mammals harvested for their meat. The problem is that there is no consistency in the sources of meat, so your cat may have a bad reaction or have food allergies and you won't know what meat source is responsible. Try to avoid unspecified sources.

Meat meal (beef, lamb), meat and bone meal: These are rendered products and, as such, are much worse than meat from unspecified sources.

Rendered meat: Meat in pet food comes from two sources: slaughterhouses and renderers. Food for people is processed in slaughterhouses, where as the parts of a slaughtered animal not fit for human consumption are processed by renderers and are used in livestock feed, pet foods and other products. *Rendering* is another term for recycling of many kinds of dead animals: the remnants of slaughterhouses; dead, diseased or dying livestock from farms; animals killed in shelters; roadkill. All these carcasses and parts are ground up and subjected to high heat to form a "rendered" product.

Meat by-products: By-products are what are left after good-quality meat is removed and includes lungs, spleen, kidneys, brain, liver, blood, bone, stomach and cleaned intestines. This is a clue that inferior meat sources have been used.

Chicken meal: Chicken that is ground or otherwise made into small particles. This does not necessarily mean an inferior origin for the chicken itself, but in order to make a dry food the ingredients have to be ground up finely enough to be made into the dough which becomes dry food.

Chicken by-product meal: Ground rendered parts of the carcass such as necks, feet, undeveloped eggs and intestines.

Poultry by-products: Heads, feet and internal organs.

Corn gluten meal (CGM): A cheap source of protein used instead of real meat, corn is an excellent food for cattle, pigs and chickens. It has no place in a cat's diet. As Dr. Hodgkins says, she's never seen a cat stalk an ear of corn.

Fish-based food: You want to avoid generic fish meal because many are stabilized with ethoxyquin (see earlier mention in this chapter), which is a harmful chemical originally developed as a stabilizer for rubber. And salmon meal comes from farmed salmon, which is raised with heavy use of antibiotics and can have significantly higher chemical contamination levels from the water they are raised in than wild salmon. Fish is generally a poor cat food.

SOME REALLY GOOD BRANDS OF FOOD

There are a number of really fine pet food companies that are making cat food you can feel confident about giving to your cat. Earlier in this chapter there is an alphabetical list of some of those food companies; however, there are smaller companies I may not know about, so don't hesitate to write to me (tracie@thecatbible.com) to tell me about others. Nothing makes me happier than being able to raise awareness of the issues about cat nutrition and to be able to make recommendations about quality products. Go on www.TheCatBible.com for a constantly updated list.

Special Diets for Health Issues

ADDING FIBER

There are several reasons why you might need to boost the fiber content of your cat's food, and there are several ingredients you can use to do it. In each case, try a teaspoon of the fiber in each meal at first, which you can increase as the cat gets used to the texture. Fiber sources include canned unsweetened pumpkin, wheat bran, oat bran, psyllium, and finely grated carrot or zucchini (which you need to prepare right before serving).

◆ Constipation, Colitis or Diarrhea
Fiber seems to help cats with all of these digestive problems, as it often does with people.

✦ Diabetes

There is misunderstanding about whether adding fiber to the diet of a diabetic cat can be helpful. Since improper diet is the cause of type II diabetes in cats, a proper diet has to be the foundation of successfully managing this disease. Many vets were trained to believe that a high-fiber dry diet can help manage a diabetic cat's blood sugar levels, but this mistaken belief has historically been put to the test and failed, according to Dr. Elizabeth Hodgkins (see the section on "Diabetes" in the medical chapter). She has proof in her own feline-only clinic, where diabetes is her specialty, that high-fiber dry food is a terrible error for diabetic cats. The high amount of carbohydrate in these foods raises blood sugar, regardless of how much fiber they contain. These vet-prescribed diabetic diets are usually called "low fat" as well as high fiber; the fat in the formula is often replaced with more digestible carbohydrate than you'd find in the regular formula, making it even worse for the diabetic cat it is supposed to be helping.

A cat with this condition needs a high protein diet, with moderate fat and very low in carbohydrate—especially those carbohydrates from cereals and grains with high glycemic indices, like corn and potatoes (this is equally true of human diabetics). Canned foods that are labeled "for the management of diabetes" are fine as long as they have 20 percent or preferably 10 percent carbohydrate.

✦ Urinary Issues (Crystals, Stones, Infection)

See the section in Chapter 13 about urinary tract problems, because altering nutrition is one of the few ways to manage the problem.

✦ Weight Loss

Decreasing the amount of canned or fresh food you give by 20 percent and increasing the amount of fiber will make your cat feel more full. You can also spread a chubby cat's food out on a big plate so that it takes her longer to eat; she may feel more full from eating more slowly. Keep the portions modest: A cat of average weight needs only 3 to 4 ounces of food twice a day.

Special Diet for Urinary Crystals or Stones

If you have a cat who has had problems with either crystals or stones in her urine or bladder, you can help manage the situation through diet. Unfortunately many vets are still suggesting that people should feed a dry kibble sold through their offices, even though recent studies have confirmed that the concept of feeding a dry diet is especially unhealthy for cats with a tendency to form crystals. Those studies showed that cats fed non-dry diets had fewer occurrences of crystals. Dilute urine is less likely to form crystals, so your cat *must* be on a totally canned or raw diet. You want as much fluid going into your cat as possible—which a wet diet provides, especially for cats not prone to drinking water. Some of the "prescription" dry diets even go so far as to include salt in their formulas to make the cats thirsty enough to drink water, which is not a natural inclination.

URINE TEST STRIPS

By periodically keeping track of the pH of your cat's urine, you will know whether it is staying in the correct range of acidity versus alkalinity so as not to encourage the formation of stones or crystals. You can buy the little dipsticks at a pharmacy (make sure you get the kind for urinary pH and not for urinary sugar testing). The tricky part is waiting for the right moment when your cat squats to pee and managing to hold the end of the stick under the flow of urine. Good luck on that maneuver! FYI: Do not expect the pH to be at a constant level; it will vary, becoming higher (more alkaline) after eating and when the cat is stressed. However, by testing now and then, you will get an idea of your cat's urinary condition, information you can share with your vet. You basically want to keep the urine not too alkaline (pH over 7)—and not too acidic either (under 6)—which means somewhere right between those two numbers. This will make sense once you get the test strips and see the graph you compare them to, sort of how swimming pool water is tested.

A Diet for Kidney Issues

A note about terminology for acute kidney disease: Dr. Elizabeth Hodgkins, the Official Vet of my radio show CAT CHAT®, prefers to use the phrase "chronic renal disease" (CRD) rather than "failure" (CRF), which sounds so dire. I like the idea of making a problem sound less alarming, but I refer to the condition both ways in this book.

In the veterinary field there is a sea change taking place in the understanding of kidney disease and diet. Many doctors are now reversing a long-held belief that feeding dry food and low-protein food was the right diet for cats with kidney issues. The new thinking is to feed all wet food—nothing but wet—and any of the high-quality canned foods or raw food is best. Compromised kidneys need fluids, but for years vets have been recommending a dry diet—which was illogical because kidneys need moisture. The need for fluids with kidney disease is why cats and dogs with chronic kidney failure (CRF) are given subcutaneous fluids—so feeding them a diet deficient in moisture would be counterproductive. Some experts believe that with an entirely wet diet, perhaps it will not be necessary to give those sub-q fluids to the cat until the kidney disease has progressed to late stage CRF.

WHAT ABOUT PRESCRIPTION KIDNEY DIETS?

There are many prescription diets available through veterinarians, but most are dry foods. While we now know that optimally every cat's diet should be based on a high quality protein, for a cat with kidney disease this is even more true: Better "fuel" in the way of protein is easier for the kidneys to work with. Corn gluten and wheat gluten are examples of protein that is not high quality; "meat by-products" are better than these two carbohydrates, but not as good as muscle meat. Look for foods that have the word "chicken" or "turkey" (not just "poultry") by-products.

There are now studies which indicate that low-protein diets *raise* creatinine levels—something you want to avoid in a cat with renal failure because it worsens the anemia and muscle wastage that are often seen with CRF.

Constipation is commonly a secondary problem for cats with CRD because they get dehydrated. Some sources suggest adding fiber to the diet because it bulks up the stool, but you have to be very cautious adding fiber to a cat's diet since it can make the problem worse. A much healthier and effective solution is to feed an all-wet diet and add some fat, which will lubricate the GI tract—a little virgin olive oil, salmon oil or even butter.

If you want to add supplements to the food of a cat with CRD, omega fatty acids are considered good for the kidneys. The B vitamins are great for combating anemia. Water-soluble vitamins are washed out, especially with excessive drinking, urination, or sub-q fluids, so supplementation can be highly beneficial. Also, if you'd like, add coenzyme Q10 (30 milligrams every other day to start). You can read about this on Dear Sally's page on Cat Chat (www.CatChatRadio.com), where she first recommended it. If you do decide to use CoQ10, note that many people keep their cats on it for life because of reported benefits for the heart—and people take it, too.

Have a look at the Feline Outreach site, which has a whole section on CRF with some good links: www.felineoutreach.org/EducationDetail.asp?cat=KidneyDisease.

If you have a cat with kidney problems and your vet is not aware of these newer ideas about the role of nutrition in managing kidney disease, consider having a phone consultation yourself with Dr. Lisa Pierson (www.catinfo.org), who will also consult with your vet on the air, reviewing a specific cat's lab work, and can recommend a diet specific to that patient.

Special Dietary Needs of Kittens

Kittens should stay with their mama until a minimum of 8 weeks of age so that they get a chance to be weaned naturally. Otherwise there is the chance the kitten will develop into a cat who has oral fixations and needs to suck on odd items throughout her life.

Kittens need a diet high in protein from quality meat sources and a good percentage of fat. Some cat enthusiasts say that a kitten needs ¼ teaspoon of butter daily while developing to meet her need for animal fat in her diet.

Kittens need to eat more frequently than grown cats because they have tiny stomachs and a fast metabolism that burns up the fuel quickly. Give the kitty a small amount at each feeding, adding more small bits until she is satisfied.

A kitten cannot be fed in the same way as an adult cat, because the little one needs more food for growth and development. Although a kitten should receive no kibble and should not be free-fed—just as with an adult cat—a kitten needs much more food more frequently. While an adult cat of approximately 10 pounds requires 6 to 8 ounces of canned food a day, a kitten can take in twice that amount. According to the feeding schedule below, you can divide up a can amongst those feeding periods and add more based on the kitten's appetite. Once she reaches 8 months of age, a kitten will be eating on the same schedule as an adult cat. You can give a kitten a small can of food in the morning, or as much as she will eat in 10 to 15 minutes, and then another can at the end of the day—more or less, depending entirely on the kitten's appetite and capacity.

Feeding Schedule for Kittens

- 6 to 10 weeks: 6 to 8 meals daily
- 10 weeks to 4 months: 5 to 6 meals
- 5 months to 7 months: 3 to 4 meals a day
- 8 months upward: 3 meals, tapering to 2 a day

Special Dietary Needs of Senior Cats

As a cat gets older, her body does not absorb the nutrients in her food as well, so you need to go back to feeding her like a kitten, with many small and nutritious meals throughout the day. You do not want an older cat to eat too much all at once because her digestion is not as efficient. Her digestive system will function best with less in the stomach to digest at one time.

VITAMINS

Add vitamins to boost the cat's system. Talk to your vet about which supplements he recommends for senior cats.

ENZYMES

Consider adding digestive enzymes to her diet. There are companies that make digestive products especially for animals (Prozyme is one of them; you can call the company at 800-522-5537 for a free sample bottle) or you can use a digestive enzyme powder sold in a health food store for people, although this may be more pricey. Put ¼ teaspoon of powdered enzymes into a little unsweetened instant oatmeal mixed with some milk, which is a treat that older kitties especially enjoy.

REDUCED PROTEIN

A cat needs less protein as she ages and becomes less active. Protein is hard on the kidneys, which become less efficient and have to work harder as a cat ages. The ideal proportion of ingredients for the senior cat's diet is 40 percent protein, 30 percent vegetable and 30 percent grain.

VEGETABLES

Adding a teaspoon of finely grated zucchini or carrot to your elderly cat's meals will give a little bit of raw vegetables (similar to what would naturally be found in the stomachs of small prey a cat would kill and eat), and the fiber they provide aids an elderly cat's digestion.

Chapter 11

CATS AND DOGS, AND CATS AND CATS: HARMONY AND CONFLICT

Dogs and Cats

Nearly half of the homes in America have both dogs and cats as pets, so despite an expression like "Raining cats and dogs," indicating a torrential storm, we know that these two species can actually coexist quite well. A dog and cat often share the same home and the same humans, and since people provide for their every need, they also sometimes share the same codependent dynamics with people. We have transformed these two species by domesticating them into what is sometimes an almost parental-child relationship with us.

Despite enormous differences in the natural behavior of dogs and cats, and in their wild ancestors, the two species can live together harmoniously and even occasionally form bonds as strong as those they have with their human caretakers. From personal experience I can tell you that cats do develop bonds with dogs and they know the difference between a dog they live with and any other dog. I used to have three cats I adopted as tiny kittens, who grew up in a country home I had that I only visited a few times a year. When I visited, I brought my two dogs, Roma, a Golden Retriever, and Amalfi, a Cocker Spaniel. No matter how much time had passed since I last was there, when I drove up with Roma and Amalfi in the car, those three cats we hadn't seen in months came out of nowhere to greet us, rubbing themselves against me and the dogs. I was amazed that any other time that people arrived with dogs in their cars, or if I brought home a dog I'd rescued, those cats disappeared into thin air—only to reappear magically within moments of the departure of the unfamiliar dog.

Differences in how dogs and cats relate: Cats and dogs are not natural enemies, but they aren't natural friends, either. A large part of what makes peaceful cohabitation possible between the two species is that they rarely compete for the same payoff from the people around them or from their environment. Dogs and cats usually don't want what is important to the other—for example, most dogs have a strong drive to achieve frequent physical closeness to their people and gain their approval, and these are not on a cat's primary agenda. When living under the same roof, both species need food and water, territory and some leadership by people, but as long as the animals are separate but equal, the potential for "sibling rivalry" and the resentment that comes with it can be avoided. After they live in the same house together over several years, the dogs and cats usually grow into an understanding of each other and learn to respect the differences in what matters to each of them.

A cat takes much longer to warm up: If your cat has not lived with a dog in the house before, expect her to have a meltdown when the dog arrives, and don't be surprised if it lasts a fairly long time. Most cats take months to adjust to having a dog around, and there's not really anything you can do to speed the process along. As long as the cat has high places to jump up onto, away from the dog, there's no danger of serious harm coming to her. She'll need those places to get away from menacing behavior from the dog, and even a physical attack. Normal defensive behaviors for a cat are hissing, arching her back and swatting, so don't be concerned if your cat does these things with a dog when she first meets him, or really anytime she is trying to get her point across.

DOGS AND CATS: LIVING TOGETHER SUCCESSFULLY

On some level, your cat may never fully forgive you for polluting her world with a canine. Some cats actually like dogs, but more frequently the best they can do is to come to accept the dog they live with, and usually just that one. A cat can go past tolerance to actual friendship with a dog, but that is unusual. Anyone who has had a mixed dog/cat household can tell you that cats are discerning about their interspecies friendships and may become really close with one dog while rejecting all others.

◆ Start Young

The most successful relationships between dogs and cats are those that begin when both animals are young, introduced as puppies and kittens, which allows them to grow up together and figure each other out. If you do not have the opportunity to have a youngster from each species, then your best bet is to pair a kitten with a grown dog, because the kitty can adapt more easily to living with a grown dog than an adult cat could. If you have a grown cat and want to add a dog to your family, your cat will usually adapt better to living with a puppy, whom she can boss around more easily.

◆ Territoriality

Dogs can be territorial about specific locations and objects, especially dominant males of terrier breeds and working breeds. Some dogs can get vicious about things such as another animal getting near their food and water bowls, setting foot in special areas of a room, trying to get on their beds or getting cozy with people of whom they're especially fond. Since a cat does not generally have that same high drive to declare ownership the way a dog does, she might not realize how fiercely some dogs will stake claim.

♦ Things That Matter Most to a Cat

Cats can also prize locations and objects, but they'll rarely fight over them and even then only with another cat, not with a dog. What *does* make a cat fiercely assertive are pathways leading to those favorite locations, attention from favorite people, play objects (especially catnip) and special food treats.

♦ Differences in the Social Order of the Two Species

While dog and cat behaviors are quite different, both species do have a pecking order—but the difference is that with cats, the ranking of who is on top is constantly fluctuating. Dogs, on the other hand, tend to establish a pecking order that remains pretty much stable unless a new addition to the pack challenges the established order. There is always an "alpha dog" in a pack; with any luck it is the human in that equation. But there is still a social order in which each dog knows his place and generally does not look for a chance to change his ranking. We know this from the studies of wolf pack behavior, which relates directly to dogs, who are their descendants.

Cats do not have a social order that is easily understood. In the wild, most big cats are solitary creatures who only come together to mate and raise their young. Otherwise, males and females live separately within their own territories (the only cat this is *not* true of is the lion, who lives in a pride, which is a kind of pack). The lifestyle of big cats in the wild helps explain the independent nature of domestic cats, who often give the impression of being indifferent to human attention. However, domestic cats have been pampered by humans who cater to their every need, and many cats have learned to crave the affection, grooming, scheduled fancy meals and affection lavished on them by their people. So while we enjoy having both these animals share our lives, it is up to us to bring them together in a way that enhances the quality of their lives, too.

INTRODUCING THE TWO SPECIES

"Let's just put them together and see what happens" is a sure recipe for disaster—it's from the same school of thought that says, "Teach someone to swim by throwing him in the water." The goal for introducing cats and dogs is to keep the animals as relaxed as possible and get them off on the right foot.

Give the introductory process lots of time. The introductory period generally takes anywhere from 2 weeks to 2 months, but it needs to be done in stages to slowly desensitize the animals to each other. Patience on your part may be hard, since you want the animals you love to love each other, but there's no rushing love. The process will take as long as it takes, and you cannot set a timetable if you want long-lasting success.

PREPARATIONS BEFORE A DOG ENTERS A CAT'S DOMAIN

Before a dog ever steps on the premises, your cat must have established safe havens and escape routes that she is familiar with and can readily use. As you will see from the instructions below, it can take quite a few days or even weeks to lay this groundwork; you can't rush into this introduction.

◆ Escape Routes: Catwalks, Perches, Cat Doors, Baby Gates

A cat needs places out of a dog's reach where she can go when she feels threatened. Perches and catwalks can give a cat real security, although not every house or apartment has places to install them. If you can, purchase or build escapes for her wherever you can reasonably do so. A cat tree is an obvious escape spot, but you can also put perches on the walls, which give your cat exercise and make a great getaway. Any home store or catalogue such as Pottery Barn has narrow shelves or ledges that are intended to prop photos, small artwork or decorative objects. You can arrange them against the wall as if they were a series of steps that reach nearly up to the ceiling and then back down again on the far side. The book *Animal House Style* by Julia Szabo has pictures of just such a series of perches she designed, which she calls Tiger Branches; they will give you an idea of how to create such a wall environment, and you can order them at www.animalhousetyle.com.

Your preparatory work is not done until your cat knows where her safe places and perches are and she is used to jumping up on them. Entice her to use these spots by baiting them with something delicious, such as bits of her favorite food, catnip, cat treats such as Dr. Harvey's Whisker Smackers (dried salmon, from www.drharveys.com) or Cherbey's tilapia jerky (dried strips of tilapia fish, from www.cherbeys.com). Sweet-talk her into jumping up to get her treat. Fish is not a recommended food for cats, but it makes a tasty treat.

◆ Baby Gates in Doorways

The cat needs to understand that she can jump right over a baby gate and that the dog cannot follow her over. Acclimate her to the gate before the dog arrives by teaching her to jump over it while you stand on the opposite side, offering encouragement and treats.

◆ Cat Doors

Cat doors can be very helpful even if your cat does not go outdoors. You can also install a cat door inside your house into the door leading to your basement or another room such as a laundry room or mudroom. You can teach your cat how use the door by giving her a chance to experience the door with your assistance. Hold the flap up so she can see straight through the opening and entice her through to the other side with a treat. After she's gone through a few times with you holding up the flap, let her get used to the feeling of the flap coming down behind her on her back or butt, the way it really will when she pushes through on her own. Hold up the flap—you should be on the opposite side of the door from her—and entice her through with more sweet talk and treats. Little by little, most cats will jump through easily, and as you let the flap down gradually, they will understand how to push the flap with their heads.

Tips on coaxing a cat through a cat door: If your cat is really reluctant to try the cat door, there are a few things you can try for further encouragement. You can duct-tape the flap open for a few days so she only has to deal with going through the opening, not pushing it open and tolerating the flap hitting her on the bottom. As an added incentive, offer her a meal on the far side of the door and make it a really delicious one. To make her more responsive to using the door, call her through and have her favorite treat waiting for her.

◆ The Cat's Necessities Have to Be up High

If they haven't been before now, your cat's food, water and toys should be up on a countertop or table for weeks before a dog arrives so that the cat knows where her belongings are and doesn't have so much to adjust to all at once when the dog enters the picture. The litter box also needs to be somewhere the dog cannot get to it—perhaps in the basement or a laundry room or extra bathroom where you can install a cat door, or tie or wedge the human door open just wide enough so that only the cat can get through.

STEPS TO TAKE BEFORE THE ACTUAL MEETING

Since dogs' and cats' noses are their best tools for investigating the world, the first step is to get each animal used to the other one's scent. To do this, use "scent socks" before the first meeting. Slide your hand into a cotton sock—a tube sock is easiest—and rub it all over the cat's face, especially on the cheeks and either side of the mouth where the scent glands with pheromones that give a lot of personal information are located. Now rub another sock all over the dog's face and body. Place the scent socks in places with positive association, such as under the other animal's food dish, for your cat on her favorite nesting place, and for the dog on his bed. Cats will often avoid the dog-scented sock at first. If you find this to be true, you can be sure that this will be a slow process—if your cat wants no part of the dog's smell, she will certainly want to avoid the dog himself.

Negative Reaction to the Scent Sock: A cat who lashes her tail as she smells the dog is upset. Continue rerubbing the dog and placing the socks around the house until the cat no longer tail lashes. For a dog who is highly aroused by the cat's odor (it may make him bark or whine), keep coming with those scent socks from the cat until the dog no longer reacts strongly to the scent. When you reach the point where the dog is no longer overly interested in the cat's scent and the cat no longer avoids the dog's scent, it is time to try actually introducing them.

THE ACTUAL INTRODUCTION

Bringing a dog and a cat together is a slow process that has to be done in stages. Keep in mind that throughout all phases of the introduction the goal is to create as many good associations and feelings for the animals about the other species as you can—it should seem to the animals that positive things happen when the other one is around.

The cat and dog won't see each other at first, but will have their first introduction to each other's scent on opposite sides of a closed door. You will be on one side with one animal, and someone familiar to the other animal will be with her on the other side. Let the animals sniff each other under the door and give them special tummy rubs, treats, toys—whatever you know will make them happy—to create a positive association with that smell. Try to sit right next to the door with one pet, but if the animal doesn't want to get that close, encourage the pet to get as close as he or she is willing while you make a big fuss over him or her.

Step 1, Start Small. Once the dog and cat are relaxed with each other on either side of the door, put the dog on a leash and prop the door open just an inch or two with a heavy doorstop on each side (even a big chair opposite the dog's side, if needed). Hold on to the leash in case the dog decides to take matters into his own hands. Practice this until both parties are comfortable with being able to see each other a little bit and smell each other directly.

Step 2, Meeting Through the Baby Gate. The next step is to set up a baby gate between the two rooms. You might still want to keep the dog on a leash in case he seems eager to scale the gate. You want to keep things calm and avoid any distractions that could escalate the tension level, so keep your own energy and voice cool. Stay with this arrangement until the cat doesn't run away and the dog doesn't get overly excited as they sniff each other through the gate.

Create an escape route for the cat. Before the actual meeting, create a "safe zone" for the cat that is out of the dog's range. Often this safe area will be upstairs for the cat while the dog stays downstairs. You need to make sure that the cat can escape somewhere up high and out of the dog's reach if she wants to bail out. In the early days, keep a long leash or long line on your dog so that if the cat takes off and his instinct to chase takes over, you can always grab or step on his leash.

The dog has to be on a leash the first time the dog and cat meet with nothing between them. If the dog is not restrained, there's a good chance the cat will bolt at the sight of the dog, the dog will follow his instinct to chase, all hell will break loose and the future of their relationship will be grim.

Keep a *Gentle Leader* with a short leash on the dog. When the dog is loose in the house with you in the first few days, have him drag a short leash at all times so you can grab the leash or step on it should he decide to take off after the cat. A sharp verbal reprimand "No!" as you step on the leash should get the idea across. If you prefer, you can keep a Gentle Leader on him with a hanging tab attached to the ring for the leash so that you can take hold of him easily and any chasing behavior can be nipped in the bud. (A Gentle Leader is a head collar, an alternative way to control a dog without yanking on his neck. This piece of equipment functions like a halter on a horse, giving you control of the dog by turning his head, rather than having to exert pressure by dragging on his neck.)

Keep the cat and dog separate for the first day or two. Leave the cat in a temporary safe room you set up, and if need be, confine the dog to a crate or small area. But after these two days, you need to have another couple of days where the two animals can see and smell each other without being able to physically interact.

Set up a baby gate at the door to the safe room. This allows the animals to see and even sniff each other without full potential for contact. It helps diffuse tension and uncertainty.

Have treats ready to reward the dog for being calm. You don't want your dog to bark at the cat or try to chase her. However, do not yell at your dog or use an angry, harsh tone to correct what may be his natural impulse to go after the cat. Instead, reward him for keeping his cool.

Practice the command "Leave it." One of the first commands you'll want to teach your dog is "Leave it" to interrupt his focus on the cat. Use the command when he and the cat are first getting acquainted, if he seems overly fixated and is staring at the cat. Some people also work on a sit-stay or a down-stay with their dog around cats.

Expect a traumatized cat at first. If there has never been a dog in the household before, be prepared for your cat to freak out when you bring in the dog. The cat will probably hiss and spit, her hair will stand on end and she'll take refuge in some unreachable spot. She may hide under a bed. She may even go on a hunger strike and not show up for meals. Being a cat, she'll show up again when she's good and ready, after she's had a good sulk and pout.

If the dog wants to chase. Most dogs are curious and have the instinct to chase a cat, although often just playfully, not necessarily to hurt her. Some cats will stand their ground, hiss, arch their backs, growl and swipe with their paws, but many times a cat will do the opposite and take off and run. The cat's flight triggers what is known as "prey drive" in a dog—the instinct to chase a small moving object. This jousting between them must be discouraged because it can end badly.

If the dog starts to lunge or to run after the cat, give a quick tug on his collar with a firm "No," then calmly tell him, "Sit." If the dog's desire to chase is really strong (if he's pulling and drooling with desire to bolt after the cat), then the reward you give him for restraining himself needs to be really big (such as a delicious piece of cheese). If the dog considers going after the cat but is easily dissuaded by your correction, then you have less of problem to fix and can also give a lower-value reward to fit the amount of effort he had to make to control his impulses.

The cat can take care of herself. A cat with claws can go on the offensive and take a swipe at the dog's face, but even a declawed cat can escape unscathed. A feline is rarely in serious jeopardy, because she can usually jump up onto something to get away from a dog or hide underneath furniture where the dog can't reach her. However, the experience can still be traumatic for the cat, so you must discourage your dog from developing a chasing/hunting habit.

The dog could get scratched in the face if he doesn't step back. It shouldn't take long for a dog of average intelligence to learn that the flying furball can be dangerous and should be shown some respect. If your cat has a face-to-face encounter with the dog, she will appear quite fearsome—she'll arch her back, hiss and lash out with her claws. Most dogs will back right off after a cat's scary display, but puppies might not get the cat's message until a swipe of the cat's paw across their nose smartens them up. However, if your adult dog shows no fear and does not shrink from the cat's display, you may have reason to worry that he could attack and harm the cat. If this is the case, you want to bring in a professional dog trainer to evaluate the situation.

◆ Loose in the House Together

Once you have gone through all the steps above and reached a place of mutual acceptance between them, it should be safe to leave the dog and cat loose in the house together *when you are there.* However, whenever you go out, you should confine the cat in a room or the dog in another room or crate, or erect a secure barrier between them. Don't leave a cat loose in the house with a dog. You never know what outside provocation or inner instincts could trigger the cat to run and the dog to chase—with possible bad consequences for one of them. You need to be there at first to help set boundaries for the dog, gently correcting him for any aggressive tendencies toward the cat or for encroaching on her territory.

Eventually, the goal is for the dog and cat to live together in cozy harmony or peaceful neutrality. But if, after several weeks of slow exposure to each other, there is still a low boil of tension or overt hostility between the animals, you'd be well advised to consult with a professional animal behaviorist or trainer to help you solve the problem, or to help determine if it can be worked out at all.

RISKY DOG BREEDS WITH CATS

Prey-driven dog breeds. Some kinds of dogs are what is technically known as "prey-driven," meaning that when a smaller animal runs off, the dog takes off after it. It would be foolhardy to consider bringing a grown dog like that into a home that already has a cat. If you are considering adding a dog to your family, find out as much as you can about that dog's attitude to cats before bringing him home to your unsuspecting kitty.

Dog breeders generally know whether prey drive is true of their breed and will usually be honest about it. They don't want an interspecies tragedy to happen. Most terriers were bred to chase and kill rodents, so a small animal such as a cat is fair game for them. In the case of a dog you are adopting, the shelter or breed rescue should have evaluated the individual dog you are considering so they have information to give you about the cat-friendliness of that individual dog. However, all dogs have a prey drive to some extent; it is just stronger in some breeds and some individuals than in others.

Pit Bulls, Weimaraners, Greyhounds, Akitas, most terriers, and many of the field-hunting breeds are considered to be prey-driven and a risk to cats. However, these breeds are just a sampling—and being on the list does not mean that all dogs of these breeds are vicious or a danger to cats. Prey-driven dogs are basically hardwired to chase anything small that runs away from or past them. Racing Greyhounds, for example, will run like the blazes after a fast-moving mechanical rabbit—and in some cases might take off instinctively after a cat on the run. While some prey-driven dogs also have the instinct to kill what they catch, many hunting dogs and breeds from the list above actually live lovingly with cats. In my own house, my 2 adopted Weimaraners, Lulu and Billy Blue, lived peacefully with my adopted cats, Bert and Ernie. My friend Antaro adopted a big Pit Bull, Obie, who is a love with her cats, and my friend's sister who is a serious cat collector had 17 cats at last count who live literally draped around a Pit Bull who loves them just as much. So much for the reliability of those listed breeds! Also, keep in mind that just because a dog breed is *not* on the list does not mean he is cat-friendly, either. Every dog is an individual and may not fit a particular mold. Don't assume anything—good or bad—until you have watched the dog (on a leash) around a cat over a period of several days for signs of whether he is "hunting" the cat.

You can help determine whether your dog has a strong prey drive by referring to the chart below. If a dog has more than one of these qualities, there's a good chance he will go after a moving cat and he won't be a good match for your cat.

SIGNS OF A DOG WITH STRONG PREY DRIVE

- ❏ Excited by moving objects
- ❏ Sniffs the air and/or ground frequently
- ❏ Stalks birds and small animals
- ❏ Shakes and "kills" toys or other objects
- ❏ Hunts or bites at your feet when you walk

TWO OR MORE DOGS CAN SPELL TROUBLE

There is a terrible phenomenon that can happen with dogs and their behavior toward cats (and other prey) when there are two or more canines around: A bloodthirsty pack mentality can take over. A dog can be totally fine alone with a cat, and while a little chasing may start when there is a second dog, all bets are off if a third dog enters the picture. It seems that if one of the dogs has the impulse to get the cat, there is what professionals call a "social facilitation process," whereby dogs that would otherwise do no harm to a cat are suddenly stimulated into a group attack mentality.

For the most part it is not advisable to bring a cat or kitten into a home that has more than 2 dogs, since 3 dogs become a pack. Each individual dog may be fine on his own with cats, and 2 dogs usually won't chase a cat, either. However, if you put *3* dogs together, that cat needs to have a good climbing tree ready. Although it is possible to desensitize your pack of dogs to a cat, it's probably not worth the effort and residual worry. Dogs can be taught to control themselves with a cat when the person in charge is there, if you have established proper rules of conduct. However, it can be a different story with those otherwise mannerly dogs when you leave the house: They may go after the cat behind your back.

I lived through this scenario myself: My 2 dog-trusting cats were almost killed when I added a third dog to my canine family. At the time, my Golden Retriever, Roma, and my Cocker Spaniel, Amalfi, had been living peacefully with my cats. After Roma died I adopted my first Weimaraner, Lulu. When I got Lulu home, I didn't like the intense stare with which she regarded the cats, and the usually trusting cats were on guard. With close supervision and obedience exercises, I got to the point where Lulu learned to ignore the cats and I felt comfortable that they were not in jeopardy. Then I adopted another Weimaraner, Billy Blue, as a companion for Lulu, and he turned out not to pose a threat to the cats, either, since his life revolved solely around when the next meal would be served.

The trouble for the cats started when I rescued a 2-month-old Rottweiler puppy who had been abandoned on the roadside in a cardboard box. From the moment the Weimaraners accepted the new youngster as a member of their pack, the older dogs began to harass the cats, chasing and cornering them. The dogs had become a hunting pack, and within a week both cats had to make an emergency visit to the vet. I found a new home for both of the cats with friends of mine, but the point is this: If you have more than 2 dogs, even of a laid-back, non-prey-driven type, you need to consider living a feline-deprived life.

GENERAL TIPS FOR CATS LIVING WITH DOGS

❑ *Bring animals together when they are young.* Kittens and puppies—or at least a kitten and a grown dog—have the best chance of making lifelong friendships.

❑ *Give your cat "vertical space" in every room.* This is cat-lingo for providing your cat with a place to escape up to, like a cat tree or other high surface such as a counter or bookcase where she can take refuge.

❑ *Establish separate sleeping areas for each animal.* They need to have their "dens" as far apart as possible, with the cat's lair always higher up. Her sleeping den should be somewhere the dog cannot reach or is not allowed to go, such as the second floor if you live in a house.

❑ *Feed the pets at different times and in different places.*

❑ *Put your cat's food and water up high.* If your cat has been eating on the floor until now, you will need to move her dish up to a counter. Even the most cat-loving, respectful dog in the world cannot pass up a dish of deliciously smelly cat food. But if you are going to get a dog and need to change the location of the food and water, do so well in advance of the dog walking in, when your cat will have everything else to adjust to.

☐ *Keep special attention and grooming private.* When you give special time to one pet, try to do it when the other one is not around to see and get jealous.

☐ *Get* Feliway *spray and plug-in diffuser.* Spraying this pheromone (described in the chapter on "stuff") can help decrease anxiety for the cat. The same company makes a similar product for dogs called D.A.P., and you may decide to use it if you feel your dog needs help taking it easy, too. However, it's more likely that your dog will need you to set firm boundaries and make it clear that he cannot cross them to harass the cat.

☐ *Let the cat set the pace.* Each cat has a unique personality and will have her own tolerance level and timetable for coping with a dog entering the household. Needless to say, your cat's pace will have a lot to do with how your dog handles the adjustment: whether he is respectful and lets the cat call the shots, or whether he is spring-loaded to take chase as soon as she jumps off the counter.

One thing is pretty certain—it is usually a very slow process. It may be months before your cat is comfortable enough in the presence of the dog to be able to walk around without constantly looking over her shoulder as though she is being hunted. However, it can also be true that one night you may come into the living room and find the two of them curled up together, snoring away peacefully!

☐ *Don't leave them alone together in the beginning.* Do not leave the dog and cat loose and alone together in the house until you are certain that they have developed at least a grudging mutual respect and can fend for themselves. Dogs and cats can learn to share the same space in friendship or at least a truce, but the peace needs to be negotiated by you from the start. The cat can fend for herself, but what you can help with is setting boundaries for the dog and gently correcting him for any aggressive tendencies toward the cat or for encroaching on her territory.

Cats and Cats: Managing a Multi-Cat Home

It seems like such a jolly idea to have a whole lot of cats—lots of beauties for you to watch and love, lots of potential friends and playmates for them. However, a multi-cat home requires a lot of finesse and work from you, and even so there may still be tension and discord amongst the cats. Remember that cats are not naturally pack or group animals; they are solitary beings designed to do their own thing, on their own terms, without restrictions or interference. Therefore, living in a group setting is unnatural and requires daily adjustments and concessions from every one of those cats. Please keep this in mind as you make decisions about how to enlarge your cat family. A Why-Not impulse from you can have disastrous consequences for some of the feline individuals you live with.

There is such a thing as too many cats—one cat too many can upset the whole apple cart and turn a sweetly purring home into a screech-fest with the fur flying. There is actually a name for people who take in too many cats: "cat hoarders." If you think you might be someone with a tendency to gather cats, keep your perspective and don't go beyond an appropriate number of cats for the size of your home and the time you will have to devote to them. Let common sense be your guide. For example, cat behaviorists will tell you that a 2-bedroom apartment is not big enough for 5 cats. If you disagree with that, you probably need to reevaluate your thinking.

There are a number of factors that can help you figure out what is going on with your colony of cats at any given time. Just as with human interactions, relationships between cats have an ebb and flow; what was working last week may be entirely different today. If you understand the elements that affect those relations, you can get a better handle on how to promote harmony and diffuse problems.

Factors Affecting Harmony Among Cats

- Age
- Size
- Sexual maturity (occurs at 6 to 7 months)
- Social maturity (occurs at 2 to 4 years)
- Number of cats in the colony
- Early socialization with littermates
- Health
- How cats were introduced
- Individual personalities
- Perception of territorial divisions
- Availability of food
- How the person handles squabbles between cats

PICKING COMPATIBLE HOUSEMATES

❑ *Littermates.* People often find that 2 kittens or cats from the same litter often make great housemates. A brother and sister are better than 2 littermates of the same sex, who might have a built-in drive to challenge each other when they hit maturity.

❑ *Choose a cat used to group living.* One of the many benefits of adopting from a shelter or rescue center is that you are able to see how each particular cat tolerates others, allowing you to pick one that can cohabit without making issues.

❑ *Avoid two males of equal age.* When 2 male cats reach social maturity at the same time—which is generally 2 to 4 years of age—they may have disputes about rank and who is top cat.

❑ *Avoid extreme personalities.* Cats who are at either extreme of the personality spectrum—those who are very timid, fearful and shy, or those who are confident, active and high-energy—may not blend as easily with other cats.

❑ *Avoid multiple Burmese cats.* Burmese are a loving breed, but they can be more territorial than other cats and therefore problematic in a group situation.

❐ *Some cats should fly solo.* Keep in mind that some individual cats whose personalities are most true to feline nature do best as the lone cat in a household.

If you keep a reasonable number of cats and things are going smoothly in your cat family, but then suddenly they go sour, one of the items listed in the chart below is probably to blame. If not, then check the chart of stress factors for cats in the behavior chapter, because any of those influences may be affecting one or more of your cats and upsetting the equilibrium.

What Can Change Inter-Cat Dynamics

- Adding or losing a cat
- Illness (which lowers a cat's status to beneath all other healthy cats)
- Sexual maturity is reached
- Social maturity is reached—this is prime time for jockeying for social position

WAYS TO INCREASE HARMONY

❐ *Create more vertical territory.* Cats need high places where they can escape to feel safe. A big, open, one-level room is a cat's worst nightmare: nowhere to hide, no vista point from which to survey it all. A cat without options feels vulnerable, and by adding other cats to the mix, you put all the cats in a position of defensive fear.

❐ *Add furniture.* The easiest way to make your cat feel more comfortable is to add one stuffed armchair to the room. With that chair, you provide multiple perches: two arms, one back, and the seat, with multiple levels, too. An ordinary chair, table or bookcase achieves the same purpose: different elevations and surfaces to occupy.

❐ *Time-shares.* You may have thought that humans invented the concept of a time-share in a resort community, but cats have been practicing time-sharing right at home for as long as they have lived with people. For example, a higher-ranking cat will lay claim to a favorite chair in the sun, and that will become "her chair"—but there is an understanding that a subordinate cat can use it when she leaves.

HIERARCHY AMONG CATS

A cat's social position in a multi-cat household is not set in stone—it is not as though there is one top cat and then everybody else takes a number, so to speak. Hierarchy among cats is fluid and dynamic, shifting subtly all the time. The rungs on the ladder are not evenly spaced, either—the feline conception of who is more important is different from the human one.

◆ The Pecking Order

The height of any vertical territory in the house is crucial to determining hierarchy among the cats. The cat who controls the highest elevations develops higher status. She can oversee the domain and have dominance over subordinates simply by dint of being physically above their eye level. This explains why a cat tree is such a valuable part of a multi-cat household, because it permits all this jockeying and layering to go on.

Territorial Claims. The top cat in a house who is top gun is the one who guards choice areas and blocks pathways and routes within the house. She also stays longer in the litter box and is the first to use it after it is cleaned.

Prime Real Estate. The cat who stakes her claim to the choice spots in the house is the *numero uno.* Such spots could be the master's bed, a chair that is in the sun or a window perch with a good view of a bird feeder.

Mounting Behavior. Even male or female cats who have been altered can still exhibit mounting behavior as a display of dominance, rather than sexual activity. Lower-ranking cats will submit to mounting by the dominant cat.

Middle-Ranking Cat. An interesting phenomenon can take place among cats who are neither highest nor lowest in a multiple-cat environment. A middle-ranking cat may constantly pick on the lower-ranked cats, creating tension in the group that may seem a mystery to you. The reason for this behavior is that a middle-ranking cat cannot stand up to the higher-ranking cat and so takes out her frustrations on a lowly cat.

◆ Determining Status: Clues to the Pecking Order
The ways that cats who live together interact reveals their relative importance or power. If you aren't entirely sure where your cats stand in the hierarchy they have determined, here are some clues.

Entering a Space. One cat walks toward the middle of the room while the other walks around the perimeter of the space, avoiding eye contact. Obviously, the first cat is the higher-ranking one.

Calmness. A cat who is not prone to nervousness will be the higher-ranking one because anxiety does not connote strength, while calmness denotes leadership.

Aggression. A cat with aggressive tendencies is *not* the dominant one. Again, the calmest cat is the one with higher rank; staying cool is powerful stuff.

Indifference. A cat who shows no interest in other cats is intimidating because not having a reaction is a sign of strength, not weakness.

Play. Even when they get quite old, many cats play games that take the form of wrestling or chasing. One cat is usually dominant in these games and comes out the "winner," but in a truly compatible relationship, cats will take turns being the chaser and the chasee, as in "Tag—you're it!"

✦ Scent Communication Between Cats

Cats have a number of ways they use scent to communicate with each other, either "leaving messages" in the environment or scent marking right on the other cat.

Marking is how cats leave "Post-Its": The main form of communication among cats is through the scents they can deposit: from urine, scat, claws, paw pads and facial scent glands.

More cats, more marking: The larger the population of cats in a home, the more urine marking you will have. Cats use marking to make statements about everything: to mark territory, to threaten, to announce their arrival or to initiate a dispute without having an actual confrontation.

Rubbing cheeks: As we've seen, cats have facial glands that release pheromones containing personal information about their age, health, sex and reproductive status. These glands are on the lips, chin and forehead, as well as the tail and paw pads.

Depositing information: If a cat wants to leave information about herself on an inanimate object, she will just use her facial glands but when cats want to deposit information on another cat they rub against them with their head and then their flank and tail.

Collecting and combining scents: Not only do cats deposit their own scent, they also engage in social behavior through which they combine their scent with that of other cats. By rubbing on another cat, they leave their information, but if the other cat is higher-ranking, they are showing respect and also gaining some social advantage by carrying the scent of a superior cat in the colony.

A familiar colony scent: Cats who live together in a colony create a scent that is a mixture of all their odors and that becomes a unifying force.

Two neutral cats meeting: When two cats approach each other and have no issues—it's simply a neutral encounter—they gather all the information they need about each other through their noses. They begin with a nose-to-nose greeting, then rub heads (depositing pheromones from their facial glands on each other), then they may lick each others' face and/or ears and finally will sniff the anal area.

The "one who is rubbed" is dominant: The cat who elicits the first rub is usually the higher-ranking cat. Lower-ranking cats often rub against more important cats as a way of seeking acceptance and gaining some sort of "feline prestige" by association with their scent, as if they are wearing "Top Cat perfume."

✦ The Pariah Cat

A cat colony can have what is called a pariah, meaning a cat who is a virtual outcast. A cat can wind up in this position as the result of low self-esteem that elicits bullying behavior from the other cats, or because her own antisocial behavior is resented and punished by the other cats. Pariah cats are often fearful, hostile cats who display defensive/aggressive behavior such as growling and hissing when other cats approach them. This is a chicken-or-egg question: Does a bully cat turn another cat into a pariah, or does an insecure cat bring out the worst in others?

Signs of a Pariah Cat

- Stays far from the other cats
- Lives on the perimeter of the territory
- Walks low to the ground in a hunched posture
- Walks with her tail wrapped around her body
- Growls near other cats
- Slinks to the food area after others have finished eating
- Is constantly picked on

Remedies for a Pariah Situation. This cycle of abuse needs to be stopped and will probably require the help of a cat behaviorist, who can suggest individualized ways to address your cat's problem. Look for links to trainers on www.CatChatRadio.com. There are some fixes that you can try yourself.

❏ *Put a bell on the collars of other cats.* By having a bell to announce their arrival or presence to the pariah, she can hear them and avoid them.

❏ *Use Feliway liberally.* This remarkable pheromone spray has a calming effect on cats and is especially valuable for this underdog situation. You should spray wherever the pariah spends the most time and also use plug-in Feliway diffusers in any of the common areas, with the goal of lowering negative emotions for all the cats.

❏ *Medications.* Ask your vet about prescribing medications that could lower anxiety and boost confidence in the pariah, thereby decreasing the reactivity of the bully cat(s).

❏ *Modify the environment temporarily.* Provide a separate living environment with food, water, a litter box and a window to look out. A barrier like a door would be the best solution because then no hostile or threatening behavior can take place. Of course, this confinement can't be permanent, and a trainer would have to take it from here, but at least it will temporarily suspend the feline war.

❏ *Go to www.spiritessence.com for natural remedies for inter-cat issues.*

FEEDING ARRANGEMENTS

You have to create a home environment where the cats feel safe and peaceful, so that none of them feels endangered by the simple decision to eat lunch. There are several options to consider in how you offer meals to your kitties.

✦ Free Feeding Is a Poor Choice

In a multi-cat home, free-feeding kibble is not a good idea, not just because it is nutritionally inferior but also because a single feeding station can create problems among multiple cats. If after reading the chapter on nutrition you nevertheless choose to free-feed, make sure you have more than one bowl and that they are positioned so that no one cat has to cross the pathway of other cats to get to the chow. Food etiquette comes into play where hierarchies are concerned, and having large quantities of kibble out all the time will only give the dominant cat(s) more opportunities to lay claim to another coveted resource and create tension and discord.

♦ Scheduled Feeding Is Best
Two meals a day of canned food is the most efficient and nutritious way to feed your cats. You will know that each cat got her due and that even the lower-ranking cats got a fair portion.

♦ Individual Bowls Promote Harmony
Each cat needs to have her own dish with her own portion of food. Try to choose a dish according to what shape each cat has shown a preference for, if it's possible to tell. It's easy to recognize the bowls that are *not* comfortable for a cat—for example, if a bowl has sides that interfere with her whiskers.

♦ Each Bowl Should Have Its Own Position
Each cat should know where you are going to set her bowl down; before long, she will go there to wait calmly for her meal. Cats thrive on routine and predictability, and dinnertime is no exception, so if you can provide a protected place for a cat to eat, you are dramatically increasing her well-being.

♦ Watch Where You Place a Bowl
There are a few spots that are inconvenient positions to put a bowl. Placing it in a corner or against a wall is no good for a cat because she may feel trapped, with her back to potential enemies.

♦ Tension Between Cats Can Be "Cured" at Dinner
If there are pecking order issues between cats, one way to defuse that tension is to put their dinner bowls far from each other, but in each other's line of sight. The theory behind this is that being able to see each other while enjoying a tasty meal will create a positive association, which over time may cancel out some of the historical problems.

INTRODUCING A NEW CAT
The circumstances under which you introduce a new cat to the resident cats will greatly influence the future of their relationship. The steps to follow may seem endless, but they are so precise for a reason: You need to be patient and methodical in order to have a meeting of the cats that happens successfully and lays a healthy foundation.

♦ Create a Safe Room
A designated safe room: If you have a room you can dedicate to the new cat for a while, that is ideal. The new cat is going to live solely in this space for as long as it takes—days or weeks—before the resident cat seems ready to accept the newcomer, as described below. In the safe room you need a water dish, a litter box and at least one piece of furniture that the cat can climb up on or hide beneath. If you have a big enough house or apartment, you might want to add a

second cat tree (assuming that your resident cat already has one). You can buy one for the new cat to use in her safe room, which afterward will become shared territory for both cats. It is great if you have a window in the safe room to give the new cat some visual entertainment.

If you don't have a whole room: Many people don't have the luxury of a whole room they can turn into a safe room dedicated to their new cat's arrival. If this is true in your case, you can convert a bathroom into a safe space. Just remember that a room with nowhere to perch and nowhere to hide is cruel to the cat, who needs both of these things.

Don't let the resident cat in the safe room. You don't want to overwhelm the new cat with your current cat's odor just yet. First the newcomer has to get her bearings and settle in before coping with the new scent.

Plug in a Comfort Zone Feliway pheromone diffuser before you bring the new cat home so that the soothing pheromones can transform the safe room into a true sanctuary.

◆ Bring the New Cat into the House

Use a Carrier with Lots of Holes. Bring the new cat into the house in a carrier with lots of holes so that your resident cat can smell her briefly as you walk right past her and into the safe room. Just give her a whiff and continue with your business, which is to get that carrier into the safe room.

Go Directly to the Safe Room. As though it's the most ordinary daily event, go right past your cat and into the safe room, closing the door behind you. Have a nice cat treat in your pocket.

Put the Carrier in a Corner. Place the carrier on the floor, open the door and put something in front of it to hold it open, but do not urge the new cat to exit. She needs to get acclimated at her own pace. Put the treat on the floor just outside the open carrier door and leave the room. Resist any urge to pat the new cat unless you have a way to thoroughly wash your hands before your resident cat sees—and smells—you, which will create resentment and jealousy during the first phase of introduction.

The New Cat Will Take Her Own Time. Don't worry about the new cat alone in the safe room—cats like to have a chance to explore and investigate on their own, and that's what she will do.

Visit the New Cat When the Resident Cat Is Busy. To avoid making your resident cat jealous, try to pick times when she is sleeping, eating or otherwise engaged to slip into the safe room undetected. Alternately, have someone else sit with your cat and give her affection, groom her or play with her while you go visit the newcomer. You don't want your resident cat sitting outside the closed door of the safe room, wondering what is going on in there with that cat you are betraying her for.

Try Not to Get the New Cat's Scent on You. Keep a terry robe in the safe room that you can slip on when you go in there so that your clothes don't get covered in the new cat's scent. Some of her odor will still get on you and your resident cat will know it, but you want to limit that as much as possible. Sense of smell is so important to cats that an odor can overwhelm them—and in the case of a new cat, it can stir up a lot of negative emotions. For the same reason, wash your hands and forearms with hot soapy water after being with the new cat so that you are not literally putting this foreign odor in the other cat's face when you go to touch her later.

• Managing the Resident Cat During the Transition

Pay Normal Amounts of Attention. Don't overwhelm your resident cat with an out-of-the-ordinary amount or intensity of emotion. We know that cats thrive on consistency and dependability, so overdoing things with a cat just sets off an alarm bell: "Something's different! Something's happening! Yikes!"

Keep Your Behavior and Tone of Voice Normal. As above, any change from the norm is cause for concern in a cat.

Camping Out at the Safe Room Door. Your cat may feel the need to guard the safe room door—to camp outside it, sniffing under the door, even hissing and growling. This is normal and nothing for you to worry about—it is just a cat's way of reacting to something foreign hidden in the house. It does not signify that things will go poorly between the cats when they are eventually introduced.

Spray Feliway Around the Door. It can ease your cat's tension and worry if the atmosphere around the door is impregnated with the good feelings that Feliway can elicit.

Your Cat Will Lose Interest. It may take days, or maybe a week or more, but eventually your cat will lose interest in the invisible cat on the other side of that door. This is the moment in the summit meeting you've been waiting for—a little apathy goes a long way toward initiating peaceful relations.

• Scent Sharing with Scent Socks
Smell is the first and most important way in which you will pre-introduce the new cat to your existing cat(s) before a face-to-face meeting. A cat's senses, in order of importance, are smell, sounds, sight and touch—so the best way to get right to the heart of it with a cat is through her nose.

"Scent Socks." Similar to what I've described in the previous section on "Dogs & Cats," you are going to imbue "scent socks" with the smell of each cat and then have the other cat sniff the sock to acclimate her to the newcomer's odor. Scent socks are a well-known technique generally accepted as the tried-and-true way to accustom 2 cats to each other before they actually meet to lessen any aggression or fear between them. The reason socks are better than towels is that a towel can be overwhelming to the cat and cumbersome for you to handle. The following is how to put scent socks to work:

1. Take 4 sweat socks or tube socks and wash them so that they have a neutral scent—no scented laundry detergent or softener.

2. Put a sweat sock over each hand and rub both hands all over your resident cat's body, especially stroking her on the cheeks and alongside her mouth.

3. Put these 2 scent-impregnated socks in the safe room, 1 in the area where the new cat sleeps or hangs out and the other near her food bowl. Do the same thing with 2 socks rubbed all over the new cat, placing them strategically in the house for the resident cat to sniff. When you see either cat approach the scented sock, give a treat; you want her to make a positive association to that smell.

4. If either cat is scared by the clean socks over your hand when you try to rub her with them, you can spread the socks on the cat's sleeping area instead so she will sleep on them and scent them that way.

5. The cats' individual reactions to the scented socks tell you a lot about how the actual introduction will go. If a cat growls and attacks the sock, you have a long wait before they can actually meet; if a cat sniffs the sock and is disinterested, that is good—you could go right ahead with the introduction itself.

6. Some cat behaviorists say that for at least 3 or 4 days you should mix the scents of the cats by stroking one cat and then going to the other and stroking her all over, mingling their smells. If the cats have been pretty mellow about the whole sock exchange, then you can try this mingling technique after the first couple of days.

◆ **Trading Spaces**

Now you are going to play "musical rooms" with your cats by switching their living spaces for about an hour. You want to do this room switch twice a day for about a week. You might want to make the amount of time spent shorter than that, depending on either cat's reaction to the switch—you want it to be a positive experience and end on a positive note, so if either cat becomes agitated you need to end the session.

First, put the resident cat in a carrier. The resident cat needs to be taken out of the picture for a moment so that the new cat can come into the house without being rushed. Have the cat in the carrier out of sight of the newcomer.

Next, open the door to the safe room. Cats are curious by nature, and the new cat has probably been dying to get out of that room and see what is on the other side of the door. However, do not pick her up and deposit her in the new territory (meaning the rest of the house). It would be frightening and disorienting to the cat to be thrust into a big space full of the resident cat's odor. Let her set the pace of how quickly she exits the safe room for a look around.

Put the resident cat in the safe room. Once the newcomer leaves the safe room, bring your resident kitty into that room and close the door, which gives her time to check out every nook and cranny where the new cat has left her scent.

The more important exploration is for the new cat. It's the new cat who has the big adjustment to make. If you have a small apartment that doesn't allow for this trading spaces, then take the resident cat in her carrier to a neighbor or friend's.

If you have multiple resident cats, do this in shifts. The new cat needs to be sequestered in another room, in a carrier or at a friend's house while her safe room is visited by the other cats. If you have several resident cats to introduce to the safe room, let the sweetest, most cat-friendly cat in first. Then you can let in other cats, one at a time, removing the previous cats depending on their personalities. What you want to avoid is having a feisty, aggressive cat come into the safe room, have a negative response to the odor of the new cat, and redirect his aggression to one of his housemates who happens to be standing there at the time.

Always give a treat or meal afterwards. Either give each of the cats a super-tasty treat right after they are returned to their original space, or time the "trading spaces" switch so that you can give them a meal right afterward. In either case, you want them to associate the experience of the other cat's smell with a wonderful treat.

✦ Promote Positive Feelings Between the Cats

Your goal during the introduction period is to promote and strengthen a friendly bond between the cats. There are a few really important rules, based on fundamental truths about cats, that you have to follow in order to make this happen. Do not make the mistake of thinking your cat is an exception because she is loving to people, or she has always been friendly to other cats, or she is timid and so won't react aggressively. Cats are cats: Individual personalities and tendencies do not change deep-seated genetic tendencies to be cautious about new cats.

Do not engage in any "secret petting." Do not get the new cat's scent on you; the jealousy it will create in your resident cat can easily turn her against the newcomer.

✦ Preparation for the Cats Being Together

Escape Routes. A cat's natural instinct when startled or cornered is to escape upward, but of course there has to be somewhere to jump up *to*. So to the best of your ability, try to create or clear several high surfaces in every room where a cat can jump up if frightened. Other times, a cat may escape by going underneath a piece of furniture: In most houses a low hiding place is an escape route that a cat can make on her own, without your assistance.

Expect Harsh Words from the Resident. Don't be a bit surprised if your usually friendly, mellow resident cat makes some pretty unpleasant noises at the new arrival. Hissing, growling, spitting—expect all of it (and be pleasantly surprised if it does not occur), because it's a normal part of the introduction process. Think of these unfriendly sounds and gestures as a kind of initiation rite: The resident cat is saying, "I'll put you through the wringer, but if you handle it and pass my tests, you'll be a member of the club."

Always Give the Resident Cat Attention First. You need to strictly adhere to the concept that the resident cat is the only one who gets attention, first and entirely, until the cats are relaxed and accept each other.

Do Not Give Affection to the New Cat "in Public." In the early adjustment period—which will vary depending on how accepting and flexible your resident cat turns out to be—you have to withhold any PDAs (public displays of affection) from the new cat that the resident cat might see or hear. This may sound harsh, but you really have to control yourself; showing affection to the new cat is a direct affront to your resident cat. You cannot give affection to the newcomer if you want the resident to accept this cat and eventually befriend her. Once that friendship has begun, you can slowly and discreetly show affection to both cats, but keep in mind to always favor the resident cat to some degree.

◆ The Moment of Truth: The Open Door

Okay—you have patiently set the scene for the actual meeting of the cats, so pretty much all you can do now is sit back and watch.

* Bring with you a pocketful of treats (to promote positive feelings while they are loose together) and a pillow (to put between them in case things get nasty). Then open the door to the safe room and stand out of the way. Let the cats go where they want and follow from a distance.

* Create a positive feeling. You can give the cats a reason to like each other by tossing a really tasty treat to each of them when they are in the same room. Toss lots of tasty treats on the first meeting, but be sure to throw them right to the cats, not in such a way that they have to run after the treats and compete for them.

* A one-minute session may even be enough. Keep it short and sweet and end on a positive note. Work your way up to an hour spent in each other's company, preferably mostly ignoring each other or pretending to.

* This can take any amount of time—the cats will determine the timetable for harmony to develop.

* If either cat is aggressive, open the safe room door and install two baby gates, one above the other, so that the gates together cover most of the opening. This allows the cats to continue to acclimate to each other without harm.

* Keep the safe room set up and continue to have the new cat to sleep there at night and put her there whenever you are not home. You must monitor their interaction for a while to feel confident that there is no underlying tension between them.

* When the cats sit peacefully in the same space, you'll know it is working. You will know you have succeeded at enabling a harmonious introduction when the two cats can sit in the same room without staring at each other (which would be a tension-filled challenge if they did).

◆ An Alternative to the Safe Room Plan: The Newcomer in a Cage

Although the safe room, scent socks and trading spaces are a proven route to harmonious cohabitation between cats, if you find this plan too difficult to follow or time-consuming for whatever reason, below you will find a shorter way to bring a new cat into your home

Disclaimer: Although I am including the following method in the interest of thoroughness, this is not a particularly kind or even very safe plan, overall.

A wire indoor cage or enclosure that you can buy or construct is another way to introduce the new cat to your family. In theory, an enclosure allows the new cat to see what goes on in the household without any other animal being able to harm her. You can use this indoor confinement when you're not going to be around.

If you don't have access to such a cage (although catalogues such as KV Vet Supply carry a few of them, and they're not very expensive), then a carrier with a wire front is a second best option because the cat can at least see out one end of it and yet is protected in the confines of the container. The enclosure should be placed in the most trafficked area of the house—like the kitchen or family room—so that the newcomer gets used to the occupants, noises and routines of the household. The goal in this scenario is to keep the new cat visible and able to see without being in harm's way—and also to be sure that she does not bolt in a panic, which could trigger the other cat to chase and set up a poor beginning for them. In theory, it will ensure that no one gets off to the wrong start or even gets hurt.

However, take note that not only does this method put the new cat in a highly vulnerable position, with nowhere to hide or escape, but it allows the other cat to harass and menace her from outside. Furthermore, it goes against the basic tenet about introducing a new cat—that she is in physical and emotional jeopardy and needs to be protected.

CAT FIGHTS

Sometimes it's hard to tell the difference between playing and fighting, or to know what to do at that moment when it crosses the line, since cats can really inflict some damage on each other.

What constitutes a good relationship between 2 cats? If cats sleep together, groom each other and greet each other calmly after one has been absent, these are important signals that their relationship is good. When cats understand each other they know how to read each other's body language and their play is bloodless.

Cats who have a strained relationship, by contrast, approach each other with tension or anxiety. There will be hisses, arched backs and other uptight signals between them (which never happens between happy, relaxed cats), and their play will reflect that discomfort. When these unhappy behaviors happen routinely during play, you can be pretty sure that fighting will follow.

• **Differences Between Playing and Fighting:**

One or Two Hisses Are Okay. More than a couple of hisses can mean it's a fight.

Hissing with Chasing Is Friendly. Play that involves simultaneous hissing and running, chasing after the other cat, can indicate a normal, friendly interchange, especially if they reverse roles at times. You may need to watch for a while to get the tone of it.

Yowling or Screaming. Vocalizations are not part of friendly play, especially loud growling, yelping or extended hissing.

Taking Turns on the Offensive. In healthy cat play, the 2 cats switch off between being on the defensive and being the playful aggressor. In unhealthy interchanges they do not take turns: One cat is always "it."

Sharing Toys. Friendly cats bat toys around between them and take turns pushing the toy around.

Scratching or Biting. In play, a cat is never injured.

Cats Bat at Each Other Gently. In happy play, cats take pot shots at each other but mix it up with leaping, wrestling and teasing.

Kiss and Make Up. When cats play and their shenanigans are over, life goes on as normal. After a fight, cats seem anxious or fearful and avoid each other.

Are Two Enemies Playing? If two cats who are normally not friendly seem to be playing, you can be pretty sure they are not and it's probably a fight.

When in Doubt, Break It Up. If you aren't sure whether 2 cats are well intentioned in their play, distract them with a positive sound—shake a box of treats, run the can opener, whatever you can do to stop them with a positive lure. By keeping it positive, there is no loss if they were actually playing, and if it was the beginning of a fight, you have intervened before it got ugly.

Signs of Not Playing Well

- One cat always chases or bullies the other.
- One cat runs for a protected spot and hides from the other.
- The cats make angry sounds.
- One cat is fearful—backing away or hissing—when the other makes motions or gestures.
- One cat does surprise attacks on the other, who runs and hides.
- Gestures are mostly hard bats, no variety.
- When it's over, cats avoid each other.

◆ What to Do About Rough Fight-Playing

If your cats display the signs of unhappy play on the chart above, *do not* let them continue to play. One or both will get hurt and at least one of them may end up emotionally traumatized, too, if it gets rough enough.

Do Not Raise the Tension Level. Yelling at the cats or throwing water on them or doing anything else that might raise the tension level is not advisable. By doing so, you run the risk of escalating an already emotionally charged situation.

◆ Dealing With Aggression and Fights

Distract the Cats with Something Positive. Call the cats for food in the tone of voice you usually use to call them to dinnertime, or run the can opener, which for many cats is their signal that lunch is served. If they associate this positive outcome with rough playing that teeters on fighting, the good reward can actually build their tolerance for each other, and with enough positive repetitions of the dinner bell ringing, it may keep that rough playing from tipping over into a danger zone.

Interrupt a Cat About to Pounce. If you see a cat plotting a sneak attack, you can interrupt the negative energy and hostility between two cats before it escalates by distracting them with a dangle or lure toy—something that will take their attention off each other. The aggressor can take out her impulse on the toy and the other cat will be none the wiser that you saved the day.

Signs of Threats. If your cats are staring directly at each other—with or without raised hindquarters—a fight is brewing and you need to interrupt it immediately. Use a toy or toss some treats to take their eyes off each other.

Put Bells on Aggressors. By "belling" your tougher cats, the less dominant ones can hear them coming and get out of the way. This precludes secret kamikaze.

Bang Pot Lids. If a fight is fully under way, you shouldn't try to break it up because you could get hurt. You need to rely on the startle factor by making a loud, sharp noise.

Ignore Both Cats After a Fight. If a fight does happen, resist any impulse you have to comfort either cat. Do not talk to or touch either one because that could be perceived as congratulating the aggressor or approving of the activity.

◆ Sudden Onset of Hostility

Redirected Aggression. This is sudden hostility that is directed at the nearest person or animal by an easily aroused cat—meaning a cat who, when agitated, will turn on whatever creature is nearby. This behavior may stem from an incident that had nothing to do with the cat on the receiving end.

Cats who have been in this situation should be separated. Keep the cats apart for a couple of days until the emotions on both sides cool down—both the aggressor and the cat who was attacked without provocation. If feelings run deep enough, they may have to be reintroduced from scratch.

Festering Feelings. If a fight erupts that has no trigger you can discern, there may have been a problem that was boiling under the surface, unbeknownst to you.

Who Started What? It's often hard to unravel who did what to whom in a sudden cat fight. The easiest solution is to separate the cats and create more vertical space in the house—if you have one cat tree, get another so there are plenty of escape options.

Apply Spirit Essence to Both Cats. There are several preparations of natural calming agents that come as oils to be rubbed onto the cats' ears. Go to www.spiritessence.com to learn more.

Consider Medication. If fights continue, especially out of nowhere, you need to get on top of the situation. Talk to your vet about the various antianxiety medications that are being prescribed for cats with aggression issues and decide together whether your bully cat is a good candidate.

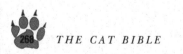

Chapter 12

MEDICAL BASICS

This chapter is intended to help you recognize and understand the physical ailments that might send you to the vet with your cat. This is not a primer for home medical care, and the information is not intended as a diagnostic tool for you to use to solve your cat's physical complaints. I say this not to avoid a potential lawsuit and cover myself but to protect you and your cat so that you don't misread her symptoms or unintentionally do her harm by not taking her to your veterinarian. Never assume that a symptom your cat has is "just like" something your cat (or another cat you had) has been through before. Where your cat's health is concerned, *assume nothing*. Let your vet be the one to tell you whether your concerns are something to worry about. It is never a good idea to just take a guess, since with medical issues in cats, 2 plus 2 does not always equal 4.

Veterinarians

When choosing a veterinarian, it's useful to know what the letters after his name mean about his training and skill. Various acronyms follow the names of veterinarians and other animal experts, so here is a list of those you are most likely to encounter.

WHAT THE LETTERS AFTER THE NAME MEAN

DVM: Doctor of Veterinary Medicine (a degree given by a four-year program at a college of veterinary medicine, and usually preceded by an undergraduate degree)

VMD: Veterinary Medical Doctorate (a degree given specifically by the University of Pennsylvania for the same training as DVM)

BVMS: Bachelor of Veterinary Medicine and Surgery (a five-year degree offered by universities in the United Kingdom and other countries but not in the United States)

MRCVS: Member of the Royal College of Veterinary Surgeons (RCVS is the organization that regulates and licenses practitioners in the UK)

BVSc, MVSc, DVSc: Bachelor, Master or Doctor of Veterinary Science (trained for research rather than for clinical practice)

DACVB or Dipl.ACVB: Diplomate of the American College of Veterinary Behaviorists (one of many specialty boards certifying veterinarians who receive specialized education and pass an exam and other requirements)

ACVS: American College of Veterinary Surgeons

AVDC: American Veterinary Dental College

CVT, RVT, LVT: Certified, Registered or Licensed Veterinary Technician (has to pass a state or federal exam after graduation from an accredited veterinary technician program)

AAFP: There are veterinarians who see only cats in their practice and most of them belong to the American Association of Feline Practitioners (AAFP). You can see if there are any such vets practicing in your area by calling 800-874-0498 or going to www.aafponline.org.

AHVMA: If you want to find a holistic practitioner in your area, go to the American Holistic Veterinary Medical Association at www.ahvma.org.

TWO DIFFERENT PHILOSOPHIES ABOUT VETERINARY PRACTICE

Just as with human medicine, there are different philosophies on how to approach wellness or preventive care for animals and what sort of medical interventions to endorse when problems arise. In American veterinary care, there are basically two schools of thought. The one that the majority of vets belong to is called the American Veterinary Medical Association (AVMA), which follows standard Western ideas about medicine and health. The second, smaller group, which is often in opposition to this traditional school, is called the American Holistic Veterinary Medical Association (AHVMA): Their training teaches natural or holistic medicine based on homeopathic remedies and on the avoidance of chemical medicines for prevention or cure.

The members of AHVMA hold views that differ from the AVMA policies on virtually every aspect of cat care, from questioning the benefits of giving routine vaccinations and the frequent use of antibiotics and other drugs to avoiding commercial dry cat foods, which many consider to be the cause of much illness. Many homeopathic vets are opposed to vaccinations on the grounds that they contain chemical agents that cause severe allergic reactions, compromise an animal's immune system, and cause emotional imbalance.

The health care philosophy that you follow for yourself will influence the choices you make for your cat. If you visit a mainstream, Western-trained doctor and have no interest in alternative health care modalities (health foods, herbal remedies, chiropractic, acupuncture, osteopathy, etc.), then you will probably follow the same course for your cat. If you gravitate toward organic foods and embrace homeopathic remedies for yourself, then you may be more comfortable with a veterinary practitioner whose training and outlook mirror your own beliefs. Myself, I tend to follow a traditional approach to medical care, with some chiropractic, acupuncture and Chinese herbs thrown in for good measure—for me *and* my pets. The majority of pet owners go in this mainstream direction, too, so this chapter is focused in that direction. However, at the end of this chapter you will find information about how to find an alternative veterinary practice.

Choosing a vet who follows one philosophy does not necessarily rule out also visiting a doctor who holds the other philosophy. You should feel free to take advantage of the theories and practice from either veterinary perspective if you have the time and flexibility to pursue differing diagnoses and treatments for your cat. Vets of both persuasions can be open-minded about their counterparts in the medical profession. Making use of other kinds of veterinary care when appropriate is referred to as "bridging." Only you can determine whether a combination of the two philosophies is best for you and your cat.

CHOOSING A VET

A veterinarian has at least two customers for every patient: the cat and her owner or owners. So when choosing a vet, keep in mind that there are two distinct versions of bedside manner to evaluate and two different kinds of communication skills that a vet needs to possess. Do you pick a vet because *you* feel comfortable or because *your cat* seems to be at ease? Or should it be a combination of both?

◆ Communication

You need to feel comfortable asking the doctor questions. If you ask a question—perhaps one that is simple or even neurotic—you shouldn't feel that you have annoyed the vet. It's not all that different from choosing a doctor for yourself or a pediatrician for your children. Do you like the way you interact with him, and does he show his expertise and compassion in a way that is appealing to you?

◆ Convenience

Does the clinic have a location and office hours that generally accommodate your schedule? Would your vet or one of her colleagues ever meet you at the clinic after hours for an emergency? Does the clinic have walk-in appointments for nonemergencies?

◆ Emergency Care Facilities

Many small animal hospitals utilize specialized emergency facilities for the needs of their clients outside of normal hours. Although this idea may not sound as comforting as being able to go to a doctor and a staff that know you and your cat in an emergency, it probably makes the most sense to have a location that is staffed and prepared for whatever may happen to your pet at odd hours.

Realistically, there's no way that even a substantial private vet practice could maintain high-quality care during office hours and also provide emergency intervention around the clock. There just wouldn't be enough qualified staff and doctors to do both well. So the question is whether your vet's emergency facility is accessible to where you live. For example, if it is more

than an hour from your house, that sounds like a long way to go in the dark with a very sick animal. If there is a closer emergency veterinary hospital, you can get your vet's opinion on whether he thinks it's okay to use it instead.

◆ Is It a "Cats Only" Veterinary Practice?

There are some vets who are board-certified feline specialists and there are some vet clinics that treat only cats. Is this important to you? The all-feline office can be nice because the cats never have to hear barking, whining dogs or endure the misery of the dog in the waiting room sniffing at the carrier door to see who is in there.

The First Vet Visit

MAKE AN APPOINTMENT IMMEDIATELY WHEN YOU GET A NEW CAT

You need a vet to see your new cat, whether you're adopting a grown cat or getting a new kitten. The doctor should meet your pet without any particular medical agenda. It's important for the vet to simply meet the kitty, and vice versa. You want that first visit to take place when there is no emergency, no serious health issue, nothing more than a routine vaccination if the cat is due for one. Unless a low-key checkup is a burden on you financially or on your schedule, that consultation allows the vet to get a sense of your cat's personality and overall health, gives the cat a chance to have a positive experience with the doctor and lets you get comfortable, too.

◆ Get Out the Feliway

Not all cats have a favorable response to Comfort Zone Feliway pheromone spray, but for those who do it can be a great help in stressful situations such as the vet's office. Prepare the cat for the vet visit by spraying Feliway in her carrier, which to some cats can make it feel safe and comfortable. Bring the Feliway with you to the vet's office because spraying it on the examination table can also make it less threatening.

◆ Ask the Vet About "Pop-In" Visits

One of the best ways to get a cat over any anxiety about going to the doctor is to randomly take her in there for a pat and a treat. It's not necessary for the doctor to see her—as long as someone from the staff gives her a tickle under the chin and a piece of chicken (or other super-tasty treat you brought with you for that purpose), before long she'll feel right at home.

◆ Other Cats at Home

If there are other cats back at home, waiting for this one to come back, be forewarned that the odor of the vet's office will cling to your kitty and the cats back at home will not appreciate it. When you get home, give your cat a chance to groom and smell like herself again before she rejoins the other cats. This will help her settle back in. A simple way to overcome the smell of the vet's is to take a towel and rub it on the cats who stayed home, then rub that towel on the returning cat so that their odors mingle.

♦ Your Attitude at the Vet's Office

How you react to the vet's office will influence your cat's experience. Make a point to be upbeat and unconcerned from the moment you enter the office until after you leave. Your relaxed attitude will have a positive effect on your cat and it will set the tone for future vet visits. This is true whether you have a small kitten who doesn't have any fear, or you've inherited a cat who becomes frantically frightened at the first whiff of the vet's office.

♦ Bring Written Questions with You

Whenever your cat isn't right, it rattles you—and with your worry and tension you might forget to ask the doctor something that really concerns you. So if you can come with a few notes jotted down about your cat's problem, it can help the doctor figure things out, and it will also help you get the answers you need in that small window of opportunity when you have the doctor's attention.

VETS WHO MAKE HOUSE CALLS

Vets who make house calls could be considered a third category of vet, defined not by philosophy or training but by where they do their work. There is even an organization that represents them, called the American Association of Housecall Veterinarians (AAHV), which lists their members online at www.athomevet.org (however, the site does not list their phone numbers or addresses).

There are several advantages to having the doctor come to you.

♦ Convenience

This is a big selling point for people with multiple pets, children or other factors that make getting out of the house a burden. If the vet comes to your house, it can save you from having to juggle your schedule to make an appointment at a vet clinic, the hassle of getting there and the amount of time lost when you have to endure a long wait. If you work from home or have other obligations there, you lose none of that travel and wait time. Instead, a house-call vet usually gives you an appointment that is within a 30- to 60-minute range (allowing for traffic, weather and other visits taking longer than anticipated) and you can carry on with what you are doing at home until he arrives.

♦ Avoiding Stress

If your cat is traumatized by going to the vet's office you can eliminate or reduce her visits there. Some cats have been so frightened in the past or are so completely terrified by the odor that other stressed or fearful pets give off in a vet's waiting area that it is very difficult to help them overcome that terror. So although you may still need to visit a vet's office or an animal hospital for problems that cannot be solved at home, you are making life easier on yourself and your pet by having routine visits at home.

◆ Avoiding Sickness

You avoid exposing your cat to illnesses if you don't go to the vet's office, where there can be sick animals. No matter how well a vet's offices are cleaned, there is still a chance of cats passing on certain illnesses to others. Avoiding this is an especially good idea if your cat's immune system has been compromised by illness or age, or if you are one of those who are referred to as "vaccination rebels," raising your cats without immunizing them against diseases or significantly limiting use of vaccinations. You'll find more on that philosophy in the vaccination section of this chapter.

◆ Home Vets Can Provide Different Levels of Service

Not all veterinary issues can be solved in your home, and blood work or other diagnostic services usually need to be taken care of in a medical office, as do many urgent situations. Some home vets work out of their trucks or vans, while others have mobile clinics in which they can do surgery requiring anesthesia. Below are some questions you should ask before scheduling a house call so that you have a sense of what to expect.

QUESTIONS FOR A HOUSE-CALL VET

- ❏ What percentage of your practice is house calls?
- ❏ What days and hours are you available?
- ❏ Do you also practice in a clinic, or are you affiliated with one?
- ❏ What services do you provide at home, and which do you not?
- ❏ How do your clients handle emergency situations?
- ❏ Do you draw blood and handle other diagnostics or lab work?
- ❏ Do you need to see the cat's previous medical records at the visit, or beforehand?
- ❏ Is there anything I need to do before you come?
- ❏ What is your policy on follow-up calls after your visit? How do you charge for that time?
- ❏ What are your fees and how do you accept payment?

Health Insurance

DO YOU NEED PET HEALTH INSURANCE?

First ask yourself whether you are a person who believes in carrying insurance in general. You may have car or homeowner's insurance, or insurance against death or disability—or you may not. Pet health insurance may be another important investment that you want to make for peace of mind—or it may seem like negative thinking and a waste of money to you. One thing is certain: Whatever it costs to insure a pet is much less than the amount your insurance will pay back if your cat has any kind of significant medical problems or procedures.

Given the enormous costs of veterinary care that rival the costs of human health care—from the lab fees to the technology that is now available to diagnose and treat companion animals—I personally don't see how you can afford *not* to have insurance. Having said that, I also realize that the cost of insurance may be out of reach for some people, who prefer to hope that their cat never gets seriously ill. And there certainly are hardy, lucky cats who sail through life without urinary disorders and other common problems that plague so many cats. If your cat happens to be so lucky, you might resent having paid insurance premiums for care you never ended up needing. However, the few hundred dollars will not seem so bad when facing one serious bill in the thousands.

FANCY TESTS AND EQUIPMENT ARE EXPENSIVE

Veterinarians often use ultrasound, CAT scans, MRIs, and X-rays to help find out what is ailing your pet—but those are just the *tests*. After those diagnostic tests are done, an operation or medications might be recommended. Would having pet insurance make a difference to you if the doctor wanted to do an MRI on your sick cat and the charge was going to be $1,000? If an MRI or a CAT scan was needed to diagnose your child, your health insurance would probably cover it—or if you didn't have the coverage, you would find a way to pay for the test. But how would you feel if the patient was your cat? Would you forgo the testing because of the cost? Would you feel frustrated or guilty about that? Or would you pay the bill and kick yourself for not having gotten the insurance? Depending on your outlook about medical care for your cat, signing up *without delay* might be the best choice for many more people than now have insurance coverage in place.

PREEXISTING CONDITIONS

Pet insurance doesn't cover preexisting conditions. If your cat has a complicated or expensive medical condition, the insurance company will request all of the cat's prior veterinary records when you make a claim, especially a large one. If a claim is made soon after you take out a policy, the insurance company will understandably want to see all of the cat's prior veterinary records and would probably refuse a claim for a problem the cat had prior to insurance coverage.

DEDUCTIBLE, ANNUAL LIMIT ON CLAIMS

Pet insurance has a deductible (sometimes you can choose how much), and different plans have different limits on the maximum they will pay each year. While insurance may not pay 100 percent of the bill, it sure beats the alternative. When you are beside yourself with worry because your pet is ailing and you have a huge medical bill on top of it, you will be so grateful for any relief of the burden that the insurance provides.

YOU PAY THE VET, THE REIMBURSEMENT COMES TO YOU

One difference between pet and human insurance is that the vet does not have to participate in an insurance plan or company, and he does not do any billing on your behalf. Some insurers ask you to get their form signed by the vet, with his diagnosis and treatment noted, and attach the doctor's bill (already paid by you). The insurance companies require that you return paperwork to them within a certain number of months for them to consider the claim, so if you're reasonably organized it shouldn't be a problem.

The positive difference between animal and human doctors is that pet insurers have no impact on the vet's medical decision-making process. Each vet does what he believes is best for

every animal without having to worry about an insurance company dictating his treatment choices (as is now often the case in human medicine).

MULTIPLE-PET DISCOUNT

If you have more than one cat (or dog), you will probably pay a reduced fee for covering all of them. The fee per animal is based on age, with older cats costing substantially more to insure than younger ones (see chart later in this section) since it is assumed that a cat will have more need for medical care as she ages. I would recommend that you not drop coverage on your older animals just because the premium goes up. Maybe you figure that an older cat leads a safer, more sedentary life, but all it takes is one bout of gastrointestinal upset—with the lab tests, possible X-rays and medication—to pay you back for the premium you paid. Your vet may also refer you to a specialty veterinary hospital that is staffed entirely by veterinarians who are subspecialists: vets who have been trained and received further degrees in ophthalmology (eyes), oncology (cancer) and other areas. I have met pet owners in the waiting rooms of these specialty hospitals who have spent $5,000 to $10,000 on their cat's care because they didn't have insurance. These are regular working people who can ill afford such enormous bills, but they view their pets as family members and will pay anything to make them well or keep them alive.

THERE IS AN ADDITIONAL PREMIUM FOR CANCER CARE

Given the high percentage of pets (dogs more than cats) who get some kind of cancer and the high cost of treating it, it's understandable that insurance companies have what they call a "cancer endorsement." You pay a relatively small additional premium, and if your pet does get cancer, you get more coverage for diagnosis and treatment.

WHAT ABOUT ROUTINE VACCINATIONS?

Many policies cover routine treatments for fleas and ticks, vaccinations, and dental care. However, for this coverage some (like the most successful one, VPI) charge an additional fee that is about equal to the cost of a cat's yearly vaccinations. It seems to me that paying extra to get that coverage is a waste of money. First of all, you might decide to pass up some of the routine immunizations anyway, especially with an indoor cat. Second, the most insurance will reimburse for a visit with vaccinations is often pretty much the same amount you pay as a premium for routine care—so the whole transaction is a wash except that you still have to fill out paperwork, have the vet's office do the same, send it in, wait to be reimbursed and so on. It seems that it might just be easier to pay for the routine office visit and be done with it.

OTHER CONSIDERATIONS

✦ Indoor Cats Have Many Fewer Ailments

Outdoor cats have higher vet bills because they can be injured by cars or other cats and dogs, and they are exposed to pathogens in the environment. So if you aren't sure whether you want insurance and your cat is indoors only, your odds of encountering a medical problem are lower.

♦ Kittens Cost More than Adult Cats

During the first year of a kitten's life, you can expect to spend about $500 on vet visits, vaccinations and neutering. So find out what an insurance company would charge you for that period and weigh it against the possible costs you will incur. Make sure that the policy covers kitten vaccinations and wellness visits, otherwise it's not as valuable.

♦ Beware of Loopholes

As grateful as I am for the existence of pet insurance companies, they are still insurance companies, and paying reimbursements is not the thing they most like to do and it is not always hassle-free. In the case of VPI, the company that I have used for years, when they refuse payment on a bill, the explanation is not clear and they require a written appeal from you (and your vet) to resubmit a request for reimbursement. A new company, Pets Best, has a more straightforward reimbursement—they pay 80 percent of costs, period.

IS HEALTH INSURANCE WORTH IT OR NOT?

It really is a person-by-person decision. I would rather pay for peace of mind and then be glad my kitty never did get sick—but that is just one person's feeling. Each person's situation and personality are different. One way to make the decision about insurance is to ask whether you would opt for expensive tests and treatment if your cat got ill. If the answer is yes, then I think the safety net that health insurance gives you has value. If the answer is no, because you do not believe that a pet should be afforded that kind of complicated medical attention, then you should pass. This is not a loaded question, by the way—there is no single right answer. Someone who would take a second mortgage on their home to try an experimental cancer treatment on a cat with only months to live does *not* love his pet more than the person who accepts his cat's medical fate as part of the natural way of things and plans to put her to sleep when she reaches the point where her quality of life is diminishing. Some would even argue that the second owner is the more self-less, compassionate, realistic one. Of course, these are two extremes; the medical problems that cats face are often less dramatic and a person's decision is often less clear-cut. You need to discover your own answer, but you should think about it before your cat ever gets ill and it becomes too late to get coverage, at least for that ailment.

WHAT DOES INSURANCE COST?

What follows are approximate, average premium costs for insurance policies in 2007. Premiums are based on your cat's age, and, as you can see, they climb steeply as your cat gets older. Like any insurance premiums, these are based on actuarial tables, which companies use to calculate how much they are likely to pay out in reimbursements so they can charge enough to come out ahead.

Even though the numbers on the chart below look substantial—and they do add up to a lot of money over a cat's lifetime—keep in mind that the amount you would pay without insurance for one ultrasound for urinary stones or even for a yearly or biennial blood panel can add up pretty impressively, too.

Annual Premiums by Cat's Age

Up to one year	$275
1 to 4 years	$300
5 to 7 years	$350
8 to 9 years	$450
10 to 12 years	$550
13 to 15 years	$650
16 to 17 years	$750
18 to 19 years	$800
20 and above	$900

This adds up to $5,075 in premiums you would pay out for a cat who lives to age 12, and $7,775 if she makes it to 16 years of age. However, keep in mind one urinary emergency can cost $2,000 or more.

CHOOSING A PET INSURANCE COMPANY

When making a decision about which insurance to use, there are a number of factors to consider. The checklist below should help you sort things out.

Evaluating Pet Insurers

- How long has the company been in business? Some are short-lived, leaving people in limbo. The longer they have been established, the better.
- Can you go to any vet? Discount plans may allow only certain providers—not a good scenario if their allowed vets are not convenient to you and/or you already have a vet.
- Who underwrites the insurance? Do they have experience handling pet claims? The company should have a good A. M. Best rating (A. M. Best is the established company that rates insurance companies from A+ to F on whether they are financially capable of meeting policyholder demands).
- Ask your vet which company he recommends, since his office will have experience dealing with all of them.
- Do they give discounts for multi-pet homes?
- Excluding preexisting conditions is common practice. Ask if previous medical conditions can be covered for an additional fee. Ask whether there are other exclusions.
- What is the waiting period? Many require a 30-day wait from the date you sign up to file your first claim.

- What is the limit (or cap) on reimbursing any one illness or injury? Most companies put some kind of cap on each medical problem during a policy term. Find out whether it is a yearly cap or a lifetime cap. For chronic issues such as joint problems, a limit for life would not be helpful since this will probably be on ongoing yearly problem.
- Are medications covered?

WHICH INSURANCE COMPANY IS BEST?

Please take the time to shop around and compare the following (alphabetically arranged) companies that offer pet health insurance. Companies may go out of business or change their policies, and policy terms vary depending on the state. So the list below is only a list to work from: You need to confirm information when you are shopping and comparing because things change. This list is not an endorsement of these companies, just a way to assist you in learning the options.

AKC Pet Healthcare Plan (www.akcphp.com, 866-725-2747) is owned by the American Kennel Club, which runs dog shows and the largest registry for purebred dogs.

PetCare Pet Insurance (www.petcareinsurance.com, 866-275-PETS) was founded in 1998 and offers coverage in 46 states, the District of Columbia and 10 Canadian provinces. It operates a variety of companies, including QuickCare, ShelterCare and Union Plus Pet Insurance. The company offers one affordable policy in partnership with PETCO for less than $10 a month. Petfinder.com (the largest adoption database on the Internet) teamed up with ShelterCare to give one month of insurance coverage to those who adopt through Petfinder.com.

PetFirstHealthcare.com (866-937-7387).

Petshealth Care Plan (www.petshealthplan.com, 800-807-6724) was introduced in 1997 and is licensed in 49 states and the District of Columbia. There are a variety of plans, all of which pay 80 percent of allowable charges after a $100 deductible. The same parent company owns a newer, similar company called Healthy Bark & Purr (www.healthybarkandpurr.com, 800-799-5852).

Petsbest.com (877-738-7237) was begun in 2005 by the man who created VPI (below). This company has a streamlined and simple equation: After deductible they pay 80 percent of 100 percent of all charges. Premiums do not go up before 7 years of age.

Veterinary Pet Insurance (VPI) (www.petinsurance.com, 866-467-4738 or 800-USA-PETS) is the country's largest and oldest pet insurance company, begun in 1982. They offer coverage in all states and, after a deductible, they pay 90 percent of the plan's benefit allowance per policy term, with charges based on a national average of veterinary fees.

OPEN A BANK ACCOUNT INSTEAD

This is a pretty clever alternative to shelling out money to an insurer every year. If you put that money away in the bank instead, you could accrue a substantial nest egg, to be touched only for your cat's medical costs. It will protect you financially from medical misfortune and at some point

it becomes "found money" if your cat doesn't wind up needing costly medical care. If you can afford to put $50 monthly into a "cat account" the total will grow impressively over a ten-year period (you should probably have the money transferred automatically because you might not do it dutifully every month). Just imagine how many thousands of dollars will be in that account if your kitty has good luck (let her "take" you on a nice vacation with what you will have saved!).

The Basics of Your Cat's Health

Because cats can get quite sick without showing particularly visible symptoms, it is important to know the basics about how your cat's body works and how to distinguish the normal from the abnormal in order to give useful information to your veterinarian. The important thing to realize about ailments in a cat is that you really need a vet to determine almost every malady. This is true for two reasons: The first is that cats tend to keep it a secret when they are not well—which springs from old survival techniques that cats had to develop so they would not appear weak or vulnerable to potential predators. Second, cats can go downhill physically fairly rapidly, so the sooner you have a professional evaluation to determine if your cat is genuinely ill, the better your chance of getting timely treatment to lessen her chance of getting critically ill.

A CAT'S VITAL SIGNS

The first thing you'll need to learn are the physical basics that will help you uncover any possible underlying medical problems with your cat. Once you become familiar with this information and have practiced checking these things on your cat, you will feel confident about evaluating whether your cat needs a visit to the vet or is just having an off day.

✦ Pulse

A rate of 120 beats per minute is the normal pulse (also known as heart rate) for a cat who is resting. However, a cat's pulse doesn't have to be exactly that number to be considered normal or healthy—the heart rate can be 10 or 20 beats more or less, accounting for individual differences. When a cat is ill, her pulse may be abnormally low or high, which is why it's important to have this information and be able to report it to your vet, should you need to contact him.

Taking a cat's pulse: You take a cat's pulse the same way you would a human's: by pressing gently with 2 or 3 fingers in a place on the body where the artery passes close to the skin. You only have to count the number of beats for 15 seconds (one-quarter of a minute) and then multiply that number by 4 to get the heart rate, which is always quoted in beats per minute. The best place to find your cat's pulse is inside her hind leg, right where it joins her body. Cats have a large artery there that you can feel easily by using 2 or 3 fingers.

Just as with taking a human pulse, you don't want to use your own thumb because it has a pulse that can interfere with your ability to count your cat's heartbeat. To get a good feel of the artery, have the cat lie down beside you and then grasp her by the haunch, with your palm on the outside of her back leg and your fingers curled up inside her haunch, where her leg and body come together. If you gently press a couple of fingers against the bone, you may be able to feel the pulse. Don't get impatient or anxious—just let your middle two or three fingers hunt around in there, not pressing too hard (which would cut off the blood supply) until you feel the *pump-pump-pump* of the cat's heart. Once you have a good feel, look at a second hand and start counting that pulse for 15 seconds. If you have any doubt about whether you've counted correctly, go ahead and count again. Now multiply by 4 to get the number of beats per minute and jot down the number so that you'll have it ready if you call the vet and he asks you for her pulse. Another reason to write the number down is because if you check her again later, you'll be able to see any changes in your cat's condition, at least from the point of view of her heart rate.

Another way of getting the pulse: Many people have a hard time feeling their cat's pulse with their fingers. Another way to get the heart rate is just to place the palm of your hand flat against the left side of your cat's chest, just behind her elbow. Cats are generally quite lean in that part of their body, so it is usually quite easy to feel the cat's heart beat against your palm.

Practice taking the pulse: Get familiar with the mechanics of finding your cat's pulse when she is well and calm. This way, if she is ever injured or sick, taking her pulse will not rattle you as you try to get this information when there is a lot going on. Your confidence will make you more smooth and effective and your cat will be reassured because she will feel that you know what you are doing.

◆ Respirations

This is the measurement of how many times per minute a cat takes a breath. You can also count the number of breaths for 15 seconds and multiply by 4. Just as with humans, medical problems can increase or decrease a cat's breathing rate. The normal respiration rate for a cat is between 20 and 30 breaths per minute. If the number is higher, that might be an indication that the cat is agitated or has been very active, while a lower respiration rate can indicate a medical problem if accompanied by other symptoms. As with so many other physical symptoms in cats, you are better off contacting your vet to determine whether you need to go in.

◆ Temperature

A cat's temperature tells a great deal about how she is feeling. The normal range for a cat's temperature is between 100.5 and 102.5° Fahrenheit (or between 38 and 39°C). Kittens have a slightly higher temperature. Taking your cat's temperature is the first step to knowing if she might have an infection or other health issue. A temperature of 105°F suggests a serious medical emergency. Other reasons for an elevated temperature can be fear or anxiety, or a reaction to medication. For example, if a cat is frightened while she is having her temperature taken, it can shoot right up to 103°F.

As you have probably imagined, it's not half as easy to get a temperature as it is to find a pulse. If you have a mellow cat who is used to being handled, then you may be able to take her temperature on your own, although having someone else to help is useful with even the most easygoing kitty. Even simple medical issues like this are a powerful reason to socialize your cat early, getting her used to all sorts of handling.

However, if you follow those instructions and watch the instructional video mentioned later, and your cat still really puts up a fight when you try to insert the thermometer, stop. Do not run the risk of getting bitten or scratched. Also, the agitation from fighting you can raise your cat's

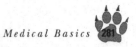

temperature even more. In most cases, if you are concerned enough to take her temperature, you will probably end up taking your cat to the vet anyway. So if your cat cannot tolerate your attempt, let the doctor handle the temperature taking when you get there.

There are emergencies where you have to take her temperature, however. If you suspect your cat has heat stroke (more on this in the next chapter), you need to determine her body temperature both right away and then again once you have started cooling her. In this situation, you will also want to get to the vet as fast as possible, but first you will need to cool down the cat and assess her status.

Monitoring your cat's temperature: Another reason you should to learn to take your cat's temperature is that your vet may ask you to monitor her temperature if she is sick. Your vet will probably want you to do this twice a day, always at about the same time. There are normal fluctuations in a cat's temperature, just as there are with a person's, so by getting two values, your vet can get a more accurate picture of what is really going on.

There is a video to help you in taking a cat's temperature. Cornell University's renowned veterinary college has a special Feline Health Center where they've produced an instructional video on taking a cat's temperature, available online at www.felinevideos.vet.cornell.edu/. (The Feline Health Center also has a wonderful newsletter called CatWatch available by mail that has timely information about cats' behavior and health. By subscribing, you help support their far-reaching work on feline health. You can order the newsletter online at www.catwatchnewsletter.com/cs, or call toll free 800-829-8893.)

Directions for Using a Thermometer. Before you get your cat involved, you will want to prepare the equipment you will need. Instead of a glass rectal thermometer, the kind people generally use on babies, you can use a plastic rectal thermometer with a digital readout. Get the "quick read" version made for babies. A plastic thermometer is much easier to use than the old-fashioned mercury type: You can read the plastic one more easily, it works more quickly (in seconds) and you don't run the risk of breaking the glass. If using a plastic one, reset the digital display; if using glass, shake down the mercury in the thermometer. Dip the end of the thermometer into petroleum jelly as a lubricant. This will allow the thermometer to slide more easily and painlessly into the kitty's anus. Set the prepared thermometer down and go get the cat.

Put her up on a surface that is level with you or get down on the floor with her. It helps if you have someone to help you by staying beside the cat with a hand underneath her stomach to keep her standing up during this process. With one hand, gently lift her tail, and with the other, gently insert just the tip of the thermometer into her anus. Move it very slowly and gently with a slight twisting motion. You will feel her sphincter muscle tighten as you insert the tip, and then she should relax. Make sure you go straight in so you don't cause her any discomfort. You only need to put the tip in. Most cats will want to put their tails back down and you should allow her to do that for the sake of comfort. You'll need to leave a glass thermometer in for about two minutes—probably the longest two minutes of both your lives! A digital thermometer will be only seconds and will beep when finished. Talk soothingly to your cat throughout the process, keeping her as relaxed as possible. When the time is up, gently remove the thermometer and wipe it off using a tissue or cotton ball with rubbing alcohol.

◆ Checking Your Cat's Scat

Scat is another word for a cat's feces, which can be an important indicator of her general health. If your cat has not been well—or is just "not right"—monitoring her scat can give your vet valuable information. The idea of studying your cat's poop may sound gross, but since you're scooping it out of the litter anyway, taking a moment to give it the once-over isn't all that much of an inconvenience.

The color, frequency and amount of a cat's scat can tell a great deal about her physical condition. First, you need to know what "normal" looks like—understanding that there are variations of normal that depend on variables in the cat's digestive system. You can't just play Sherlock Holmes of the Litter Box by looking at it: You need to know particulars about the cat's habits and patterns.

The color of normal feces depends on what a cat has eaten and how much bile is in her stool. Normal color can vary from beige to dark brown and even occasionally have a greenish or orange shade to it. A gray, cement-like color is not commonly seen but could be a sign of a bile duct obstruction, which could signal problems with the pancreas or gallbladder. Stool that is very dark or the color of coffee grounds could mean that your cat is bleeding internally, which could indicate ulcers, kidney, liver or bowel problems. Feces with streaks of blood can be the result of bleeding from the rectum or large intestine.

The consistency of a healthy cat's feces should have no variation from normal, which is that the stool should be solid enough that scooping it leaves hardly anything behind. Also, there should be no mucus or blood on the scat.

The frequency is also predictable from cat to cat—anywhere from once to three times a day. For example, if a cat's habits change from that daily schedule, a vet can get a good idea of where the problem may lie in the cat's body.

Although keeping a sharp eye out for changes in your cat's bowel movements may not appeal to you, it is a valuable tool to pick up abnormalities in your cat that might otherwise go unnoticed.

◆ Blood Pressure

Taking a cat's blood pressure is a relatively new phenomenon and not one that is done frequently by vets. BP's are difficult to do on cats and the stress it causes them actually causes their blood pressure to go up, which then gives a false high reading. The medical cases in which getting a blood pressure reading might have value to a vet are with a geriatric cat or one who has diabetes, hyperthyroidism or CRD (chronic renal disease, often called CRF—see that section in this chapter). It would be fairly pointless for a veterinarian to attempt taking a cat's blood pressure as part of a routine physical exam, and certainly not on a young, healthy cat, as well as being counterproductive since it creates a negative association for the cat with going to the vet. Because of the extra time and care that is required to take a BP on a cat, most vets will charge extra for this.

How to Know If Your Cat Is Sick

If your cat has any one of the symptoms on the list below, it isn't necessarily a reason to worry or visit your vet, unless it is really pronounced and unusual for her. Observe her behavior, see if the

symptom goes away and notice whether other symptoms accompany it. This list is valuable to you as a tool to aid your vet because it will help you get a sense of what information matters. You are the guardian of your cat's health, and one of the best things you can do is be observant of her normal routines and habits when she's feeling good—everything from when and how much she likes to eat to how often she uses the litter box. This way you'll know if something is up with her, based on changes in her behavior and habits.

THREE THINGS THE VET WILL WANT TO KNOW

When you think your cat just isn't right and you decide to visit the vet, there are three pieces of information that can be helpful to have prepared for the doctor: (1) a clear description of the problem, (2) how long the cat has had it and (3) how frequently the problem occurs. While this may sound ridiculously simple, you'd be surprised how many people don't pay close enough attention to the obvious.

The list below contains those signs that might signal a problem with your cat's health, giving you a heads-up to keep an eye on her.

Symptoms to Watch

Unusual breathing: shallow; labored; fast; *with open mouth* (see vet immediately)

Change in coat appearance: greasy; thinning; dull; dry; bald patches; mats of hair

Change in behavior: anything that differs from her normal habits: not playful; nervous; aggressive; listless; cranky; fearful; hiding

Change in appetite: cats don't eat the same amount every day, so a fluctuation in consumption is normal (hot weather, stress and recent snacks all ruin appetite), but difficulty eating, weight gain or loss or refusal to eat are serious

Change in drinking habits: consuming more or less water than usual; drinking from unusual places such as the shower or sink

Change in urination: going more or less frequently; going outside of the box; straining; crying when urinating; blood-tinged urine; change in odor; *unable to urinate* (see vet immediately)

Change in bowels: going outside of the box; diarrhea; constipation; foul smell; amount of stool; blood or mucus in stool

Drooling excessively: bad breath

Flatulence: passing gas, odiferous or not

Coughing: depending when it started, how often and long it lasts, it can be a minor irritation or a sign of serious illness

Limping or pain walking: check that nothing is stuck in the paw pad

Sneezing: ask same questions as with coughing to determine if a temporary irritant or more serious

Vomiting: usually not serious since cats routinely vomit hair balls or food (if they eat too fast, too much or weather is very hot or cold); *however*, if she repeatedly vomits food hours after consumption, or if vomitus is *not* food, then note frequency and describe the vomit

Frequent swallowing: can be relevant to vomiting and may precede it

Withdrawing from social situations: facing the wall can be a sign of depression, stress or feeling ill

Hiding, sitting in litter box, pressing her head against something—all signs of pain

Change in skin: inflamed or irritated; flaky and dry; scratching; change in color or texture; bad odor; cuts or bruising; swelling; lumps

Crying, howling: excessive vocalizing

Sleeping a lot: normal after a big meal, in spring and fall during shedding season, but can also mean fighting off infection or a weakened condition

Stumbling, staggering or tilting head: possibly serious, *immediate vet visit*

Seizures: other neurological changes such as tremors, palsy

Temperature change: fever or low body temperature; shivering

Discharge from nose, eyes or ears: describe color, consistency; pawing at face; shaking head

MAKING LIFE COMFORTABLE FOR A SICK KITTY

When your cat does not feel well or is recovering from an illness or operation, you can lift her spirits and speed her recovery by knowing about the ways she'll need some special TLC during her healing period.

◆ Keep Her Warm and Quiet

The best place for a cat to get better is a peaceful part of the house, away from loud noises or comings and goings. Set aside your kitty's recuperation area and make sure everyone knows it is off-limits to children, dogs, visitors, workers and others. Play some classical music in the cat's space to give her additional calming vibes. Make sure the space isn't chilly and that there are no drafts, since a cat can have a hard time maintaining her body temperature when she isn't moving around much while recovering from physical problems.

◆ Use a Heating Element

If your cat seems cold to the touch or is shivering, you can put a warming element in bed with her. You can purchase a heating pad made especially for pets that goes on or under a pet's bed and maintains a constant low heat (most larger pet stores carry them, as do any of the good pet catalogues such as KV Pet Supply, Drs. Foster & Smith, or Dog.com), or you can use a human heating pad on the lowest setting. You can also use a hot water bottle wrapped in a towel, or a beanbag type of heat producer made for people that can be warmed in the microwave. So you don't risk burning your cat, always be cautious with heat from any source by using low heat and fully wrapping the heat source in a towel.

◆ Cover the Cat's Bed in a Towel

In order to keep your kitty clean and dry, put a towel over her bed that you can change in case of spilled medicine, food, leaking urine or diarrhea or if she comes back from the litter box not quite clean and soils the bed.

◆ Help Keep Her Clean

Often when a cat is sick, she doesn't have her usual strength or motivation to look after her own cleanliness. However, because cats are normally so fastidious, being unable to groom themselves properly can be stressful. Besides brushing her gently every day when she is ill, have some old washcloths nearby that you can dampen in warm water to gently wipe her face after she eats or wipe medication that spills on her fur. If she urinates on herself, you need to clean it off with a wet cloth because the urine can irritate her skin; the same goes for diarrhea. If your cat has long hair and this problem happens more than once during her recovery, you can clip the hair short around her backside to make cleaning easier and more complete.

HANDLING A SICK CAT WHO IS AGGRESSIVE

Some cats become fearful or aggressive when they are in pain, especially if they have sustained an injury. A cat doesn't know why she is in pain and she may be frightened or confused by it. Her instinct may be to flee, and anything you do to restrain her may elicit an aggressive response of biting or scratching. If you have to put her into a carrier to take her to the vet in this condition, you need to protect yourself before and during transport.

Approach her from above when putting her in her carrier, not face-to-face because it can cause a defensive reaction. Rub her chin and stroke her head gently before proceeding; if you can calm her and gain her acceptance of your presence, you will avoid getting her really worked up and ready to fight you.

◆ Use Gloves

If you have leather or suede gloves (for gardening or tending a fire) put those on to protect yourself. Even winter gloves work, and they will fit more closely, allowing you more control. Your face and eyes are particularly vulnerable if you lean closer to inspect the injury, so make sure she cannot lash out to bite or scratch you before you get close.

◆ Pick the Cat Up by the Scruff

If you think a cat may fight you, you can pick her up by the scruff of the neck the way her mother did back when she was a kitten. This tends to make a cat more passive in her reaction and it will help you protect yourself. You don't want to hold her entire weight with just that one hand, so put a hand lightly underneath her back feet to give her some support there, but not so much that she can spring off your hand.

WRAP HER IN A TOWEL OR BLANKET

If your cat is panicked or struggling, you can make things easier on both of you by putting a small blanket or thick towel over her to subdue her before you pick her up or medicate her. First give her a moment to settle down inside the security of the covering, then gently gather her up, tucking the loose ends of the towel or blanket underneath her. You can also swaddle a cat in a towel by placing it over her back and then wrapping it around her chest and legs so that only her head and neck are sticking out. This can actually make her feel more secure and you will be protected from any attempts to escape or scratch. Make sure her head is exposed once you get her settled so that she does not suffocate. In the next chapter, there is a step-by-step guide to wrapping a cat when you are not rushed in an emergency: look in Chapter 13 under "How to Wrap Up a Cat."

IF THE CAT IS STILL UNPREDICTABLE

Do not let your guard down until you have her in a carrier or box: She can still lash out at you in fear or confusion, depending on what is wrong with her. As much as you are concerned about her condition, keep your personal safety in mind with everything you do to help her.

Stress

You may be surprised to learn that many cats experience stress in everyday life—and when a cat is ill or nervous, her perception of what is stressful may even be magnified. Although some stressors in your cat's environment are beyond your control to alleviate, there are others that you can easily soften or eliminate by becoming aware of them. What follows is a chart of all the things that can be stressful to cats, and may be especially difficult for a cat who is sick or recovering from an illness. When caring for a recovering cat you conserve her energy and support the healing process by minimizing her other stresses.

SOURCES OF STRESS FOR A SICK CAT

- ❑ **Environmental change.** Moving from vet to home and then being confined in a small area such as a bathroom is tough on a cat, who thrives on predictability and sameness. While she is healing, fill the cat's zone with her bed and familiar objects, including clothing of yours.
- ❑ **Unexpected movements.** Don't approach your cat without warning when she is in this fragile state. Use your voice to announce your presence, before you touch her or give her medication.
- ❑ **Loud noises.** Cats are always sensitive to noise, but now you want to quiet even human voices that are loud or piercing. Keep sound soft and soothing: Try playing classical music in the cat's recovery space.
- ❑ **Intense odors.** Eliminate sharp smells such as cigars and cigarettes, room deodorizers, cleaning products or other airborne chemicals. Run a HEPA filter or fan on very low if odor source cannot be controlled.

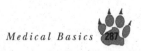

Medical Basics **287**

❑ **Being caged or crated.** A cat experiences this as being trapped with nowhere to hide, so place a brown paper shopping bag, with the edges cuffed back, on its side in the cage to give her a space to which she can retreat.

❑ **Pain.** Vets now know that cats *do* experience pain, and doctors will dispense pain medication. Be sure you give the medicine as instructed to keep your cat as pain-free as possible.

❑ **Soiled by medication, vomit or feces.** Cats are fastidious, so the inability to keep themselves clean is distressing. Use a warm washcloth to wipe off anything right away.

❑ **Your emotional state.** Your cat will pick up on whatever you are feeling so try to keep positive thoughts and energy when around your cat.

❑ **Strangers.** If the cat was at the vet, she's already had enough strange hands on her. At home, limit the number of visitors and keep it to people she already knows.

❑ **Being left alone.** The only thing worse than the presence of strangers is the absence of familiar people. Limit your time away from home; have someone familiar stop by.

❑ **Being restrained for procedures.** Being held down is traumatic, but sometimes it's necessary at the vet's. If *you* have to hold her down for treatment, be light and quick.

Emergency Checklist

Abdominal pain, indicated by pawing at her stomach, getting into a praying position, refusing to let her stomach be touched (possibilities: internal bleeding or inflammation; organ problems).

Bleeding from an opening in the body such as ears or eyes, or spurting/pulsing from a cut, indicating an artery has been cut. Apply moderate pressure for a full 5 minutes; if it doesn't stop, bandage firmly and transport.

Blindness that comes on suddenly—bumping into things, fearful to walk because she is walking into things—is a critical emergency (detached retina, glaucoma).

Change in gum color—normally pink, they can quickly go pale (shock, anemia or internal bleeding), blue (difficulty breathing), yellow (disorder of blood, liver or gallbladder) or red (shock or serious infection).

Difficulty breathing—labored or audible wheezing is an emergency (possibilities: asthma; heart/lung problems; respiratory illness or inhaling something toxic).

Difficulty defecating—straining to relieve herself, especially if she vocalizes during the effort (can be constipation).

Difficulty urinating can be a urinary tract infection or obstruction (if the latter it is a male problem and an absolute emergency, since a male cat who cannot pass urine around a blockage can die if not attended to immediately).

Lameness that comes on suddenly to limbs or inability to use them, or sudden back/neck pain (bone infection or fracture; cardiac problems; circulation problems).

Seizures, whether convulsions, spasms, twitching, disorientation to where the cat is, warrant a careful look.

Staggering like a drunk (infection of middle ear, neurological disorder or poisoning)

Vomits more than once especially within an hour, especially if bloody (possibilities: swallowed something; intestinal disturbance; poisoning; liver or kidney disease)

Tips for Handling Emergencies

Stay cool: your calm demeanor helps the cat and other helpers (who should be limited to only one or two).

Delegate responsibilty: someone else can call the vet to say you're coming while you deal with the cat.

Wear protective gloves: a frightened or hurting cat can scratch or bite.

Take it easy: be very gentle and take it slowly; there's a chance you can hurt her more by moving quickly.

Have your cat's records available: so you are able to grab them in case you go to an emergency facility and not your regular vet. There may be lab tests in there and other pertinent details.

Chapter 13

ILLNESSES AND MEDICAL CONDITIONS

This chapter is organized alphabetically and includes most of the common physical problems and illnesses that can befall cats. The purpose of this chapter is to give you descriptions of the various physical problems with some of the usual treatments for them. In no case does this mean I am helping you to diagnose your cat or to treat her; that is the job of your vet, and your vet alone. This is intended as a reference you can go to for a brief, clear description of the most common conditions that your cat may have. It cannot replace the expertise of your vet, who can only properly evaluate your cat's situation by seeing and touching the animal herself. Because a cat can go from feeling fine to being "iffy" to becoming very sick in a very short period, it is never a wise choice for you to guess or wait it out where medical issues are involved. Do not be casual when your cat just isn't feeling right; while the symptoms of different ailments in cats are often quite similar, the consequences can be devastating if not treated promptly by a veterinarian.

On medical topics where there is controversy about how to treat a condition, I have included the differing perspectives to keep you abreast of the factors that may influence the advice, information or care that you get.

Note: My apologies in advance for using the male gender when referring to vets in this book—especially when several of my female friends are actually vets, including Dawn Stelling, the medical advisor on this book. But since I opted to refer to cats in the female gender throughout the book, it seemed only fair (and less confusing) to refer to vets as gentlemen.

Allergies

Cats can have allergic symptoms at certain times of the year, with runny eyes and nose and sometimes with sneezing, the way people get seasonal allergies. This means a cat might be responding to airborne pollen or dust. You can be pretty sure that it is an allergic reaction if it is not accompanied by other symptoms such as lethargy, loss of appetite or fever. Cats can also develop allergic skin problems that may be caused by an allergic response to an insect bite (including fleas and mites), a fungus or a food. Chemicals in household cleaners or paints can also cause an allergic skin reaction, or the response can show up as upper respiratory symptoms.

Another suspected cause of allergies that has only recently been identified is giving multiple vaccines all at once or repeated vaccinations frequently to a cat. It is a newfound realization in the traditional veterinary field that routine vaccination is a possible cause of allergies (not to mention cancer). Homeopathic vets have always been strongly opposed to the practice of frequent immunizations, maintaining that it was an unnecessary assault on a cat's immune system. It has taken years, but now the American Veterinary Medical Association (AVMA) and many of their members who follow mainstream medical philosophy have come to understand that overinoculating a cat has detrimental consequences. Talk to your own vet about ways you might be able to minimize or eliminate the frequency and multiplicity of vaccinations, depending on your cat's age and lifestyle.

Other possible causes of allergies in a cat are inbreeding purebred cats, which can predispose them to allergies. As for the connection between feeding dry food with colorings and preservatives and a cat developing allergies, please read the nutrition chapter in this book to learn how detrimental it is to feed cats a diet based on processed, commercial dry food.

Anal Sacs

Cats have two anal sacs located in the tissue of their anal sphincter. The sacs themselves are the size of a bean and are connected by a thin tube to either side of the anus itself, where the tubes have openings no bigger than the head of a pin. The ducts transport a smelly, thick liquid that is usually excreted when the cat has a bowel movement. The exact purpose of the liquid is not known, since cats function fine without anal sacs, but it is guessed that the fluid is either a lubricant for the feces or a way to leave a personalized "calling card" and mark territory. However, since urine is already a potent marker, this conjecture seems unlikely. Anal sacs give modern cats quite a bit of trouble, and it is believed that these glands are a leftover from a prehistoric version of the cat who must have needed them for some real purpose.

What can go wrong with anal sacs is that the fluid is not excreted and builds up inside the sacs, causing irritation, inflammation and eventually even an impaction with infection. You will know something is wrong if your cat bites and licks at her anal region much more than for normal grooming, and you may also see that the area is red and swollen. You will need to take your cat to the vet, where he or a veterinary technician will relieve this pressure by gently squeezing the area around the anus to expel the trapped fluid. After the blockage is relieved, your vet may inject an antibacterial solution into the ducts and/or tell you to apply hot packs to the area until the swelling goes down. For cats who have a chronic problem with their anal sacs, it is sometimes necessary to remove them surgically.

Arthritis

Degenerative joint disease (DJD) is the official name for arthritis in cats. Just like for us, arthritis is the erosion of cartilage in the joints so that bone rubs against bone, making movement difficult and painful. However, because cats are masters at concealing pain (which goes back to their wild origins and the need to mask any weakness or vulnerability from predators), you should have your vet check your older cat for arthritic changes in the joints. The vast majority of old cats suffer from some degree of joint degeneration: X-ray studies show that 90 percent of cats 12 years and older have signs of DJD, while about a quarter of even young cats have some degeneration in their joints. The only purebred cat at special risk for arthritis is the Maine Coon.

SIGNS OF DJD

Again, because cats mask their pain it isn't always easy to spot the symptoms of arthritis, but they are what you would logically expect: stiffness, especially when getting up from lying down, and reduced activity level. If it hurts to get up and down and to walk, a cat will understandably do less of both. You may notice her legs becoming thinner as she exercises less and her muscles atrophy. You may also see that a cat who used to leap up onto counters now has trouble making it up onto a chair.

A cat with DJD may groom less because she cannot bend as well; she may have accidents outside the litter box because it is difficult for her to get in there. She may become cranky and not want to be groomed or patted because of the pain. However, you aren't likely to see a pronounced limp, or favoring of one leg; in cats, arthritis typically affects both sides of the body equally since pain often originates in the spine and front legs.

Because it is hard to elicit the signs of DJD in the doctor's office, a vet may ask you to videotape your cat at home under relaxed circumstances so he can observe the extent of the arthritis. X-rays could give him the same information, but it's preferable to avoid putting the cat through that ordeal, as well as the substantial cost to you.

TREATMENT FOR DJD

There is no cure for arthritis in cats, any more than there is for people who suffer from it, so one course is to lessen the inflammation by using natural compounds such as glucosamine and chondroitin. Go to www.platinumperformance.com for a feline supplement that many listeners to Cat Chat have found helpful. When that doesn't give relief, there are chemical anti-inflammatories and narcotic pain relievers. You and your vet together will have to decide what treatment to use and when to use it for your cat.

Asthma

Asthma is the most common of the respiratory disorders that affect cats. An asthma attack is a constriction of the airways that can happen to a cat when she is just resting or when she is active. You will see her stop whatever she is doing and her breathing will suddenly become labored.

THE SIGNS OF ASTHMA

The most common sign is rapid, labored breathing, which can progress to the cat holding her mouth open, trying to take in more air. You can see the effort in her chest and abdomen as she tries to get more air into her lungs. There can also be a wheezing sound when the cat exhales: This signals a more severe asthma attack and is a sign that you should go to the vet. If the cat is coughing repeatedly and showing signs of weakness, these are also signs of a serious condition requiring medical intervention. Another sign of bronchial stress from chronic asthma is that the cat may retch repeatedly, as though she is trying to cough up a hairball.

WHAT MAKES ASTHMA WORSE

An outdoor cat is more likely to suffer from asthma because she is exposed to more potential allergens, but an indoor environment can be dangerous for a cat with asthma, too. Indoors there can be vapors and chemicals from household cleaners, cigarette smoke and household dust, and

the dust from kitty litter so use one of the dust-free versions such as the environmentally friendly Feline Pine or World's Best Cat Litter. To lessen the danger of your asthmatic cat having an attack, remove any potential allergens you might have in your house, vacuum frequently with a high-quality filter bag and consider putting air filters in the rooms where the cat spends the most time.

TREATING ASTHMA IN CATS

Asthma is not curable, but it is manageable with treatment based on how severe the condition is—sometimes a corticosteroid drug to reduce inflammation of the bronchi but preferably an inhaled medication (bronchodilator) to open up the airways. You vet will discuss all the options with you and come up with a management plan to keep your cat comfortable and safe.

Cancer

Cancer is the number one natural cause of death in older cats: It kills 50 percent of cats who die after 10 years of age. Despite this miserable statistic, cancer is also the one of the most treatable diseases compared to kidney failure or heart problems. Choice in cancer treatments for cats is constantly improving, making advances parallel to those for human cancer. In many cases there are numerous choices that can extend your cat's life—and *quality* of life—even once cancer is diagnosed.

WHICH CATS ARE AT RISK FOR CANCER?

Some purebred cats are at greater risk for lymphoma (the most common cancer in cats), specifically Siamese, Himalayans and Persians. Another risk factor is exposure to tobacco smoke—studies show that secondhand smoke can kill anyone exposed to it, so cats should not be confined to smoky indoor environments.

THE MOST COMMON CANCERS

◆ Lymphoma

Lymphoma represents about 30 percent of all feline cancers; it is the most prevalent kind of cancer in cats. It is a disease of the lymph system that affects the white blood cells, like non-Hodgkin's lymphoma in people. There are both slow-growing and fast-spreading types of lymphoma, which can afflict young and old cats. Outdoor cats are more susceptible. Cats with FELV and FIV are more at risk for lymphoma.

What can be done for it? Since lymphoma can occur anywhere and is a systemic cancer, chemotherapy is the usual treatment. Chemotherapy is done weekly for 6 to 8 weeks, and then every other week for 2 years—or as long as the cat lives. Without chemo, a cat will usually live about 3 to 6 months, whereas with chemotherapy 70 percent of cats respond and live another 7 to 12 months following treatment, while 30 percent live 2 years or more.

✦ Skin Cancer

Skin cancer is the second most common cancer in cats and accounts for about 25 percent of the overall cancer rate. White or light-colored cats are at greatest risk, with noses, eyelids, and ear tips as the most affected parts of their bodies. Outdoor cats who bask in the sun, especially during the midday hours, are the most vulnerable. Mast cell tumor is a relatively common type of skin cancer in cats under 1 year of age; it appears on their lips, face and neck, usually as lumps under the skin. Keep your cat out of direct sunlight between 11 A.M. and 2 P.M.

✦ Mammary Cancer

Mammary cancer is one of the most deadly kinds of cancer that cats can get. An aggressive tumor in the mammary glands can spread quickly to lymph nodes and the lungs. Although it is only the third most common cancer, mammary cancer represents 20 percent of the cancers that female cats get. What makes this cancer so deadly is that 85 percent of these cases are malignant, growing quickly, spreading to areas throughout the body and coming back even after surgery to remove them.

Risk Factors: Mammary cancer is usually seen in older cats, between 10 and 12 years old, although it can strike at any age and has been seen in kittens less than a year old. Siamese cats have a much higher risk than other breeds, from double the risk to 4 times more than the average female cat. Of all the cats afflicted by this cancer, 95 percent of them are female.

Detecting It: Early stages of breast cancer are painless and the cat seems fine, so you want to aggressively check your female cat to catch any possible cancer very early. Once a month do a breast exam on your cat, just as women are encouraged to do for themselves. Ask your vet to show you just how to do it, but basically you'll run your fingers up and down your cat's nipple lines and feel around the lymph nodes in her armpit area.

Finding even the smallest lump on a cat—as small as a peppercorn—is reason to visit your vet. You need to have that lump professionally evaluated since this kind of cancer is so deadly. After finding a lump, don't delay that vet visit because this cancer can spread quickly, to the point where there is nothing the doctor can do to help. Caught early and treated aggressively, a cat can live for 2 to 3 years, although 65 percent of tumors recur within a year. The smaller the size of the tumor when surgery is done, the longer the survival time. A growth that is 2 cm or smaller is associated with a survival time of more than 3 years; a 2–3 cm tumor has a survival time of more than 2 years; a tumor larger than 3 cm when it is discovered usually only gives a survival time of 4 to 9 months.

Why some cats get this cancer is unknown to oncologists, some of whom believe that genetics does not seem to play a role. However other veterinary oncologists have found that Siamese are at greater risk. And while other types of cancer have been linked to agents in the cat's environment, with mammary cancer this does not appear to be the case.

By spaying your cat before her first heat, you can prevent this disease. You want to do it *before* she reaches sexual maturity, which is when breast tissue, which is most vulnerable to mammary cancer, develops. Spaying can also be effective against the cancer if it is done within the first 2 or 3 heat cycles.

Removing the cancerous tissue surgically is the first step in treatment. Most vets will recommend a radical mastectomy, which entails removing the entire mammary chain (there are 4 glands on each chain) on whichever side, right or left, the tumor occurred. Sometimes both chains have to be taken out—and removing the lymph nodes from the armpit or groin is often recommended, too. Hormone therapy is not useful. While radiation can be effective, this part of the cat's body is hard to successfully irradiate. Some vets use chemotherapy after surgery, which increases the survival rate. Treatment is once every 3 weeks, for 5 or 6 treatments.

◆ Oral Cancer

Oral cancer is fairly common in older cats, with squamous cell carcinoma (SCC) being the most common. It occurs in the mouth, with lesions in the nose and ears. Unless diagnosed early, surgery is unsuccessful because these tumors in the mouth are invasive and can spread.

For a small mass, the tumor must be surgically removed; for a larger mass, a combination of chemotherapy and radiation is generally the only option. For radiation, treatment is once a week for a month; for chemo, once a week to once every 3 weeks, depending on the protocol. If the lesion is small, the outlook is good; sadly, the prognosis is not good for a large tumor.

◆ Brain Tumors

A cat's brain is pretty small—about the size of a Ping-Pong ball—but its anatomical features and functions are virtually identical to those in our brains. Brain tumors in cats are rare, and the good news is that 60 percent of brain tumors in cats are meningiomas, which are benign and grow slowly. Without surgical removal they can be fatal, but surgery usually results in a total cure.

Two other types of brain tumors can afflict cats. Lymphosarcomas (caused by the feline leukemia virus, or FeLV) grow quickly; pituitary gland tumors grow inside that small organ in the brain. While often benign and slow-growing, tumors in the pituitary gland can't be surgically removed because of their location and they will eventually grow and become fatal to the cat.

◆ Fibrosarcoma

Fibrosarcoma is cancer of the fibrous tissue that holds bones, muscles and organs in place. The symptoms are lameness, joint swelling, loss of appetite, increased salivation and bad breath. This is the cancer everyone is worried about because it can be caused by vaccinations: It often occurs or recurs at injection sites. Scientists have not yet discovered why this deadly reaction happens, but the incidence is so common that some vets are now vaccinating as low down on a cat's leg as possible. The reasoning is that should cancer occur at the site of a vaccination, it is possible to amputate the limb to save the cat's life. This is a gruesome thought, but pragmatic. If cats need vaccinations to protect them against deadly diseases, and cancer could develop at the site, it is preferable to vaccinate in an area where the cancer could be removed.

Treatment begins with surgery and a wide, deep removal of the mass, and then combination therapy if the mass was large. Radiation is done for 3 weeks, and chemotherapy is done every 3 weeks for 5 treatments. The odds of survival are 5 months if no medical treatment is followed, 18 months with surgery alone, and as much as 30 months if all 3 treatments are combined.

◆ **Bone Cancer**

Bone cancer is rare in cats, with osteosarcoma being the type of feline bone cancer that accounts for 70 percent of it. This cancer is very malignant and aggressive in cats, and the prognosis is not good. The treatment is amputation of the affected limb to prevent spreading.

SIGNS OF CANCER

While some cancers have no symptoms, there are a variety of symptoms of cancer that you should know about so that you can alert your vet immediately. The earlier the cancer is detected, the better a cat's chance for survival. Many of the signs and symptoms of cancer are similar to those in humans, and almost any symptom can occur in cats, depending on the body part affected. The number one sign of cancer is weight loss and poor appetite.

Cancer Warning Signs

- Sudden weight loss or loss of appetite
- A sore that won't heal
- A lump or swollen area that doesn't go down
- Difficulty urinating or defecating
- Diarrhea, bloody stool
- Blood in urine
- Coughing
- Blood from mouth
- Difficulty breathing
- Low energy, lethargy
- Irritability

Reducing Your Cat's Cancer Risk

- Spay females early—before the first heat.
- Keep light-colored cats out of the sun, especially during peak hours.
- Discuss with your vet keeping vaccines to a minimum.
- Keep cats away from tobacco smokers.
- Do not feed tuna fish, which may be linked to cancer in cats.

TYPES OF TREATMENT FOR CANCER

Cancer care has become so sophisticated for pets that often doctors will want to try several treatments together, combining surgery, radiation and chemotherapy. Of course, it depends on the type of cancer your cat has, and what stage it is in, but there are advanced treatments for feline cancer that can be as successful as treatments for human cancer. Obviously, results will depend on the location of the cancer, the kind of cancer, whether it has spread and the overall health of the cat.

◆ Should You Go to an Oncologist?

There are veterinarians who are cancer specialists, called *oncologists,* just like the subspecialty for human doctors. Many vets will refer a cat with cancer to one of these specialists, who have the diagnostic equipment, treatment facilities and specific training and practice in those skills. A veterinary oncologist will work with your primary vet to come up with a treatment plan to care for your cat at this difficult time. If your vet has a working relationship with an oncologist who is not too far away geographically—and whose fees you find out about ahead of time and can afford—then going to a specialist is certainly an option to consider. But of course much depends on how far advanced your cat's cancer is and whether you want to put your cat and yourself through a long process that is costly in time, money and the cat's stress from side effects, travel to the doctor and so on.

◆ Chemotherapy

Chemotherapy drugs attack cancer cells, preventing them from growing or spreading. The side effects of chemo in humans can be devastating, but they are often milder in cats, who are actually given the very same drugs, just in smaller doses. Oncologists tailor the amount of chemotherapeutic drugs given and the length of treatment to cause the least discomfort to the pet while stopping the cancer's progress. The use of sophisticated chemotherapy is one reason you might want an oncologist involved in the case; your cat can benefit from a specialist's experience in finding the right balance between slowing or stopping the cancer cells while not harming the normal cells and the cat's comfort.

Side Effects. Oncologists usually won't talk about the downside of chemotherapeutic drugs, which can have an immediate adverse affect on a cat's body, particularly the gastrointestinal tract. Loss of appetite is the most common symptom, along with nausea, vomiting and loose stool. The side effects usually last 3 to 5 days; if they are pronounced, the doctor may be able to prescribe antinausea medication or antidiarrhea pills. Some cats also develop a low white blood cell count, which puts them at risk for infection, so a cat will always have her blood checked while she is undergoing chemotherapy. Depending on the potential side effects of the drug being used, other blood tests may need to be done to monitor your cat's kidney or liver function.

The Cost Is Substantial. A full round of chemotherapy for a cat starts anywhere from $1,500 to $2,000 and can often cost much more. *If* you have pet insurance, and *if* you signed up for the additional cancer coverage, you will still need to contact the company to find out how much of the chemo bill it will cover.

What Does "Remission" or "Success" Actually Mean? Oncologists have a quite different definition of their success rate than you might. For example, if you were told that 50 to 60 percent of cats with lymphoma achieve complete remission, wouldn't you think that means your cat will be cured forever if she is in that fortunate group? This is misleading because in the language of veterinary oncology, that remission will last only 6 to 8 months, and the cat may still die. Only 10–20 percent of cats with lymphoma will still be in remission 1 year later—and we don't know if these are the cats whose cancer was caught the earliest, when it had spread the least. The point is, when you make a decision about cancer treatment you need to have all the facts so that logic, not wishful thinking and emotion, informs your decision to do the best thing for your cat.

◆ Surgery
This was the first treatment used on cancer and is still responsible for most cancer cures. The difference in today's cancer treatment is that surgery is very often combined with radiation and/or chemotherapy for a more aggressive attack on the disease.

◆ Radiation Therapy
Radiation is a cancer weapon that has been around for decades, for treating humans as well as animals. Radiation is aimed at the site of the tumor and the surrounding 2 or 3 inches of healthy tissue. In order to minimize the negative side effects from the radiation, cats are usually given small doses over several weeks.

◆ "Cancer Diet"
Some oncologists prescribe a diet high in fat and low in carbohydrate for their patients, which they believe can slow down the growth of tumors. So far, studies have not shown this to be effective. However, a high-protein, low-carbohydrate diet for dogs with cancer *has* shown effectiveness, so there has to be merit to the connection between diet and cancer, even though no clear guidelines have yet emerged for cats. Nonetheless, a high-carbohydrate diet of dry food is never healthy for any cat, much less one fighting off cancer. Please read the nutrition section for a full understanding of this.

A SAMPLING OF CANCER CARE RESOURCES
Most veterinary colleges have cancer departments with ongoing research studies, clinical trials and sometimes treatment services for individual pets owners. This is by no means a comprehensive list, but just a sampling of the many organizations and facilities that cater to companion animals with cancer. If you live anywhere near Tufts, Cornell, UC Davis, University of Pennsylvania or any of the great veterinary schools, do not hesitate to call up and see whether they have a treatment program your cat might fit into or whether they have an oncology department able to treat individuals.

Abramson Cancer Center of the University of Pennsylvania, www.oncolink.org

Animal Cancer Care, www.animalcancercare.com.au

Animal Cancer Foundation, www.animalcancer.org

American Veterinary Medical Association (AVMA), Vaccine Associated Feline Sarcoma
Task Force, www.avma.org

The Argus Institute, www.argusinstitute.colostate.edu

Colorado State College of Veterinary Medicine and Biomedical Sciences,
www.csuanimalcancercenter.org

Veterinary Oncology and Hematology Center, www.oncovet.com

Colds

Upper respiratory infections can become quite serious and may require veterinary care.

SYMPTOMS ARE SIMILAR TO HUMAN COLDS

Colds in cats last about the same amount of time as they do in humans, 7 to 10 days. They are referred to as *upper respiratory infections* (URIs) and cause sneezing, runny nose, coughing, wheezing, oral ulcers and red watery eyes with a discharge. Cat colds usually occur when multiple cats
are in close contact, such as in a shelter or a boarding facility. The most common type of feline
cold virus is the feline herpes virus (FHV), which produces the cold symptoms just mentioned
(not sores the way herpes does in people). There is another cold virus in cats called FCV (for feline calicivirus), which causes similar mild cold symptoms. Both can become more serious.

TREATING A COLD

It is common for a cat with a cold to refuse to eat or drink, because a cat smells her food before
eating and if her nose is stuffed up she can't smell anything. If this lasts longer than a day or two,
you need to take her to the vet because dehydration can set in within a couple of days and her
body will use its fat stores for energy, causing other complications. Because of all this, a cold in a
cat can become a health hazard and has to be watched very carefully, so you have to be prepared
to get her to the vet on short notice. Therefore it is not the cold itself that is a danger but the resulting effect on the cat's system if she doesn't eat.

   If your cat will eat and drink, she will be more relaxed and comfortable at home if you can administer the medications your vet has prescribed. If her nose is really stuffed up, you can wipe it
gently with a warm, damp cloth to help relieve the congestion. However, if she won't take in food
or liquid, your vet may feel she would be better off in the clinic, although the stress of being in a
cage away from home also has to be considered.

HOW TO PREVENT A COLD

Be sure you don't carry home germs if you have been to a shelter, a vet's office, a boarding kennel or even a private home with cats; at the very least, wash your hands in case any of the cats were
carrying germs. If you were around any cats with cold symptoms, before touching your own cat

you might even want to change your shoes and wash your clothes if you had extended contact with a sickly cat.

COLD VACCINES

Some vets will give vaccines against colds to kittens and 1 year-old cats, and then a booster every 3 years after that. You'll have to discuss with your vet whether he is a proponent of giving these vaccinations, despite general concerns about the dangers of vaccines to cats.

If you have been sick, don't worry about giving your cold to your cat because you cannot—nor can you catch a cold *from* your cat. In general, cold viruses are species-specific, meaning that they cannot transfer from one species to another. However, colds can be spread very easily among cats, so if you have more than one in your household, get your sick cat to the doctor before the infection passes to your other cat(s).

Constipation

When a cat is constipated her stool is hard and dry and retained in the colon, making it hard to pass. Most cats have at least one bowel movement a day—those who normally have one only every couple of days are the ones who are most likely to suffer from constipation. The typical profile of a constipated cat is a middle-aged (6-year-old) male cat, with short-haired cats being more likely to become constipated than long-haired ones.

CAUSES OF CONSTIPATION

Most cats don't take in enough fluids because they are on dry food. This can lead to constipation, especially if combined with any of the other contributing factors, such as hairballs, reaction to medication or trauma to the pelvis.

HOW TO TELL IF YOUR CAT IS CONSTIPATED

The absence of stool in the litter box is not something everyone notices, but it's actually really important to keep an eye out for changes in litter box habits because they can indicate problems with your cat's health. If the cat is not producing feces or the stool is in rock-hard little balls, your cat is constipated and you should do something about it before it creates a serious health problem. Besides noticing how much stool is in the litter box, there are other ways to detect constipation.

STAGES OF CONSTIPATION

◆ Occasional Constipation Becomes Chronic Constipation

If you don't alleviate a cat's constipation, her bowel movements can become even more infrequent and difficult. Hairballs are often the culprit; long-haired cats are especially prone to them, as are short-haired cats who live with them, since they may groom each other. If your cat is having serious hairball problems, she will be vomiting hairballs and you'll also see hair in her stool. In

Signs of Constipation

- Lack of daily bowel movement
- Straining to defecate
- Crying out while passing stool (it hurts when it's hard and dry)
- Squatting in litter box for extended time before or after passing stool
- Feces are hard little pieces
- Stool is black and/or bloody
- Vomiting

cases like this, the solution is frequent use of a hairball prevention product (like Petromalt) that you smear on a cat's foot so she will lick it off. You can also put a dab of butter in her food.

If your cat does not pass stool for one day and she has no other underlying health problems, you can try any of the constipation remedies from the chart at the end of this section. If they do not relieve the cat so that she can have a bowel movement, then you will need to see your vet, who may administer an enema and/or an IV of saline solution to rehydrate her. The doctor will also check for hairballs or other illnesses.

If your cat has gotten to the point where she has not passed stool for more than a day, talk to your vet about giving her a laxative gel, which you should use only on your vet's advice. One thing people often don't know is that laxatives should be given at least 2 hours before or after meals, never mixed with food; a brand without sodium benzoate (or benzoate of soda) is preferable.

✦ Obstipation: The Cat Is Having No Bowel Movements
With obstipation, or fecal impaction, stool is stuck in the colon. Do not try any remedies yourself at home. Get your cat to the vet, who will give an enema or an oral laxative; he may even have to do a procedure to remove the stool manually.

✦ Megacolon: The End Stage of Constipation
This is a condition where the colon becomes so enlarged that it cannot expel the stool, which becomes trapped there. It can happen to cats in middle age (around 5 or 6 years old) and may require surgery to remove that part of the dysfunctional colon.

MAKE A HOMEMADE STOOL SOFTENER
First check with your vet before offering the following concoction to your cat, but it's unlikely that the doctor would be opposed to it. You'll be mixing together some high-fiber ingredients, which your cat will eat as a treat. Mix 1 tablespoon of any vegetable/meat baby food, ½ teaspoon of melted butter, ¼ teaspoon of fine or powdered bran, and about 1 teaspoon of a product such

Remedies for Constipation

- Add fiber to the food: 1 teaspoon canned pumpkin or ¼ teaspoon finely ground psyllium husks.
- Add 1 teaspoon finely ground raw carrot to the food 3 times weekly.
- Mix ½ teaspoon powdered or fine bran with ½ teaspoon butter and give as a treat.
- Avoid dry food entirely.
- Have ample fresh water in a couple of locations to encourage drinking.
- Feed canned food or freshly prepared high-moisture-content food.

as Metamucil that contains ground psyllium husks. Add at least 2 tablespoons of water to this mixture and offer it to your cat. If she isn't interested, sprinkle some brewer's yeast (or nutritional or flaked yeast—all available at health food stores) on it to enhance the flavor.

Declawing

The surgical removal of a cat's front claws is a highly emotional and controversial topic. Almost every organization governing cats—from veterinarians to the Cat Fanciers' Association—has condemned this operation, and yet uninformed people still choose to declaw their cats without fully understanding the extent to which they are mutilating their cats' feet. Those who defend the operation say that without it, some owners would abandon their cats or put them to sleep because of household damage from scratching. These same apologists for declawing claim that it is better for a cat to be declawed than to be homeless or euthanized. This section will give you all the available information on this topic so you can come to your own conclusions about the best way to humanely handle any issues with your cat's claws.

HOW DECLAWING IS DONE

This surgical procedure to amputate a cat's nails from her front paws is performed under general anesthesia. In order to remove the entire nail base, the ends of a cat's toes are cut off, right up to first joint—if you want to compare it to your own hand, imagine the cut being at your first knuckle, so you'd lose the entire joint above your nail. Consider the vital importance to a cat of her paws to walk, jump, climb and play, then also consider what that mutilation would do to every waking minute of her existence.

Four different procedures can be used for this operation. The first method uses a nail trimmer similar to the guillotine-type trimmer used for cutting a dog's nail. After a tourniquet is placed on the cat's leg, the trimmers are positioned over the joint behind the nail. By squeezing, the joint is opened enough for the trimmer to get in and amputate the toe; then the incisions are closed with sutures or surgical tissue glue and tightly bandaged. This is the least favored declawing technique because of complications such as hemorrhaging, pain and infection and also because often the bone is often not properly amputated and the claw can regrow, causing a lifetime of pain and lameness. The American Animal Hospital Association discourages the use of a nail trimmer for this operation.

The second method also involves placing a tourniquet and using a scalpel blade to cut the bone at that joint. The wound is closed similarly and the paws are wrapped tightly for at least 24 hours. This method does not usually create the problem of improper amputation and regrowth of bone, but there is more bleeding and pain.

The third method is the newest and doesn't require a tourniquet or bandages—it uses a carbon dioxide laser to do the amputation. An intensely focused light beam removes the claws instead of a scalpel, causing less bleeding, scarring and pain. It has gained popularity with some vets as being more humane because the laser seals the nerve endings and cauterizes the blood vessels to stop bleeding. It is a shorter operation requiring less anesthesia and recovery time. While there are vets who will do only laser declawing, many caution that you need to find a doctor with a lot of experience because in the wrong hands a laser can do great damage.

The fourth method of declawing is an alternative to cutting the bone. In a flexor tendonectomy, with the cat under general anesthesia, the vet cuts the tendon that attaches to the end of the toe. There is no tourniquet or bleeding, but bandages are put on cats older than 4 months. The severed tendon keeps the claw permanently sheathed; the cat still has her claws, and for the rest of her life you have to frequently cut them or they can curl under and grow into her foot pad. Also, long-term arthritis is a complication of tendonectomies, which is why the American Veterinary Medical Association does not recommend them. Many vets say that this solution is little better than just trimming your cat's nails every week.

THE CASE AGAINST DECLAWING

◆ The Emotional Reaction
Declawed cats become defensive because they have difficulty climbing to escape danger and they cannot defend themselves against dogs or other cats. This makes them nervous, vulnerable and in a state of constant stress. They may withdraw from social interaction, exhibiting shyness in new circumstances and a terror of the vet clinic. Declawed cats tend to defensively bite more quickly and more often, since they no longer have claws to use as a warning or weapon. This is a reason that a declawed cat is *not* always a safe pet for children, despite what people might assume. Claws are the first line of defense for a cat—remove them and you take away an essential survival and communication tool.

◆ The Physical Downside
The amputation performed when declawing a cat is the equivalent of what is done to people who are tortured: It is a kind of dismemberment. There are those who say that a declawed cat can have a gradual weakening of the legs, back and shoulders because she cannot walk

normally, but this is not common. These detractors of declawing compare the cat's condition to having clubfoot, with her posture altered, forcing her to shift her weight to her back feet. The tourniquet used during surgery can also cause nerve damage that makes the cat walk abnormally.

Those vets who perform declawing say that if it is done on a young cat at the time of neutering, recovery will be swift and easy. Regardless of whether that judgement is true, some vets are declawing cats way past kittenhood. The age at declawing apparently correlates to the amount of pain and emotional reaction to the operation, but I hope that what you have read here would give you misgivings about a vet recommending declawing at any age.

OFFICIAL DISAPPROVAL FOR DECLAWING

The Cat Fanciers' Association of America, which regulates cat shows, will not allow declawed cats into competitive events and issued the following statement: "CFA recognizes that scratching is a natural behavior for cats and that cats may be defenseless without full use of their claws. Scratching damage to household furnishings can be minimized or avoided by routine clipping of the claws, the use of claw covers and by redirecting the cat's activity to acceptable surfaces (a scratching post)." They go on to say that declawing is an elective medical procedure with no benefit to the cat and that the pain associated can have behavioral or physical effects. You can read the full position paper and get more information at their Web site, www.cfa.org.

The American Association of Feline Practitioners (vets who specialize in cats) has declared that the procedure is not medically necessary. The group urges veterinarians to educate cat owners with a truthful explanation of what declawing is like for the cat. The AAFP position papers included many of the same points against declawing as the Cat Fanciers' Association statement, mentioned above. You can read the organization's full statement online at www.aafponline.org/declaw_statement.htm.

Declawing is illegal in many countries in Western Europe and around the world, including Denmark, Finland, Germany, the Netherlands, Sweden, Switzerland, the United Kingdom, Australia and New Zealand.

MY PERSONAL REMORSE ABOUT DECLAWING

I can only claim ignorance as my own defense for subjecting two of my sweet kitties to declawing. I had moved from the West Coast to the East Coast with 2 cats and 3 dogs and had rented a house during the transition. The cats were going to town on the couches and I did not know enough about cat trees and how to make a scratching post inviting, so they continued to destroy the landlord's furniture. The local vet told me that declawing was a swift and simple procedure and that within days the cat would forget it had happened. Let me tell you, my friends, that you never want to have my experience of watching two previously happy and frisky cats come home from this procedure and be physically and emotionally destroyed by it.

When I brought those cats home, their front feet were obscured by enormous layers of bandaging. They could barely walk on those bandages, but even when they were removed, they walked so gingerly on their feet that the floor might as well have been covered in hot coals—which may be what it felt like to them. They slunk against walls as they went. They stopped being affectionate or wanting contact; it seemed like a combination of pain, sadness and stress at having been mutilated. It was months—many months—before it didn't hurt me to watch them walk. One of the cats ran away at the first opportunity and we never found her; the other resigned himself to his disability, a shadow of his former self. It was the most cruel and senseless thing I have ever inflicted on an animal, and while I blame the vet for underplaying the seriousness of the operation, I also owed it to them to do my homework before inflicting that mutilation on them. Since I cannot make it up to those two poor souls, at least I can shine an honest light on this barbaric procedure for all the kitties still out there, walking on their own four feet.

I can't tell you what percentage of declawed cats react this way, but after reading the above description, do you really feel okay even asking that question? If you have had the experience of living with a declawed cat who did not seem to suffer extraordinarily—or you are told by anyone at all that it "really isn't that bad"—I urge you with all my heart to reconsider.

Diabetes

My independent research over several years has convinced me that most cats are being fed the wrong food and it is to blame for many of their physical woes, with the potentially fatal disease diabetes at the top of that list. However, once my radio show CAT CHAT® began on the Martha Stewart Channel of Sirius Radio, I was contacted by a cats-only veterinarian, Dr. Elizabeth Hodgkins, who was excited to learn that I was getting the nutritional message she believes in—"wet food only"—out to a larger audience. I discovered that she is "the cat's meow" where feline diabetes is concerned: known as the "savior of diabetic cats" by the many cat lovers whose kitties she has cured of diabetes (when found early enough) or helped live a long, healthy life with the disease. Dr. H. became the Official Vet of CAT CHAT® and I, and my listeners, will always be grateful for her generosity of time and spirit in teaching us all the right nutritional path for all cats—wet food only—with diabetic ones benefiting the most. Some of what you will read in this section may contradict what your own vet tells you. Although I have no desire to interrupt a good relationship between anyone and their veterinarian, I urge you— I beseech you—to ask your vet to look at Elizabeth Hodgkins' Web site, www.yourdiabeticcat.com, and then contact her directly since she is eager to explain her theories, describe her clinical experience and give support in following it to any vet.

Diabetes is one of the most common endocrine (or glandular) disorders in cats. Diabetes can strike a cat at any age but it generally affects middle-aged, obese, neutered male cats. The only breed of cat more susceptible than others is the Burmese, 1 in 10 of which get diabetes after 8 years of age.

WHAT CAUSES DIABETES

Although no one knows the cause of it for sure, some of the suspected reasons for a cat becoming diabetic are because she is genetically predisposed, has a hormonal imbalance or has disease of the pancreas, or it is the result of taking certain medications. However, one of the prime—and completely preventable—causes of diabetes is that most people are mistakenly serving their cats a fundamentally incorrect diet of dry food. Feeding a carbohydrate rich diet to an animal who is an "obligate carnivore"—which simply means she must eat meat—is undoubtedly the cause of type II diabetes in cats. This is a health epidemic that we have created for cats in the past decade or two, by giving our feline companions an endless supply of dry bagged kibble to crunch on. Please read the nutrition section of this book so you can learn how to "think outside the bag," and utilize that knowledge either to correct your cat's diabetes or to keep it from developing.

HOW DIABETES FUNCTIONS

When your cat has diabetes, her pancreas doesn't make enough insulin, the hormone necessary to control glucose (sugar) levels in the blood. The process begins as food is digested and sugar enters the bloodstream. This blood sugar, as it is called, is essential for the body's energy, growth and repair, but it is the insulin from the pancreas that allows sugar to get from the bloodstream into the tissue cells—like those in muscles—where the cat's body needs it. If there isn't enough insulin, the sugar remains in the bloodstream, where it is useless to the body, and then gets filtered out in the urine. A lot of water goes out with the sugar, which is why diabetics produce a large volume of urine. All of this is true of diabetes in humans, too.

THE EFFECT ON A CAT'S BODY AND METABOLISM

Because they are producing so much urine, cats who are diabetic (or borderline diabetic) drink an excessive amount of water to avoid getting dehydrated. And because the body of a diabetic cat lacks the insulin to convert the sugar in the bloodstream into usable fuel for the muscles, the body automatically switches to using its own fat and protein as a source of energy. This is why diabetic cats usually lose weight as a result of the disease—yet overweight cats are more likely to get diabetes in the first place (the same is true with people).

DIAGNOSING DIABETES

This disease is actually easy to catch because the classic signs are so obvious: The cat drinks enormous amounts, urinates copiously, has a good appetite and loses weight. If you notice any of these symptoms, particularly all at once, you need to make a vet appointment right away. The vet will do blood and urine tests, which will show a high sugar level in the blood and the presence of sugar in the urine if your cat is diabetic. Once in a while, the classic signs aren't so clear and even the lab tests aren't definitive, but there are further tests the vet can do to make the diagnosis.

TREATMENT FOR DIABETES

Many doctors believe that diabetes cannot be cured, but Dr. Hodgkins would disagree because she has done just that with many cats. If diabetes is caught early enough while the pancreas is still healthy, the disease can be stopped in its tracks by feeding wet food exclusively. More advanced diabetes can be treated and kept under control with a combination of diet and the correct type of insulin in the correct amount (see below), not unlike the way people control their diabetes. In many cats, switching to a high protein diet along with a daily insulin injection can actually cause a remission in the disease within weeks. In the early stages of treating the disease, your vet may also want you to monitor your cat's blood sugar to see how she is responding. Many cats who need insulin shots in the beginning may no longer need them after the first few weeks or months, so it will be important to check the cat's blood glucose level, as explained below.

• Diet: High Protein, Low Carbohydrate

The fastest route to controlling diabetes is to eliminate all dry food from your cat's diet, which gives her system the correct ingredients to function properly. By feeding a diet of no more than 20 percent carbohydrates you will also reduce the amount of fat on your cat's body, a very good thing since obesity is another trigger for diabetes, along with other health problems. While there are commercial diets sold by vets that are specifically formulated for cats with diabetes, you may be surprised about the quality of the ingredients—furthermore, feeding any dry food to a cat only exacerbates the problem of giving an incorrect food. After reading in the nutrition chapter about what is in those bags of commercial cat food, you may decide to switch to a good canned food since really we're just talking about feeding lots of protein, which is what a cat would be eating if guided by her own instincts.

• What If Your Cat Is Hooked on Kibble?

Some cats get so accustomed to dry food that they are known as "carbo-junkies" by Feline Foodies (as I lovingly call those cat lovers who are dedicated to getting the word out about the dangers of dry food). Whether or not your cat has learned to love carbohydrates, they are an unnatural ingredient for a cat's metabolism, as you read in the nutrition chapter. Dry cat food can contain up to 50 percent carbohydrates from rice, corn, wheat and soy, none of which belong in any cat's optimal diet, which should be little more than a simple mouse.

With so many cats relying on kibble as their main food, it may be a radical change to switch your diabetic cat to canned food. Please read the nutrition chapter so you can learn why a carbohydrate-heavy, all-kibble or mostly kibble diet is unhealthy for even the healthiest cat. That chapter will clarify how we, as consumers, have been misled by cat food manufacturers into believing that dry food is healthier, when the only health it really promotes is that of the pet food company's balance sheets. As you will see, the fact is that cats are carnivores who need real protein—either raw, cooked or in a can—as their main food. In the nutrition section you will also find a checklist of how to wean your cat off kibble and onto canned food if she doesn't seem to like it at first. Just remember that with a diabetic cat you should always consult with your vet about any changes you want to make in her diet to accommodate her diabetes.

• What Kind of Insulin to Use?

Despite the fact that many vets use a synthetic human insulin called Lantus, or glargine, for cats, Dr. Hodgkins has found that PZI (protamine zinc insulin) is by far the most effective medication for a diabetic cat since it is formulated from beef and pork insulin molecules, which are closer to a cat's natural insulin than the human version. She believes it is because of this that Lantus gives unpredictable effects and is not as effective in controlling the cat's blood sugar levels. To learn more about this—and Dr. H's methods for keeping a cat's blood sugar lower than other practitioners are doing—go to www.yourdiabeticcat.com.

◆ **Giving the Insulin Injection**

Many people are squeamish about the idea of giving an injection to their diabetic cat, but once you get the hang of it you'll see that the injection is easy to give and causes no discomfort to your cat.

◆ **Checking Your Cat's Sugar Levels**

Most cat lovers will tell you that going to the vet's office is a nerve-wracking experience for their kitty, so having to make frequent trips there to check a diabetic cat's blood sugar levels is both stressful to the cat and time-consuming for her human companion. Therefore home-testing is the best way to go when managing your cat's diabetes. Dr. Hodgkins recommends using a glucometer made for human diabetics to check their own blood sugar levels. She has a link on her Web site that will teach you how to check your cat and maintain the low blood sugar levels she recommends, which she has found can lead to getting a cat off insulin entirely. See www .felinediabetes.com/bg-test.htm.

Diarrhea

Diarrhea may be a sign of several different disorders—but if it only happens once or twice, it doesn't have to be a cause for concern. The intestinal upset may just be a reaction to something that will pass out of the cat's system in 24 hours. However, diarrhea that lasts longer than a day can dehydrate a cat, and if not corrected it can lead to shock.

SOME "NORMAL" REASONS FOR DIARRHEA

Although it can be a symptom of a disease or serious illness, diarrhea can also be a reaction to a change in diet (which is why dietary changes should be made slowly and gradually), and it can come from overfeeding or from a new source of water. If the cat goes outdoors, the stomach upset could be from eating prey, garbage or even poison that has been put out for rodents (more good reasons to keep your cat indoors). Cats are also lactose intolerant, meaning that they cannot easily digest dairy products, so a bowl of milk will often bring on a bout of diarrhea (in some cats more than others). An emotionally sensitive cat can also get diarrhea just from a stressful event, such as going to the vet or any of the items on the stress chart in Chapter 5.

WHAT TO DO ABOUT MILD DIARRHEA

Any diarrhea that doesn't fit the warning signs on the chart below will probably pass on its own in a day or two. Your vet may want to give you a mild product for feline digestive upset, but *do not even think of using human over-the-counter products.* The newest Kaopectate formula and any diarrhea product with bismuth subsalicylate (such as Pepto-Bismol) can be poisonous to a cat. Most vets will suggest withholding food for 24 hours so the digestive tract can empty out and calm down. A wonderful powder called Bio-Sponge from Platinum Performance (800-553-2400) works wonders.

If your cat has any of the symptoms on the following chart, you should call the vet and see if he wants to see her right away.

Diarrhea Requiring a Vet Visit

- It continues more than one day.
- It is bloody or contains mucus.
- It is black or any color other than brown.
- It is accompanied by fever, vomiting or lethargy.
- It has a foul odor.

Digestive Problems: Inflammatory Bowel Disease (IBD)

Cats with recurring digestive problems may have a serious disease called inflammatory bowel disease, or IBD (not to be confused with the human illness irritable bowel syndrome or IBS). In cats, inflammatory bowel disease is thought to be an overreaction to the normal bacteria in the intestine, which play an important part in normal digestion. In a cat with IBD, her immune system does not tolerate those bacteria and attacks them, causing inflammation. IBD is the most common cause of gastrointestinal distress in cats and can lead to severe illness or cancer if not treated, so you need to be on alert.

SYMPTOMS OF IBD

A cat with this disease will have symptoms that come and go periodically—this on-and-off quality is typical of IBD—primarily chronic vomiting and diarrhea, but also abdominal pain, intestinal gurgling, frequent passing of gas, loss of appetite, weight loss, difficulty defecating and blood or mucus in the stool.

THE CAUSE OF IBD

Nobody is sure what makes a cat's immune system attack the friendly bacteria, but it may be hereditary. To reduce the risk of the disease in any cat, experts suggest keeping your cat away from any potentially unclean water that might contain bacteria, especially water outdoors that has been standing in puddles. Having worms in the stomach, an overgrowth of certain bacteria and allergies to particular food proteins may also trigger the inflammatory response.

DIAGNOSING IBD

Because the symptoms of IBD are variable and can fluctuate, a vet has to diagnose it one step at a time. After testing blood and fecal samples and deworming, a doctor may put your cat on an experimental diet to see if she is allergic to or intolerant of any particular foods. If all of those tests are inconclusive, then to make a definitive diagnosis of IBD a cat has to be given an endoscopy—under anesthesia, a tube is passed into the digestive tract to take samples.

TREATMENT FOR IBD

This ailment is not curable, but 90 percent of cats respond well to a diet and drug therapy, usually some form of cortisone. The goal is to get the cat off the medication as soon as possible and maintain her healthy digestive system with diet alone. However, even a cat who is doing well may relapse into periods of more vomiting and diarrhea and will have to go back on additional medical therapy.

Ears

EAR MITES

All cats have some ear mites but they become a problem when there is a large infestation, causing the cat to scratch incessantly at her ear. These tiny parasites feed on the lining of the ear and when there is a large quantity they cause irritation and a dark brown, smelly discharge. Ear mites are commonly found in kittens—adult cats are much less likely to be infested with them—and they are extremely contagious. You want to get the afflicted cat to the vet as quickly as possible for medication and to keep the mites from spreading to other household pets. Any other cats or dogs in the household need to be treated with the same ear drops your vet will give you for the carrier cat.

◆ Signs of Ear Mites

There's a good chance your cat has ear mites if she holds her ears flat against her head, scratches at them constantly and shakes her head as if to get something out of her ear. The outer ear will be inflamed, and inside the ear there will be a dark, thick, nasty-smelling discharge, although some cats can be infested without any visible symptoms.

◆ Treatment for Ear Mites

Get your cat to the vet just as fast as you can so you can relieve her intense itching and keep her from mutilating herself as she scratches and claws at her face and ear. You also want to catch the condition before it turns into a serious infection, otitis externa (see below). Do not attempt to clean out her ear on your own until your vet shows you the safe and effective way to do it.

OTITIS EXTERNA

This inflammation and infection of the outer ear must be treated with antibiotics before it has a chance to travel to the middle or inner ear, where it can permanently damage a cat's hearing and balance. The vet will examine the black gook coming out of your cat's ear to see whether ear mites are present, as well as to check for other parasites, bacteria or fungi, all of which can cause similar symptoms. Depending on what your vet discovers to be the underlying cause of the inflammation, he will give appropriate treatment.

Eyes

If there is any discharge from your cat's eyes, she should go to the vet. If eyes are red-rimmed, squinting or closed; running with fluid, bloody discharge or discharge of any color; or if there is brown-stained fur around the eyes, these are all signs that an eye has been injured, has a foreign body in it or is infected. Bloody discharge indicates a seriously deep wound to the eyeball and is an emergency situation requiring a vet visit at whatever hour it is discovered.

Chronic eye discharge in Persian and Himalayan cats is a different story because it is usually caused by a congenital deformity causing blocked or malformed tear ducts on cats with the distinctively flat faces of these breeds. The breed's facial conformation can also result in more dirt or dust getting in the eyes.

Siamese cats with flat straight noses also are prone to chronic eye discharge because of the shape of their faces, which can become exaggerated as the result of breeding choices by some breeders. With repeated breeding and inbreeding to achieve a certain look in a Siamese, the end result is that there is not enough room in the skull for normal tear ducts. If your cat falls into this category, your vet should be able to help you give her some relief from this permanent irritation.

Fatal Diseases

There are seven deadly viruses that attack cats. There are vaccines to protect against some of them (see the end of this listing), but for others there is no prevention. These illnesses all go by acronyms that are irritatingly similar, since all start with *F* (for *feline*) and have two or three other letters beside it. These are the main diseases that cause suffering and death for cats and tragedy for the people who love them.

FPV: FELINE PANLEUKOPENIA VIRUS

The name for this virus derives from the Greek and means "lack of white blood cells." The illness is lethal and highly contagious and is also known as feline distemper. It attacks the cells lining the intestines and begins with fever, vomiting and diarrhea, then progresses to central nervous system damage and sudden death. Kittens are most susceptible to it and it can wipe out entire litters in shelters or other crowded conditions.

FHV: FELINE HERPES VIRUS

This disease causes severe upper respiratory distress, with sneezing and troubled breathing. A cat with this disease can suffer from loss of appetite that leads to malnutrition since the nasal congestion interferes with her sense of smell. This is another virus common among kittens living in crowded conditions because it is passed in secretions from the respiratory tract, where the virus attacks. Kittens can be infected by their mothers because this disease is transmitted through licking and mutual grooming.

FCV: FELINE CALICIVIRUS

This is another upper respiratory virus that also affects the oral cavity. Like FHV, it is transmitted through respiratory and oral secretions and is readily spread among cats through grooming. It is similar to FHV in every way except that with this virus, cats develop sores and ulcers in their mouths. Vaccines have been developed to lower a cat's chances of becoming infected with FCV, but if a cat has spent enough time around other sick cats, she can still come down with it.

FELV: FELINE LEUKEMIA VIRUS

This highly contagious virus causes a serious infection that leads to several other horrible diseases. Three percent of cats who appear to be healthy, and a much greater percentage of those who are obviously sick, have this virus, which is a major killer of cats throughout the world. FeLV leads to the development of lymphosarcomas, cancerous tumors made up of white blood cells. Cats pass this illness through licking each other and through biting, and an infected cat who is pregnant will pass it to her babies.

A simple blood test will show whether your cat is a carrier of this virus: A positive test means that she should be isolated from all other cats. All cats who test negative for FeLV should be vaccinated as early in life as possible. Vaccinations consist of a series of two initial injections and a yearly booster.

However, a positive test does not mean your cat is necessarily going to get sick and die. Some cats can fight off the virus and develop immunity to it, although there is no definite way to know which cats those will be. Sadly, other cats do become infected and die from infectious diseases able to attack their weakened immune systems. There is no treatment once a cat is infected, which is yet another reason to keep your cat indoors, away from potentially infected cats who might be wandering around.

FIP: FELINE INFECTIOUS PERITONITIS VIRUS

This highly contagious viral disease is usually deadly. It occurs mostly in cats between 6 weeks and 5 years of age, although most victims are less than 2 years old. It is sometimes called the "purring disease" because kittens who have it snuggle and purr constantly, perhaps to keep warm since they run fevers. Older cats can also become susceptible to it when their immune systems weaken with age.

There are two forms of this disease. The "dry" form causes small inflamed lesions that spread throughout the organs, while the "wet" form causes fluid to accumulate in the chest and abdominal cavities. Although it is very contagious, only 5 percent of cats in multi-cat households actually develop FIP—the cats in your household probably already have the harmless intestinal version of the virus, which does not cause illness. However, once a cat shows symptoms of the virus, she will live only a short time.

There is no prevention or cure. An FIP vaccination was developed, but it was too controversial because of side effects; most vets and researchers don't think the vaccine is beneficial. This disease is very difficult to diagnose and there are no reliable tests for it.

Many experts believe that stressors trigger the development of FIP in kittens who are genetically susceptible to the virus. If this is true, then watch out for any of the stress factors on the chart in Chapter 5, "Your Cat's Emotions." Regardless, everyone should try to minimize the stressors in their cat's environment as much as reasonably possible.

Many cats don't show signs of FIP in the beginning except maybe for mild upper respiratory problems such as sneezing, watery eyes and nasal discharge. Then there are also all those symptoms that could fit any of the deadly viruses: loss of appetite and weight, vomiting, diarrhea, lethargy and depression.

FIV: FELINE IMMUNODEFICIENCY VIRUS

This is also known as "cat AIDS," because it can weaken a cat's immune system and make her vulnerable to many other opportunistic diseases. This disease is not contagious to people (for more on diseases that can be passed between our species, see Chapter 8). The virus resides in a cat's saliva and is transmitted when an infected cat bites an uninfected one. Most cats who have it are feral (more on them in Chapter 14) and male, which should at least tell you that your cat might be safe if she doesn't fall into those categories. Signs of the disease include loss of appetite, weight loss, high fever, sores in the mouth, chronic diarrhea, skin infections and upper respiratory symptoms. Some affected cats can have periods of pretty good health and then the illness takes hold again.

The American Association of Feline Practitioners (vets who specialize in cats) issued guidelines for which cats should be tested for FIV, although it is routine practice to test any cat before she joins your household.

Test for FIV If Your Cat . . .

- Has never been tested before
- Roams freely outdoors
- Is an unneutered male
- Has been exposed to an FIV-positive cat
- Has fought with another cat
- Lives with other cats who haven't been tested
- Is sick and exposure can't be ruled out
- Is being considered for adoption

For information on FLUTO, FUS, *see* Urinary System Problems.

RABIES

This virus causes a fatal disease of the central nervous system. It is more frequently reported in cats than any other domestic animal and can be spread to humans or other animals via a bite. Wild animals also carry rabies. Vaccinating your cat against the disease is required by law in most states. Some states like California do not require it for exclusively indoor cats, but check your local rules.

There are a number of reasons to give your cat as few vaccinations as possible. Most vaccines do not prevent infection, but merely lessen the severity should your cat be exposed to any of them. More important, cats can develop cancer at the site where vaccines are administered, a fairly recent realization by veterinarians. Several of these vaccinations are given as a 3-in-1 injection, which in itself may raise the chance of a deadly reaction at the site. Although statistics show that only a very few cats develop sarcoma at the injection site, nonetheless vets are now advised to give vaccines as far down a front leg as possible—presumably because if cancer does develop, that part of the leg could be amputated, since immediate surgical removal is recommended.

The injections for FPV, FCV and FHV have routinely been given to cats on a yearly basis. However, the American Veterinary Medical Association reported in 2004 that it was no longer necessary to give these 3 vaccinations on a yearly basis because their protection actually lasted 2 years or longer. Vets now recommend that to protect against vaccine-associated sarcoma, *a cat should receive as few injections in a lifetime as possible.* Instead of routinely having your cat vaccinated every year, you and your vet should discuss your cat's risk factors for infection to come up with a safe plan, based on her specific lifestyle and age. For example, there is no valid reason for a cat who lives completely indoors to receive certain vaccines. Vaccines have been divided into "core" and "non-core," meaning those that are considered necessary basic vaccinations and those that may be needed depending on a cat's lifestyle. However, you still must have a clear discussion with your own vet about the benefits of each vaccine compared with the risks.

Kidney Disease

This is the number one medical problem of older cats, but there is good news. While this can be a fatal condition in dogs, when kidney disorder is diagnosed early and properly managed in a cat, she can often live a long time with it.

The kidneys are the organs that deteriorate first in a cat as she ages. They undergo a gradual decline and the cat seems generally ill. The most common signs of kidney disease are that she will drink more, urinate more and lose weight. She may also have bad breath and mouth ulcers, vomiting and poor appetite.

If caught early (by an observant owner who brings the cat to the vet), kidney disease can usually be managed with a radical change in diet, usually one with lower protein. Depending on the severity of the condition, some cases can be managed with home care that includes injections of fluids under her skin to flush out the waste products in her system that her kidneys can no longer properly process.

Medications and How to Give Them

One of the great challenges of taking care of a cat is trying to give her medication. There are so many techniques and gadgets and equipment to assist you in this daunting task—probably because it is so frustrating when our cat is sick and needs to have the medicine we have spent time and money procuring, but she insists on spitting it out or clawing us to shreds in the process. Twenty years ago I rescued a tiny, sickly gray kitty, Grigio, who had a showdown with me over every life-saving medication I tried to administer. Having teetered on death's door for weeks as a wee thing, Grigio is now over 20 years old and still hanging in there. So don't give up on your violent, obstinate cat when it comes to medicine—there are so many good ways to help make the process, which I outline on the pages that follow, less stressful for both of you. Before I go into the choices, just a word on antibiotics, which are given to cats for so many illnesses and yet can make a cat pretty miserable in the process of making her well.

ANTIBIOTICS

Antibiotics are drugs used to treat infections, and they have saved countless lives, in the human world as well as in the animal one. But one of the downsides of antibiotics is that when they destroy bacteria, they are not selective: They kill all the bacteria in a cat's system, good and bad alike, particularly the valuable bacteria that the digestive system needs to function properly. Without the "good" bacteria, a cat can get diarrhea and feel generally lousy.

When a cat has to take antibiotics, ask your vet about giving her a *probiotic* to take alongside them to replace the "good" bacteria in her gut. A good probiotic is one that contains live acidophilus, to replace those "friendly" bacteria so that she doesn't get the tummy troubles that antibiotics so often cause. This is true for dogs and yourself as well: Any creature being treated with antibiotics will benefit from getting a probiotic during and for at least two weeks after antibiotic treatment has ended.

What's the best way to give a probiotic? Yogurt with live acidophilus is the best way to get those probiotics into your cat's system, but some cats will not tolerate the taste. You can try to introduce yogurt to your cat by adding a teaspoon or two of organic, cultured yogurt to each meal, but since her appetite may already be dampened by taking the antibiotic, she may not be interested in eating at all, or she may be put off by the flavor or texture of the yogurt. Commercial yogurts from the supermarket are so doused with sugar and additives that they bear very little resemblance to the "real thing," whether for your cat or yourself because they lack the live acidophilus that the gut needs. You can purchase a high-dose probiotic supplement at any health food store—the best ones have live cultures and are kept refrigerated. Most health food stores have a lot of probiotics to choose from, so check the chart on the following page to make a good selection for your cat. The acidophilus comes in capsule or liquid form: Use the capsule if you don't think she'll finish all the food you would put the liquid on.

How much should you give? It is safe to use any probiotic supplement marketed for humans. Give the full dose suggested for humans for two weeks, beginning when you start the antibiotics, and after that reduce to about half the amount for a couple of weeks afterward for maintenance. At times of stress or illness, or whenever antibiotics are administered, give the full human dose.

Qualities of a Good Probiotic

- Has large enough amounts of viable organisms to have a therapeutic effect (at least several billion, not just millions, colony-forming units [CFU], per serving)
- Live organisms are guaranteed—not only at time of manufacture but throughout the shelf life of the product
- Does not contain fillers, sweeteners or preservatives
- Be sure to give probiotics 2–3 hours after the antibiotics, otherwise the "good" bacteria will be killed off by the antibiotic, rather than being replaced afterward

GIVING PILLS

This is probably the hardest way to give medicine to your cat, so I will give it the most attention. There are a variety of ways to administer a pill, and there are products designed to help you do it. You want to prepare yourself and your cat in advance so that the ritual is calm, organized and not miserable for her. By setting things up in advance you make things easier and avoid struggle or fear from the cat.

Before giving a pill, trim your fingernail short on the index finger of your dominant hand so that it won't scrape the back of your cat's throat or her palate while you are placing the pill in the back of her mouth. Be sure to wash your hands first; it is simply the polite thing to do. This may sound obvious, but you'd be amazed how many of us do not think of *our* hygiene for the sake of our cat. Remember that if you have just put on hand cream, have just chopped onions or have any other offensive smell or flavor on that hand, it will make your cat resist the pill and want to avoid the whole enterprise.

◆ Make It a Positive Association
Rather than creeping up on your cat and trying to shove a pill down her throat, making both of you anxious and causing a struggle, begin with some stroking time. Before you get into the best position to give a pill (described below), massage and stroke around your cat's neck, cheeks and ears. At times that have nothing to do with medication, get your cat used to accepting your touch all around her face and neck, even when she is being held in a fairly restrictive way, so that it becomes something pleasant for her.

◆ Be Patient but Swift
You need to develop a mental plan of how you are going to present this pill. If you first have a mental picture of easily opening her mouth and popping that pill in, it will go more smoothly because you have rehearsed it in your mind. Pick the right moment to start; then don't hesitate, just go for it. Your confidence and swiftness will be much less nerve-wracking for your cat than if you are nervously making false starts and mumbling apologies to her.

✦ Position Is Everything

There are two basic positions to try for giving pills: you on the floor, or the cat on a counter. If you are fairly limber and comfortable on the floor, then you can kneel down on a carpeted area to cushion your knees, sit back on your heels and open your legs enough to make a small V. Position the cat between your legs and with her back to you so that if she tries to back away, she just moves against you. If that doesn't sound comfortable, you can put the cat on a counter so you don't have to get down on the ground. You still want to cradle her against you with your nondominant arm so that when you go to give the pill, she is securely held in place.

✦ Have the Pill Ready

Forget about hiding the pill in food—cats have a sense of smell so sharp they can sniff out that pill even if it's got ham wrapped around it. And if she doesn't smell the pill first, she will sense it the minute she goes to chew the "trick treat," and then you will have lost her trust and created resistance for your next attempt. You can make the pill more slippery by coating it with butter. It will go down the cat's throat more easily, but it will also be more slippery for your fingers to grasp, so you have to decide which is more important for success. You can also coat it with a bit of the hairball medication paste for lubrication, which has a pleasant taste for the cat, too.

✦ Head Tilted, Mouth Open

So you can visualize what you need to accomplish, imagine the way a baby bird receives food from its mother. So, in whichever position you have chosen, put your palm on top of the cat's head and tilt it back just slightly—not too far or she will resist.

You need to use both hands to get this right: Hold the cat's head with your nondominant hand, fingers pointing in the direction of her nose, and place your thumb on one side of her mouth and your middle finger on the other side. Applying pressure to her lips against her teeth, open her mouth partway.

✦ Inserting the Pill

Hold the pill in your dominant hand, gripping it between your thumb and index finger, and use the middle finger of that hand to pry the cat's mouth open a little more. By pressing your middle finger gently but firmly against her lower jaw, you can get her mouth open enough to scoot that pill in with the index finger, gently pushing it against the back of her throat.

Don't hold her head back or hold her mouth shut. Doing either of those things actually inhibits a cat from swallowing. You can massage her throat slightly, but don't restrict her jaw since she needs to have her teeth apart to swallow. You will know that you have been successful if the cat's tongue darts out and licks her nose, which is a sure sign she has swallowed the pill. If she coughs afterward, the pill probably went down the windpipe. Let her go so that she can cough it up. You want to let her dislodge that pill so it doesn't block the windpipe or start to dissolve there and cause irritation.

Blowing in a cat's nose will also cause her to swallow.

HOW TO WRAP UP A CAT

Wrapping a cat in a towel is the most efficient way to restrain her while you are giving her medication. It is actually a kind thing to do: It prevents her from engaging in the panicked fight-or-flight reflex and allows you to do what you need to do without either of you getting hurt. The goal of wrapping is to immobilize the cat, but within the limits of comfort so she feels secure, the way a swaddled baby might. You want to end up with her legs and body all wrapped up, the towel ending below her chin, so that only her head is exposed.

Tips on Cat Wrapping

- Don't think of this as something negative; imagine it as a chance to show love to your cat. Stroke and snuggle her once she is wrapped up.
- Use as little restraint as possible. Being held too tightly will upset a cat and make her struggle.
- Notwithstanding the above tip, wrap the cat firmly; if the towel is loose, she may try to break free.
- Move decisively and quickly so that before the cat can react with panic, she's already wrapped up, feeling safe and snug.
- Speak quietly and reassuringly before and during the wrap-up.
- Do not stare directly at her while wrapping, since this is a threatening gesture.
- Use an old, thin towel—thick and fluffy doesn't let you get a snug wrap.

STEP-BY-STEP CAT WRAPPING

1. Lay a big, old, thin bath towel on a flat surface.

2. Place the cat across the towel in the middle, so the longer sides are on either side of her.

3. Hold her by the scruff of the neck so she will not fight you.

4. Fold up the short portion of towel in front of her feet and behind her tail.

5. Fold over one long side to cover her back and wrap on top of the short bits, incorporating her front feet.

6. Tuck any extra over her hind end and then snugly underneath her body.

7. Keep the towel tight against her chest and right up under her chin as you pull it snug.

8. Now fold over the other long side, securing down any loose bits and pulling it tightly over the towel already covering the cat's side and chest.

9. Secure the end of the towel by tucking it behind the cat's head, if that gives a snug anchor. If not, hold that last, unwrapped end of the towel in your hand as you simultaneously keep hold of the scruff of her neck with the same hand—gently but firmly, which discourages struggling. Now you can use your other hand to do what you need to do—or enlist the help of a brave friend or family member to do the honors as long as you keep the cat still.

GIVING EYE AND EAR MEDICATION

If you use the wrapping method to administer eye drops, ointment or ear drops, you can avoid wrestling with your cat and you will have her eyes and ears readily available for attention. Since your cat won't be struggling against you, this makes it safer for both you and your cat; you won't run the risk of harming her eyes if they are not a moving target.

GADGETS TO HELP GIVE MEDICINE

Pill Pockets are edible pouches into which you pop the pill to be given. In tests done by *Catnip*, a monthly newsletter, they proved popular with the cats who like treats. Be careful not to get the odor of the pill on the outside of the pocket. A bag of 45 costs about $7 at some vets' offices and most pet stores.

Tube pill dispensers require a little practice from you. You put the pill into a long plastic tube dispenser that goes into the cat's mouth and pops the pill into the back of her throat. Once you get the hang of it, using a dispenser can be easier than trying to get your finger into the back of your cat's throat. If the cat struggles, you'll have problems even with a dispenser, so wrapping the cat as described above is always the best option. Ezy Dose is a well-known brand and is available at all pet stores and even some supermarkets and pharmacies.

Droppers and syringes, available at pharmacies and pet stores, can be used to give liquids by mouth. Just stay away from any made of glass, which could break if the cat bites down.

Compounded medications can be made by many veterinarians. This is a simple process by which doctors can transform an often nasty-tasting pill that a cat will not tolerate into a tasty flavored liquid (tuna, beef or bacon) that she will willingly eat.

Neutering and Spaying

In order to fully appreciate why there is such a dedicated campaign by everyone who loves cats to get them neutered, you need to know how the desire to reproduce negatively affects the behavior and personality of cats.

TOMCATS AND NEUTERING

Unneutered male cats, known as tomcats, often cause day-to-day problems both with their aggressive personalities and with their personal habits, particularly spraying. Tomcats tend to be more territorial than unneutered males. They view more territory as their personal turf and wander farther, therefore frequently challenging other cats and winding up in bloody fights.

◆ Problems with Other Cats

An unneutered male will challenge other male cats and often wind up needing emergency trips to the vet for stitches. These wounds can later become infected, and the biting and scratching during catfights also pose a threat of spreading infectious diseases such as FeLV and FIV. Neutering would eliminate almost all of this, since most catfights involve tomcats.

◆ Problems in the House

Urine spraying is the worst habit of an uncastrated male cat, especially because the urine of an unneutered male has a more pungent odor.

◆ Problems with People

Tomcats can get wound up when you caress or groom them, building up a level of emotional intensity that can spill over and cause scratching, biting and sexual mounting behavior toward people. At times, a tomcat will bite your hand as you are petting him, or otherwise threaten or frighten you.

◆ Benefits of Castration

Once castrated, a male cat will stop spraying indoors—in most cases, he will spray only outdoors (if he has any access to the outside world)—and his urine will lose that intense odor. There's also less chance of stimulation turning into aggression from him when you're giving him affection or playing with him. Probably the greatest benefit of neutering is that it makes a cat more friendly and sociable with people and with other cats. Neutered toms are more playful and actually demand more attention from us because they have been freed from the intense drive to patrol and procreate.

◆ The Actual Procedure

Castration of a male cat involves a brief anesthesia and is done in a few minutes. When the cat wakes up he can go right home, and life goes on as before, no longer interrupted by all that nasty tom behavior.

FEMALES AND SPAYING

◆ Menstruation and Pregnancy

Do not expect any information in this book about female heat cycles, menstruation or pregnancy, regardless of how all-inclusive the book is otherwise. There are millions of unwanted cats and kittens in this world, and perfectly sweet, healthy, beautiful ones are killed in droves every day. There is no excuse to even contemplate breeding a cat unless that is your profession or avocation, in which case you know what you need to know or other breeders will take you under their wing. It is thoroughly unacceptable for anyone else to have unspayed or unneutered cats, especially people who claim to love cats. The widespread murder of tens of thousands of cats in our country alone is a crying shame that can be halted the day that all cats except for purebred breeding stock are neutered. Conscientious breeders are the first to agree with that and carry it out on their own non-show cats and even some they do exhibit, which is permitted.

◆ What Effect Does Spaying Have?

What is the female reproductive cycle? A female usually comes into heat twice a year; however, if the female is not bred, she will come into heat again within a week or two, and then over and over again if she is not impregnated. The unspayed female is a drama queen who can make life miserable because in addition to her loud wailing, she may also rub against objects, roll around on the floor, point her hindquarters invitingly in the air and generally try to be the center of attention.

The personality of a female cat is not as heavily influenced by neutering as the male's is, but spaying does prevent the loud and incessant calling that we hear from unneutered females when they are in heat and driven by instinct to seek a sexual partner. The loud calling for a mate happens mostly at night and can be intolerable for owners and neighbors. Some of the very vocal Asian breeds of cats (Siamese and Burmese) are even more verbally demonstrative, making an unspayed female of these breeds even more difficult to bear.

◆ The Age for Spaying

Females usually come into heat for the first time around 4 or 5 months of age. Most vets like to spay before the first heat because it lowers the chance that your cat will get deadly mammary cancer later in life. However, the age range for a kitten to reach sexual maturity is enormous—anywhere from 3 to 18 months. This means that an individual kitten can come into season before you arrange to have her spayed, so be very careful not to let her out of the house if she comes into heat. A female in heat is compelled to look for a tomcat to impregnate her.

By the way, don't project any associations that go along with the human experience of sexual reproduction on your cat. People make a terrible mistake when they mistake their cat's powerful drive to mate as some warm and fuzzy desire on a cat's part to experience motherhood and raise a family. Cats do not have those human emotions; instead, they are driven by basic instincts, as are all animals, to eat, to stay alive and to breed. The drive to reproduce is powerful because it ensures the continuance of the species, but getting pregnant has no emotional component for cats. Intercourse is actually painful for females, as anyone who has lived above an urban alley with strays can tell you. The consummation of the sex act sounds a lot like someone being murdered, which is due to the fact that the tomcat's penis is actually barbed, ensuring that it stays in when it goes in—but when he pulls it back out, that is why you hear those wails of agony from the female.

The Behavior of a Cat in Heat. A cat in heat is a miserable creature—she will act restless and nervous with strange facial expressions that seem angry or frightened, while sticking her butt up in the air in front of other cats, kneading the ground and making an array of intense crooning or calling sounds. She seems inhabited by demons—and often sounds like it. In fact, the first heat for some kittens can last for weeks and your cat's calling can become so unbearable for you and neighbors that you may want to ask your vet to spay her even while she's in heat. This is not difficult and many vets will agree to it for everyone's peace of mind—and to eliminate the possibility that she will instinctually find her way out and get pregnant.

◆ The Procedure Itself

The uterus and ovaries are removed in a short operation under anesthesia. The wound is small, requiring only a stitch or two, often with self-dissolving thread, or stitches the vet will remove in about a week.

◆ What If She's Already Pregnant?

A cat can be spayed in her first trimester of pregnancy, which will obviously terminate the pregnancy. However, surgery at this stage is a high-risk procedure since the uterus is active and more likely to bleed, so you might want to consider looking for homes for the kittens instead.

Obsessive-Compulsive Behavior

Cats can engage in the same behavior over and over again, which is then referred to as *obsessive-compulsive*, just as it is in human behavior. For example, a cat who excessively grooms herself, which some will do to the point of creating open wounds, is engaging in obsessive behavior which is a compulsion for her—once she starts, she doesn't seem to be able to stop herself. The behavior itself can become an addiction for her, the reason being that some compulsive behaviors release endorphins, which are natural opioid compounds in the brain. These compounds themselves are addictive, and so the repetitive behavior itself becomes addictive because doing it is what triggers the pleasurable compound. Your vet may be able to help you break your cat of habitual compulsive behavior by using drugs that block the effects of those endorphins in the brain, thereby interrupting the cycle of addiction. Also consider natural remedies from www.spiritessence.com.

Oral Problems

Your cat may paw at her mouth, stop eating, drool or have bad breath, all possible symptoms of *gingivitis*—gum inflammation, the same as can happen to humans with dental problems. Another oral problem is called *stomatitis*, which is inflammation of the entire mouth. There are several possible reasons for these painful conditions, either specific to the mouth or indicative of a larger physical problem. If you notice these symptoms, schedule a visit to your vet to begin the process of finding out the cause of the inflammation and controlling it.

Parasites and Pesticides

Cats can be infected by many different kinds of parasites, and many can cause diseases. *Worms* are internal parasites that may sound disgusting or dirty, but they are a natural part of a cat's life and can be easily treated by your vet. *Fleas* are a problem that can take over your house as well as your cat if you don't keep them in check, and they can transmit a disease called bartonella to them. *Mos-*

quitoes carry the devastating disease known as heartworm, which is a silent killer, but they are easily prevented with the right products. *Ticks* are fortunately less of a problem because cats groom themselves so effectively and are not susceptible to Lyme disease or other tick-borne illnesses.

SOME THOUGHTS ABOUT CHEMICALS ON OUR CATS

The conundrum about pesticides is that while they are a health risk to humans and animals, they can also keep away deadly diseases and physical discomforts. We use chemicals to deny parasites the "free lunch" they take off our pets while transferring diseases, yet we pay a price by exposing our cats to the toxic chemicals to protect them. Keep in mind that because cats constantly lick their fur, they therefore ingest the chemicals, which move through the intestinal tract, filter through the liver and kidneys and are eliminated in urine and feces.

In America, pesticides are often used on plants or animals until they cause enough damage to be banned—at which point another chemical replaces them until the ill effects of *that* product are documented and it is banned in turn. Those in charge of testing and regulating the chemicals we use in the environment consider some level of damage to be "acceptable." So each person has to decide for himself what amount of risk he is willing to take: Products designed to protect our cats against parasites may cause a bad reaction in some cats, and they are also perilous to small children. While proponents of alternative health care make a passionate case against pesticides, I don't see how most of us can avoid them until there is another way to effectively eliminate fleas, ticks and the misery they bring. Weigh the risks and benefits of using pesticides on your pet, depending on her state of health and lifestyle, and use the smallest amount necessary of those chemicals to keep her safe and comfortable.

The active ingredients in pesticides you put on your cat—imidacloprid, fipronil, permethrin, methoprene, pyriproxyfen—have all been linked to serious side effects. These ingredients are neurotoxins, carcinogens and teratogens, and they've been shown to cause nervous system damage, cancer, fetal damage and organ damage in laboratory animals. Several of these products warn on the label that cats that have close physical contact with dogs treated with products are at special risk of toxic exposure themselves. Just think how dangerous and powerful a product must be if a cat can get sick just by rubbing against a dog who has been treated with it. "Inert ingredients" in these products can be as toxic and damaging as the active ones, but current regulations do not require the inert ingredients to be rigorously tested, or even listed on the products. This means there may be undisclosed toxic ingredients in these products, in addition to the ones we know have caused adverse effects on mice, rats and dogs in laboratory tests.

FLEAS AND HOW TO CONTROL THEM

These horrible little insects can live in your house while feeding periodically on your cat's blood. It isn't really the flea bite that causes the problem, it's the flea's saliva that causes skin irritations. For a cat who is particularly allergic, the bites can become a major problem. The cat will lick and bite at her irritated skin, causing what is called a "hot spot," which in turn can become infected—and this can mean multiple vet visits with a variety of medications.

Make sure you treat all animals in your home, because dog and cat fleas are interchangeable and if one of your pets has fleas, all are affected (even though some may not scratch if they have less reaction to the bites).

Fleas spend only a small part of their time feeding on you or your pets. The rest of the time, they are laying eggs in your house and yard that will hatch into more fleas just waiting to procreate. Fleas reproduce year-round in many parts of the United States and can thrive indoors even when the weather is cold outside. If your cat goes outside or other animals have access to your property, you have to attack the fleas not just on your cat but also in your yard and in your house. Adult fleas are the ones that bite, but you also have to kill developing fleas before they reach adulthood to avoid a big infestation, especially in the hot months when fleas do their multiplying.

Sprays and foggers contain ingredients with a quick-kill component to destroy adult fleas, along with an insect growth regulator (IGR) that keeps the immature eggs from developing. However, they are highly toxic to the environment and to people, so you cannot safely bomb your house or yard. It is more responsible and environmentally friendly to focus your attention directly on your cat and to clean your house as rigorously as possible until the life cycle of the fleas has ended by using the on-cat products described below.

The sure way to eliminate fleas is to keep to a set regimen: Vacuum the house daily (put a flea collar in the vacuum bag to kill any fleas or their larvae), wash the pet's bedding frequently and keep using flea products on your cat every month.

◆ The Choice of Products

Caution: Please read the manufacturer's warnings carefully. Never use multiple flea products at one time. For example, giving your cat a flea bath and putting a flea collar on her is a dangerous combination.

On-Cat Products. You can use a monthly topical product that you apply between the shoulder blades so that it enters the cat's bloodstream without her being able to lick it. These are so effective that you often do not have to treat the environment with powerful pesticides. The two best-known products of this kind are *Advantage* (imidacloprid), which kills all fleas on the cat within 12 to 24 hours, and *Frontline* (fipronil), which kills adult fleas, repels fleas and can also be used on kittens over 12 weeks old.

Other products that target fleas are *Revolution* (selamectin), which is available only through your vet and has numerous benefits: It controls fleas by causing a sort of neuromuscular paralysis in the insects, and it also prevents heartworm, ear mites, scabies and ticks. It kills adult fleas and also prevents eggs from hatching. *Sentinel* is a flavored pill that protects against fleas, heartworm and intestinal parasites (worms) by preventing their eggs from hatching, although it is not labeled for use in cats. Sentinel does not kill adult fleas, so its effectiveness won't be seen for several weeks if you have a flea infestation and you'll need a spray to kill the fleas that are already populating your cat. *Interceptor* also takes care of heartworm and intestinal parasites at the same time.

Program (lufenuron) can be given as a monthly pill or a once-every-six-months injection; it does not target adult fleas but kills flea eggs and reduces the population. *Capstar* has to be taken every day as part of a total flea prevention program, but used in a higher concentration under your vet's supervision it can also be used to kill off severe flea infestations in a few hours. It can even be given to kittens from 4 weeks of age.

Bio Spot is a topical flea product that prevents flea eggs from developing and protects against ticks and mosquitoes. It is available in pet stores and many people use it, but because of reports of adverse reactions, it may not be safe for use on cats.

With any of these products, please work with your vet to come up with a safe and effective treatment plan tailored to the area you live in and your cat's lifestyle.

◆ What Does Not Work Against Fleas

Flea baths used to be a common treatment, but with the development of pesticides, baths are now considered fairly useless. The fleas get washed out of your cat's fur, but their cousins will jump right back on as soon as the cat is dry, and they can still infest the cat's bedding and the household carpeting.

Flea dips can be toxic to cats and are not in use anymore, despite anything you might read about then. *Warning about Persians:* Persian cats are hypersensitive to the chemicals in flea dips, which can kill them. Never dip a Persian, but occasional flea shampoos or sprays are all right if absolutely necessary.

Chemical flea collars have gone out of favor, both because there were health questions about putting the anti-flea toxin right against your pet's skin and because more effective, less toxic and longer-lasting products have been developed.

Flea sprays are useless because cats detest being sprayed, and even if you could completely spray your entire cat, she would proceed to immediately lick it all off, filling herself with the pesticide.

Electronic flea collars have never been proven to do anything.

Nutritional supplements such as garlic, brewer's yeast and B vitamins provide no protection against fleas, despite claims to the contrary.

MOSQUITOES AND THE DISEASES THEY SPREAD

◆ Heartworm

Heartworm is a potentially fatal disease that any cat can get in a geographic area where mosquitoes breed. Heartworm may show no serious outward signs in a cat, or the signs can seem like many other feline illnesses—but it can be devastating. It's unclear why vets do not usually educate people about this risk to cats, who need every bit of protection they can get from it, even cats who stay mostly indoors. Please go to the American Heartworm Society (www.heartwormsociety.org) for more information.

Geographical Need. Please note that heartworm is a vastly undertreated illness in cats. In whatever areas dogs are being protected from heartworm, cats should also be on a preventive medication, especially if you live in an area where mosquitoes breed. Heartworm tests for cats are not reliable, so you need to evaluate your cat's need for protection with your vet based on the prevalence of mosquitoes where you live. Illness is less likely in the Northeast than in the southeastern states, where it is best to consistently keep your cat on heartworm medication.

The Disease Itself. Dogs are the hosts for heartworm disease, and can have immature heartworm larvae circulating in their blood. The illness is spread to other animals when a mosquito draws blood from an infected dog and the insect takes in the microscopic larvae with that blood meal. Over 2 to 3 weeks the larvae develop inside the mosquito; when they reach the infectious stage and the mosquito feeds again on another dog or on a cat, the insect transmits the infectious larvae into the bloodstream of the new host. It takes months for the worms to develop, traveling through the animal's body until they reach the right side of the heart and the arteries of the lungs. In cats, the main location where heartworms grow is in the lungs, despite the name of the parasite.

How to Know If Your Pet Is Infected. Because heartworms can take years to develop, and blood tests on cats are inconclusive about whether the worms are in their bodies, testing becomes pointless. Years ago, it was thought to be dangerous to give preventive medication against heartworm to animals already infected. However, that is no longer a worry. Since there is no way to know through outward signs or from a blood test whether a cat has been infected, it is recommended to protect all cats with preventive medication.

Preventive Medications for Heartworm. Feline practitioners are alarmed because unlike dogs, 65 percent of whom are given medication, fewer than 5 percent of all cats are on heartworm prevention. Since there is no way to be certain that a cat has not been infected, and there is no effective treatment, the only way to keep a cat safe is to have her on preventive care. Think of it as polio in people—preventive medication was the only option. There are three equally effective medications available that need to be used every month, year round. Heartgard for Cats (ivermectin) is a chewable tablet, while topical solutions to put on the skin monthly are Revolution (selemectin) and Interceptor (milbemycin oxine).

Increased Risk of Heartworm When Traveling. Because so many people choose to travel with their dogs and cats, the incidence of heartworm is spreading, and the illness can now be found across most of the United States. Many dogs and cats have immature heartworm larvae in their blood, unbeknownst to anyone. All it takes is for a mosquito to bite them, and then for them to contaminate local pets, who can then in turn pass on the heartworm to pets in other areas as soon as a mosquito there transmits the disease.

Texas has a much greater number of heartworm cases than any other state in the country. In a study conducted by the American Heartworm Society (www.heartwormsociety.org), Texas had nearly twice as many cases as the next most infected state, Florida, followed by Louisiana, North Carolina, Georgia, Mississippi, Tennessee, South Carolina, Alabama, Indiana, Arkansas, Missouri, Illinois and Michigan. But when you take into consideration how many people on the East Coast spend winters in Florida with their pets and then bring them back up north, you can see how easily the disease can spread across state lines. The only responsible way to keep your cat and others from becoming infected is to keep her on heartworm medication year round.

◆ **West Nile Virus**

The only way West Nile virus can be transmitted is when mosquitoes feed on birds that are carrying the virus and then pass the disease to humans and other animals by biting them. The virus cannot be transmitted directly between animals, or from animals to people. Wild birds and horses are the only animals identified as carriers of the virus; the risk to pets is very low. The best way to prevent West Nile is to reduce the chance of your cat being bitten by mosquitoes.

REDUCING YOUR CAT'S EXPOSURE TO MOSQUITOES

• Keep pets indoors during early morning and evening hours, when mosquitoes are most actively flying around, if you live in an area where mosquitoes are prevalent.

• Consult with your vet before applying any repellent to your cat because it is considered unwise. There are pyrethrin-based flea sprays with directions for use in cats, but many vets do not advocate using them.

• Do not use mosquito products intended for people. Many insect repellents designed for human use contain a chemical that can cause serious illness in cats.

• Do not use any product containing DEET, which research has shown to cause serious adverse effects in pets.

• Avoid citrus oil extracts (citronella) and essential oils; some cats are sensitive to these products.

• If pesticides are sprayed in your area, keep your cat(s) indoors with the windows shut tight during spraying and for several hours afterward.

INTESTINAL WORMS

Although the idea may be sickening, it is quite common for cats and kittens to have a variety of parasitic worms in their intestinal tracts. There are tapeworms, roundworms, whipworms and others—all of which can be identified by your vet from fecal samples. Depending on the kind of worm that is using your cat's body as a host, your vet will give you a deworming medication to kill off the parasites. Talk to your vet about how often he recommends that you bring in a stool sample for testing, since cats are regularly exposed to these parasites. Worms are not life-threatening to cats as long as they are regularly banished with medication.

Skin Problems

There are a lot of reasons cats develop skin problems and you should not try to diagnose them for yourself—only your vet can do the tests necessary to determine what is bothering your cat's skin and what treatment is going to work. The categories under which skin problems fall are:

Parasitic: caused by fleas, lice, mites; the most common of the skin problems.
Fungal: caused by yeast and mold infections like ringworm.
Neoplastic: skin cancer.
Nutritional: caused by deficiency in diet.

Seborrheic: comes from overproduction of keratin, resulting in blackheads, scales and crusting on chin and lips; related to feline acne.

Viral: cats with FIV and FeLV can be infected by viral agents.

Bacterial: from scrapes, bites or scratches; can develop into an abcess (a pus-filled wound).

Hormonal: caused by a malfunction of the thyroid or pancreas, which produce hormones.

Immunologic: an allergic reaction to pollen or dust.

Thyroid Disease

Hyperthyroidism, or an overactive thyroid caused by a tumor on the thyroid gland, is one of the top three diseases from which older cats suffer.

SYMPTOMS OF THYROID PROBLEMS

The cluster of signs that distinguishes thyroid disease includes constant hunger yet weight loss, increased thirst, increased urination and high blood pressure. The cat is also often in a hyperactive state, with nighttime crying and aimless pacing. A physical exam by your vet will let him feel whether either lobe of the thyroid gland is enlarged, whether your cat has high blood pressure and whether a blood test shows elevated thyroid levels.

TREATMENT OF THYROID PROBLEMS

The most common treatment is for the cat to be given thyroid pills twice a day, but considering how difficult it is to "pill" a cat, you may want to opt for the choice of surgery to remove the offending lobe of the gland. This option is often ultimately less expensive than a lifetime on thyroid medication. The use of radioactive iodine to treat thyroid disease is much less common because there are attendant risks for the human caretakers, since the cat's feces and urine will be radioactive afterwards.

Urinary System Problems (FLUTD, FUS)

Cats are prone to problems with their bladders and their urethras (the tube leading out of the body from the bladder). These problems are often all lumped together as FLUTD, or feline lower urinary tract disease (which is also known as FUS, or feline urologic syndrome). They can happen to cats of any age, and although females get inflammation as often as males, males can get obstructions because of their long, narrow urethras and are unable to pass the crystals, while females rarely get an obstruction since crystals and stones can pass right out.

The problems generally stem from crystals that form in the urine, causing inflammation of the bladder and/or urinary tract lining or blockage of the urethra so that the cat cannot urinate at all. Urinary blockage is a true medical emergency: If it goes untreated, it can be fatal in a male cat. You need to always be on the lookout for symptoms of urinary problems before they become a life-threatening crisis, which is one reason cats should not be left home alone for extended periods of time.

BLOOD-DETECTING LITTER

A lower urinary tract infection can quickly become a life-threatening blockage in a cat, but it's almost impossible for you to see one of the important clues to a problem: blood in the urine. There is a litter than combines blood-detecting granules with Odor Lockers litter—a small packet of blood-detecting granules comes with the litter, which you stir in. When the white granules come into contact with blood in the urine or stool, they turn blue—giving you an early warning to contact your vet right away. This allows you to get help for your cat before the condition escalates to the point that the cat is having symptoms. The product is available at most pet stores, or you can visit their Web site, www.odorlockers.com, or call them toll-free at 888-223-8199 for more information.

Signs of Urinary Problems

- Straining when using the litter box
- Blood or pink-tinged urine (see Odor Lockers, above)
- Crying out or distress when urinating
- Change in urine color or odor
- Expelling small amounts of urine
- Inability to urinate at all
- Urinating outside the litter box
- Frequent trips to litter box (often without wetting much)
- Incontinence (leaking urine)
- Licking genitals frequently
- Abdominal (stomach) tenderness or distension
- Loss of appetite and/or loss of weight
- Change in attitude: restlessness, irritability, depression

TWO KINDS OF URINARY CRYSTALS

The crystals or small stones that develop in a cat's urinary tract can be of two kinds: The most common is called *struvite;* the other is *calcium oxalate.* It's important to have your vet identify which type your cat has, since each is managed with a quite different diet. There are commercial cat diets that claim to prevent the formation of struvite crystals by maintaining a more acidic pH in the urine. However, the conundrum is that highly acidic urine can actually *cause* the other type of stones, calcium oxalate, to form. Calcium oxalate stones form as a by-product of a cat's metabolism of protein, and they are more likely to form in acidic urine, so keeping a cat's urine crystal-free can be a delicate balancing act. The role of diet in crystal formation is crucial (see below).

Urinary stones are painful, costly to treat and life-threatening, so you and your vet need to know for sure what you are dealing with in order to find the best possible treatment for your kitty.

CANNED VERSUS DRY FOOD

The best diet for a cat who is prone to stones is one that eliminates dry food. Canned food is 75 percent water, which ensures that the cat is consuming a good amount of liquid. In nature, cats do not need to drink much water since they consume their liquids through the blood and bodily fluids of the animals they eat. This would explain why cats on all-kibble diets frequently develop urinary problems and constipation as a result of the dehydrating effects of dry food.

The other fact about commercial kibble that is rarely discussed and vets may not even know about is that dry cat foods with their high plant content actually *cause* a very alkaline urine pH. Alkaline urine causes an unnatural environment in the bladder that can lead to inflammation and stones. The normal urine of a meat-eating animal is acidic (a pH lower than 7.4), which is a healthy pH for the bladder, whereas alkaline urine is higher than 7.4 and can lead to stone formation and urinary tract infections, too.

Ironically, dry cat foods are sprayed with an acidifier that manufacturers have discovered makes the kibble more appealing to cats (for unknown reasons). The acidifying spray, which attracts cats to the kibble, happens to also help balance the alkaline effect of the food. However, the whole thing is a manipulation of what would be a naturally balanced urine pH if a cat ate her natural diet of meat. It should be clear that you can keep your cat out of this dietary/urinary vicious cycle by avoiding kibble entirely and keeping her on a healthy, all-wet-food diet.

MEDICAL TREATMENT FOR URINARY TRACT BLOCKAGE

If your cat cannot urinate or is struggling to do so, the vet may insert a catheter into her bladder to empty all the urine. After examining the cat, the doctor might give IV fluids if she is dehydrated (one of the main causes of FLUTD). The doctor will do whatever is necessary to remove the crystals blocking the urinary system after determining what kind of crystals they are, which can include further testing or even surgery if necessary.

Maintaining long-term wellness and preventing the formation of further crystals involves a change in diet to wet food exclusively, an increase in exercise and keeping the cat's weight down. If you can stimulate her to drink more water, too, that is further insurance against crystal and stone formation.

INCREASING WATER INTAKE

Urine that is greatly diluted—as opposed to concentrated—has less chance of developing crystals or stones. In theory, the goal for a cat with a tendency toward crystal formation would be to encourage her to drink as much water as possible, except that for most cats, drinking water is not a natural habit. Feeding only wet food already goes a long way toward satisfying a cat's natural need to acquire her moisture through her food, which in nature would be comprised of 75 percent fluids.

Making the water more inviting is one way to stimulate a cat to drink more. Change the water frequently in your cat's bowl, and wash the bowl out carefully without leaving a soap residue— this may encourage a few more sips than usual. Some cats seem inspired to drink from water "fountains" that have flowing water that recirculates—these pump-driven electric water bowls are costly; they take up a good deal of floor space and may not trick a clever cat into drinking anyway. It would be a shame to invest in one and discover your cat is not so easily manipulated.

The other often-heard advice is to make the cat thirstier by giving her a diet that includes salt. There are commercially prepared prescription foods that do just this, but it seems unhealthy and backward thinking to give her a dry food that is already dehydrating and then to add sodium (salt) to counteract this by driving her to drink more. And all this dietary seesawing is just to compensate for feeding her food in a bag and getting back to where she would be if she hadn't eaten dry food in the first place.

OTHER FACTORS CAUSING CRYSTALS AND STONES

The dilution of the cat's urine is certainly important, and when a cat consumes only canned or raw food, she has dilute urine; a higher volume of urine means she will empty her bladder more frequently, all of which will make it less likely for crystals to form. The other considerations in what causes stones are environmental lifestyle issues, like a cat's activity level (more is better) and stress level (less is better).

SPECIALIZED COMMERICAL FOODS FOR URINARY STONES

A number of commercial cat food manufacturers have come out with prescription-diet dry foods intended to prevent urinary stones. Many veterinarians are recommending them based on the companies' own claims of success. I suggest that you be willing to make your own decisions about ongoing healthy nutrition for your cat, now that you are equipped with some knowledge about the way dry food can cause stones—even if another dry food claims to be able to cure them.

Royal Canin is a pet food that is well-known abroad but has only recently come to the United States, where the company has made a particular effort to promote its cat food. They have a food in both dry and wet form they call Urinary S/O that is aimed at cats and reducing the occurrence of *both* types of urinary stones. Previous attempts by food companies to modify a cat's diet to guard against production of struvite stones by creating an acidic environment in the bladder often led to the creation of calcium oxalate stones. This new food was formulated to increase the amount of urine a cat produces—but by artificially making the cat thirsty to increase drinking, something not natural to cats, as explained earlier. The canned version of Royal Canin Urinary S/O is a higher quality food, if only because it is not kibble. The company's own studies showed no stones returned in nearly 90 percent of cats with previous stones who were fed the food in the can—while in 40 percent of cats who were fed the dry version, stones recurred. Their own studies show the negative effect of kibble, even one presumably made for a specific reason. However, there was no study to see whether a cat fed a normal diet of canned food would have done as well or even better than a cat eating the veterinarian-prescribed canned food. There are many cat nutritionists who believe that eliminating dry food prevents stone formation.

Eagle Pack makes a "Hairball formula" dry food that some experts claim keeps their cats crystal-free. This company's foods are all formulated to create a target urine pH of 6.0—which is considered the ideal pH to keep urinary stones from forming. However, a basic knowledge of the problems with dry food would deter many from feeding a cat a product like this.

C/D is a well-known prescription food formulated to influence the composition of the urine to prevent crystals from forming. It is prescribed by vets because the food has been successful at discouraging crystal formation. However, there are certified animal nutritionists who will not recommend C/D as a long-term food because of the poor quality of its ingredients. While this food may reduce crystal formation, the nutrition experts do not view it as a fair trade-off to sacrifice good overall health.

CRANBERRIES AND THE URINARY TRACT

It was once thought that adding cranberries to a cat's diet increased acidity in the urine, keeping it in a low pH range and preventing urinary problems. However, it turns out that the benefits were not because of the acidifying properties of cranberries. Instead, it is believed that cranberries help by discouraging infection-causing bacteria from growing on the walls of the bladder and urinary tract. However, the most common bladder problems in cats—straining, painful urination and stones—are usually not related to bacterial infections. So while you might be interested in putting powdered cranberries in your cat's food, there's no telling if it would be beneficial, and cranberries are a fruit, which should be avoided in cats because they can cause problems with blood sugar.

Vomiting

Cats throw up for a lot of reasons, and longtime cat owners will tell you that they will also throw up for no good reason at all. Vomiting is a natural reflex for a cat, some more than others, so it helps to know your own cat's tendencies. If she gets hairballs frequently and throws up trying to cough them up, you can give her some Petromalt or other intestinal lubricant as a hairball remedy. If your cat is vomiting persistently or acting ill in any other way, take her to your vet.

If your cat throws up every once in a while but otherwise seems healthy and normal, it's probably just a case of mild tummy troubles. If a cat throws up once, it doesn't require any response from you. If she throws up a second time in one day or night, however, you might want to call your vet and describe to him (or the vet tech who answers the phone, who probably hears this sort of thing frequently) what the cat's vomit looked like. This allows the vet to decide whether the cat needs to come in for an office visit or should just take it easy at home. Your vet will usually advise that you take away food for 12 to 24 hours to give the cat's stomach a chance to rest and repair, followed by a bland diet such as white chicken meat for a day or two. It's usually considered fine to make water available during the period when you are resting her upset stomach.

HAIRBALLS AS A REASON FOR VOMITING

Self-grooming causes a cat to swallow a lot of her own hair, which becomes a hairball in her stomach. Most of it passes through the system and exits in the stool, but if it gets matted up in the stomach, it has to come back out the way it came in, hence a fair amount of hacking and heaving for the cat to expel it by vomiting. But if a cat has a lot of hair in her gastrointestinal tract, it can obstruct the esophagus, the stomach or the small intestine. And if large quantities of hair wind up in the large intestine, it can cause inflammation and/or constipation. The sound of a cat hacking up a hairball is pretty disgusting, and it must be pretty uncomfortable for her, too.

Vomiting That Requires a Vet Visit

Vomiting blood or a black coffee-grounds-like substance—internal bleeding

Vomiting a foreign object—requires X-rays to see what is left inside

Vomiting worms: bits of stringlike roundworm can come up, especially in kittens (vet will give deworming medicine)

Vomiting but unable to defecate—intestinal blockage, could be very serious

Vomiting feces—same as above, requires emergency care

Projectile vomiting (it shoots out)—serious indication of tumor or blockage

Vomiting more than once a week—could be a disease such as irritable bowel syndrome

Vomiting more and more frequently—see idiopathic vomiting (below)

Preventing hairballs from forming. You can minimize the formation of hairballs by grooming your cat with a good brush at least twice a week, to reduce the amount of hair that she swallows. You can also give a lubricant preparation such as Petromalt every week. The idea behind these medications is that they will make the swallowed hair slippery so it will pass through the intestine more easily. Based on your vet's advice, you can decide how often to administer the paste (usually an inch-long piece is smeared on her paws so she will lick it off) and see whether that diminishes hairball formation. Make sure you only use a product formulated for hairballs—don't try to use mineral oil or fish oil, which can be swallowed incorrectly and go into the cat's lungs instead of her stomach.

EATING TOO FAST OR OVEREATING

In a multi-cat household, cats may feel a sense of urgency to finish all their food quickly—or to eat as much as possible. This competitive eating can drive some cats to gobble down not only their own food but that of their housemate(s), and this can cause vomiting. The best solution is to feed the cats with eating issues in separate locations so their eating is regulated by their own appetites and not a contest with another cat.

NIBBLING ON "CAT GRASS"

Cats enjoy and/or have a physical need to eat grass to stimulate and cleanse their digestive system. Supply your cat with a little planter of cat grass from the pet store as a nice perk of being a house cat. But expect some vomiting to follow grass eating, since it is thought that one of the reasons cats eat grass is to induce vomiting.

INCREASINGLY FREQUENT VOMITING

There are some cases where a cat starts out throwing up every month, then every week, then nearly every time she eats. At that point the vet needs to do a full workup on the cat, including prescribing a hypoallergenic diet. If none of that makes a difference, your cat may have a condition called *idiopathic vomiting syndrome*. A cat with this condition seems in good spirits and does not lose weight, but vomits with increasing frequency. Your vet may have some different solutions to try, but one that has been tested is giving a cat a decreasing dosage of the dog birth control pill Ovaban, which can function as an anti-vomiting drug.

Euthanasia

Although cats are stoic about physical ailments, when a cat is nearing the end of her time with you, there are ways to know that she is ready to go. If you know what to look for, euthanasia is an option that allows you to make the decision about the right time to end her life. Because cats do not cry out or make noises of pain, people often don't realize that their cat is giving out until it is too late. As your vet will tell you, if your aging cat is getting weaker and you wait too long, her lungs may fill with fluid until she is gasping for breath and weak from dehydration. To avoid making her wait until she has reached that miserable point, and especially if you have a senior cat who has been going downhill, keep an eye out for the symptoms on the following chart. Doing this does not put you on a ghoulish death watch, but rather ensures that your older cat will have a good quality of life and then a peaceful, painless end.

When the end is near, a cat will have more than one of the symptoms below:

Signs That the End Is Near

- *Confusion*—Can't find her bed or litter box
- *Purring constantly* for no apparent reason
- *Eyes unfocused*—Staring at nothing
- *Weakness*—Staggering, leaning against walls or furniture, collapsing
- *Sitting or lying in litter box*
- *Lying or crouching with head over water or food dish*
- *Rapid breathing, lips parted*
- *Abdominal effort with breathing*
- *Cold ears, paws, legs*—temperature below 100.5°F
- *Refusing warmth* even though cold
- *Not acknowledging your presence or attention to her*

WHEN THE TIME COMES TO LET GO

Putting a cat to sleep is a painful and difficult decision, but one that most owners have to face at some time. However, your cat does not suffer the emotional turmoil you do—she doesn't know what you are considering, so don't imagine that she knows anything when she gives you a "long look." Neither will she suffer physically when the time comes, since euthanasia is a painless procedure that takes very little time—the cat is unconscious within seconds of the first shot, and after that her heart stops.

Euthanasia is the medical word for what we usually refer to as "putting a cat to sleep" and the cat *does* just close her eyes and seem to go to sleep. As difficult a decision and experience as it is for us, it is actually a gift to an ailing, suffering pet. It is our final act of selflessness and love.

✦ Modern Medicine Can Make It More Difficult

Advances in veterinary care can make the difficult decision to put a cat to sleep even more difficult. New procedures and medications make it possible to prolong the life of an old cat—even a very sick one. Almost every medical intervention available to people—from cancer treatments to pacemakers—is now available to pets.

✦ Does the Medical Care Enhance Quality of Life?

Is prolonging her life good for your cat? Even with all the advanced medical techniques and treatments available, this does not mean that every owner should necessarily be trying to get them for his cat. What if your cat can gain only a few weeks or months of life from a procedure that will take a great deal of your time, emotion and money? A family member or a medical provider may be able to help you find a proper perspective that takes into account your cat's physical and emotional state, as well as your own. You have to ask yourself the tough question: "Am I doing this for me, because I cannot stand the idea of letting my cat go, or do I believe it will result in some more months of quality life for her?"

✦ Will Medical Intervention Just Prolong Suffering?

Even if money or your time were of no consequence, in any medical situation with an older cat who is very sick you have to question whether you are doing the right thing by putting her through radiation, chemotherapy, dialysis or operations. The trauma, pain and possible long confinement or repeated hospital visits should be weighed against a peaceful end to her life at home with you, in some cases with medication to alleviate her suffering. Sometimes the most humane and loving thing to do is to allow your cat to end her life swiftly, with dignity and your attentive affection, rather than medically prolonging it with teams of medical professionals.

✦ What About *Your* Quality of Life?

Complex medical treatments cost a great deal of money (even pet insurance only goes so far) and can involve multiple days of dropping off and picking up your cat and handling her reaction to the treatment. Ask yourself whether you can handle the emotion, time and cost demanded of you in such a situation. If you have a human family who needs you, a job you have been neglecting or other demands on your resources, please give them the weight they deserve in your decision-making process. Just because you are *willing* to go into debt to pay for some special treatment for your cat does not necessarily mean you *should* do it, if what you are considering will only buy some less-than-great time for your sick cat.

Do not feel guilty or defensive about your decision. If your cat is really sick or has a terminal disease, more often than not it is a blessing to be able to offer her the privilege of leaving this world on a good day, or at least to be able to shorten the number of bad days.

✦ How to Know When the Time Has Come

"Playing God" Is a Burden. Deciding when it is time to euthanize your cat is really a big responsibility. There is no perfect time or correct way to do it.

It's a Deeply Personal Decision. Each owner will have her own guidelines and conscience to guide her to make the best possible decision. Don't let anyone push you either way, but you may need to talk it through with someone to feel at peace with your decision. Be aware that the experience of your cat's illness (or advancing age) may trigger complicated and painful memories of a person or previous pet in your life who was once at a similar juncture. Dealing with your cat's imminent death, especially death preceded by pain and suffering, may stir up your feelings about that earlier time, so to the best of your ability try to make decisions for your cat that are separate from those intense memories. Only you know what is right for you and for your cat—and if you are not sure, then discuss it with your vet or someone close to you who will give you feedback based on respect for your situation and your outlook on life.

More Bad Days than Good. Many people try to decide when the time for euthanasia has come by determining whether their cat has reached the point of having more bad days than good ones. They ask themselves: "Is she having more pain than pleasure? Can she no longer do the things she loves? Is she suffering from physical pain or a loss of dignity because of incontinence, not being able to climb stairs or falling down?"

"She'll still eat," other people say, thinking they cannot justify ending the life of a sick or old pet who is still eating. Just because a cat continues to eat doesn't necessarily mean she's feeling good or has a good quality of life; eating is merely a survival instinct. You owe it to her to take other things into consideration to decide whether she may be ready. If you wait until your cat will no longer eat, you may have waited until she is suffering significantly—even though she does not show the pain.

WHERE SHOULD THE END COME?

✦ Staying Beside Your Cat

Deciding whether to be with your cat when she is put to sleep depends on your feelings. You can prepare yourself for anything unusual that might happen by looking at the list later in this section. Certainly your cat would feel more relaxed and comforted to have you by her side, but if you feel you cannot stand being there, then you have to follow your instincts. Also, if you feel you might break down uncontrollably and become really emotionally distressed before she is gone, you don't want her to pick up on your anxiety and become agitated, too.

✦ Euthanasia at the Vet's Office

Most veterinary offices have a lot of experience with putting pets to sleep, so they are well aware of the emotional intensity it creates for owners and their families. You may fear that you will break down when you are putting your cat to sleep, but that is natural and normal, and your vet and the staff understand. Or if you are the kind of person who keeps it all in and doesn't show any emotion,

you may be concerned that the staff will think you don't care. It is understandable to feel self-conscious about how you will handle it. Vets have seen many kinds of reactions. They know how much people's pets mean to them, and they will not judge the way you deal with your grief.

Some animal clinics have a euthanasia room that allows you privacy and the chance to make your cat's passing a personalized, spiritual experience. Some people light candles or incense, play music or have others present. With the help of a compassionate veterinarian, euthanasia can be an almost spiritual emotional event, or a peaceful relief for you if your aging cat has been ill or suffering. Even in a regular room at the vet's, you can personalize the experience in whatever way makes it more bearable for you.

✦ Euthanasia at Home
You may feel more comfortable having your cat put to sleep at home. This may be because you want the privacy or because your cat is really anxious about going to the vet under any circumstances and you don't want her final moments to be frightening. Most veterinarians will make arrangements to come to your home before or after hours if your cat has been a longtime patient. If your vet cannot assist you because you live too far away or there are other practical impediments, the doctor should be able to inform you of a mobile vet whose practice is based on home visits.

Some people fear having the memory of the cat's death in their house, even if they feel it would be easiest for her to be put to sleep there. They worry that they will always look at the spot where it took place and be emotionally haunted by it. The decision of where to end your pet's life is one that only you can make.

✦ Plan a Special Time Together
Assuming that your cat is well enough, you might want to plan a special "farewell time" together with her, depending on where you live, what your cat's pleasures usually are and her condition, even if it makes you more sad.

THE LOGISTICS OF THE PROCEDURE

✦ You Don't Have to Go in the Main Entrance
If you have made an appointment ahead of time to have your pet euthanized, most veterinary hospitals will not expect you to go in the main door and sit in the waiting room. If they do not inform you ahead of time of an alternative entrance, ask them where it is so you can bypass the other cats and people out front and be shown right into a room.

✦ Where to Actually Do It
If you want to hold your cat on the examination table and stand beside her, that is fine, but being up on the table makes many cats anxious, so it might be preferable to get down on the floor with her. Depending on your own physical mobility and how alert your cat is, it may be best to have her lie on a blanket on the floor, where she can be put to sleep with you sitting or kneeling next to her, or holding her in your arms. If so, you should wear clothes that allow you to sit comfortably on the floor beside her. Your vet will undoubtedly accommodate your wishes.

◆ Bring a Blanket or Ask If They Can Provide One

Some vet offices will provide a blanket or bedding for your cat, which they can use to lift and wrap the body afterward, if you are going to transport her. You may want to bring a familiar blanket or quilt for her to lie on—one that you would want her to be wrapped in afterward if you plan on taking the body home. However, if you are going to leave her body for cremation, burial or disposal, the blanket should be one you are willing to forfeit.

◆ First She Will Get an Injection to Calm Her

Before beginning, some vets will insert an IV catheter into the cat's leg. Although this is an additional medical procedure, some vets like to use it so that they don't have to locate the vein later on to inject the fatal dose. Once you are settled in with your kitty—whether you cradle her head or just stay nearby stroking her and perhaps speaking to her—the doctor will give her a shot of tranquilizer. You may find it helpful to have the doctor tell you what he is doing each step of the way, along with how it might affect your cat. If so, ask him beforehand if he would do this.

The tranquilizing shot may sting a little and get a pain reaction from your cat, but that's the worst that will happen. Within moments, she will be heavy-lidded and groggy, and she may close her eyes. Vets say this is a nice mental zone for the cat to be in. Sometimes the cat will give a big sigh (of what may seem to us to be relief) as the tranquilizer enters her bloodstream. Some cats may appear to be agitated or excited; this is called "involuntary excitement," during which the cat can't control her reflexes, but this is a rare reaction. The sedative affects the brain, so the cat appears agitated but is not experiencing any distress.

◆ An Overdose of Anesthesia

Next, the doctor will inject an overdose of anesthesia in the cat's vein, and she will drift away very quickly. So before that medication is injected, you'll have a final moment in which she'll still be conscious (even though she is groggy and super-relaxed) if you want to say any last words to her.

First, the doctor will prepare the cat's front leg for the injection. (If an IV catheter was placed this preparation is not necessary.) He will place a tourniquet or press a finger against the bone high up on her leg and may shave a small patch of hair below it if necessary. Then he will slide the needle directly into the vein—the cat will probably not feel it since she may already be asleep at this point from the sedative. Then the anesthetic medication will take your cat out of her suffering forever. She may look as though she is in a very deep sleep and she is completely unconscious at this point, perhaps still breathing very slowly, with only seconds before the drug takes effect. The cat's brain and feeling will go first, although the heart muscle may continue a little past that point. The doctor will listen to the cat's heart with a stethoscope to be sure it has stopped. Once it has, the doctor will often say something like, "She is gone now."

◆ Time Alone with the Body

You may want to spend some time with your cat's body. For some people the lifeless body may seem gruesome, but for others being with it is an important first step in the grieving process. This is not entirely different from the feelings and realities that people have to grapple with when a

Possible Physical Reactions to Euthanasia

- At the end, the cat may have spasms, twitches or tremors.
- Her tongue may protrude out of her mouth.
- Her eyes may open partially and seem to be rolled back into the sockets.
- She may exhale all the air left in her lungs with what seems to be a sigh (but at this point she is actually dead and feels nothing).
- She may make a "last gasp," the final contraction of the chest muscle (but she's completely unconscious and not experiencing distress or anything else).
- The bowels may evacuate or the bladder empty (the body releases everything).
- The abdominal contents may gurgle.
- Fluid or blood might drip from the nose or mouth (depends on the cat's illness).
- Some breaths may continue past brain death (the last part of the brain to go regulates breathing).

person they love dies. If you are afraid of what your cat will look like afterward, be assured that this is a peaceful way to go and that your cat's expression and body will reflect that.

◆ Odd Things to Expect During Euthanasia

Some unsettling things may happen at different points during the euthanasia process, and it can be reassuring to know ahead of time what they might be. These physical events are simply the body letting go, since whatever you may think of as the spirit or soul is gone by then.

WHAT TO DO WITH THE REMAINS

There are three ways that people can deal with their cat's body, and it is a good idea to consider the options and make a decision ahead of time. You may be too emotional to think very clearly after your cat is put to sleep, and it can be a relief to have made a plan beforehand. You can leave her body behind, you can take her home to bury or you can have her cremated and receive the remains.

◆ Leave the Cat's Body at the Vet Clinic

If burial at home is not allowed where you live or is not practical, your vet can arrange for the body to be picked up and disposed of. If this is the most practical choice for you, you can still have a memorial without the body (see below).

There is usually a disposal fee (approximately $50) for leaving your cat's body at the vet's. Some doctors will absorb this fee out of consideration for your feelings, although you should know that the vet certainly has to pay to have the body removed.

◆ Have Her Body Cremated

For 2007, the cost of cremation was $200 or more in most areas; the service is provided by a company that will ship you the container of ashes within a few weeks. Some people worry that the ashes are only from their cat and not mixed with the remains of other animals. Depending on where you live, there are some crematories that allow people to wait (but not watch) while their animal's body is cremated, and then they receive the ashes right there.

♦ Take the Cat's Body Home for Burial
Every local area has its own rules about whether burial is allowed on residential land. If it's not allowed where you live, you may know someone in a more rural setting who would let you bury your cat or her ashes on his or her land.

♦ Pet Cemeteries
You can also arrange to bury your cat's ashes or body at a pet cemetery. You might be surprised to learn that there are 400 such pet cemeteries at various locations throughout the United States, and you can get details about them on the Web site of the International Association of Pet Cemeteries and Crematories (www.iaopc.com).

A pet cemetery can offer a wide range of services, everything from burial or cremation to predeath planning, caskets, urns and monuments, funerals and memorial services, silk or seasonal flowers and concrete vaults. These facilities charge a wide range of prices for burial and funeral services, anywhere from $350 to over $2,000, depending on the plot, the casket, the headstone and the ceremony you may choose.

When choosing a cemetery, make sure it is deeded so that there can never be future development on the land, and also find out whether the facility has funds set aside to maintain the grounds.

A SAMPLING OF SOME BETTER-KNOWN CEMETERIES

Hartsdale Pet Cemetery & Crematory, Hartsdale, New York, 800-375-5234, petcem.com
Hinsdale Animal Cemetery, Willowbrook, Illinois, 630-323-5120, petcemetery.org
The Memorial Pet Cemetery, Roseville, Minnesota, 651-646-6821
Oregon Humane Society, Portland, Oregon, 503-285-7722, oregonhumane.org
Pet Heaven Memorial Park, Miami, Florida, 305-223-6515, pet-heaven.com
Smoke Rise Farm Pet Cemetery, Azle, Texas, 817-444-2221, smokerisefarmpetcemetary.net
S.O.P.H.I.E., Inc. (Save Our Pets' History in Eternity)/Los Angeles Pet Memorial Park, Calabasas, California, 818-591-7037, lapetcemetery.com

GRIEF OVER LOSING YOUR CAT
You may be surprised at how intensely you, or others around you, react to the loss of your cat. If you weren't expecting such a depth of feeling, you may be uncomfortable about it, perhaps feeling self-conscious to have been so attached to an animal. The grief that some people experience over the loss of their cat is more profound than the grief they have felt for people they have lost, which can be disturbing. It may help you to better understand this intense emotion if you realize that for many of us, when we lose a cat what we feel is the end of that whole era of our lives that the cat lived through with us. So we aren't just mourning the loss of our devoted kitty, we are also

grieving for all those years we shared with her, and the personal and professional ups and downs during which she was by our side.

Accept your grief as a testament to the depth of your feeling for your cat; the profound way in which she enhanced your life is commensurate with the depth of your sadness in losing her.

✦ The Six Stages of Grief

If you have suffered a profound personal loss before, you may be familiar with what psychologists have identified as the six stages that people go through when they are grieving. Everyone does not necessarily experience all of these emotions, and they don't always appear in this order:

Denial. This reaction can begin while your cat is still alive—you may be in disbelief when you are told she is injured or has a disease that may take her life. If her death was sudden and you had little or no time to prepare yourself for the loss, a natural reaction is to question your veterinarian's competence. You may voice doubts about whether your vet was right in his diagnosis or whether he made good choices in care and gave you good information. You may "doctor-shop" the way terminally ill people are known to do, looking for a more optimistic evaluation of your cat's condition. This is an example of being in denial about the prognosis for your pet.

Before seeking out alternative or non-Western therapies, drawn by stories of "miracle" cures, you might be better off if you stop to question the logic of these stories. If herbal medicines or offbeat ingredients could truly cure cancer, you can be pretty sure that there would be widespread, successful use of them in the mainstream medical community.

Guilt. Owners commonly feel guilty about deciding to euthanize a cat, and this guilt can be made worse depending on the circumstances of the cat's death and whatever part human choices played in the decision. For example, "If only I'd taken her to the vet sooner . . ." is a thought many of us have had after our cat was diagnosed with a deadly illness. Even if an earlier diagnosis would not have saved her life, it is natural to wonder if our tardiness in seeking medical attention allowed the disease to flourish. If your cat is killed by a car because someone carelessly left a gate, fence or door open, you may feel guilty about it or angry at whomever was the careless one.

Anger/Blame. You may experience illogical, angry feelings as part of the grief process and you may place blame all over the place—on caregivers, family members, friends and anyone else who was part of the end of your cat's life, whether it was the person driving the car that hit your cat, or the assistant at the vet's office who handed you back your cat's collar after euthanasia.

Bargaining. This is another stage of grief that some people experience when they have cats who are gravely ill. It is a primitive sort of superstitious "deal" that you might make with yourself that if your cat recovers you'll promise to do something specific (give up some personal pleasure, make a contribution to a charity) or effect some sort of change in general (pay more attention to your cat, be nicer to people at work.)

Depression. When the reality of your cat's death sets in, which for some people will be soon after the death and for others may be months later, after experiencing other stages of grief, then the sadness will take over. The depression people feel about their lost pets can provoke reactions that are every bit as intense as for the loss of a loved person: crying, eating disturbances, withdrawing from activities, lethargy, sleeping too much. Some people may feel that life has no meaning and that there is no reason to go on living without their beloved kitty. If thoughts of suicide enter the pictures, these must be taken seriously, whether or not other people can understand and respect that the loss of a loved animal might drive someone to end his own life. This phase of grief, when depression sets in, is when people often seek out professional help, because of how much pain they are feeling, but also because they're having trouble dealing with day-to-day life. *If your feelings are this intense, they could be dangerous and you should seek help from a professional.*

Acceptance. During this final stage of grief, the pain will have lessened, and although sadness about your cat may come in waves for a long time, you can resume most aspects of your everyday life. All of the feelings mentioned so far can still surface, but usually with less intensity and for a shorter amount of time. You may still cry about your cat for weeks or occasionally for years to come; your sadness about losing her may hit you when you least expect it. Allow yourself these feelings—don't judge yourself and don't try to repress these sentiments—because they are normal and healthy. It might make your intense sadness easier to accept if you view it as an expression of how deeply you loved your cat.

◆ Rituals and Grief

There is a social reason for many of the rituals surrounding death in human society. Just as rituals help when a person dies, they can help people coping with a cat's death. You might want to consider whether having a structured expression of grief would make you feel more at peace and satisfy a need to celebrate your cat's place in your life and heart. There are any number of ways to ritualize your loss.

A Memorial to Your Cat. If you have a yard, you may want to set aside an area and plant something special as a tribute to your kitty. You can also order a memorial marker engraved with your pet's name and dates and a message (see the list at the end of this section). You can also make a contribution in your cat's memory to a local animal rescue group or shelter. Another way to remember your cat is to make a gift in her name to the veterinary school that your veterinarian attended; most schools have provisions to take contributions in this way. This allows you to celebrate your pet by helping less fortunate companion animals or furthering research, while showing gratitude to the doctor who cared for her during her life.

Some Other Ways to Commemorate Your Pet. Have a tree planted (www.treegivers.com, 800-862-8733); donate a public bench locally in the cat's memory; have a memorial service; make charitable donations in your pet's name to a local animal rescue organization, to a national animal welfare group such as the Humane Society of the United States (www.hsus.org, 202-452-1100) or to a veterinary research program (such as those at Cornell or Tufts), or to the Morris Animal Foundation (www.morrisanimalfoundation.org, 800-243-2345), which funds veterinary research.

Place a Memorial Stone in Your Garden. Companies that provide these services are available on the Internet or through advertisements in the back of cat magazines such as *Cat Fancy*. One reliable company I have used repeatedly for lovely and affordable stones is Carved Graphics at www.carvedgraphics.com.

RESOURCES FOR PET MEMORIALS, URNS AND COMMEMORATIVE KEEPSAKES

All Pets Crematory and Remembrances, Stamford, Connecticut, 203-967-4949, toll-free 866-334-PETS, www.allpetscrematory.com

OldYeller.net Pet Memorials, San Francisco, California 415-558-9977, www.oldyeller.net

Rock-It Creations, Council, Idaho, toll-free 866-Z-ROCK-IT, www.rockitcreations.com

Personal Creations, Burr Ridge, Illinois, toll-free 800-326-6626, www.personalcreations.com

Whisper in the Heart, Antioch, California, 925-755-WITH, www.whisperintheheart.com

Forever Pets, Inc., St. Paul, Minnesota, toll-free 888-450-7727, www.foreverpets.com

My Cherished Pet, Henderson, Kentucky, 888-830-6412, www.mycherishedpet.com

The Pooka, Ulen, Minnesota, 218-596-8360, www.thepooka.com

RoxAnn's Glass House, Commack, New York, 631-266-3167, www.glassbyrox.com

◆ Find a Sympathetic Ear

Seek out friends who understand the importance of your pet's love and your loss. It may be that your best company will be other pet owners—others who have lost a pet can be particularly empathetic to what you are experiencing. Don't belittle your grief. Your cat was a member of your family, your loss is very real and your sadness is legitimate. Don't let anyone else belittle the pain you are feeling because it's "only" about an animal—non-cat-owning friends can fail to recognize that your cat may have been your constant companion, or even closest friend, for years. They don't mean to sound callous and insensitive, but they can be nonetheless.

◆ Pet-Loss Support Groups and Hotlines

The Web site www.petloss.com started in 1992 as an online pet bulletin board designed to pay tribute to departed pals and share solace and advice. This Web site has attracted hundreds of thousands of visitors, and there are now dozens of other Web sites devoted to pet loss. Reaching out for compassion and guidance from those who have had a similar experience and understand your grief is an excellent way to cope and get support.

Over the past decade, telephone hotlines, and in some cases e-mail hotlines, have emerged as part of a growing social recognition that it isn't "just an animal" people lose when their cat dies. The human-animal bond is being taken seriously, and people's grief is being shown respect and compassion. Several veterinary colleges have hotlines that are manned at no charge by students in veterinary medicine at the colleges. They are not professional counselors but receive special

Pet Loss Support Lines

Chicago Veterinary Medical College, 630-603-3994
Colorado State University, 970-491-4143
Cornell University, 607-253-3932
Grief Recovery Hotline, 800-445-4808
Iams Company Pet Loss Support Hotline, 888-332-7738
Iowa State University, 888-478-7574
Michigan State University, 517-432-2696
Ohio State University, 614-292-1823
Pet Grief Support Service (Arizona), 602-995-5885
Tufts University, 508-839-7966
University of California at Davis, 800-565-1526, 530-752-4200
University of Florida, 800-798-6196, 352-392-4700
University of Illinois, 877-394-2273, 217-333-2760
University of Minnesota, 612-624-4747
University of Pennsylvania, 215-898-4529
Virginia-Maryland Regional College of Veterinary Medicine, 540-231-8038
Washington State University, 509-335-5704

education in grief counseling. In theory, this not only means that grieving people are helped, but that the next generation of vets will be that much more capable of dealing with the emotional needs of their human "patients." The vets-to-be learn important interpersonal skills and insight and gain valuable experience for the future while helping pet owners through a dark time.

Hotlines. Except for the 24-hour service offered by Pet Grief Support Service in Arizona (see below), phones are generally manned only from 6:00 P.M. to 9:00 P.M. (local time). If you leave a message and number, expect a call back collect. You don't need to call the one that's geographically close to you; you'll probably feel better just by reaching out to someone who understands what you're going through.

Pet Loss Grief Counseling on the Web. The American Veterinary Medical Association Web site is www.avma.org, and they have grief counseling under "Goodbye My Friend." Animal Love and Loss Network is an organization of pet loss counselors (www.alln.org). The Delta Society has information about counselors and links to support groups 425-226-7357 (www.deltasociety.org).

◆ Cats and Their Grieving
Cats also grieve over the loss of a close family member, human or animal. In addition to death, this can also include other human "disappearances" caused by divorce, a child going off to

school and so on. We don't know whether cats understand that a person or animal has left and is never returning or whether it is just the upset in the household routine, but they can be profoundly affected. If the cat loses a person with whom she was closely bonded, it can be months before she is totally herself again. If she loses a companion cat or dog, she can mourn, too.

The Surviving Cat(s) and Euthanasia. A theory has floated around that the cat(s) left behind after a housemate is euthanized should stay with the dead cat's body for hours. These advocates say that the other cat(s) will be scared, fascinated or disinterested, but that eventually it may help them to pay their "last respects." But there is no proof from wild cats that any mourning goes on in their species, so why would we try to impose this fairly macabre concept on our house cats? There are even some advocates of having your other cat(s) present for the euthanasia itself, but to me this is a ghoulish idea, possibly even cruel to the cat(s) left behind, for whom it could be distressing and even traumatic to witness the death of their companion.

Obviously we cannot know what, if anything, death means to a cat, but why risk doing the wrong thing? Go with your own instincts. Don't do anything that makes you uncomfortable, since your remaining cat(s) may not have any need to spend time with a dead body in order to grieve and move on.

Cats are individuals with reactions that are not always predictable: One companion cat may not react at all to his departed pal's death, whereas another may be devastated when her housemate dies, and go into a deep depression and stop eating. Because you could say that, on some level, cats are as varied about experiencing and expressing grief as we are, it is inappropriate to impose some funereal ritual on them.

Easing Your Cat Through Her Grief. A cat may need help getting through her grieving process, so here are some suggestions of ways to support and understand your cat as she goes through this transition. Give your cat more time and attention than you ordinarily would, but don't overdo it and focus so much emotion on her that she gets "hooked" on the grief-related behavior. Keep the surviving cat's schedule as consistent as you can—it is a comfort to her to stick to the routines she had before, which include mealtimes, exercise and grooming. Add some new elements into the cat's life to give her something to focus on. Get her a great new climbing tree or wall perches rubbed with catnip or some new lure toys you can use to play with her. Don't let her lie around depressed. If she has lost her appetite, go ahead and indulge her with some tasty additions to her usual fare.

Chapter 14

A LITTLE OF EVERYTHING ELSE

This chapter is the place for all the miscellaneous topics, a mixed bag of issues that are every bit as important as those with chapters dedicated to them, but just not substantial enough to need a whole section to themselves: senior cats; training (particularly leash training); feral cats; cat care when you travel; and lost and found.

Senior Cats

The cat population is getting larger all the time. More than half of the cats in our lives are older than 6, and at age 8 they are officially considered seniors. Understanding the issues facing our older cats and being prepared to deal with them will make the transition easier for both species.

The major health concerns for older cats are arthritis, cancer, dental disease (including cancers in the mouth), diabetes, hyperthyroidism, kidney failure and urinary tract diseases.

SIGNS THAT YOUR CAT IS GETTING OLDER

We all know that as we humans get older we tend to slow down a bit—we're slower to react, slower-moving—and this is as true of our cats as it is of us. It's helpful to know about some of the specific signs of aging in cats because it will help you to understand that changes in your cat after about age 10 are natural. Some possibly strange behaviors are a normal part of a cat's aging process, and accommodating your routines and household around them can make the golden years more mellow for you and your senior kitty. As your cat's muzzle turns a little whiter, what follows are the things to be on the lookout for.

◆ Low Energy, Slow Motion

A cat's metabolism slows down as she gets older, so she may have less zip. Add that to the normal aches and pains of creaky arthritic joints, and you have a cat who is moving slowly in everything she does. You should be taking her to the vet for a checkup twice a year, for lab tests to rule out physical problems such as thyroid imbalance (usually hyperthyroidism), diabetes, kidney problems and other metabolic issues. If you have *not* been following the recommendation to take your senior cat to the vet twice a year, then right now is definitely a good time to make an appointment to have her checked out.

◆ Can't Handle Temperature Change

The older she gets, the less a cat is able to adjust her inner thermostat. In a hot climate or during the summer months she will need a cool place to chill out, and a cozy, warm spot is ideal during the winter.

◆ Lots of Snoozing

Older cats sleep a great deal; it's the natural course of things. Cats sleep a lot at the beginning of their lives when they are kittens, and again when they are seniors.

◆ "Senior Moments"

If you see your cat start off down the hall and then stop as if she's wondering where she was going . . . that may be exactly what she's doing. It's really not that different from what happens to people as we get older and our brains have those cloudy moments. (It is both distressing and comical to go to the garage and not have any idea what the heck you went there for—especially when you've finally just found the cordless phone in your *refrigerator*, where you last left it.) So be understanding of your aging cat's confused moments when she can't remember where she was going.

◆ Wandering Off

Because of the absentmindedness mentioned above, it is not safe to allow an older cat to be unsupervised outside. Leaving aside the whole indoor/outdoor debate, even if you live deep in the country and your cat has always had outdoor freedom, now is the time to start keeping a close eye on her outside. Think of treating her as you would your slightly senile grandmother if she wanted to go for a stroll—you wouldn't want to deny her the pleasure, but neither would you want to risk her getting hurt or disoriented. With your cat at an advanced age, you basically need to be physically outside any time she goes out, observing and following her if she goes off on her own—or you may choose to be even more cautious and keep her indoors all the time. With any freedom outside there is a chance that she will get lost: Unlike in earlier times, she can lose her bearings and end up unable to find her way home, even if she isn't far away. If you don't want your old girl to have to forfeit her fresh air and sunshine, look for ways to construct an outdoor cat patio in Chapter 4.

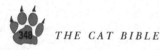

✦ Fear of Noises

Your cat may have been tolerant of loud sounds when she was younger, but now she may run and even hide at sounds that didn't used to affect her, such as banging pot lids, lawn mowers or electric appliances. This heightened sensitivity is normal for an aging cat.

✦ See Less, Hear Less

Old folks of every species lose some of their sight and hearing as they age. This can be true of your cat; be aware that she may not hear you calling her or may not see things as well as she once did. This should help explain some of the perplexing things that she does nowadays.

✦ Change in Socializing Patterns

If your cat shares your home with other cats, as she gets older her relationship with those cats may change. Generally, older cats withdraw from other cats, especially in their sleeping habits. They stop sleeping with the other cats, even if they have always curled up together at night. On the other hand, a cat who withdraws from other cats may become much more affectionate toward people—even to the point of being clingy—and may sit purring in your lap for long periods.

✦ Litter Box Issues

It is not uncommon for an older cat to start her visit to the litter box by urinating in it but then step outside the box to defecate. Nobody is sure what causes this lapse—arthritis is sometimes blamed for inappropriate elimination, but if she can get in the box just fine to urinate, then clearly mobility is not the issue. See Chapter 7 for solutions to litter box problems.

✦ Grooming Problems

A cat's nails get brittle and cannot retract easily as she ages, and it becomes difficult for her to remove the outer sheath. You can help with this by trimming her nails twice a week so they don't get out of hand.

SENIOR CAT CHECKLIST

Without making yourself crazy, it's a good idea to keep a much closer eye on your older cat than you may ever have before. Warning signs of mental or physical problems that can affect aging cats are clear, giving you a chance to seek medical help early if you do see any of these symptoms—and perhaps stop the problem from progressing. You should also be aware of the ways in which getting older is taking its toll on your cat's body and temperament. If you do see any of the changes on this checklist, it is well worth it to talk to your vet about them. I am not including any of the possible reasons or causes for these changes because this list is *not* intended as a tool for you to diagnose what is going on with your senior cat—that would be foolish and even pose a health hazard to your old-timer if you guess wrong. You don't need to know *why* things are changing; your vet will figure that out. You just need to be a watchdog (excuse the expression) to report on what is changing.

 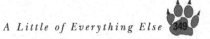

♦ The Three Most Common Medical Problems for Seniors

In descending order, the medical ailments that befall cats are kidney disease, thyroid disease and diabetes. Have a look in the alphabetical listing in Chapter 13 so you know the symptoms to look out for in order to catch them early. These disorders are treatable in older cats, and cats can live a long time with these problems when they are properly managed.

Changes in Your Older Cat

- Spatial disorientation (doesn't seem to know where she is)
- Wandering in unfamiliar areas
- Staring into space or at a wall for long periods
- Less playful
- Sleeping a great deal
- Changes in sleep cycle
- Sudden, prolonged unprovoked vocalization
- Unusual changes in appetite
- Weight loss or gain
- Indifference to water or drinking a lot
- Change in amount of urine produced
- Unusual stool—diarrhea, strange color, bloody
- Elimination outside the box (usually defecation)
- Change in skin or coat—dry, oily/greasy, flaky
- Stiffness/pain getting up, lameness/pain moving around
- Lumps anywhere, especially around the head and neck
- Inside the mouth: odor, red gums, growths, tongue problems
- Continuous coughing or sneezing
- Increasingly cloudy eyes—some is normal, more could mean cataracts
- Scratching ears—smelly or red inside

EMOTIONAL ASPECTS OF OLD AGE

We are now aware of the many vicissitudes of old age that affect our senior cats, and we are finding ways to ease the transition to the golden years of their lives. Years ago, people didn't pay as much attention to the odd behaviors that crop up in older feline citizens—but then again, we weren't always as concerned about the changes that older humans go through, either. Some of these quirky changes can be quite troublesome, such as the ones below.

♦ Senility

The outward signs of a cat who is getting senile are similar to the signs of senile dementia and Alzheimer's disease in people: confusion, lack of physical coordination and inappropriate

behavior. In fact when an autopsy is performed on an elderly cat, the physical changes in the brain are similar to those of people who died of Alzheimer's or dementia. Up to 80 percent of all cats over 16 show signs of senility.

◆ Nighttime Calling

Calling out in the middle of the night—a persistent, loud howling and screeching—is one of the most frequently reported strange behaviors of older cats. In some cases, it can occur constantly between midnight and dawn. Although this heartbreaking calling usually takes place at night, it can also happen anytime the cat is seeking reassurance or affection. When it first happens, you may jump out of bed with a pounding heart, fearing that your older cat is in terrible pain or some sort of jeopardy. However, you will undoubtedly discover the old gal just pacing around, not in need of anything in particular. It's as though she just needed to check in with you, get a reassuring cuddle in the long, dark, lonely night and then curl back up to sleep.

Nobody knows what triggers this mournful nighttime calling, but it is probably related to a vague anxiety and disorientation when an aging cat just doesn't feel right. Some people think it may come from a premonition by the cat that the end is near.

Beware of Letting an Older Cat "Teach" You to Come. Your older cat does not call out for you at night to purposely to trick you; she does it because of a confused emotional need, but beware of how you respond. If your cat discovers how quickly she can get you running to her side, her calling may become a purposeful act if you let it. Nighttime calling may begin with no purpose, but if your cat perceives that she is successfully "training" you to come running to her cries, she may turn you into a sleep-deprived slave to her whims.

Some Solutions to Nighttime Calling. Learning not to run to your cat's side when she cries out will help preserve your sleep and sanity, but it is also the best thing for your cat's sake. If you jump up and pander to those "nightmares" of hers, it is ultimately a validation that something really is wrong, and you can make her think she needs you there. When you come at her first cry, what you have done is rewarded her for crying out. Instead, if you don't jump up or respond in a dramatic way, your calm demeanor may reassure the old gal and lessen the frequency of her outbursts—she may even regain some of her earlier confidence and tranquility.

If your cat has not traditionally slept in your bedroom, as she gets older and begins to exhibit this sort of dependent, anxious behavior, you might want to consider allowing her to sleep in your room with you. Many people deal with the situation of nighttime calling by putting the cat's favorite bed right next to theirs. This way if your cat becomes disoriented or agitated and starts to holler for you in the middle of the night, you don't have to get out of bed; you can reach down and stroke her for reassurance.

Another solution is to place a baby monitor where the cat usually sleeps. When she cries out, you can talk to her soothingly over the intercom to calm her, rather than getting up. However, this will only work if her hearing is still good enough to hear your voice through the speaker!

Other suggestions include: Get a heated sleeping pad made especially for pets and put it on the cat's bed; this can give her comforting warmth while easing the aches and pains of older joints. Keep a radio turned on low to classical or easy-listening music, which can be soothing and lessen the possibility that distress is about feeling so alone. Turn on night-lights or a few table lamps so that when the cat is wandering around, dazed and confused in the dark of night, at least she can see where she is, even if she isn't sure where she is going. Cats see best at dusk, not in the pitch dark, and in addition, their vision diminishes as they get older.

MAKING THINGS A LITTLE EASIER ON HER

Here are some suggestions about ways you can make life more comfortable for your aging pussycat:

- ❏ Have a routine and stick to it. That will be a source of comfort to her.
- ❏ Do not think of introducing a new dog, cat or kitten. These are stressors she does not need and would have trouble coping with.
- ❏ Provide ramps and stepstools leading onto any bed or couch she enjoys.
- ❏ Make litter boxes easily accessible. Provide at least twice as many as you had when she was younger, and make sure they are easy for her to get in and out of.
- ❏ Bring her bed, litter box and feeding area closer together than they were previously. Despite cats not liking their food and litter box to be close together, the convenience factor of this proximity outweighs that instinctual dislike.
- ❏ Play gentle games to stimulate her mind and maintain mental agility.

Teaching and Training Cats

For any creature, the process of learning anything requires patience and a willingness to do it wrong and try again. Cats do not generally have the temperament to put up with frustration. A cat's reaction to a frustrating situation might be: "If at first you don't succeed, don't worry about it—just walk away and find something better to do, like lick your fur." The "try, try again" part just isn't for felines—they tend to yawn when they are in a situation that has no obvious route to a payoff. A cat must get an immediate and valuable treat from you in order to make the effort worthwhile for her. Knowing that you have a challenge in this area can be half the fun; if you have a mellow, interactive cat, you might want to experiment with ways to teach her, in which case this section has some pointers for how to do it.

TEACHING A CAT TO DO WHAT WE WANT

People have the idea about cats that they are very hard to train to do what we want because it doesn't interest them to do so. It's true that it is generally difficult to teach a cat anything, but if you are motivated to try, then you need to understand what makes a cat tick and work within that framework. Part of the reason it's so difficult to teach a cat is because it's nearly impossible to find something as a reward that will motivate a cat. Unlike with dogs, who will happily perform for a tasty morsel or a special toy or playing a game, working for a reward does not ring the bell for cats. Many cats appreciate attention and affection (in limited amounts), a cozy warm place to curl up or a special morsel of food, but with cats there is no easy way to offer these elements for a result, which is the generally accepted module of teaching by bribe or reward.

Cats generally follow their own track in life: They are not interested in pleasing us or performing for us. This independence and lack of interest in our approval is a central part of their "catness" and makes them so fascinating and alluring to us—but it makes training difficult.

POSITIVE REWARDS

◆ Food Treats
Food is pretty much the only physical reward you can offer a cat. If your cat responds to food when offered as a thank-you for doing what you want, then make sure that you give it right away, every time that the cat does what you wanted. Food rewards will be more effective if given when your cat is hungry, so plan to work before meals. Having established mealtimes makes it easier to know when she will be hungry. However, you don't want your cat to be so hungry that she is super-excited by the treat and is overly focused on the food instead of on understanding and learning what you are trying to teach her. Starving your cat by withholding all food and then dangling something tasty in front of her only works for cat-food commercials. What each cat considers a special treat varies quite a bit: What is heaven to one cat may mean nothing to another. Try each of the treat choices below and see which one your kitty loves best. But keep in mind that a cat has a small stomach (about the size of quarter), so treats should be no bigger than an unpopped kernel of corn or you'll fill her up.

Food Treats Cats Love

- Chip of cheese
- Sliver of sardine
- Tidbit of tuna
- Choice bit of chicken
- Dab of butter
- Smidge of meat baby food

◆ Catnip or Other Favorite Toy
If you have a frisky young kitten or a cat who is fun-loving and always ready for a game, then you may find good results using play as a reward for doing what you want. It really depends on the individual cat.

PUNISHMENT
Threats and punishment used to be an integral part of teaching—"spare the rod, spoil the child" was an attitude that prevailed for any training, whether of a person, dog or horse. However, using

negative reinforcement methods has since been found to be a *deterrent* to learning—it usually backfires and creates resistance, fear and distrust. Punishment is now generally frowned upon in any learning environment. Where cats are concerned, the effects are even more dramatic because using force or fear to try to get a point across can actually shut down communication on every level between the cat and the person dispensing the harshness, effectively destroying that relationship. In order to teach your cat anything, you must move slowly, gently and patiently. Or, for the sake of your relationship with your cat, walk away immediately if you don't think you can maintain that mind-set.

• Don't Raise Your Voice

Don't make threatening motions, either, and certainly never strike a cat. If you do any of these things, you may irreparably damage your relationship with your cat right then and there—and even come away with some nice claw marks as a future reminder of your mistake.

• Find a Deterrent

The best way to train a cat to stop doing a behavior you don't approve of is to create a deterrent that makes the behavior itself unpleasant for her. The deterrent must seem to the cat to come as a direct result of the forbidden place the cat has gone or what she has done. She cannot see you as the enforcer. You don't want to make a cat afraid of you or have her associate the negative reinforcement with you—it needs to appear to come from the action or location itself.

Booby Traps. To keep a cat out of some forbidden territories, you have to rig up a booby trap ahead of time to deter her from returning there in the future. For example, tie together empty soda cans and line them up on a kitchen counter so that they clatter down when the cat tries to jump up there.

Spray of Water. Another effective training technique is to spray a cat with water when she scratches her claws into furniture or jumps up on a forbidden table or counter. However, your timing must be perfect, because the water has to come so suddenly that the cat does not see it coming or connect it to you.

Loud Noise. A sharp, sudden noise will stop a cat in the middle of whatever she is doing. This is a good tool to use in a situation where you want to stop a cat from doing something that normally is not an issue, like to deter her just this once from going someplace you don't want her to go. You can drop a pot lid on the ground or create some clattering noise that does not seem to come from you.

A Hiss Sound from You. Making a *sssss* sound is a good deterrent because it is familiar to cats, who themselves use a hiss to signify displeasure. Although it comes from you, it does not cause physical discomfort or fear, so there is no danger of you being painted with the brush of being a bad guy.

Clapping Your Hands. A young kitten who is just learning what is acceptable behavior will accept you in the position of the mama cat who tells her what to do. When the cat is going somewhere you don't want, such as the kitchen counter or tabletop, walk toward her clapping your hands together briskly, saying "No!" at the same time. You are using the hand clapping as a nonphysical way of "pushing" her away from what she is doing. If your cat ignores you and continues on her mission, clap your hands again, but make sure you keep your voice neutral; do not raise your voice or let it sound angry.

◆ Don't Be Bossy

Cats do not respond well to being pushed around. Asserting your authority can be valuable in training dogs or horses, but it backfires with cats, who will not put up with that nonsense. You'll anger or alienate your cat if you bring along concepts such as obedience, discipline or respect for authority.

◆ Be Patient

Without patience you are doomed to fail. You cannot rush the process of teaching a cat. Nothing is going to happen on your timetable. Since cats cannot tolerate their *own* frustration, you can be darn sure they are not going to put up with *your* impatience.

TEACHING YOUR CAT TO WALK ON A LEASH

Leash training a cat has several applications. The first is that if you live in an urban area or densely populated suburban setting, a leash and harness allow your cat outside without danger of her running away, being run over by a vehicle or being attacked by dogs or other cats.

◆ Is Your Cat a Good Candidate for a Leash?

Leash training is so much easier if you start when the kitten is young because then it will be a normal aspect of her life: the fun of exploring the outside environment while physically connected to you. Although cats do not naturally want to walk on a leash, they can learn to do it and enjoy short explorations with you. Some cats will be unwilling to accept a harness and leash; some just panic when anyone tries to get a harness on them; other cats will not be able to cope with the outside world. For these types of cat, the better option is to stay home and be an indoor cat, doing what they please. But for those cats who can handle a harness and aren't afraid of the outside world, going for walks is great mental and physical exercise.

Some of the purebred cats generally known to do well on a leash are the Siamese, Burmese, Maine Coon and Bengal breeds. A cat with an easygoing personality tends to be easygoing about most everything, which is the kind of cat personality that is most adaptable to wearing a harness and going for walks. Starting leash training with a kitten is the easiest of all, but if you want to teach your adult cat to walk, it helps to evaluate the cat's personality before undertaking this adventure. See the chart below to determine whether your cat is a good leash candidate.

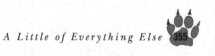

A Little of Everything Else 355

An Easygoing Cat Accepts . . .

- Being picked up
- Hugs or cuddles
- Toenail clipping
- Being given medication
- New sights and sounds
- Visits from strangers

◆ **Advance Preparations Before You Begin Leash Training**

Choose a Safe Room. You need to have a small room where you can begin getting your cat used to the harness and leash. It should be a fairly uncomplicated space, such as a bathroom, so that she can't escape or get stuck behind furniture if she bolts or panics. Even an easygoing cat may have an initial panicky reaction to having a harness around her or a leash trailing behind. A smaller, unfurnished safe room means fewer things to hide behind (you'd be at risk of getting scratched or bitten if you reached under or behind to extract her) and less opportunity that she could get her leash caught on some piece of furniture if she decides to leap over it. Either scenario would just make her more panicked and create a negative reaction to the leash, the opposite of what you're trying to accomplish. If your bathroom isn't large enough to move around in comfortably, then pick the smallest room you can and take out any furniture that might become obstacles to your cat's calm acceptance of the harness.

Make the Harness a Positive Experience. You want her to have only good, fun associations with the harness. Be ready with the treat your cat loves best so that when you buckle the harness on her it always means something good is happening. Tasty treats can help achieve that goal. If your cat isn't interested in food treats, then pull out her very favorite toy for a quick play session when you put the harness on.

Distraction Works During the Adjustment. If your kitten seems to have any issues with the harness, then be prepared to take her mind off it with something she really enjoys as soon as you pull that harness out. Right as you buckle it on, give her that little salmon treat or special tickle where she loves it.

Know What Makes Your Cat Smile. Before you start training, it helps to have a clear idea of what puts a smile on your kitten's face. Is it a special cat treat such as dried salmon or chicken, or a taste of cheese or human baby food? Is there a toy she just can't resist? (If so, save it for special circumstances like this.) Or does she bliss out when you use her favorite brush? Whatever rings your cat's bell, *that* is what you want to have ready to make leash training a happy experience.

You'll use it during the adjustment period to distract her, whether when you first buckle on the harness or start to practice with the leash itself.

Assume That Things Will Work Out. If you have a positive, calm, can-do attitude, it will help the process along. Just know that in most cases even cats who have a rough beginning with leash training will eventually get used to it and wind up being cats who take walks.

End the Training Session on an Up Note. Have your cat's favorite treats ready for her when you take the harness off.

◆ Directions for Using a Leash and Harness

These are the basic instructions to leash walking, which will be covered in more detail in the pages that follow. You'll need to buy a harness, a short leash for training (or an old dog leash cut short) and a long leash you'll eventually be using for walks, about 6 to 8 feet, but no longer than that or you won't be able to manage it. See the chapter on "Stuff" for information about a new harness and attached leash from Premier (which makes Gentle Leader for dogs).

1. First Get the Cat Used to Wearing a Harness. A harness is a much safer and ultimately more comfortable option for walking a cat than trying to use a leash with a collar. Buy a harness that is soft, adjustable and flexible and put it on the cat for short periods while the cat is indoors. Remove it if the cat becomes agitated—or better yet, note how long a cat can tolerate the harness before she gets uncomfortable, and take it off *before* she begins to resist wearing it. If your cat doesn't like the harness at all, try putting it on just before you feed her so that she connects the harness with something pleasurable.

Get your kitten used to the harness slowly. The best beginning you can give your kitten is to start out by putting on the harness for only a few minutes at a time. Gradually increase the amount of time she wears the harness around the house, starting with only a couple of minutes several times during a day, and work your way up to 30 minutes a day.

2. Use the Harness Without a Leash. During the adjustment period don't attach the leash to the harness since all you're doing at this point is getting your kitten or cat comfortable with the feeling on her. Let her wear the harness at first without attaching a leash or in any way manipulating her by the harness; you don't want her to feel trapped. During this time you're not actively demanding anything of the cat, just her compliance in having the thing on at all.

3. Next Attach a Short, Light Leash. As soon as the cat accepts the harness, you can attach a very short, light nylon leash to it. Let her drag it around for a few minutes so she can get used to the feeling of something being attached to the harness. You can move the leash around so that she swats at it, which makes it her toy.

4. Put on the Longer Leash and Pick It Up. When your cat is used to dragging the leash around, the next step will be for you to pick up the leash and follow her around. Keep in mind that your cat runs this show and decides where you go: You need to drop any ideas you may have about being in charge.

5. Walk Around With Her Indoors With the Harness and Leash. Start off with short walks for up to 10 or 15 minutes. Be sure to stuff your pockets with especially tasty treats and disperse them liberally during this period to reinforce that good things happen when the harness is on. However, at this stage you're not holding the leash nor influencing where the cat goes while wearing it.

6. Let the Cat Take You for a Walk. Don't put any pressure on the leash or try to pull her anywhere. Let her get accustomed to being attached to you; once she accepts that physical sensation, use a particularly succulent food treat to entice her to come along with you. If she won't walk forward with a nice piece of chicken held in front of her, then try a feather on a stick or a catnip toy you can dangle to get her to follow you around.

7. Next Put Some Pressure on the Leash. The cat needs to experience the feeling of light tension from you on the other end of the leash. You can gently pull on the leash with a little pressure, until the cat accepts this as a normal feeling, but it goes without saying that you should not be dragging the cat anywhere. The cat should accept that you put some pressure on the leash, and even allow you to gently steer her course. You're not looking for the kitten to obey you or go where you want; you just want her to accept the feeling of the connection of the harness and leash between you.

8. Move to a Larger Indoor Area and Practice There Before Going Outdoors. What the cat will be learning is that you are going to be close to her when she walks and that it is normal for her to feel some tension on the leash.

9. Trying It Outdoors. Once your cat is used to going around with you attached to her in the house, you're ready to try an outdoor foray. The area you pick for your first outdoor outing with the harness should be safe and quiet. The best location would be a quiet, fenced-in yard where you could take the kitten to explore without any chance of escape. Follow her around holding the leash for 5 or 10 minutes. Most cats will adjust to this controlled way of exploring the outside world.

If your cat has already been exposed to the many sights and sounds beyond your door, she has a greater chance of adapting to the challenge of taking walks outside. See the chart earlier in this section to get an idea of whether your cat will be a good candidate for this experiment.

◆ Fearful Reactions to Leash Walking Outdoors

A cat who has been relaxed and confident walking on a harness and leash in the house may surprise you by freaking out when she steps outside. There are so many new sights and sounds on a suburban street or city sidewalk—people, cars, strollers, bikes, dogs on leashes, children, buses, you name it!

A cat's natural reaction when frightened is to flee—which is true for many animals, of course.

If you have a fearful or timid cat who panics when you expose her to the big, bad world out there, you need to have someplace for her to escape and take refuge, even if it means bringing her travel carrier along.

• **Tips About Harness and Leash Walking**

Don't Ever Leave a Cat Unattended Wearing a Harness. Without supervision a cat can get hurt or frightened if the harness gets hooked on something and traps her.

Do Not Let the Cat Walk out the Front Door. When you are going outside with the cat, *carry her* over the threshold, both when going out and coming back in. Better yet, if you have an alternative exit from the house other than the front door, use that, but still carry her. You don't want the cat getting comfortable with the idea that she can walk through an open door. Put her harness on at a distance from the door so that she does not associate the harness going on with being allowed to leave on her own. When you return home, carry her back inside and go to that same area away from the door to remove her harness after the walk.

Don't Go into Busy, High-Traffic Areas or Places Where There Might Be Dogs. If possible, avoid areas of high congestion where there are many things that could frighten a cat. The harness is enough for the cat to get used to without adding external fear factors.

You're Not Trying to Make the Kitten Obey You or Go Where You Want. This is not about obedience; leash-walking a cat is just a safe way to let a cat be outside and explore the world.

Stay Out for as Long as the Cat Seems to Be Happy. But always keep hold of the leash. You don't ever want to risk losing the cat because she gets spooked and takes off, even in a fenced yard. Fence or no fence, a frightened cat will get away and may never come back. If the cat gets fidgety, she's had enough and it's time to go back inside.

Don't Start What You Don't Intend to Continue. If you take your indoor cat out on a harness and she loves it, you pretty much have a moral obligation after that to make a habit of taking her out whenever possible. How unkind would it be to give her a good long look at the outside world and then close her back indoors without more visits to that fascinating world out there?

Cat Care When You Travel

The official name for a boarding facility that takes cats is a *cattery*. Although some are quite nice, being taken to a cattery is really stressful for a cat. Most cats are really better off in their own homes being visited once (or preferably twice) a day. Furthermore, cats can pass illness to other cats very easily, so this risk factor is also worrisome.

ALTERNATIVES TO A COMMERCIAL CATTERY
(BOARDING FACILITY)

◆ Enlist a Neighbor, Friend or Family Member

Bring home a wonderful and extravagant present for the person willing to be your cat nanny, visiting the cat once or twice a day—or, even better, staying over at your house.

◆ Create a Local Group of Cat Enthusiasts

You can form such a network yourself by asking local veterinarians and pet stores if you could put a sign up on their boards with your name and phone number and something like "Share Cat Sitting with Your Friends and Neighbors." All it takes is three or four people who don't live far from each other to barter time among themselves and look in on each other's cats.

◆ Sign Up for an Online Community such as PawSpot

The Internet is global, but some Web sites have found a way to be as local as your corner store. The site www.pawspot.com is an animal-lovers' community designed for people to create their own personal pet-sitting network. You create an e-mail list of friends and neighbors you can turn to for reciprocal cat-sitting—you visit my cat, I'll visit yours—so with one click of your mouse you can ask for a hand with your cat or lend one to a friend or acquaintance.

◆ Hire a Professional Pet Sitter

Believe it or not, there are thousands of professional pet sitters, many of whom belong to national organizations that collect dues from them, offer conferences and provide a central clearinghouse where potential clients can find them by geographical location. NAPPS (National Association of Professional Pet Sitters) is one such group and is a nonprofit organization run by its own members. The group and its members can be reached at www.petsitters.org.

The obvious benefit of a sitter who comes to your house is that your cat's routine is not disrupted, and we know how important predictability and stability are to a cat—especially if she will also be dealing with the stress of your absence.

A pet sitter usually charges by the visit, so if you have multiple cats, the cost can be lower than a cattery that charges a daily rate per cat. Here are some questions you should ask a pet sitter, who, as a professional, will expect to answer them.

It is not a waste of time to follow up on the names the sitter gives you. However, when you reach the reference, ask no more than four or five questions so that you are not a pain in the neck. A few questions should suffice: "When did this sitter work for you and how did it work out? Have you recommended her to friends? Was there anything that didn't seem quite right or made you uncomfortable?"

Questions for a Pet Sitter

- Are you bonded and insured?
- How long have you been a pet sitter?
- Is there another sitter who covers for you if necessary?
- Do you charge by the pet, the visit or the amount of time? Does this include travel?
- What do you do on a visit besides scoop the litter and give meals?
- Is this your only job? If not, what hours are you free to make the visits?
- Do you have three recent referrals?
- What veterinarian(s) do you use yourself or for emergencies?
- Do you have a cat or other pets yourself?

IF BOARDING IN A CATTERY IS YOUR ONLY OPTION

If none of the possibilities above is available to you and a commercial boarding facility is where your cat needs to go, then there are ways to help you choose a cattery that will take good care of your kitty so you can have peace of mind on your travels.

You must visit any cattery you are considering; avoid any place that will not allow you to have a look, because it is likely to have something to hide. Proprietors of clean, well-run facilities are only too glad to show them off. Keep in mind that you are not there to judge the *person's* household condition, personality or lifestyle; the only thing that matters is whether their cattery is clean, inviting and comfortable.

Because cats can pass disease and illness so easily to others, a cattery must be set up in a highly hygienic way, which explains some of the questions on the checklist below. Some questions may seem over the top to you; however, the risk of contagion is so high among cats that you cannot be careful enough. The chart below covers the most important qualities to look for:

Checklist for Catteries

What They Should Require of Customers

- Vet certificate stating the cat's good health and vaccination history
- List of personal information about your cat's habits and issues
- Contact list for you
- Name of a local person as your proxy in case of emergency
- Extra payment for obligatory daily grooming of a long-haired cat

What You Should See for Yourself

- Clean and pleasant-looking
- Odor-free (especially no smell of urine)
- Other cats look relaxed and well-nourished
- Clean litter pans and feeding bowls for each cat
- Individual units for each cat (unless they're from the same household)
- Plastic barriers between units (also called "sneeze barriers") to prevent contact between confinement areas
- No communal gathering place where all cats could have contact
- A double-door system (like in a jail) so that a cat cannot escape if she accidentally gets out the first door

Feral Cats

What *feral* means is "a domestic animal that has reverted to a wild state." Feral cats are the descendants of cats who were once people's pets but now live outside human homes and care. The social issue with feral cats is that they are viewed as a problem on a number of levels in the neighborhoods where they take up residence. Some people complain that these cats destroy songbirds and other small prey; some say they are a health hazard to other pets; others complain that feral cats can cause traffic accidents by running into the streets. And those who look after feral cats just want to catch them, neuter them and return them to live peacefully in the colonies they have created for themselves. The guardians of feral cats are deeply motivated and dedicated individuals, some of whom work with small groups of like-minded people, and they devote a great deal of time and their own funds to looking after feral colonies and trying to educate others. I hope this section will serve to do the same.

HOW DO CATS BECOME FERAL?

A domestic cat can develop into a feral cat or can be born wild. Cats can become feral in a number of ways: Either a cat can be abandoned by her people and wind up fending for herself, or she can get lost and wind up the same way. Once a cat has returned to the wild and procreates, the offspring are truly "born wild" because they do not have any experience of sharing a home or interacting with people.

HOW FERAL CATS LIVE

Feral cats tend to live in groups, or colonies, which can range in size anywhere from a few cats to hundreds of them. They generally congregate in areas where they have shelter and a source of food—which would mean where there are fishing boats, restaurants or hotels, or industrial locations that generate scraps the cats can live on. Feral cats can also survive in rural areas or anywhere that attracts an ample supply of small rodents and birds for them to hunt.

PEOPLE DEVOTED TO THE FERAL CAT SOLUTION

Feral cats all over the world tend to attract people who make it their business—in some cases even their life's work—to feed, neuter and meet the medical needs of these cats who live outside direct contact with people. There is a wide range of the kinds of people who adopt colonies of feral cats; the different backgrounds and motivations of these cat-lovers are not easy to categorize. One thing that is consistent is the amount of time, planning and money it requires to look after a colony of feral cats. Their shared goal is to *trap, neuter* and *release* feral cats, which is referred to as TNR.

There is a cliché that lonely little old ladies are the primary friends of the undomesticated cats that are living wild, but the range of feral devotees is much greater than that. Some are sophisticated, chic world travelers, like my dear friend Eleonora, who has adopted a feral group outside her apartment building in Rome, Italy, a city famous for its stray cats. Eleonora captures them in humane traps for neutering and other medical care and then releases them back to their colony, where she feeds them twice a day. She has even managed to civilize a number of them to return to domestic status and live out a lush life in her rooftop apartment surrounded by a wide terrace abundant with plants. I am grateful for what she has taught me about feral cats, and others like her who do this despite social disapproval.

EAR TIPPING FOR IDENTIFICATION

If you see a cat with one ear that is cut off at the tip, this mark is the universal symbol for a feral cat who has been spayed or neutered and then released again. This symbol is used by vets who work with people who look after feral cats. The tip is taken off their ear while the cat is under anesthesia to be neutered and does not cause any distress to the cat. Ear tipping allows volunteers to immediately recognize cats who have already been sterilized.

DON'T CONTRIBUTE TO THE FERAL CAT POPULATION

◆ Don't Lose Your Cat

This may sound absurd to you (you must be thinking, "How could *my* loving kitty ever become wild?"), but most feral cats once had ancestors whom somebody loved and cared for. Cats get lost and are often never found—in fact, many are never even looked for (see what a sad problem this is at the end of this chapter, under "Lost and Found"). Please take steps to keep your own cat safe from escape and properly ID her with a microchip (see below) and a name tag, or she could wind up being one of these homeless cats scratching to survive.

◆ Neuter Your Cat

By now everybody knows there is no excuse not to neuter a pet cat, but if you need one more reason, it's because once loose, an unneutered cat will create litters of kittens, contributing to the feral cat situation.

◆ Confine Your Cat

Unless you live in wide-open country, it's dangerous to let your cat have the freedom to roam; even there, be careful because cats have lots of natural enemies. Chapter 4 tells you about the various enclosures you can create to allow your cat to safely enjoy the outdoors.

◆ Microchip Your Cat

A cat should always wear a tag with your name, but with a safety breakaway collar there's always the risk that the collar can do exactly that—and then your cat could lose her connection to you and become just another stray. This is why a microchip is so important for a cat. It is a tiny chip that your vet inserts painlessly under her skin at her shoulder blades. Nowadays shelters and vet's offices have a scanner they automatically use to determine whether any lost pet has been microchipped, allowing them to immediately find the owner.

◆ Volunteer to Help Feral Cats

If you are interested in helping the feral cat population, there are groups that can teach you how to trap, neuter and release homeless cats and become their guardians afterward. To find a training course in effectively dealing with the homeless cat situation, visit one of the Humane Society of the United States Web sites at www.humanesocietyu.org/workshops_and_classes/tnr.html. There are several well-known feral cat groups from which you can get information about how to be part of the solution to the feral cat problem. Each community has its own issues, but these groups are full of people to help with the answers. Alley Cat Allies, 1801 Belmont Road, NW, Suite 201, Washington, D.C. 20009, 202-667-3630, www.alleycat.org; Alley Cat Rescue, P.O. Box 585, Mount Rainier, MD 20712, 301-699-3946, www.saveacat.org; No Kill Solutions, www.nokillsolutions.org.

Lost and Found

One of the saddest things about lost cats is that the people who love them wait for days before they initiate a search plan—by which time it is often too late. What is disturbing to people in the animal shelter community is that if a *dog* in these same households were to get lost, his people would go into high gear. People search high and low when the dog is the beloved animal family member who has gotten lost, anxiously leaving no stone unturned to bring their pooch back home. The professionals don't understand why people do not feel the same level of concern and use the same effort to get their cats back. People love and cherish their cats as much as their dogs, but there is a grossly mistaken idea that cats are clever and self-sufficient and will come back on their own. That is far from the truth. House cats have few survival skills outside the home, which is the only place they can live safely.

When people don't make a serious effort to find their lost cats, the cats can wind up unclaimed in shelters, where they are often euthanized for lack of room, or they get hit by cars or are killed by other animals. The Humane Society of the United States in Washington, D.C., the nation's largest animal protection organization, recommends two Web sites dedicated to explaining how to look for your lost kitty and successfully bring her home: The HSUS is *not* a government agency (as some people mistakenly think, probably because the words "United States" are in the name and it is based in Washington)—it is a nonprofit organization that mobilizes funds and manpower across the country (and even internationally) to protect the welfare of all the animals whose lives we touch. Go to the Web sites, www.safecats.org and www.catsinthebag.org. I recommend that you visit them, both for their constantly updated and thorough information and to learn more about the HSUS, and give them your support.

Do not wait for your cat to return on her own. This is the worst assumption that people can make. If your cat could get home on her own, she would already be there, safe and warm and with a full tummy. Instead, she is out there somewhere, hungry, thirsty, dealing with weather conditions and perhaps hurt. Being lost is not something a cat chooses to do. She needs you to find her, the sooner the better.

If your cat gets lost, do not give up hope. You need to keep looking, using the techniques here and anything else you learn on www.safecats.org. Don't quit looking after a few days and think it's useless; many pets are found weeks or months later. You need to continue actively looking, just as you would hope to be looked for if you got lost on a hike. How would *you* like it if the people who supposedly cared about you went back to their daily routines and said, "He'll find his way back when he's good and ready"?

FINDING A LOST CAT INSIDE THE HOUSE

A cat who has been spooked by something she saw or heard can go into serious hiding. She can also get stuck somewhere in the house—cats explore in the most amazing nooks and crannies and can get trapped. If your cat has been somehow injured, her instinct will be to lie low and wait it out, when of course medical care is what she really needs. Take a flashlight and look in the following places.

Indoor Hiding Places

- Behind washer and dryer
- Behind refrigerator or stove
- Inside closed pantry
- Inside linen cupboard
- Inside closets (shelves above or cubbies below)
- Inside a TV cabinet
- Inside a cupboard or armoire
- Under a platform bed
- *Inside* box springs or mattress (look for torn lining as entry point)
- Bookcase, even *behind* books
- Dresser drawers (and behind drawers, even if they are shut)
- In the chimney
- In heating ducts or vents
- In the attic

The sooner you start looking, the less ground your cat will have covered if she is on the move, so do not delay. Do *not* think, "Well, I'll leave for work and we'll see if she's back by nightfall." Give up an hour of work and get cracking—you are your cat's guardian and your timely effort to find her may be the difference between her life and death. A cat who has access to the outdoors all the time (which is something you really need to reevaluate) already has hiding places and knows her way around, but an indoors-only cat is as vulnerable as a human toddler outdoors; she is terrified and has no idea how to protect herself.

◆ Check All Possibilities Close to Home First

She May Be Hiding Nearby. A terrified cat will probably not come when you call her. Bring a box of treats outside and shake it, but even if that sound would ordinarily induce her to come running, once she's frightened she may not budge. You're probably going to have to see where she is and get her out of there.

Look Inside Sheds and Garages. Check not just your property but ask neighbors if you can check around their houses. Look on the edge of the property in brush or landscaped shrubbery, and under decks and crawl spaces.

Check Under Front Stoops. Cats can die underneath a front porch when they go in after prey of some kind and cannot get back out. Often the ground falls away under wooden front steps and porches, so while a cat may be able to slither under the steps from the outside, there is not room enough for her to maneuver to exit because she is trying to climb up a downward slope and then out a very narrow opening. If she starts digging, that just makes it worse because the ground is already eroded.

Check Neighborhood Construction or Relocation. If any nearby houses are having work done on them, the cat may have gotten trapped in there among the construction debris or closed into an area she cannot get out of. If neighbors have recently moved in or out, she may have slipped through open doors that closed behind her.

Dusk Is a Cat's Prime Time. Go out to look for your cat at dusk, which is when she might emerge from wherever she has been hiding. A cat's internal clock—and her eyes—are programmed for hunting as the light is fading. This is also a dangerous time because people driving have not yet put on their headlights and they may have trouble seeing a cat in the dim light, when human eyes see the least well.

Call Quietly for Your Cat. A timid cat is not going to respond positively to anxious yelling. Call in a restrained voice, and bring a sound that might stimulate her and bring her out of hiding, like a box of treats you can shake or a can of cat food to tap on with a spoon.

THE CAT BIBLE

◆ Call Local Radio Stations
Radio stations in some towns announce lost pets as a public service.

◆ Change Your Outgoing Message on Your Answering Machine
Leave a new message saying something like, "If you're calling about the cat, thank you *so* much. Please leave word when and where you saw her. Please leave your name and number in case I have questions and so I can thank you afterward. Thanks again so much!"

◆ Put an Ad in the Local Paper
Many newspapers have reduced rates or no charge at all for their "Lost Pets" column. You should also look under "Found Pets," because good citizens who find a pet will go to the trouble of putting up a notice or taking an ad.

◆ Make Flyers Using a Good Photo
Local print shops are accustomed to printing up lost animal flyers, but with the sophistication of computers, you should be able to paste a photo of the cat right onto a document and print it yourself. Using a color photo is more costly, while a black-and-white photo is often less clear but you can make more of them less expensively.

Put "Lost Cat" above the photo. Include a short description (color, markings, hair length if relevant) and your phone number. If you have a timid cat, you don't want them to scare her off, so write, "Cat will run if approached! Please call instead." Do *not* put a reward amount. People do not return or report found cats for the money—those who would are not to be trusted anyway.

Put flyers up everywhere you can. The more the better, where flyers are concerned. Tack them up in the office, grocery store, vet's office and of course on poles and trees around where she was last seen.

◆ Beware of Your Own Safety
Unfortunately, scam artists and pranksters love lost-pet situations. You need to protect yourself from scam artists—horrible people who prey on the emotions of people with lost pets, and have found ways to profit from their desperation.

Do not include your name or address on the flyer, and beware of including too many descriptive details. Withhold some information. Do not describe every detail; for example, do not describe her collar.

Beware of anyone claiming to be a truck driver. An old trick is to call and say, "I was passing through your town and your cat was hurt. I took her to a vet and then kept her with me. As soon as you reimburse me for the vet bill I will ship the cat to you." If you weren't so upset about your cat, you'd realize how ludicrous this scam is, but people get taken in by it all the time.

Ask for the person's phone number and say you'll call right back. Criminals aren't going to want you to have their number, but if they are careless and their number comes up on your caller ID, be sure to write it down.

Ask for a very detailed description of your cat. This is why you leave out details on your flyer—so that the finder can fill in the blanks. Ask what her collar looks like.

Demand a photo of the cat and a copy of the vet bill. This is where they will surely hang up on you if they are tricksters.

✦ Set a Humane Trap

A cat who has never been outside may just be too terrified to come out of hiding when you call for her. You can put out a humane trap—the kind used by animal control to catch raccoons and that guardians of feral cats use for TNR to trap cats in order to neuter them and return them to their territory. You should be able to borrow such a trap from a local feral cat group (your vet may know of one), or even ask the animal control people if they will lend you one of their traps (which go by names like Havahart).

You can find out how to effectively and safely use a trap at www.neighborhoodcats.org. But here are some basics:

Bait the Trap with Food. Open a can of the smelliest cat food you can find and drip some juice from the can near the entrance to the trap. Drop a small amount of food just inside the open door of the trap, and a small bit of food within the trap leading to the back. Place a large portion of food at the back end of the trap so that the cat has to enter completely and will trip the trap door when she reaches the food in the far back.

Spray Feliway on the Trap. This calming synthetic hormone may reassure a cat as she approaches the trap and help make the trap less forbidding.

Put a Piece of Your Clothing in the Trap. Take clothes you have worn for hours against your skin and put them in the trap to make it more appealing.

Put the Trap Out After Dark. Cats are nocturnal, so this is the most likely time for her to come slinking around.

If you don't have the time or energy to do this yourself, spend the bucks and call up a pest control company. They are skilled at painlessly catching wild animals, and their traps and techniques work just as well with cats. They will usually come within the day, which is what you want—and often more quickly than you could organize getting a trap some other way. They will also know the best placement of the trap.

✦ Stay in Touch with Your Local Rescue and Shelter

Take the time to visit and call the shelter(s) in your area every day—and then after a week, do so every other day. Tell them that the cat is still lost. You have to keep trying. Don't worry about being a pest. You don't have to apologize for calling or visiting frequently. This is what they are there for: to reunite people and their pets. The staff should appreciate your efforts—they wish more people were like you. Shelter workers in most places have to deal with the heartache of euthanizing healthy, sweet pets because nobody claims them. If they can reunite one cat with her person, it makes their job more meaningful.

AFTERWORD

Today, the cat is *the* favorite house pet in the United States, and cats have outnumbered dogs (the previous favorite) for a decade or more. Those of us involved in the veterinary profession are seeing unprecedented numbers of well-cared-for felines living alongside people who are often willing to do anything and everything necessary to give their pets long, healthy, and happy lives. This desire to care for a pet's every need has resulted in some significant improvements in health and longevity for cats, in a way that I could never have anticipated when I graduated from veterinary school in 1977. For example, the increasingly common indoor existence enjoyed by cats has reduced the incidence of most infectious diseases within cat populations and has curtailed death and injury to cats from automobile accidents, attacks from dogs or wildlife, or other sources of trauma. More routine spaying and neutering of household pet cats has also positively affected the number of abandoned and neglected cats in shelters put to sleep.

Unfortunately, while so much is better for cats today, they have also paid a price for the heightened level of attention they receive from their devoted owners. That price is loss of health from such detrimental influences as poor nutrition in the form of commercial dry cat food diets, excessive and potentially life-threatening vaccination practices, and a general failure to understand the cat's needs and behavior as distinct from any other pet species. When owners fail to understand a cat's unique needs, it can ruin the health of the cat and damage her relationship with her loving guardians.

Virtually all of the major lethal feline diseases—obesity, diabetes, bladder problems including inflammatory cystitis, kidney failure, hyperthyroidism, inflammatory bowel disease, and perhaps even some forms of cancer—are directly related to mistakes that loving humans make in caring for their felines. Ironically, these are not mistakes of neglect or abuse, but mistakes made by following the conventional wisdom advanced by pet care experts. How can it be that the "best" information available from the most knowledgeable sources for cat health care is so seriously flawed? The answer lies in the rather haphazard approach our society has taken to developing its knowledge about cats and their care, reflected especially in the uncontrolled influence that the multibillion dollar pet food industry has on pet owner beliefs.

Decades ago, cats were not considered pets; they were thought of as workers around the property, in charge of controlling the vermin population in a ranch, farm, or neighborhood setting. We humans provided certain protection to the local cats in exchange for the service of ridding our homes and towns of disease-carrying and grain-consuming rodents. In this particular symbiotic relationship, it was not necessary, and not even particularly desirable that cats become true pets. Because a cat's work required that it retain all of its keen wild-hunting instincts and hunger, it was left outdoors, seldom fed from the household larder, and generally encouraged to remain feral in all aspects. To be of service to humans, it was necessary that the cat remain just as it was before the relationship with humankind began. The cat's sole value in its relationship with people was to eliminate the creatures that robbed the community of its harvest and, in the process, assist in the management of vermin-facilitated disease, like the black plague.

As feral cats have been domesticated, beginning with the ancient Egyptians and continuing into the present day, their personalities have become more docile. This shift in personality was, and still is, largely a matter of socialization, rather than deliberate domestication that occurred with dogs, cattle, and the like. This simple process of socialization has not changed the cat's unique, primitive metabolic and nutritional needs, and the workings of the cat's mind and body remain intensely prehistoric, molded through thousands of years of selective environmental pressures into the perfect carnivore, the top predator of its environment. Nothing that humankind has done to harness the useful qualities of this predatory mammal has changed that in any way.

These special and ancient characteristics distinguish the cat from all other animals in our lives. In our past failures to understand these characteristics as we bring the cat into our homes and hearts, we have begun a process of unwitting harm. Today, we rush to live our lives at breakneck speed, placing trust in the tidal wave of consumer marketing that inundates us hourly from all corners. This misplaced trust has led us to inflict a poisonous lifestyle upon our felines, even as we believe that we are doing everything possible to keep them healthy and happy.

Fortunately, new sources of insight and cat-inspired guidance are becoming available to assist the devoted cat lover. *The Cat Bible* is here to teach you, in more complete ways than ever before, how to truly understand your cat. These tips will open up wide avenues of enjoyment and improve quality of life for cat and owner alike and allow us to start caring for our cats in ways that will increase their lifespan. What can possibly be better than that?

—Elizabeth Hodgkins, D.V.M., Esq.

Dr. Elizabeth Hodgkins is a renowned veterinarian with a cats-only practice in Southern California, called the All About Cats Health Center. Her pioneering work on diabetes in cats has earned her an international following. Dr. Hodgkins also breeds and shows Ocicats, which you can see at www.sunstoneocicats.com. She is the official veterinarian for *Cat Chat* on the Martha Stewart Living channel on Sirius Radio.

ACKNOWLEDGMENTS

My first and foremost thanks go to the fine people at the Humane Society of the United States in Washington, D.C. Kathy Bauch has been a supportive friend and professional source of reassurance and support to me, all the way from *The Dog Bible* right through to this book. Wayne Pacelle, the head of the HSUS, is an inspiration to all those who work with him as well as to everyone interested in animal welfare: He lives his life eco-friendly and vegan, and shows up on every level for the animals. My greatest thanks go to the companion animal expert at HSUS, Stephanie Shain, who honored me by writing the foreword to this book. Stephanie is passionate about the place of cats in our lives, and she was eager to take on the demanding task of reading every word for accuracy and completeness. I am relieved to say that her corrections were few, but often the subtle difference between one word and another makes a meaningful difference. I am really proud to have passed muster with Stephanie, because cats have no greater champion.

The whole family at Martha Stewart Living Radio has been so supportive with my weekly show, *Cat Chat* on Sirius Radio. The cat lovers of America and I both owe them a big thank-you for giving me such a wonderful opportunity. Dr. Elizabeth Hodgkins has been so wise and generous in joining me regularly on the air and helping me answer questions behind the scenes, too.

Dr. Wallace Smith at WLIU-FM has been a great guide and mentor in producing my live weekly show *Dog Talk* on his NPR station, but I have to acknowledge him here since his greatest love is for his two wonderful cats (and I don't even think he minds if the *Dog Talk* fans find out).

Dr. Dawn D. Stelling was kind enough to vet the medical chapters in the book for correctness. It was wonderful to have the wisdom and experience of a vet who has helped me with many of my own animals, as well as to have a professional with whom to talk through some of the controversial topics. Dawn's generosity in giving the book her time meant even more given that she has three small children (and a very supportive husband) along with a full-time veterinary practice.

I'd like to acknowledge the lifelong commitment to cats of my dear friend Eleonora Brown, who rescues abandoned cats wherever she goes in the world (and she travels *a lot*), as well as the feral colony she has adopted and cares for in her hometown of Rome, Italy. From watching her over the years, I have learned so much about what a modern-day St. Francis might be like. Leo raised my awareness of the plight of friendless alley cats decades before I ever undertook this book—and way before feral cats became an identified topic in animal welfare.

My editor, Jessica Sindler, cut her teeth at Gotham on this book and was never daunted by the size of the task at hand. I can imagine that everything else will seem like a piece of cake after this mountain of words! Her own love of cats must explain in some part her tireless and always cheerful support and good eye. And it was comforting to know that my senior editor, Erin Moore, was watching over us with an equally feline-loving eye. Beth Parker in Gotham publicity was a wonderful cheering section, and my dear agent, Robert Lescher, was with me all the way.

I have so many friends who cheered me on regardless of how much I moaned about never being able to finish a book that seemed to get bigger the more I researched. Who knew there would be this much to say about cats?! Friends I am so lucky to have: Carolyn Arnold, Kirsten Benfield, Loring Bolger, Bob Celentano, Sharon Dauk, Jean Guest, Jill Jakes, Adrienne Kitaeff, Libby Langdon, Fran Lubin, Joan Rivers, Yvette Ruby, Diane Saatchi, Aimee Sadler, Karen Turetski and—on a nearly daily basis—Lisa Charde (I defy anyone to find a more true-blue friend and this is my public promise to take her with me to Chicago when Oprah invites me back on her show). Familial thanks to my father, Hotch; his sweetheart Va.; my sister Holly; and my brother Tim, to whom this book is dedicated because he always has my back.

My Web master Jack Passarella and my e-mail master Jim Fryman are both maestros in the truest sense and really good writers in their own rights. I would be sunk without them.

Finally, I'd like to salute two monthly newsletters from veterinary schools that have interesting, intelligent and useful articles you won't find anywhere else. I got a lot of the up-to-date medical information in the book from these two publications. Neither publication takes any advertising, which I think is the most reliable way to feel comfortable that a source of information is open-minded, honest and fair. When no money changes hands, hands cannot be dirty—at least that's the way I see it.

Catnip is the newsletter of the Cummings Veterinary School at Tufts University and can be had for $40 a year by writing to P.O. Box 420235, Palm Coast, FL 32142 or calling 800-829-8893.

Cat Watch is published by The Feline Health Center at Cornell University's veterinary school with articles of interest for the general cat-loving population. A subscription costs the same as *Catnip* and is also published by the same company in Florida. You can also go to www.catwatch-newsletter.com/cs to subscribe for $40 a year, or contact them at the same toll-free number and land-based address as *Catnip*, above.

INDEX

injuries
   and hypothermia, 74
   purring and self-healing, 60
instinct
   hunting as, 51, 79
   prey-drive, dogs, 250–51
   scratching, functions of, 145–46
   See also wild, cats in
insulin, diabetes treatment, 308–9
Interceptor, 325
intermittent rewards, 119
International Cat Association (TICA)
   contact information, 32
   functions of, 18
   registration of litters, 31
Internet
   CatChatRadio.com, 242
   cat-related organizations, 32
   grief counseling for cats, 133
   Humane Society of the United States, 16
   pet-loss support sites, 345
   purebred rescue groups, 32
   TheCatBible.com, 239

J
Jacobson's organ, 56
Just 4 Cats Outdoor Safety Enclosure Plans,
   102
JW Easy Groom, 97
JW Pet Company, 97, 205

K
Kaopectate toxicity, 309
kava toxicity, 222
kibble
   avoiding, 211–12, 221, 223–25, 308
   and dehydration, 224
   and diabetes, 306–7
   and obesity, 220–21
   prescription diets, 241
   and skin/fur problems, 211–12
   taurine requirements, 218
   for urinary tract disease, 332–33
   and urinary tract problems, 218, 224, 331
   weaning cat from, 228–29, 233–34, 308
kidney disease. *See* chronic renal disease
kill shelters, 15–16
kindle, 33
kitchen
   counter, jumping on, 184
   safety precautions, 64–68
kitten(s)
   belly up, 114
   brushing teeth, 214
   catnip, avoiding, 88
   climbing behavior, 141–42

development of. *See* kitten development;
   socialization
feeding, 35, 220, 242–43
feline herpes virus (FHV), 312
feline infectious peritonitis (FIP),
   313–14
feline panleukopenia virus (FPV), 312
grooming, 204
in home. *See* home safety; home, cats in
kneading, 52
later personality, 18
littermates, compatibility of, 254
minimum time with litter, 13, 26
ownership, disadvantages, 13–14
physical problems, signs of, 14
scent marking, 168
scratching by, 147–48
sex of cat, determining, 13
temperament, warning signs, 14
kitten development, 34–39
   air-righting reflex, 39
   eye color, 46
   eyesight, 46
   feeding, 35
   hot/cold sensitivity, 58
   kitten to cat transition, 37
   and later dependency, 185
   litter box, use of, 165–66
   minimum time with litter, 13, 26
   mother cat, role of, 36
   movement and age, 34
   play, 104–5, 143
   and purring, 59
   sensitive period, 34
   sleep pattern, 54
   smell, sense of, 55–56
   spaying, age of, 322
   teeth, 52
   weeks 1 through 14 milestones, 37
   See also socialization
kitten mills, 23–24
Kitty Hoots Crackler, 110
Kitty Tease, 108
Kitty ToothWipes, 215
Kitty View, The, 102
Klaw Kontrol, 102
kneading, emotional state, 52, 115
knives, dangers, 64, 66
KV VetSupply, 83

L
labels, food, 237–39
lactose intolerance, 231, 309
lameness/staggering
   and arthritis, 293
   as emergency, 288

routine. *See* predictability
Royal Canin Urinary S/O, 332
rubber plant, 65
runs, 101
Russian Blue, personality traits, 21

S

safe room, 74–77
   coming out, time for, 76, 77
   Feliway, use of, 75–76, 261
   hiding places, providing, 75, 77
   and home remodeling, 70
   kitten-safety, 76
   and leash training, 356
   new cat introduction, 259–64
   in new house, 124–25
   setting up room, 77–78
saliva/salivation
   and allergies, 178, 180
   drooling, 52, 115, 284
   and eating, 52
   rabies, 196
salmonella, raw diet, 235
sand as litter, 157
scent glands. *See* pheromones/scent glands
scent marking
   cat-to-cat communication, 45, 116, 168–69, 257
   functions of, 168–69
   multiple-cat household, 257
   rubbing against leg, 45, 56, 114, 225
   rubbing with head, 75, 115, 167–69
   scent, cat detection of, 56, 168
   and scent glands. *See* pheromones/scent glands
   with urine. *See* Spraying
scent socks, 248, 261–62
schefflera, 65
scoops/scooping, litter, 163–64
Scottish Fold, personality traits, 21
scratching, 145–50
   and cat scratch fever, 196–97
   functions for cats, 103, 146, 167
   interventions, 146–50
   by kittens, 147–48
   Soft Paws solution to, 150
scratching posts, 103–4
   benefits to cats, 103, 146
   homemade, 103
   kitten use of, 147–48
   in multiple-cat household, 148
   old posts, keeping, 149–50
   placement in home, 103–4, 146–47, 149
   in safe room, 76
   scratching pads, 149
   teaching cat about, 104, 146–48
scruff, lifting cat, aggressive cat, 286
seborrhea, blackheads on chin/lips, 210, 329

seizures
   as emergency, 288
   and hyperthermia, 72
   as warning sign, 285
Selkirk Rex, personality traits, 21
senility, senior cats, 116, 350–51
senior cats, 347–52
   aging, signs of, 347–50
   chronic renal disease, 315
   comforting, tips for, 352
   hyperthermia risk, 73
   as indoor cats, 80
   litter box issues, 162, 166
   nighttime calling, 351–52
   nutritional requirements, 243
   ramps for, 102, 352
   senility, 116, 350–51
   thermal cat cushion, 83
   vocalizations, 116
senses, 45–51
   ears and hearing, 45–46
   eyesight, 46–48
   hot/cold sensitivity, 58
   smell, 55–56
   taste, 56–57
   touch, 57–58
sensitive period, 34
Sentinel, 325
separation anxiety syndrome (SAS), 125–27
   at-risk breeds, 125
   medication for, 126–27
   soothing cat, 126–27
   and spraying, 171
   symptoms, 125–26
Seventh Generation, 91
sexual aggression, 135
shadowing, 127
shampoo for cats, 205
shearling mat beds, 83
shedding
   seasonal cycles, 203
   and stress, 203
shelters, 14–17
   evaluating, 16–17
   kill or no-kill, 15–16
   lost cats, checking for, 368
   quality, signs of, 16
show-quality cats, 31
shrieking, emotional state, 43
Siamese
   cancer risk, 294
   coloration, 12
   eye discharge, 312
   eyesight, 48
   fabric-eating, 130
   leash training, 355

tongue
    roughness, 57
    spitting out problem, 62
    and taste, 57
    utility of, 51
Tonkinese
    personality traits, 22
    and separation anxiety syndrome (SAS), 125
tooth brushing, 52–53, 214–15
    dental products, 215
    procedure, 214
tortoiseshell coloration, 12, 34
tote bag carrier, 85
touch, sense of, 57–58
    and footpads, 49, 58
    touch receptors, location of, 57
    touch spots, 57
    whiskers, 58
toweling cat
    aggressive cat, 287
    procedure, 319–20
    to put in carrier, 87
toxoplasmosis, 197
toys, 107–12
    bells, dangers of, 63
    boredom, preventing, 77, 105, 107, 126
    catnip-filled, 88, 89, 110
    everyday objects as, 111, 188
    for human/cat play, 107–11
    in safe room, 77
    for solitary play, 110
    types to avoid, 111–12
Track-Less Litter Pearls, 158
Traditional Cat Association, 32
training cats, 352–59
    fears, desensitizing, 119, 121–23
    leash training, 355–59
    punishment, avoiding, 353–54
    rewards, 117, 353
    stopping problem behaviors, 354–55
tranquilizers, for separation anxiety syndrome (SAS), 126
travel
    boarding cats, 359–62
    heartworm risk, 327
treats
    commercial, avoiding, 228
    food treats, 353
    freeze-dried, 228
    hiding as game, 111, 126
    high-quality brands, 228, 247
tricolored cats, 34
trilling, emotional state, 43
trusts, planning for cat, 201–2
tuna, avoiding, 230, 297
Turkish Angora, personality traits, 22

Turkish Van
    affinity for water, 61
    personality traits, 22
Tuxedo coloration, 12
Types A and B personality, 11

U

Ultimate Scratching Post, 103
unneutered cats
    petting aggression, 139–40, 321
    spraying, 170, 321
    tomcats, problems with, 320–21
upper respiratory infections
    feline herpes virus (FHV), 312
    See also colds
urinary tract crystals
    calcium oxalate, 230, 330
    and foods/diet, 230, 240
    and magnesium, 230
    struvite, 230, 330
    urine testing, pH strips, 241
urinary tract disease, 329–33
    blood-detecting litters, 158, 330
    commercial foods for, 332–33
    cranberry remedy, 333
    crystal formation. *See* urinary tract crystals
    emergency treatment, 329
    and kibble, 218, 224, 331
    and litter box issues, 153
    medical care, 331
    symptoms, 330
    water, encouraging drinking, 331–32
urination
    diabetic cats, 307
    difficulty, as emergency, 288
    in house. *See* house soiling
    marking behavior. *See* spraying
urine, normal pH of, 331

V

vaccinations
    allergies, cause of, 291
    cancer at injection site, 296, 315
    cold prevention, 301
    feline calicivirus (FCV), 313, 315
    feline herpes virus (FHV), 315
    feline leukemia virus (FeLV), 313
    health insurance coverage, 276
    holistic view, 291
    overinocculation problem, 291
    rabies, 314
    routine types, 314
vacuum
    desensitizing fear of, 119
    flea elimination, 325
    house cleaning, 181–82

Valium, 126, 175
Van
    coloration, 12
    See also Turkish Angora
vegetables, for senior cats, 243
Verbasis, 158
veterinarian(s), 269–74
    academic degrees, 269–70
    choosing vet, 271–72
    euthanasia, 337–40
    finding breeders, 27
    first visit, 272–73
    and health insurance, 9–10
    house calls, 273–74
    philosophies of care, 270–71
vibrissae, 211
vinegar
    bath rinse, 209, 211
    cat-friendly cleaning, 91
    cat hair control, 98
viral infections
    colds, 300–301
    feline calicivirus (FCV), 312
    feline herpes virus (FHV), 312
    feline immunodeficiency virus (FIV),
        314
    feline infectious peritonitis (FIP), 312
    feline leukemia virus (FeLV), 312
    feline panleukopenia virus (FPV), 312
    rabies, 314
    skin/fur problems, 210, 329
visitors, 198–200
    dangers to cats, 68–69
    interaction with cats, 122, 200
    new persons, feline needs, 199
    and spraying, 170
    stranger anxiety, 120–23
vital signs. *See* health status
vocal cords, and purring, 59
vocalizations, 59–60
    and breed, 116
    cat in heat, 322
    ending chattiness, 117
    and grief, 132
    nighttime calling, 350–52
    purring, 59–60
    senior cats, 116
    and separation anxiety syndrome (SAS),
        125
    sounds/meanings, 43, 60, 117
    and stress, 117
vomeronasal organ, 56, 168
vomiting, 333–35
    and constipation, 301–2
    emergency treatment, 289, 334
    grass consumption, 236, 334

and hairballs, 236, 333–34
ideopathic vomiting syndrome,
    334–35
and inflammatory bowel disease,
    310–11
as warning sign, 285

W
washer/dryer dangers, 68
wastebasket precautions, 66
water
    affinity and breed, 61
    bathing cats, 60–61
    playing with, 60–61
    swimming, 61
    toilet water warning, 61
water, drinking, 218–19
    changes and illness, 284
    diabetic cats, 307
    encouraging, guidelines for, 219, 331–32
    and tongue, 51
    for urinary tract disease, 331–32
    water bowl, placement, 219
weather conditions, hyperthermia/hypothermia,
    72–74
web sites. *See* Internet
weight loss
    and inflammatory bowel disease, 310
    See also appetite, loss
West Nile virus, 328
wet food. *See* canned/wet food
wheat-based litter, 158
whipworms, 328
whiskers
    body language, 39–40, 43
    and hunting, 58
    number of, 58
wild, cats in
    food hiding, 144
    grooming, 187
    hunting/prey. *See* hunting
    independence of, 113–14, 246
    marking/territoriality. *See* scent marking; spraying,
        territoriality
    maternal/paternal behavior. *See* father cats; mother
        cats
    meals per day, 219
    physical contact, lack of, 200
    rubbing, mutual, 168
    social order, 246
    water drinking, 218
    See also feral cats; instinct
wild cat crosses
    Bengal, 22
    personality of, 22
Wild Kitty Cat Food, 228

will, planning for cat, 201–2
Windex, 64
windows
    drapes, climbing on, 142
    marking/spraying near, 170, 174
    observation cube, 102
    safety precautions, 65–66, 68
    window perches, 96
wind-up toys, 109–10
wood chip litter, 157
wood tar, 90
wool, ingesting. *See* fabric-eating
World's Best Cat Litter, 158, 294
worms
    deworming, 328
    kittens, 14
    roundworms, passed to humans, 196
    types of, 328
    vomiting, 334
wrapping cat. *See* toweling cat

X
X-O odor remover, 92, 172

Y
Yesterday's News, 158
yogurt, 316–17
yowling, emotional state, 60, 265

Z
Zero Odor, 91–92
Zig-N-Zag ball, 110
Zoom Groom, 205
zoonoses (cat-to-human illnesses), 195–98
    cat scratch fever, 196–97
    preventing, 198
    rabies, 196
    ringworm, 196, 198
    roundworms, intestinal, 196
    salmonella/*E-coli*, 235
    toxoplasmosis, 197

ABOUT THE AUTHOR

TRACIE HOTCHNER IS THE AUTHOR OF *THE DOG BIBLE: EVERYTHING YOUR DOG WANTS YOU TO KNOW* (Gotham Books, 2005) and the million-copy bestseller *Pregnancy & Childbirth,* for which she appeared on national talk shows ranging from *Today* to *Oprah.* Tracie's two areas of pet expertise have made her a national radio personality twice over. She hosts two live weekly call-in shows: *Cat Chat* on the Martha Stewart Living channel of Sirius Radio and *Dog Talk,* her own NPR show, produced by WLIU-FM at Southampton College.

Tracie lives in East Hampton, New York. Visit her Web sites at www.TheCatBible.com and www.CatChatRadio.com.